T5-CVM-266

NUMERICAL LITERARY TECHNIQUES IN JOHN

SUPPLEMENTS TO
NOVUM TESTAMENTUM

VOLUME LV

LEIDEN — E. J. BRILL — 1985

NUMERICAL LITERARY TECHNIQUES IN JOHN

The Fourth Evangelist's Use of Numbers of Words and Syllables

BY

M. J. J. MENKEN

LEIDEN — E. J. BRILL — 1985

ISBN 90 04 07427 9

PRINTED IN THE NETHERLANDS BY E. J. BRILL

CONTENTS

PREFACE

The publication of a dissertation is a landmark in one's theological studies. It is a fitting occasion to thank those who have guided one along the way leading up to this point. First of all, I wish to express my gratitude to Prof. Dr. J. Smit Sibinga, who directed this thesis at the University of Amsterdam. I am indebted to him for much, and learned a great deal from his skill and acumen. His inspiration is clear throughout the present study. I would also like to mention the other members of the committee, instituted by the University of Amsterdam, that accepted the thesis: Prof. Dr. G. Bouwman, Prof. Dr. K. A. Deurloo, Prof. Dr. J. J. A. Kahmann, and Dr. H. J. de Jonge. I thank my other theological teachers, especially those who taught me New Testament exegesis and cognate matters, at the Amsterdam School of Catholic Theology, the University of Amsterdam, and the Pontifical Biblical Institute at Rome.

I am grateful to Prof. Dr. A. Ollongren, who helped me in mathematical matters, together with his collaborators of the *Centraal Reken Instituut* of the State University of Leiden.

I like to thank Mrs. K. M. Court for her correction of the English text.

My gratitude goes to the editors of *Novum Testamentum* for their willingness to include the book in the series Supplements to Novum Testamentum.

The publication of the book in this series was made possible by financial aid from the *Radboudstichting Wetenschappelijk Onderwijsfonds* and the *Stichting Priesteropleiding Bisdommen Haarlem en Rotterdam.* I thank both foundations for their support.

Finally, I wish to express my thanks to the entire community of the institute where I am employed at present, the School of Theology and Pastorate at Heerlen, for its interest and encouragement. It is a pleasure to work in an atmosphere of comradeship.

The manuscript of this book was completed in February 1983. External factors caused some delay in its being printed.

Brunssum, The Netherlands
November, 1984

M. J. J. Menken

ABBREVIATIONS

The system of abbreviations used here is that of the 'Instructions for Contributors', *Biblica* 63 (1982). Beside it, the following abbreviations are used:

Barrett	C. K. Barrett, *The Gospel according to St. John*. An Introduction with Commentary and Notes on the Greek Text (London 1978^{2})
Bauer	W. Bauer, *Das Johannesevangelium* (HNT 6; Tübingen 1933^{3})
Bauer, *Wörterbuch*	W. Bauer, *Griechisch-Deutsches Wörterbuch zu den Schriften des Neuen Testaments und der übrigen urchristlichen Literatur* (Berlin 1958^{5})
Becker	J. Becker, *Das Evangelium nach Johannes* (Ökumenischer Taschenbuchkommentar zum Neuen Testament 4; Gütersloh/Würzburg 1979-1981)
Bernard	J. H. Bernard, *A Critical and Exegetical Commentary on the Gospel according to St. John* (ICC; Edinburgh 1928)
Blass-Debrunner-Rehkopf	F. Blass-A. Debrunner, *Grammatik des neutestamentlichen Griechisch*, rev. by F. Rehkopf (Göttingen 1976^{14})
Brown	R. E. Brown, *The Gospel according to John*. Introduction, Translation and Notes (AB 29-29A; New York 1966-1970)
Bultmann	R. Bultmann, *Das Evangelium des Johannes* (MeyerK; Göttingen 1968^{19})
Haenchen	E. Haenchen, *Das Johannesevangelium*. Ein Kommentar, ed. by U. Busse (Tübingen 1980)
Hoskyns-Davey	E. C. Hoskyns, *The Fourth Gospel*, ed. by F. N. Davey (London 1947^{2})
Lagrange	M.-J. Lagrange, *Évangile selon saint Jean* (EB; Paris 1936^{5})
Liddell-Scott	H. G. Liddell-R. Scott, *A Greek-English Lexicon*, rev. by H. Stuart Jones and R. McKenzie (Oxford 1925-1940^{9})
Lightfoot	R. H. Lightfoot, *St. John's Gospel*. A Commentary, ed. by C. F. Evans (London 1956)
NA^{25}	*Novum Testamentum Graece*, ed. by Eb. Nestle-Erw. Nestle-K. Aland (Stuttgart 1963^{25})
Odeberg	H. Odeberg, *The Fourth Gospel*. Interpreted in Its Relation to Contemporaneous Religious Currents in Palestine and the Hellenistic-Oriental World (Uppsala 1929; repr. Amsterdam 1968)
Schnackenburg, I, II, III	R. Schnackenburg, *Das Johannesevangelium* (HTKNT 4; Freiburg etc., I 1972^{3}, II 1971, III 1976^{2})
Schneider	J. Schneider, *Das Evangelium nach Johannes*, ed. by E. Fascher (THKNT-Sonderband; Berlin 1976)
Schulz	S. Schulz, *Das Evangelium nach Johannes* (NTD 4; Göttingen 1972)
Strathmann	H. Strathmann, *Das Evangelium nach Johannes* (NTD 4; Göttingen 1963^{10})
Van den Bussche, *Boek der tekens*	H. Van den Bussche, *Het boek der tekens*. Verklaring van Johannes 1-4 (Het vierde evangelie 1; Tielt/Den Haag 1961^{2})
Van den Bussche, *Boek der werken*	H. Van den Bussche, *Het boek der werken*. Verklaring van Johannes 5-12 (Het vierde evangelie 2; Tielt/Den Haag 1962^{2})
Van den Bussche, *Jezus' woorden*	H. Van den Bussche, *Jezus' woorden bij het afscheidsmaal*. Verklaring van Johannes 13-17 (Het vierde evangelie 3; Tielt/Den Haag 1960^{3})

Westcott	B. F. Westcott, *The Gospel according to St. John*. The Greek Text with Introduction and Notes (London 1908; repr. Grand Rapids 1954)
Fs.	Festschrift
OCT	'Oxford Classical Texts' = Scriptorum Classicorum Bibliotheca Oxoniensis
S	syllable(s)
Sin	*Codex Sinaiticus*
Teubner	Bibliotheca Scriptorum Graecorum et Romanorum Teubneriana
W	word(s)

TEXT-EDITIONS USED (SOURCES AND TRANSLATIONS)

a) *Bible*

Biblia Hebraica Stuttgartensia, ed. by K. Elliger-W. Rudolph (Stuttgart 1967-1977)
Septuaginta, ed. by A. Rahlfs (Stuttgart 1935)
Novum Testamentum (Oxford 1889; = Textus Receptus)
Novum Testamentum Graece, ed. by J. J. Griesbach (Halle/London 1796-1806[2])
Novum Testamentum Graece et Latine, ed. by C. Lachmann (Berlin 1842-1850)
Novum Testamentum Graece, ed. by C. Tischendorf (Leipzig 1869-1872[8])
The New Testament in the Original Greek, ed. by B. F. Westcott-F. J. A. Hort (Cambridge/London 1881)
Das Neue Testament, ed. by B. Weiss (Leipzig 1894-1900)
Novum Testamentum Graece, ed. by Eb. Nestle; from 1914[10] by Erw. Nestle, from 1952[21] also by K. Aland (Stuttgart 1898[1]-1963[25])
Die Schriften des Neuen Testaments in ihrer ältesten erreichbaren Textgestalt, ed. by H. von Soden (I Berlin 1902-1910; II Göttingen 1913)
Novum Testamentum Graece, ed. by A. Souter (Oxford 1910, 1947[2])
Novum Testamentum Graece et Latine, ed. by H. J. Vogels (Düsseldorf 1920, Freiburg 1955[4])
Novum Testamentum Graece et Latine, ed. by A. Merk (Rome 1933, 1964[9])
Novi Testamenti Biblia Graeca et Latina, ed. by J. M. Bover (Madrid 1943, 1959[4])
The Greek New Testament, ed. by K. Aland-M. Black-B. M. Metzger-A. Wikgren (New York etc. 1966)
The Greek New Testament, 3rd ed., ed. by K. Aland-M. Black-C. M. Martini-B. M. Metzger-A. Wikgren (New York etc. 1975)
Novum Testamentum Graece, ed., after Eb. Nestle and Erw. Nestle, by K. Aland-M. Black-C. M. Martini-B. M. Metzger-A. Wikgren (Stuttgart 1979; = *NA*[26])

b) *Jewish Literature*

The Apocrypha and Pseudepigrapha of the Old Testament in English, ed. by R. H. Charles (Oxford 1913)
The Testament of Abraham, ed. by M. R. James (TextsS II/2; Cambridge 1892)
Die Texte aus Qumran, ed. by E. Lohse (Darmstadt 1971[2])
Josephus, ed. by H. St. J. Thackeray-R. Marcus-A. Wikgren-L. H. Feldman (LCL; Cambridge, Mass./London 1926-1965)
Philo, ed. by F. H. Colson-G. H. Whitaker-R. Marcus (LCL; Cambridge, Mass./London 1929-1962)
Ps.-Philon, *Les Antiquités Bibliques*, ed. by D. J. Harrington-J. Cazeaux-Ch. Perrot-P.-M. Bogaert (SC 229-230; Paris 1976)
The Mishnah, transl. by H. Danby (Oxford 1933)
Der Babylonische Talmud, ed. by L. Goldschmidt (Berlin etc. 1897-1935)
Sifra or Torat Kohanim, ed. by L. Finkelstein (New York 1956)
Mekhilta d'Rabbi Simᶜon b. Yochai, ed. by J. N. Epstein-E. Z. Melamed (Jerusalem 1955)
Mekilta de-Rabbi Ishmael, ed. by J. Z. Lauterbach (Philadelphia 1933-1935; repr. 1961)
The Midrash Rabbah, transl. into English ... unter the editorship of H. Freedman and M. Simon (London etc. 1939; new compact edition 1977)
Seder Olam Rabba, ed. by B. Ratner (Vilna 1897)
Pirke de Rabbi Eliezer, transl. by G. Friedlander (London 1916; repr. New York 1971)
Targum Ps.-Jonathan on Exodus, ed. by A. Diez Macho in *Biblia Polyglotta Matritensia* IV/2 (Madrid 1980)
The Passover Haggadah, ed. by N. N. Glatzer (New York 1953, 1969[2])

c) *Early Christian Literature*

Die apostolischen Väter I, ed. by F. X. Funk-K. Bihlmeyer-W. Schneemelcher (Sammlung ausgewählter kirchen- und dogmengeschichtlicher Quellenschriften 2,1,1; Tübingen 1970[3])
The Odes of Solomon, ed. by J. H. Charlesworth (Oxford 1973)
Acta Apostolorum Apocrypha, ed. by R. A. Lipsius-M. Bonnet (Leipzig 1891-1903)
Irénée de Lyon, *Contre les hérésies*, ed. by A. Rousseau a.o. (SC 100, 152-153, 210-211, 263-264; Paris 1965-1979)
Origène, *Commentaire sur saint Jean*, ed. by C. Blanc (SC 120, 157, 222, 290; Paris 1966-1982)
Eusebius, *Praeparatio Evangelica*, ed. by K. Mras (GCS 43; Berlin 1954-1956)
Romanos le Mélode, *Hymnes*, ed. by J. Grosdidier de Matons (SC 99, 110, 114, 128, 283; Paris 1964-1981)

d) *Pagan Literature*

Homeri *Opera*, ed. by D. B. Monro-T. W. Allen (OCT; Oxford 1912-1946)
Euripides, *Ion*, ed. by W. Biehl (Teubner; Leipzig 1979)
Thucydidis *Historiae*, ed. by H. Stuart Jones (OCT; Oxford 1900-1901; repr., with apparatus criticus emended and augmented by J. E. Powell, 1942)
Aristophanis *Comoediae*, ed. by F. W. Hall-W. M. Geldart (OCT; Oxford 1906-1907[2]; repr. 1970)
Isocratis *Orationes*, ed. by F. Blass (Teubner; Leipzig 1910-1913[2])
Platonis *Opera*, ed. by J. Burnet (OCT; Oxford 1900-1907)
Aristotelis *Opera*, ed. by I. Bekker, 2nd ed. by O. Gigon (Berlin 1960-1961)
Die Schule des Aristoteles, III: Klearchos, ed. by F. Wehrli (Basel/Stuttgart 1969[2])
Euclidis *Elementa*, ed. by E. S. Stamatis (Teubner; Leipzig 1969-1977)
Theocritus, ed. by A. S. F. Gow (Cambridge 1950)
Diodori *Bibliotheca historica*, Libri I-XX, ed. by F. Vogel-C. T. Fischer (Teubner; Leipzig 1888-1906)
C. Sallustii Crispi *Catilina-Iugurtha-Fragmenta ampliora*, ed. by A. Kurfess (Teubner; Leipzig 1954, 1981[3])
P. Vergili Maronis *Opera*, ed. by R. A. B. Mynors (OCT; Oxford 1969)
Cornifici *Rhetorica ad C. Herennium*, ed. by G. Calboli (Edizioni e saggi universitari di filologia classica 11; Bologna 1969)
Dionysii Halicarnasei *Opuscula*, ed. by H. Usener-L. Radermacher (Teubner; Leipzig 1899-1929)
Sex. Propertii *Elegiarum libri IV*, ed. by R. Hanslik (Teubner; Leipzig 1979)
Vitruvii *De architectura libri decem*, ed. by F. Krohn (Teubner; Leipzig 1912)
Ps.-Hippocrates, *De decentia*, in: Hippocratis *Opera* I/1, ed. by J. L. Heiberg (Corpus Medicorum Graecorum; Leipzig 1927)
Plutarch's *De Iside et Osiride*, ed. by J. Gwyn Griffiths (University of Wales 1970)
P. Cornelii Taciti *Libri qui supersunt*, ed. by E. Koestermann (Teubner; Leipzig 1961-1965)
(Ps.-)Demetrius, *On Style*, ed. by W. Rhys Roberts (Cambridge 1902; repr. Hildesheim 1969)
Heronis Alexandrini *Opera quae supersunt omnia*, ed. by W. Schmidt-H. Schöne-J. L. Heiberg (Teubner; Leipzig 1899-1914)
Nicomachi Geraseni Pythagorei *Introductionis arithmeticae libri II*, ed. by R. Hoche (Teubner; Leipzig 1866)
Alexander, *De figuris*, in: *Rhetores Graeci*, ed. by L. Spengel (Teubner; Leipzig 1853-1856)
Theonis Smyrnaei philosophi Platonici *Expositio rerum mathematicarum ad legendum Platonem utilium*, ed. by E. Hiller (Teubner; Leipzig 1878)
Herodiani technici *Reliquiae*, ed. by A. Lentz (Leipzig 1867-1870)
Luciani *Opera*, ed. by M. D. Macleod (OCT; Oxford 1972-1980)

Hermogenis *Opera*, ed. by H. Rabe (Teubner; Leipzig 1913)
Aquila Romanus, *De figuris sententiarum et elocutionis liber*, in: *Rhetores Latini minores*, ed. by C. Halm (Leipzig 1863)
Diogenis Laertii *Vitae philosophorum*, ed. by H. S. Long (OCT; Oxford 1964)
Anthologia Graeca, ed. by H. Beckby (Tusculum-Bücherei; München 1957-1958)
Corpus Inscriptionum Graecarum, ed. by A. Böckh a.o. (Berlin 1828-1877)
Vitae Vergilianae antiquae, ed. by C. Hardie (Oxford 1966)

INSTRUCTIONS TO THE READER

The division of verses into parts a, b, c, etc., agrees with the division by means of punctuation marks in *NA*[26]. Subdivisions are indicated by *a*, *b*, *c*, etc.
A slanting stroke (/) indicates the addition of the figures in one column. The total appears on the right side of the stroke.

INTRODUCTION

1. *Structural analysis of biblical texts*

Biblical books are the final products of long developments of tradition. Consequently, they can be approached in two ways: as bearers of previous tradition, and as final products. The first approach has been the dominant one in much research that has been done in biblical studies during the first half of this century; methods associated with it are literary criticism and form criticism. The second approach has become increasingly important during the past three decades of this century; it has to be associated with methods such as redaction criticism and various kinds of structural analysis[1]. The present study is to be situated within this second approach.

As is well known, both form criticism and redaction criticism start from a separation of tradition and redaction. In form criticism, this separation is carried out in order to obtain the traditional materials used by an author; then these are investigated to trace their previous history. In redaction criticism, the redaction, being an author's[2] own contribution to his literary product, is the main object of research. The redactional share of an author comprises quite a set of operations: the addition and omission of words, clauses, sentences, stories and statements, the introduction of changes into the available materials, the arrangement of the materials within a framework. These operations may be motivated by stylistic, poetic, theological reasons; they give us an impression of an author's interests, his theology, the people for whom he wrote, their situation and problems. The way an author deals with his materials can be established rather precisely when we know the tradition available to him, as is the case with the Gospels of Matthew and Luke, whose authors knew and used the Gospel of Mark, at least according to the Two Document Hypothesis. Elsewhere, the redactional share can be deduced with some probability from the observation of an author's literary and theological idiosyncrasies, and of tensions within the text. It should be stressed, however, that the final author is responsible not only for his own contributions to the materials he used, but also for the traditional materials which he has incorporated into his text, because it is he who decided to retain certain parts of the tradition and to omit others[3]. So the final author is responsible for the entire literary product which comes from under his hands. When redaction criticism is carried through in a consistent way, it leads to a view of the biblical text as something intended by its author to be a meaningful and coherent unit[4].

The way is open, then, for a search of the structure of this meaningful and coherent unit. The word 'unit' can be understood on different scales, extending from a whole book to a single scene or part of a letter or even to a single sentence. The Gospel of Matthew, e.g., is a unit; on a smaller scale, the Sermon on the Mount (Matt 5-7) is a unit in its own right; within this unit, the Beatitudes (Matt 5,3-11) constitute a unit, which is, in turn, made up of smaller units: the single sayings 5,3.4.5 etc. On each scale, a unit is made up of various elements. A clause is made up of words, a sentence of clauses, a scene of sentences, a story of scenes, a gospel of stories. Now 'unity' among the elements of a certain text may be established in various ways, e.g., by — temporal or logical — sequence, by formal likeness, by likeness of content, by antithesis. To return to the example adduced above: the elements of Matt 5,3-11 are connected by likeness of form as well as of content, because they all begin with μακάριοι. Within this series of connected elements, the verses 3 and 10 are connected in a closer way, as both end with the clause ὅτι αὐτῶν ἐστιν ἡ βασιλεία τῶν οὐρανῶν. The structure of a unit, or the composition of a unit, to use a term which directs attention more to the editorial activity of the author, is the whole of the connections between the elements of that unit.

This use of the term 'structure' coincides only partly with the use of the term in so-called 'structuralist exegesis', i.e., exegesis in which models of text-analysis stemming from structuralist linguistics (as developed by, e.g., V. Propp, R. Barthes and A. J. Greimas) are applied to biblical texts[5]. In this structuralist approach, interest is focussed mainly on 'deep structures', defined by D. Patte in this way: 'those structures which offer their potentialities in quest of actualization to the author's (...) creativity and which are also constraints limiting the author's creativity', or 'the constraints which impose themselves on any author or speaker'[6]. To illustrate this with an example: it is a structuralist conviction that all personages and things playing a role in all possible narratives can be reduced to six structural constants or 'actantial roles', viz., sender, subject, object, receiver, helper and opponent, and that there is a fixed pattern of relationships between these six roles[7]. This pattern of six actantial roles constitutes a 'deep structure'.

It will be evident that the structuralist definition of 'deep structure' differs from my definition as given above. There is, however, agreement between my definition and the concept of 'surface structure', also used in structural exegesis, of which B. van Iersel gives the following definition: 'the arrangement of the text which consists in correspondences on a lexical level, i.e., similarities and oppositions in the meanings of individual words and groups of words, and also similarities in sound'[8]. In both definitions, the structure of a text is its individual shape, created by its author and perceptible for its readers.

In recent years, much energy has been invested in determining the shape of individual passages and even of whole books of OT and NT. The exegetical relevance of this quest for structures will be evident: insight into the relationships between the various elements of a literary unit is an important step in understanding the unit in question. The structures displaying symmetry which have been found in biblical texts (and also in extra-biblical literature) can be reduced to a few basic types. S. Bar-Efrat has proposed recently four main types: the parallel pattern (A-A'), the ring pattern (A-B-A'), the chiastic pattern (A-B-B'-A') and the concentric pattern (A-B-C-B'-A')[9]. These four patterns can be reduced, in fact, to two really basic types: the parallel pattern (A-A') and the concentric pattern (A-B-A'). Bar-Efrat's chiastic pattern is a combination of the parallel and the concentric pattern (the middle part is divided into two parallel halves), and his concentric pattern is only an extension of what he labels ring pattern. Other combinations and extensions are, of course, possible.

Other structures simply display a sequence of elements which are connected chronologically, geographically or logically (A-B-C-D etc.), or a rather common scheme of story-telling containing introduction, narration proper and conclusion. In every single case, the structure of a literary unit is to be analysed on the basis of the indications present in it, starting from the most evident and objective ones, such as changes of persons, of place and of time, and literal repetitions.

The results of efforts to analyse biblical texts along these lines have been recorded in numerous publications. I adduce only a few examples out of an immense series. In the field of OT studies, efforts have been made to analyse the literary structure of Exod[10], Judg 13-16[11], 2 Sam 10-20 and 1 Kgs 1-2[12], Hos 2[13], Jonah[14], Ps 1[15], Ps 46[16], Ps 90[17], Ru[18], Cant[19], Qoh[20], Dan 2-7[21]. Examples of NT books and passages to whose structure has been given attention are Matt[22], Mark 2,1-3,6[23], Mark 10,46-13,37[24], Mark 13[25], Luke-Acts[26], Luke 1-9, 22-24[27], Luke 2,41-51a[28], Luke 24,13-35[29], John[30], John 1,19-5,47[31], John 18-19[32], Rom 4,16-18[33], Rom 5-8[34], 1 Cor 1,17-2,2[35], 1 Thess[36], Heb[37], Jas 2,14-26[38], Jas 2,18-19[39], 1 John[40], Rev[41]. Special studies have been devoted to the use of chiastic and concentric structures in OT and (part of the) NT[42], and to the use of parallelism in OT and NT[43].

A similar interest in the shape of individual passages and books can be observed concerning literature from Greek and Roman antiquity, witness a number of studies in this field[44]. Several of the techniques to compose a text which are supposed to have been used, have been described in antiquity[45].

It should be stressed that the structural analysis just described looks for the *individual* form of a text. In that respect it differs from form-criticism, where interest is focussed on the form a text shares with other texts, e.g., the form of a parable, of a miracle story. Nevertheless, both kinds of form may coincide, at least partly: the formal characteristics a text shares with other texts may be used as (part of) the form of this individual text. It is also possible that difference in literary genre (the form a text shares with other texts) is used in the composition of a text. So in Matt the literary genre of the discourse is used to structure the gospel: five full discourses (5,1-7,27; 10,5-42; 13,1-52; 18; 24-25), each one of them followed by more or less the same formula (7,28; 11,1; 13,53; 19,1; 26,1), are put in Jesus' mouth and give structure to Matthew's Gospel.

2. *Size and proportion in ancient literature*

a) *Ancient theories about size and proportion in works of literature*

In analysing the structure of biblical texts and texts from classical literature, it has been often observed that the size of the parts of a literary unit plays a role in the structure of that unit. There are several testimonies from antiquity suggesting that the relationship between parts of a literary unit should be a relationship of proportion in size. Greek rhetors had their theories about the καιρός, the 'due measure', and the συμμετρία, the 'due proportion' of what they had to say. Isocrates, for instance, inserts in his *Helena* an encomium on Theseus (18-29), which he has to break off in the middle of the account of Theseus' deeds, because he sees himself ἔξω φερόμενον τῶν καιρῶν, 'going outside the due measures' (29). At the end of the very long prooemium of his *Panathenaicus*, Isocrates states that he sees himself ἔξω φερόμενον τῆς συμμετρίας τῆς συντεταγμένης τοῖς προοιμίοις, 'going outside the due proportion prescribed for prooemia' (33). In the same oration, Isocrates inserts an encomium on Agamemnon (72-89), against the end of which he sees himself put before a dilemma: either τῶν καιρῶν ἀμελεῖν, 'to neglect the due measures', or to omit essentials about Agamemnon. Isocrates prefers the former possibility: at the cost of the συμμετρία τοῦ λόγου, 'the due proportion of the oration', he will speak in agreement with Agamemnon's importance, though he knows the weight of the reproach of ἀκαιρία, 'the absence of due measures' (85-86)[46].

In Plato's theories about the beautiful, the due measure and proportion are essential elements (see *Gorgias* 506 D; *Philebus* 64 E; *Sophista* 228 A; *Timaeus* 87 C). In his *Phaedrus* 264 C, Plato applies these principles to a work of art in language:

> δεῖν πάντα λόγον ὥσπερ ζῷον συνεστάναι σῶμά τι ἔχοντα αὐτὸν αὑτοῦ, ὥστε μήτε ἀκέφαλον εἶναι μήτε ἄπουν, ἀλλὰ μέσα τε ἔχειν καὶ ἄκρα, πρέποντα ἀλλήλοις καὶ τῷ ὅλῳ γεγραμμένα.
>
> 'Every discourse should be put together as a living being, having its own body, so that it is neither without a head nor without feet, but has a middle and extreme parts, written in a way that they fit to each other and to the whole.'

Μέσα and ἄκρα are mathematical *termini technici*, indicating the inner and outer elements of a proportion (see e.g., Euclides, *Elementa* 6,16); ἄκρον καὶ μέσον λόγον τεμεῖν is an expression to indicate a division according to the golden section, i.e., a division of a given whole into two parts so that the proportion between the smallest and the largest part is equal to the proportion between the largest part and the whole (Euclides, *Elementa* 6 Def. 3; 6,30). It seems, then, that Plato aims at mathematical proportions in the proper sense.

Similar theories about a literary work of art can be found in Aristotle. In his *Poetica* 1450b-1451a, he writes:

> ἔτι δ'ἐπεὶ τὸ καλὸν καὶ ζῷον καὶ ἅπαν πρᾶγμα ὃ συνέστηκεν ἐκ τινῶν οὐ μόνον ταῦτα τεταγμένα δεῖ ἔχειν ἀλλὰ καὶ μέγεθος ὑπάρχειν μὴ τὸ τυχόν· τὸ γὰρ καλὸν ἐν μεγέθει καὶ τάξει ἐστίν.... ὥστε δεῖ καθάπερ ἐπὶ τῶν σωμάτων καὶ ἐπὶ τῶν ζῴων ἔχειν μὲν μέγεθος, τοῦτο δὲ εὐσύνοπτον εἶναι, οὕτω καὶ ἐπὶ τῶν μύθων ἔχειν μὲν μῆκος, τοῦτο δὲ εὐμνημόνευτον εἶναι.
>
> 'Again: to be beautiful, a living creature, and every whole made up of parts, must not only present a certain order in its arrangement of parts, but also be of a certain definite magnitude. Beauty is a matter of size and order.... Just in the same way, then, as a beautiful whole made up of parts, or a beautiful living creature, must be of some size, but a size to be taken in by the eye, so a story or Plot must be of some length, but a length to be taken in by the memory' (transl. I. Bywater[47]).

Aristotle also gives rules for the size of smaller elements of a discourse: period and colon should be neither too short nor too long (*Rhetorica* 1409b). In that connection he states that prose that is arranged in periods is easy to follow, as it is easy to remember,

> τοῦτο δὲ ὅτι ἀριθμὸν ἔχει ἡ ἐν περιόδοις λέξις, ὃ πάντων εὐμνημονευτότατον,
>
> 'and this because language when in periodic form can be numbered, and number is the easiest of all things to remember' (*Rhetorica* 1409b; transl. W. Rhys Roberts[48]).

Some three centuries later, we meet similar statements in the works of Dionysius of Halicarnassus. The *Rhetorica* ascribed to him contains a warning against digressions causing one καιροὺς ὑπερβαίνειν, 'to go beyond the due measures', and against faulty disposition; in this warning the passage from Plato's *Phaedrus* quoted above is referred to (10,3). In his *De compositione verborum*, Dionysius deals with the γλαφυρὰ σύνθεσις, 'the elegant composition', which requires

> καὶ τὰ κῶλα τοῖς κώλοις εὖ συνυφάνθαι καὶ πάντα εἰς περίοδον τελευτᾶν, ὁρίζουσα κώλου τε μῆκος, ὃ μὴ βραχύτερον ἔσται μηδὲ μεῖζον τοῦ μετρίου, καὶ περιόδου μέτρον, οὗ πνεῦμα τέλειον ἀνδρὸς κρατήσει· ἀπερίοδον δὲ λέξιν ἢ περίοδον ἀκώλιστον ἢ κῶλον ἀσύμμετρον οὐκ ἂν ὑπομείνειεν ἐργάσασθαι,
>
> 'that the cola are well woven together and that they all end in a period, while it determines the length of a colon which will be neither shorter nor longer than what is proper, and the length of time of a period which a full breath of a man will master; but it might not endure the making of a speech which is not periodic, or of a period which is not divided into cola, or of a colon which is disproportionate' (23).

Elsewhere, Dionysius tells us that Isocrates, in order to obtain equal size and rhythm in his periods, often lengthened parts of his speech with useless expletive words (*De Isocrate* 3; cfr. *De compos.* 22, ed. Usener-Radermacher, p. 97 l. 10 sqq).

In the *Bibliotheca historica* of Diodorus Siculus we meet several remarks, in which the author states that the size and disposition of what he writes are determined by symmetry and by fixed measures (see I 8,10; 9,4; 41,11; II 31,10; IV 5,4; 68,8; VI 2,3; cfr. XX 1,5). A similar statement is found in, e.g., Sallust's *Bellum Iugurthinum* 19,2: Sallust thinks it better to remain silent about Carthago than to say too little, 'quoniam alio properare tempus monet', 'because the due measure (tempus = καιρός) urges to hasten to another subject'. It seems, then, that for at least a number of classical authors size and proportion of the parts of a text were things to take account of in composing a literary work[49].

b) *The line as unit of measure in ancient literary works according to modern scholarship*

In view of the testimonies quoted above, it is not astonishing that efforts have been made to detect whether literary works from antiquity meet the standards formulated by Plato and others. A rather obvious way of measuring texts is to count lines. This, however, can be done and has been done in two different ways: lines can be counted in a printed text-edition of a prose work, and poetic lines can be counted. In the former case, the line is an artificial modern criterion imposed upon ancient texts; in the latter case, it is a measure used by the ancient author himself. A few examples will give an impression of the results for both kinds of analysis. The materials analysed are divergent, in character, in time and in cultural milieu. Firstly, some examples of analysis by means of a count of lines in a printed text-edition of a prose work.

1.1. A quantitative analysis of Isocrates' *Panegyricus* has been carried out by F. Seck[50]. Its results can be summarized in the following scheme, in which the figures to the right indicate numbers of lines in the Benseler-Blass-edition of Isocrates:

A	parr. 1-14	prooemium		86		
B	15-132	epideictic part		905		
Ba		15-18	transition		28	
Bb		19-99	encomium on Athens		638	
Bb^1			19-50 introduction and deeds of peace			246
Bb^2			51-99 deeds of war			392
Bc		100-128	apology of Athens		214	
Bd		129-132	transition		25	
C	133-186	symbouleutic part		456		
D	187-189	epilogue		23		
	sum total			1470		

The proportion of epideictic part and entire speech is a proportion according to the golden section: B:sum total = 905:1470 × 5:8,12, 5:8 being the proportion of the larger part of a whole divided according to the golden section to that whole as given in *Scholium* 73 ad Euclidem 2,11[51]. That means that the proportion of the epideictic part (B) to the rest of the oration (A + C + D) is 905:565 = 8:5. The same proportion rules between the two parts of the encomium on Athens: Bb^1:Bb^2 = Bb^2:Bb = 246:392 = 392:638 = 5:8. Between epideictic part (B) and symbouleutic part (C) there is a proportion of 905:456 = 2:1, and between the encomium on Athens (Bb) and the apology of Athens (Bc) there is a proportion of 638:214 = 3:1. The transitions (Ba and Bd) are of almost equal size: 28 and 25 lines. The prooemium has approximately three times the length of the epilogue (86 and 23 lines respectively). The important paragraph 99, where the claim of Athens to leadership in the war against the Persians culminates, is in the middle of the entire oration.

1.2. It might be expected that Plato's *Phaedrus* meets the requirements formulated in it for a literary work of art. And so it does, according to F. Pfister's analysis[52]. This dialogue is made up of two main parts (230 E-259 D and 259 D-278 B, separated by a framework-passage 259 A-D; the outer framework 227 A-230 E and 278 B-279 C is left aside), of approximately 1045 and 645 lines respectively. The body of the *Phaedrus* is, then, divided into two parts according to the golden section: 645:1045 = 1045:1690 = 5:8. The first main part comprises a speech of Lysias (told by Phaedrus) and two speeches of Socrates; each speech is followed by a conversation, of equal size in each case. Lysias' speech is as long as the preceding introduction to the entire dialogue. Both speeches of Socrates are made up of a part in which the foundations are laid and definitions are given, and a part in which Eros is reproved (in the first speech) or praised (in the second one). In the second speech, both parts are of equal size. This speech in its entirety is as long as the speech of Lysias, the first speech of Socrates and the two ensuing dialogues together. So, reproof of Eros (230 E-243 E) and praise of Eros (243 E-257 B) are of equal length. The same size has the first section of the second main part (259 D-274 B), containing — after determination of theme and definitions (259 D-262 C, of the same size as each one of the conversations in the first main part) — the praise of the good and the reproof of the bad Logos.

Plato's *Respublica* has been analysed in a comparable way. K. Vretska[53] examined from it 8,1-9,3 (543 A-576 B), counting lines in Ast's edition of 1822, and found that Plato attaches outstanding importance to the middle of a section, both on a large and on a small scale. He situates his essential thoughts there, or he gives a certain splendour to the middle by symbols or symbolic thoughts. O. Apelt[54] found that the passage about the king-philosopher (473 D) is the middle of Plato's *Respublica*.

1.3. The third example of quantitative structural analysis, where a line of printed text is used as smallest unit, concerns the NT. Recently, F. G. Lang[55] proposed a division of the Gospel of Mark into an introduction and five parts, which he defended by means of — as well as other considerations — a count of lines, in the *NA*^{25}-edition. These are the main results of his count:

introduction	1,1-13	29 lines	
part 1	1,14-3,6	155	
2	3,7-8,21	505	(14 in 3,7-12, 246 in 3,13-6,6a and 245 in 6,6b-8,21)
3	8,22-10,45	264	
4	10,46-13,37	280	
5	14,1-16,8	282	
sum total		1515	

Part 2 amounts to exactly 1/3 of the sum total, part 1 to approximately 1/10. The size of part 3 is (without the healing story 8,22-26 which introduces it, counting 12 lines) 1/6 of the sum total, and parts 4 and 5 are of almost equal length.

In passing, Lang gives a rapid analysis along the same lines of other NT writings, including the Gospel of John. He divides it into three parts: chs. 1-6, 7-12 and 13-20, with a size of 624, 636 and 641 lines of text in *NA*^{25} respectively[56].

The above examples suggest that quantitative structural analysis is a useful and promising way of detecting the structure of a work of literature. An important point of criticism, however, which should be raised against them, is that the unit of measure used, a line in a printed edition, is too inexact to yield results which can be judged to be more than, at best, approximate: these lines can be of inequal length, as to the number of words and syllables they contain. Moreover, the ancient authors themselves did not write in lines of a printed edition[57]. A count of lines leads to more precise results in poetic texts, where the line is a unit used by the author himself. Some further examples:

2.1. A poetic text displaying a structure in numbers of lines is Vergil's *Bucolica*. Its numerical pattern has been analysed by P. Maury[58], O. Skutsch[59] and J. Van Sickle[60]. I shall give here some of the results at which Van Sickle, building on the work of his predecessors, arrives.

First of all, *Eclogae* 1-9 display a pattern of concentric symmetry: *Ecl.* 5 is the central element, *Ecl.* 9 corresponds to *Ecl.* 1. *Ecl.* 2 and 8 and, similarly, *Ecl.* 3 and 7 and *Ecl.* 4 and 6 belong together. Now, firstly the sum total of lines of *Ecl.* 1 + 9 is equal to that of *Ecl.* 4 + 6, and secondly, the sum totals of *Ecl.* 2 + 8 and *Ecl.* 3 + 7 are also equal. According to the number of lines *Ecl.* 5 is the numerical centre of *Ecl.* 1-9: what precedes (*Ecl.* 1-4) is of the same size as what follows (*Ecl.* 6-9). The book as a whole divides 'into two equal halves (accepting Skutsch's exclusion of E. viii 78) ... precisely at the point towards the end of the fifth that harks back to the second and third, that well known "sign of chronology" that initiates a process of pointed reflection on the first halfbook (E. v 85-90 = B. 415-20, out of 828 lines)'[61]. In scheme:

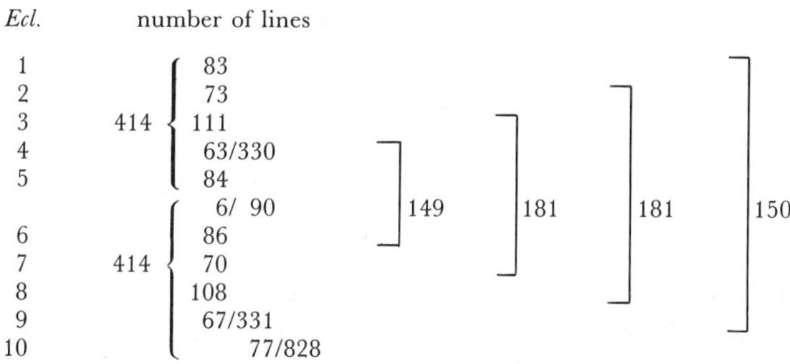

Ecl.
number of lines
1 83
2 73
3 414 111
4 63/330
5 84
6/ 90
149
181
181
150
6 86
7 414 70
8 108
9 67/331
10 77/828

Three *Eclogae*, placed at regular intervals, contain Arcadian themes: in *Ecl.* 4, 'distant hope of poetic victory in Arcadia' (lines 58-59); *Ecl.* 7 is a 'report of two Arcadians competing on Italian ground', and *Ecl.* 10 is a 'report of full cast of Arcadian characters in Arcadia itself'. The number of lines of these three *Eclogae* are three sequential multiples of 7: 63, 70 and 77[62].

Numerical patterns are also detected by Van Sickle in the various *Eclogae* in themselves. Donatus' *Vita Vergilii* 15 informs us that Vergil 'inter cetera studia ... maxime mathematicae operam dedit'. It seems, then, that he determined the structure of at least part of his poetic works in a mathematical way.

2.2. Another example of a poetic text in the composition of which a similar technique has been observed is Propertius' *Monobiblos*. It has been analysed by O. Skutsch[63], who divides this work into five groups of poems; the first four groups contain each five poems. Group A^1 comprises poems 1-5 and has a size of 89 distichs (in poem 1, two lines have to be inserted after line 11). Poems 6-9 (nr. 8 is divided into two poems, 8A and 8B) make up group B^1, with a length of 71 distichs. Group B^2 (poems 10-14) counts 70 distichs. Group A^2 (poems 15-19) has a size of 88 distichs. So, group A^1 and A^2 are of almost equal size; the same is valid for B^1 and B^2. Evident literary correspondences can be detected between A^1 and A^2, and between B^1 and B^2. The fifth group, C (poems 20-22), constitutes a kind of coda; it contains three poems, consisting of 36 distichs. So, the two A-groups together have the same length as the two B-groups together with the C-group. We have here again a clear instance of numerical arrangement of a text.

2.3. The structure of poetic parts of the OT has also been analysed by means of a count of stichs, verses (made up of one, two or three stichs) and strophes (made up of one or more verses). The problem in this case, however, is that the units of count are determined by various scholars in various ways. Consequently, the results of numerical analysis differ considerably[64]. There are, of course, specimens of OT poetry where numeric arrangement is quite clear, such as Ps 119, made up of 22 strophes, of 8 verses each; the strophes are arranged, moreover, according to the 22 letters of the Hebrew alphabet, in such a way that in each strophe all 8 verses begin with the same letter. A comparable though less elaborate arrangement is found in other alphabetic poems: Ps 37 is made up of 22 strophes of two verses each; Pss 111 and 112 consist each of 22 stichs of 3 or 4 words (5 words only in 112,1b; the headings 111,1a and 112,1a are left aside); Prov 31,10-31 has 22 verses of two stichs (an exception is 31,15, with three stichs), displaying synthetic or synonymous parallelism. Lam is made up of 5 songs of 22 members each. Lam 1-4 are alphabetic poems; in Lam 1, 2 and 4 the first letters of each strophe make up the alphabet, while in Lam 3 all three verses of each strophe begin with the same letter. In Lam 1-3 each strophe has three members[65], and each member is made up of two stichs. The strophes of Lam 4 consist each of two members of two stichs, and Lam 5 is made up of 22 verses of two stichs[66].

Another example of an OT text with a structure displaying numerical aspects is the book of Qoh. In contrast with the poetic texts from the OT dealt with above — it is a disputed question whether Qoh is a specimen of Hebrew poetry; the Massoretes, at least, did not apply to it the poetic system of accents[67] —, the basic unit of measure in Qoh as it has been analysed by A. G. Wright[68], is the Massoretic verse. Referring to his earlier analysis of the literary structure of Qoh by conventional means[69], Wright advances

> 'some additional data of a numerical nature, hitherto unnoticed — namely, that the versification of Ecclesiastes comes from the original author, that he has counted his verses and built the text on specific numerical patterns, that he has signalled those numerical patterns in his work, and that an appeal to verse count as an index of structure is legitimate and will be necessary in any future analysis of this book'[70].

According to Wright, Qoh is made up of two main parts: 1,12-6,9, entitled by him 'Qoheleth's Investigation of Life', and 6,10-11,6, 'Qoheleth's Conclusions'. The first part is preceded by the title of the book (1,1) and a poem on toil (1,2-11), and the second part is followed by a poem on youth and old age (11,7-12,8) and the editor's epilogue (12,9-14). Both 1,1-6,9 and 6,10-12,14 have a size of 111 verses, so the whole book has a length of 222 verses. Excluding the editor's epilogue 12,9-14, the size of the book is 216 ($=6^3$) verses; 216 is the numerical value of the clause *hbl hblym hkl hbl*, 'vanity of vanities, all is vanity', which includes the book proper in 1,2 and 12,8[71]. In 1,2 this clause is preceded by *hbl hblym...*, so we meet there three times the word *hbl* in the singular. The numerical value of *hbl* is 37; three times 37 makes 111, the number of verses of the first and second half of Qoh, the editor's epilogue included. Moreover, the word *hbl* occurs 37 times in the entire book, when its textually dubious occurrence in 5,6 or 9,9 *secundo loco* is left aside. The first word of this book originally made up of 216 verses is *dbry* (1,1), the numerical value of which is 216; both author (1,1) and editor (12,10-11) use this word as a synonym for the whole book. The body of the book (2,1-11,6), i.e., the book without title (1,1), inclusion (1,2), opening poem (1,3-11) and introduction (1,12-18) on the one side and without final poem (11,7-12,7), inclusion (12,8) and editor's epilogue (12,9-14) on the other, is made up of two parts, with a division at 6,9/10; both parts have a size of 93 verses, which is $2\frac{1}{2} \times 37$ (considering that 37 is an odd number, and that only entire verses can be counted). What precedes the first part (1,1-18), has a size of 18 verses, $= \frac{1}{2} \times 37$. What follows the second part, had originally a size of 12 verses (11,7-12,8); the editor added 6 verses in order to achieve 18 verses here also. It seems, then, that the measure used in the computation of the size of Qoh was 37 verses, called a *hebel* by Wright, as 37 is the numerical value of *hbl*. The entire book, the epilogue included, has a size of 6 *hebel*'s: 5 for the body of the book (*hbl*, in singular and plural, occurs 5 × in 1,2), divided into twice 2½ *hebel*'s, and one for the framework. Because the verse is the smallest unit of count in Qoh, and because of the balance of 93 over against 93 verses in the body of the book, the 5 *hebel*'s for the body of the book amount to 186 instead of 185 verses, and the *hebel* for the framework amounts to 36 instead of 37 verses. If Wright's analysis holds true, Qoh is a clear example of a book construed by means of numerical techniques.

The second series of examples, in which the poetic line or the Massoretic verse is the unit of count, compares favourably with the first series: the analysis of the text's structure is carried out here with a measure used by the author himself, and the results are more exact and more objective than those of the first series.

c) *Indications for the use of word and syllable as unit of measure in the transmission and the making of ancient works of literature*

Ways of counting which are at least equally exact and objective as a count of poetic lines are a count of words or a count of syllables. In these cases, the unit of count is (mostly) unequivocal; these ways of counting are applicable to all kinds of texts, poetry as well as prose. They have been used by the author of the Fourth Gospel, as I shall try to show in this thesis.

1. There are, first of all, indications that in antiquity a count of words or syllables was used in the transmission of works of literature.

From the Greco-Roman world we know the phenomenon of stichometry. The size of texts was calculated in στίχοι, lines. In prose texts, a στίχος or standard line was used with the length of a hexameter: 15 or 16 syllables. Numbers of στίχοι were mentioned in manuscripts, and served also as a measure in determining the price of manuscripts. Since the στίχοι had an equal number of syllables, the syllable was the basic unit of count in this system[72]. Proof for the use of stichometry in prose texts is found since the 4th century B.C. (see, e.g., Isocrates, *Panathenaicus* 136; from later times Dionysius of Halicarnassus, *De Thucydide* 10.13.19.33; Josephus, *Antiquitates Judaicae* 20,267). Several papyri contain stichometric indications[73]. Stichometric information is found in P46[74], in the manuscripts belonging to *f*13[75], and in other Greek biblical manuscripts[76], as well as in some canon lists[77]. The count of lines, when handled in an exact way, made it also possible to check whether a text had been copied correctly as far as its size was concerned.

In the transmission of the text of the Hebrew OT[78], words were counted, as well as verses and letters, in order to secure the text from corruption. The *Massorah* offers several pieces of information concerning numbers of verses, words and letters of the biblical books.

In b. Qidd. 30a these counting activities are ascribed to the Sopherim, i.e., the scholars of the pre-Tannaitic period, by means of a popular etymology of their name: 'The ancient ones are called Sopherim, because they counted (*hyw swprym*) all letters of the Torah'. Then we are told that they established the middle letter, the two middle words and the middle verse (*pswq*) of the Torah, and the middle letter and middle verse of the Psalms. There follows a discussion about the problem whether the middle letter and middle verse of the Torah belong to the first or to the second half. Among the participants in this discussion are mentioned R. Joseph (b. Chiyya, died 333) and Abayye (died 338/339), while Rabba b. Bar Chana (± 280) is referred to in the discussion. The latter is reported to have said, that 'they' (presumably the ancient ones), confronted with the problems discussed, fetched a Torah scroll and counted. The possibility to do the same in the present discussion is dismissed by R. Joseph as far as the count of letters is concerned with the argument that 'they' were experts in the *scriptio defectiva* and *plena*, whereas the participants in the present discussion are not. Finally, the teaching of the Rabbanan concerning the number of verses of the Torah, the Psalms and the Chronicles is mentioned.

It would be imprudent to consider the etymology of the name Sopherim and the activities ascribed to them as historically reliable information[79]. Nevertheless, the passage from the Talmud gives some clues for a dating of the counting activities in question:

a. To judge by the names of the rabbis mentioned in the passage, the idea that the ancient ones counted words, letters and verses, was current in the second half of the 3rd century. This is confirmed by b. Sanh. 106b, where R. Isaac, ± 300, is said to interpret the participle *spr* in Isa 33,18 *primo loco* as 'one who counts the letters of the Torah'.

b. By that time, the counting activities in question already belonged, at least partly, to the past: its results are part of the tradition, and R. Joseph is not able any more to test the tradition about the middle letter of the Torah, because he does not possess the knowledge required to do so.

The habit to count letters, words and verses in the Hebrew OT should, therefore, amply antedate the second half of the 3rd century[80]. Whether it goes back to the actual Sopherim or not, is a question to be left open here[81].

2. So far, we have only indications for a count of syllables or words in the transmission of texts. There are a few hints that it was also used in the making of texts.

The Peripatetic Clearchus (before 342-half of 3rd cent. B.C.) tells about a game, in which the participants firstly speak to and answer each other in a metre agreed upon, πρός τε τούτοις ἕκαστον εἰπεῖν ὅσων ἂν προσταχθῇ συλλαβῶν ἔμμετρον, καὶ ὅσα [ἀπὸ] τῆς τῶν γραμμάτων καὶ συλλαβῶν ἔχεται θεωρίας,

'and besides this, each one says a metrical verse of so many syllables as has been prescribed, and all which the theory of letters and syllables holds' (Fragment 63,I = Athenaeus X 457 C).

It seems reasonable to suppose that, in order to be used in a game, the 'theory of letters and syllables', part of which was the making of verses in a prescribed number of syllables, should have been rather common, at least in certain milieus[82].

A second indication for the use of numbers of syllables and words in the making of texts is supplied by rhetoric theories, in which the phenomenon of the isocolon is dealt with[83]. An isocolon is a sentence or clause, or a combination of sentences or clauses, which consists of equal cola or members; mostly these members display the same sequence of parts of the sentence, in which case they have an equal number of words. In several descriptions of the isocolon, it is said that its members should have an equal or almost equal number of syllables. Aristotle says very succinctly:

παρίσωσις δ'ἐὰν ἴσα τὰ κῶλα.

'*Parisosis* is making the two members of a period equal in length' (*Rhetorica* 1410a; transl. W. Rhys Roberts).

In *De elocutione*, ascribed to Demetrius of Phaleron but really dating from ± 100 C.E., we read:

εἶδος δὲ τοῦ παρομοίου τὸ ἰσόκωλον, ἐπὰν ἴσας ἔχῃ τὰ κῶλα τὰς συλλαβάς, ὥσπερ Θουκυδίδῃ, ''ὡς οὔτε ὧν πυνθάνονται ἀπαξιούντων τὸ ἔργον, οἷς τε ἐπιμελὲς εἴη εἰδέναι οὐκ ὀνειδιζόντων''. ἰσόκωλον μὲν δὴ τοῦτο.

'Under the heading of symmetry of members comes equality of members, which occurs when the members contain an equal number of syllables, as in the following sentence of Thucydides: ''This implies that neither those who are asked disown, nor those who care to know censure the occupation.'' This is an instance of equality of members' (25; transl. W. Rhys Roberts).

The quotation from Thucydides (1,5) is made up of 16 + 16 syllables[84]. An example from Isocrates (*Helena* 17) is given, after a definition of the *parison* (= isocolon), by Alexander, *De figuris* 26 (2nd cent. C.E.):

παρισόν ἐστιν, ὅταν δύο ἢ πλείονα κῶλα συνενωθέντα μάλιστα μὲν καὶ τὰς συλλαβὰς ἴσας ἔχῃ, ἀλλά γε καὶ τὸν ἀριθμὸν τὸν ἴσον ἐν πᾶσι λαμβάνῃ, ὡς ἔχει τὸ Ἰσοκρατικόν·
''τοῦ μὲν ἐπίπονον καὶ φιλοκίνδυνον τὸν βίον κατέστησε, τῆς δὲ περίβλεπτον καὶ περιμάχητον τὴν φύσιν ἐποίησεν''.

> 'There is a *parison*, when two or more united cola have above all their syllables equal, but obtain also in all their parts equal rhythm, as the passage from Isocrates quoted above has:
> "Of him, he rendered the life painful and adventurous,
> of her, he made the nature admired and fought for".'

In the example adduced by Alexander, the parallelism is perfect, and both clauses have a size of 19 syllables, or 8 words.

The principle of an equal number of syllables in the members of an isocolon is formulated somewhat less strictly in a passage which is older than the two just quoted, and which has, moreover, an interesting continuation, viz., *Rhetorica ad Herennium* 4,20,27 (dating from ± 50 B.C.):

> conpar appellatur quod habet in se membra orationis, ... quae constent ex pari fere numero syllabarum. hoc non denumeratione nostra fiet — nam id quidem puerile est —, sed tantum adferet usus et exercitatio facultatis, ut animi quodam sensu par membrum superiori referre possimus.

> 'A *conpar* (= isocolon) is called that which contains in itself members of speech ... which should consist of an almost equal number of syllables. This will not happen by our counting — for that is childish —, but only the use and training of the ability will bring it about that, because of a certain sensitivity of the mind, we are able to word a member equal to the preceding one.'

The author of this rhetorical work does not only give a definition of the isocolon, but he also tells us that making an isocolon is a matter not of simply counting syllables, but of sensitivity, to be developed by practising and training. We may presume that for the ancients the making and perceiving of an isocolon was far more natural and usual than it is for us. And there is no reason why what is said here about the isocolon, should not be valid also for other kinds of numerical balance and symmetry in literary works of art from antiquity, at least when this balance and symmetry are present in an utterance not exceeding the size of a period[85].

In the *De figuris sententiarum et elocutionis liber* of Aquila Romanus (3rd cent. C.E.), we meet the requirement that the members of an isocolon have an equal number of words, whereas a *parison* allows of an unequal number (23-24).

So far, no direct indications have been found for the use of numbers of syllables or words in the making of texts, the size of which exceeds a few clauses. The indications found concern only the making of small quantities of text, whereas the indications for the use of numbers of syllables or words in large quantities of text concern only the transmission of texts. We should not forget, however, that our knowledge of ancient theories concerning literary techniques is limited, and that a large part of what we know about literary techniques which were applied in antiquity, is based upon induction. Patterns of highly sophisticated concentric symmetry have been detected in many ancient works of literature, but — as far as I know — a theoretical description of such patterns from antiquity is still missing. Likewise, the question whether numbers of syllables and words have been used in the composition of literary works can only be answered by close examination of these works. The indications discussed above are, at least, quite compatible with possible positive results of such an examination.

d) *Quantitative analysis in modern biblical scholarship: word and syllable as unit of measure*

Now we must look for the role of numbers of syllables and words in the composition of literary works from antiquity. Positive results of an analysis of their literary composition in terms of numbers of syllables and words would constitute the proof of the theory that authors built their works in that way.

In the field of biblical studies, research of this kind has been carried out in the past decades. Some of its results will be summarized here, in order to lay down a basis for similar research into the Fourth Gospel.

Several scholars make use of a count of words or syllables in their analysis of literary units from the Hebrew OT. In dealing with the role of the number 7 in Gen 1,1-2,3, U. Cassuto[86] observes among many other things that Gen 1,1 has a size of 7 words, that Gen 1,2 has a size of 14 (= 2 × 7) words, and that the seventh paragraph of this unit, about the seventh day (2,1-3), has a length of 35 (= 5 × 7) words; this paragraph contains, moreover, three successive clauses, in which the expression 'the seventh day' occurs, of 7 words each (2,2a.2b.3a). To these observations, P. Beauchamp[87] adds the following ones: Gen 1,3-31 (about the six days of creation) is made up of 207 + 206 words, for 1,3-19 (the first four days) and 1,20-31 (the fifth and sixth day) respectively. The 207 words of 1,3-19 consist of 69 + 69 + 69 words, for 1,3-8.9-13.14-19, about the first and second, third, and fourth day respectively. Both halves of 1,3-31 contain 5 utterances of God introduced by *wyʾmr* (in 1,3.6.9.11.14 and 1,20.24.26.28.29).

A count of words (and also of clauses and sections) is used by F. Langlamet[88] in his analysis of passages from 2 Sam and 1 Kgs. He applies it to reconstructed previous stages of the text as well as to the text in its present state. On both levels, he distinguishes in his counts between narrative and discourse. He discerns symmetry and balance in the arrangement of the text in numbers of words, and a preference for certain numbers, such as round numbers (numbers divisible by 10), and multiples of 9 and 11. He tries to explain the use of certain numbers of words by the size of the columns in which the text was written.

Examples of a count of words in 1 and 2 Kgs are given by J. Smit Sibinga[89]. 1 Kgs 19,1-18 contains 160 words of narrative; in 19,7-8 the 'second time' and 'forty days and forty nights' are mentioned, and 2 × (40 + 40) = 160. 19,1-3 and 19,4-6 have both a length of 50 words; 19,7-11a and 19,11b (beginning with *whny*)-14 have both a size of 75 words. In 2 Kgs 2,23-25 it is told that two bears tear 42 boys to pieces; this short passage has a size of 44 (= 42 + 2) words. 2 Kgs 8,1-6 is made up of 88 words of narrative and 44 words of discourse. I convinced myself that 1 Kgs 18,20-46 has a size of 452 words, which number is the sum of two figures mentioned at the beginning of the story: 450 prophets of the Baal, and two bulls (18,22-23).

A similar phenomenon has been observed by Smit Sibinga in Exod 24. There, 'the sum total of the cardinal numbers equals the total number of words: 70 + 1 + 12 + 12 + ½ + ½ + 70 + 6 + 40 + 40 = 252'[90]. So, in several of the OT passages just mentioned, there is a relationship between the size of the text, measured in numbers of words, and the numbers mentioned in the text itself.

D. N. Freedman[91] makes use of syllable-counting in his analysis of the metrical structure of poetic texts from the OT. This method is 'relatively objective and simple' (relatively of course, as we are not always certain about the division into syllables of Hebrew words because of our defective knowledge of historical morphology and phonology of the Hebrew language), and it is 'designed to describe accurately the metrical structure of the poem under consideration.... Without insisting that the Hebrew poets consciously or deliberately counted syllables in composing their works, we observe that their poems exhibit patterns with a degree of regularity and repetition which is best captured by a syllable-counting process'[92]. These patterns concern not only verses and strophes, but also entire poems. I adduce an example to illustrate Freedman's method. In Ps 137[93], both introduction (137,1-2) and conclusion (137,8-9), making up together an inclusion because of the mentioning of 'Babel' in 137,1.8, contain 5 metrical units, of 7, 8 or 9 syllables. The introduction has a size of 37 syllables, the conclusion of 38. The body of the Psalm has three parts: 137,3.4-6.7. First and third part are both made up of four metrical units, and have both a size of 27 syllables. The central part (with a chiasm at its centre, 137,5-6a) is exactly as long as first and third part together: 8 metrical units, 54 syllables[94].

A scholar who incidentally uses a count of syllables on a small scale is L. Sabottka, in his translation of and commentary on Zeph[95]. Two examples: Zeph 1,4-6 is made up of three lines of 10 syllables, followed by lines of 6, 6 + 5, 11 + 6, 17 + 5 and 22 + 6 syllables, displaying in this way a regular growth[96]. Zeph 1,15-16 consists of 6 stichs of 7 syllables, all of them beginning with *ywm*, which word is used 7 times in these two verses[97].

A count of syllables or words is also used in the analysis of the literary composition of NT passages. I begin with three instances of incidental use of this method. In J. Schniewind's commentary on Matt[98], we are informed that the series of Beatitudes in Matt 5,3-10 is made up of two parts: 5,3-6 and 5,7-10, about the waiting and the being respectively of those who are said to be blessed, and that both parts have an equal number of words (36). E. Bammel[99] supposes that in 1 Cor 15,3c-5 Paul incorporates into his letter an older formula of confession which originally ended with ὤφθη in 15,5. This formula of four members, in which first and third member display *homoioteleuton*, as do also second and fourth member, is made up of 10 + 3 + 10 + 3 words. H. J. de Jonge[100] observes that in Luke 2,41-51a, a pericope of 170 words, 'the word μέσῳ in 46 is the 85th word and the phrase ἐν μέσῳ τῶν διδασκάλων therefore forms the mathematical centre of the pericope'. He adds an observation of J. Smit Sibinga which concerns the concentric structure of the pericope: the sum total of words of the first two (2,41-42.43) and last two elements (2,49-50.51a) of the concentric structure is equal to the sum total of words of the three middle elements (2,44-46a.46b-47.48), viz., 85 words.

There are a few scholars who make the count of syllables or words into a major tool in their structural analysis of passages from the NT. J. Schattenmann[101] analyses a series of NT texts he considers as 'prose hymns'. The authors of these hymns did not, according to Schattenmann, take into account the quantity of syllables, but only the number of syllables, using in this way not metre but a free rhythm and following in this respect the general tendency of the period[102]. Such hymns are often made up of two parts, one about God and one about man, with a central word standing in the middle[103]. Good examples are Phil 2,6-11 and Col 1,12-20. The hymn Phil 2,6-11[104] is made up of two parts: 2,6-8, about Jesus humbling himself though being equal to God, and 2,9-11, about his being exalted. The central word is σταυροῦ at the end of 2,8. When in 2,9 τό before ὄνομα is omitted (with D F G Ψ *Mehrheitstext* Clement Origen), both parts are of equal length: 90 syllables. In the hymn Col 1,12-20[105] Schattenmann transposes 1,13-14 behind 1,18a, where the words τῆς ἐκκλησίας are omitted as being a gloss. In this way he obtains a hymn with two parts: 1,12.15-18a, a 'Logos-hymn', and

1,13-14.18b-20, a 'Christ-hymn'. Both parts have a size of 151 syllables; the first part has a size of 78 words, the second one of 75 words.

Unfortunately, Schattenmann's analyses are weakened by at least two circumstances. Firstly, he inclines to a rather careless use of textual criticism and literary criticism: his decisions in both fields are too often obviously motivated only or at least mainly by the fact that they yield results which fit well into the numerical schemes proposed (cfr. his transposition of Col 1,13-14, mentioned above). To avoid a vicious circle, one should have more arguments than only this one. The other weakness of Schattenmann's work concerns the date and origin of some theories about the meaning of the various numbers he detects. Many numbers get in his theory a special religious significance, mainly derived, it seems, from gnostic speculations. He seems to suppose that the authors of the NT 'prose hymns' were aware of these theories and used them — which remains, in my opinion, something to be proved.

If one wants to show that authors made use of numbers of words and syllables in constructing their text, one should not burden one's argument with unproved hypotheses in the field of textual or literary criticism, or concerning the significance of numbers. The two other authors whose publications will be discussed here meet this requirement. J. Irigoin[106] analyses the text of the Prologue of the Fourth Gospel (John 1,1-18) as printed in *NA*^{25}, in two different ways: by counting all syllables (he considers the *iōta* at the beginning of Ἰωάννης 1,6.15 and of Ἰησοῦς 1,17 to be a separate syllable), and by counting only stressed syllables[107]. These counts result in a bipartition of the Prologue into 1,1-8 and 1,9-18; both parts display an A-B-A'-pattern. For the two counts, the schemes are as follows:

1,1-4	75 syllables	A		1,1-3b[108]	20 stressed syll.	A
5	22	B		3c-5	14	B
6-8	75	A'		6-8	20	A'
9-13	138	C		9-13	40	C
14	50	D		14	14	D
15-18	139	C'		15-18	41	C'

In order to assess the value of this analysis, Irigoin inquires whether this division is in accordance with the contents of the Prologue. A number of data suggest it is. John the Baptist occurs in A' and C', whereas A and C are about the Logos. In the first part, there is an antithesis between A, about the eternal Logos, and A', about the man John. In C, the section about the refusal of the light (1,9-11) is (almost) as long as the section about the acceptance of the light (1,12-13): two times 69 syllables, or 21 and 19 stressed syllables. D is considered to be the synthesis of the entire Prologue. Its elements return in C', which part can also be divided into two sections, beginning with John the Baptist and Moses respectively: 1,15-16 and 1,17-18, of 71 and 68 syllables or 22 and 19 stressed syllables respectively.

Irigoin has difficulty with the difference between the two counts in the division of 1,1-5: does A end with 1,4 (so the count of all syllables) or with οὐδὲ ἕν in 1,3 (so the count of stressed syllables)? From the point of view of contents and style, both divisions can be defended. In the former case, B deals with the antinomy of light and darkness and begins, just as D, with καί, and the present tense φαίνει contrasts well with the preceding preterites. In the latter case, 1,3c-5, about the Logos, source of life and light and contrasted with darkness, is a unit, made up of four sentences, connected by evident *concatenatio*, and by the conjunction καί. It seems to Irigoin that for the time in which the Fourth Gospel was written a rhythm based on stressed syllables is more probable than the other kind of rhythm, to judge from what is known of later (especially liturgical) poetry. After all, Irigoin shows a slight preference for the count of stressed syllables, but he remains very cautious and hesitating in this choice. A rhythm based on stressed syllables seems fitting for this passage, with its hymnic character. A count of all syllables need not surprise us in view of the practice of stichometry which was widely used in the Hellenistic world (see above, p. 12).

A few remarks concerning Irigoin's study have to be made here: 1. His study clearly shows that numerical regularity and balance are present in John 1,1-18: numbers of syllables and of stressed syllables are essential to the way in which the text was composed. 2. The fact that two different structures seem to be present in one text is perhaps not too embarrassing[109]. It is not inconceivable that one passage (in the present case John 1,3c-4) fulfils more than one function. The important thing in such a case is to show that both structures are supported by indications in the text, a thing which Irigoin does. 3. Irigoin considers — without further explanation — the *iōta* at the beginning of Ἰωάννης and Ἰησοῦς as a separate syllable: in the historical Greek language, *iōta* always is a vowel. However, grammarians of the NT seem to be agreed that in such transcriptions of Semitic proper names the *iōta* functions as a semivocal[110], and should not be read as a separate syllable.

A consequence of this last remark is a slight change in Irigoin's scheme for the structure of John 1,1-18 in numbers of syllables. I would propose the following figures:

1,1-4	A	75	
5	B	22	
6-8	A'	74/171	
9-11	C		69

12-13		69/138
14	D	50
15-16	C'	70
17-18		67/137/325/496

The symmetry of Irigoin's scheme is hardly reduced by this operation; only A' is now shorter than A by one unit. The sum totals which appear for the two parts and for the entire Prologue become interesting in this count: 171, 325 and 496 are triangular numbers, of 18, 25 and 31 respectively; 496 is, moreover, a 'perfect' number[111]. Furthermore, 496 is the numerical value of μονογενής (40 + 70 + 50 + 70 + 3 + 5 + 50 + 8 + 200 = 496), a qualification of Jesus which is important in John; it occurs twice in the Prologue (1,14.18), and also elsewhere in John (3,16.18) and 1 John (4,9)[112].

Irigoin's analysis suggests anyhow that a count of syllables might be worth while also in studying the composition of other passages of the Fourth Gospel.

A NT passage which is analysed by Irigoin in the same way, is the *Magnificat* (Luke 1,46-53)[113]. There also, Irigoin finds that both a count of all syllables and a count of stressed syllables only lead to schemes of structure which are in accordance with the contents of the text, even though here the difference between the two schemes is greater than in the case of John 1,1-18. In this case, too, Irigoin is inclined to consider the count of stressed syllables the more important one.

A third scholar who makes a count of syllables and words into a major tool in his analysis of NT (and other early Christian) texts is J. Smit Sibinga. He bases his counts on the text as printed in *NA*[25], and considers Ἰησοῦς as a dissyllable. In a communication to the 'Journées Bibliques' of Louvain in 1970, he discussed 'a literary technique in the Gospel of Matthew'[114]: consciously and consistently, the author of the First Gospel 'arranged his text in such a way, that the size of the individual sections is fixed by a determined number of syllables. The individual parts of a sentence, the sentences themselves, sections of a smaller and larger size, they are, all of them, characterized in a purely quantitative way by their number of syllables'[115]. Out of the series of Matthean passages investigated by Smit Sibinga, I adduce one small but clear example of application of this technique. Matt 8,19-22 contains two apophthegms on following Jesus. The scene has a very simple structure: twice, a statement of a follower of Jesus is followed by a saying of Jesus himself. The first half is made up of 12 + 8 = 20 syllables for the narrative in 8,19a.20a, and 17 + 43 = 60 syllables for the direct discourse in 8,19bc.20bc; together 80 syllables. In the second half, the narrative amounts again to 12 + 8 = 20 syllables (for 8,21a.22a); now the discourse has a size of 21 + 19 = 40 syllables (8,21bc.22b). For the entire episode 8,19-22, we obtain 40 syllables of narrative, and 100 syllables of discourse[116]. Smit Sibinga observes that frequently in Matt the number of syllables of individual scenes (or of combinations of scenes) is a number divisible by 100, 50 or 10; often also, either the narrative or the discourse of a scene amounts to such a number. We shall see that this technique has also been applied by the author of the Fourth Gospel.

In another contribution[117], Smit Sibinga subjects Matt 24-25, the apocalyptic discourse, to a closer inquiry, and points out that the technique of syllable-counting has been applied there both on a smaller and on a larger scale. In a recent article[118], he investigates text and composition of Matt 14,22-33, the story about Jesus walking on the water, and finds that several numerical literary techniques have been used in that episode: a count of the various forms of the verb, a count of words and a count of syllables. The count of words especially leads to interesting results[119]. The story contains 31 words of discourse, and 155, = 5 × 31, words of narrative. Within the story, several small units of 31 words are discernible: 14,22-23a; 14,24-25 and 14,26-27. Moreover, 14,27, Jesus' self-revelation to his disciples, constitutes exactly the centre of the episode, when it is measured in numbers of words: this verse of 12 words is preceded and followed by 87 words.

Mark 3,1-6, the story about Jesus healing a man with a withered hand, is another passage in the composition of which numbers of words are essential, according to Smit Sibinga's analysis[120]. This short narration displays a concentric structure. 3,1-2.6 constitute the framework, in which 3,2 and 6 are corresponding: there, the action of the Pharisees is recorded. The healing is told in 3,3.5b-d (from λέγει onward). In 3,4-5b (up to αὐτῶν included), the dispute between Jesus and the Pharisees is recorded. Corresponding are Jesus' double question in 3,4a-c, and the double participial statement about his action and emotion in 3,5ab. In the middle we have the short phrase: 'but they remained silent', 3,4d. This concentric structure, together with the correspondent numbers of words, can be rendered schematically as follows:

3,1	frame, *a*	13								13
2.6	frame, *b*		11						15	26
3.5b-d	healing			13				13		26
4a-c.5ab	dispute				14		12			26
4d	no answer					3				3

All three combinations of corresponding parts amount to 26 words; the healing is reported in 13 + 13 words. The introduction 3,1 has a size of 13 words. The literary structure of the story also finds expression in numbers of words.

Many instances of syllable-technique are detected by Smit Sibinga in Acts[121]. Frequently, episodes are made up of two halves which contain an equal number of syllables. There are also several instances of *isopsepha* in Acts, where the number of syllables of an episode or speech is equal to the numerical value of an important name or word occurring in or related to the passage in question (such as we found concerning John 1,1-18, where both the number of syllables and the numerical value of μονογενής are 496). Peter's speech in Acts 2,14b-36, e.g., is made up of two equal halves: 444 syllables in 2,14b-24, and again 444 syllables in 2,25-36. Their sum, 888, is the numerical value of the name 'Ιησοῦς — a number which was famous in this quality in the second century, witness Irenaeus' *Adversus haereses* 1,15,2[122].

Of some importance for our present purposes is also Smit Sibinga's analysis of 1 John[123], because 1 John is very closely related to the Gospel of John. The technique of syllable-counting has been applied there on various levels. Some small sections amount to such numbers of syllables as 100 (2,18-19; 3,9-10), 150 (3,13-16; 5,14-16), 125 (2,15-17), or 75 (4,11-12)[124]. In several cases, logical structure and pattern of syllables fit or suit each other. A clear and simple example is 5,14-16, made up of 80 syllables for 5,14-15, and 70 syllables for 5,16[125]. A larger section which amounts to a round number of syllables is 3,1-12: it has a size of 500 syllables, made up of 320 syllables for 3,1-8 and 180 for 3,9-12[126]. Smit Sibinga even draws up a plan for the whole letter on the basis of syllable count. He distinguishes three parts: 1,1-2,26; 2,27-4,6; 4,7-5,21. First and third part are of equal length: 1450 syllables, over against 1370 syllables for the second part[127].

Finally, I mention — without going into detail — Smit Sibinga's analysis of Melito of Sardis' Περὶ Πασχα[128], where he discerns application of syllable count: 'It is well known that Melito, and other writers of the Asianic school, sometimes determined the length of parallel sentences according to the number of syllables. Now the same principle determines the size, the structure and what I would like to call the balance of larger sections, both their internal order and their respective dimensions.... Melito, then, shaped the parts of his Homily so as to fill out a certain number of syllables: a round number, or a symbolic number, a square or "triangular" number, or a number that for some other reason could interest an arithmetician'[129].

From the above survey, it seems probable that in antiquity numbers of words and/or syllables were used in the composition of literary works, and that this phenomenon was not confined to only one cultural milieu[130]. A count of syllables and/or words may be a help, then, both in textual criticism and in the analysis of literary structures.

3. *Plan of the present study concerning the fourth evangelist's use of numbers of words and syllables in the composition of his text*

It is the hypothesis of the present study, that the author of the Fourth Gospel used not only conventional literary means, but also numbers of words and syllables in the composition of at least large portions of his text. He measured, according to this hypothesis, literary units and their various parts in numbers of words and syllables, and connected parts of a literary unit by means of relationships between numbers of words and syllables. This was one of the ways in which he shaped his text.

The hypothesis will be tested in five portions of the Fourth Gospel, in which the main literary genres which occur in this gospel are represented[131]: sequence of narration, dialogue and monologue, represented by chs. 5 and 6, and also by 9,1-10,21; extensive and dramatically shaped story, represented by ch. 9; long monologue, represented by 10,1-18 and ch. 17; series of connected scenes, represented by 1,19-2,11. A selection of passages from the gospel proved necessary for various reasons. A thorough analysis of the entire Fourth Gospel would outgrow the limits of a thesis. Moreover, in order to test a hypothesis such as the one proposed here, it is essential that one employs literary units of limited size. It is also important that the passages in question do not present too many textual problems which could hamper the analysis. The conclusions of this investigation will, strictly speaking, be valid only for the passages just mentioned. However, a proof of the hypothesis for these passages would arouse a very strong suspicion that the technique of word- and syllable-count has been used in other passages of John as well.

A problem which poses itself before the actual analysis is: which text to use? Modern editions of the Greek text of the NT try to approximate the original Greek text as well as possible, but nevertheless they display a considerable number of differences between each other. The most obvious solution is to take an edition which is the median of the various modern editions, and to take into consideration always the possibility that the text which is printed in this edition does not coincide completely with what the evangelist originally wrote. When I started my research, the choice of an edition which met the condition of being the median of modern editions was not very difficult. It fell upon *NA*[25], which edition is, in fact, the average of three authoritative editions from the end of the preceding century and the beginning of this century, those of Tischendorf[8] (1869-1872), Westcott-Hort (1881) and B. Weiss (1894-1900). About Nestle's editions of the Greek NT (up to the 25th included) it was written recently: 'The majority text which he [i.e. Eb.

Nestle] formulated corresponded not only to the views of nineteenth century New Testament scholarship on the text of the New Testament, but to those of twentieth century scholarship as well'[132].

In the meantime, *NA*^{25} has been succeeded by *NA*^{26}[133], which edition is, as far as its wording is concerned, identical to *UBSGNT*^{3}. Where *NA*^{25} and *NA*^{26} are in agreement, I follow their common text[134]; instances of difference between the two editions which affect numbers of syllables and words will be discussed in order to arrive at a well-considered decision about the reading to be adopted. After all, one should not forget that only a restricted number of variant readings influence a count of syllables and words. For this count it does not make any difference whether two clauses should be connected by καί or by δέ, or whether the order of words should be changed or not.

A second preliminary problem concerns literary criticism. Several scholars are of the opinion that the text of John as we know it (that is, without 5,3e-4 and 7,53-8,11) is not identical with what the author originally wrote: parts of the text are supposed to have changed places, and other parts are supposed to be later redactional additions. To mention a few examples concerning the passages discussed in this book: there are scholars who hold that the order of chs. 5 and 6 has been reversed, that parts of ch. 7 (7,15-24 or 7,19-24) originally belonged together with ch. 5, that 5,28-29 and 6,51c-58 (or 6,48-58) are redactional additions, that 10,1-18 originally belonged together with 10,26-28. None of these theories has gained even an approximation to universal adherence; even for ch. 21 the matter is by no means settled, whether it should be considered as an epilogue which does belong, or as an appendix which originally does not belong, to the Fourth Gospel[135]. It seems to me that (without denying *a priori* the possibility of transpositions and additions), generally speaking, a) these theories find support in the textual tradition in only very few cases; b) they are too often based on preconceived ideas about the evangelist's views (e.g., that he would know only a present eschatology, or that he would be critical towards sacraments), or about the logic of his narration; c) as far as they are theories about later additions, they are hardly supported by stylistic arguments; d) as far as they are transposition theories, they mostly fail to explain convincingly how the present order of the text came into being. One had better leave the text as it is, and, with C. H. Dodd, 'assume as a provisional working hypothesis that the present order [i.e. of the Fourth Gospel] is not fortuitous, but deliberately devised by somebody — even if he were only a scribe doing his best — and that the person in question (whether the author or another) had some design in mind, and was not necessarily irresponsible or unintelligent'[136]. We shall have to see whether a count of words and syllables will confirm Dodd's working hypothesis.

The method of analysis which will be followed is, at least in principle, very simple. The count of syllables and words does not present many problems[137]. The few problems, e.g., concerning Greek words beginning with *iōta*, and concerning some Greek transcriptions of Semitic proper names, will be dealt with at the beginning of the discussion of the passages in which they present themselves for the first time.

The results of the counting work constitute the raw materials to be analysed. Before doing so, a thorough analysis of the literary structure of the passages in question by conventional means is necessary. This analysis comprises, essentially, three steps:
1) delimiting a literary unit;
2) determining the sections of which it is made up;
3) establishing the relationships between these sections.
These steps ought to be carried out on various scales, as there are various scales of literary unity (see above, p. 2, where Matt 5-7 is adduced as an example).

Then the decisive step of the analysis follows: the literary structure as detected by the conventional literary analysis is transposed, 'translated', into numbers of syllables and words, to see whether the literary structure is also discernible in these numbers. If it is, the hypothesis has been proved. If it is not, the hypothesis does not hold. It is also possible, of course, that aspects of literary structure which were hitherto unnoticed may come to light by means of a count of words and syllables; however, the count should be used in that way only when it has been established with some certainty that the composition shows, let us say, numerical features.

At this point the question of the criterion should be raised. When do we conclude a literary structure is to be discerned or recognized in the figures representing either the number of words or of syllables of a text? The definite answer to this question can be given only by the analysis of the selected passages itself. Nevertheless, some examples may be given in advance:
— The size of a literary unit amounts to a round number of words or syllables ('round' to be understood as: divisible by 50).
— Either the direct discourse or the narrative[138] of an episode amounts to a round number of words or syllables.
— One small but important part of a literary unit, e.g., an important saying of Jesus or an OT quotation, contains exactly the number of words or syllables which this unit has above a round number (I term this technique the 'surplus-technique').
— Within a literary unit, corresponding parts are of equal length, or their sum total amounts to a round number of words or syllables, or their numbers of words or syllables have a common factor.

— Certain basic numbers have been used in a literary unit, i.e., many figures occurring in its numbers of words and syllables are multiples of the same number.

These and similar numerical phenomena are evidence of a numerical technique on the part of the author. Many variations occur in the application of this technique — as is also the case in the application of conventionally known literary techniques. The numerical aspect may seem artificial and mannered, but the evidence of the texts is such that it deserves our attention and our respect.

4. *Ancient theories about numbers*

Finally, a few things have to be said about numbers that in antiquity were considered as somehow significant. In the above examples only round numbers were mentioned. These are obviously significant for every user of the decimal system; and Greek-speaking people in antiquity were users of the decimal system, hardly in their way of writing numbers, but certainly in their way of pronouncing them[139]. There were, however, other kinds of numbers as well which were given special significance, and which seem to have been applied in John. In documenting the ancient ideas about significant numbers, I will pay special attention to Philo, because of both his interest in numbers[140] and his cultural and temporal vicinity to the Fourth Gospel.

Three kinds of natural numbers, related among each other, which, because of their special character, attracted attention from arithmeticians in antiquity, are triangular numbers, square numbers and ἀριθμοὶ ἑτερομήκεις, 'rectangular numbers', i.e., numbers which are the product of two successive natural numbers (e.g., 6, being the product of 2 and 3)[141]. A triangular number is the sum of a series of successive natural numbers beginning with 1 (see n. 111 above), a square number is the sum of a series of successive odd numbers beginning with 1, and a rectangular number is the sum of a series of successive even numbers beginning with 2. It seems that the Pythagoraeans were already interested in these numbers (cfr. Aristotle, *Metaphysica* 986a); the interest is anyhow old[142]. The categories of numbers in question are mentioned by Aristotle, *Metaphysica* 986a; 1092b[143]. They are discussed extensively by later arithmeticians who systematized older arithmetical knowledge: Nicomachus of Gerasa (± 100 C.E.), in his *Arithmetica introductio*, 2,8,1sqq, and Theon of Smyrna (first half of the 2nd cent. C.E.), in what is left of his *Expositio rerum mathematicarum ad legendum Platonem utilium* (ed. Hiller, pp. 26-38).

Interest in such numbers can also be observed elsewhere. In his *De Iside et Osiride* 75, Plutarch tells that the highest oath among the Pythagoraeans was the so-called τετρακτύς or 36, which they called also 'the universe' because it was the union of the first four odd and first four even numbers. Lucian, in his *Vitarum auctio* 4, informs us about Pythagoras' conception of 10 as triangular number of 4. There, he puts Pythagoras upon the stage among the philosophers to be sold. In a dialogue with one of his potential buyers, Pythagoras tells this man that one of the things he will teach him, is counting. The buyer says that he knows to count, whereupon Pythagoras asks him how he counts. The answer is: 'One, two, three, four'; then Pythagoras interrupts him and says: 'What you think to be four, that is ten, and a perfect triangle, and our oath'. Apparently, the public in the dialogue and Lucian's readers were supposed to understand this allusion to 10 as the triangular number of 4; this may show the spread of this way of thinking in antiquity. Philo, too, often points out triangular numbers; as such are indicated 10, 28, 36, 55, 120 and 300[144].

That square numbers come into being by addition of successive odd numbers beginning with 1, and rectangular numbers by addition of successive even numbers beginning with 2, is remarked by Philo, *Quaestiones et solutiones in genesin*, 2,5.12.14; cfr. 3,49. Square numbers to which Philo pays special attention are 4, 9, 36, 49, 64 and 100[145]. Rectangular numbers especially indicated by Philo are 6, 56, 90 and 110[146]. The first twelve square and first twelve rectangular numbers are summed up in *Quaest. et sol. in gen.* 2,5.

It will be evident that there are certain relationships between the categories of numbers just described. A triangular number, being the sum of successive numbers, is the half of a rectangular number, being the sum of successive even numbers. An example: 36, triangular number of 8, is the half of the rectangular number 72 ($= 8 \times 9$). In Nicomachus' *Arithm. introd.* 2,12, and Theon's *Exp. rer. math.* p. 41 Hiller, we are informed that the sum of two successive triangular numbers is a square number. Again an example: the sum of 28, triangular number of 7, and 36, triangular number of 8, is 64, square number of 8.

Cubic numbers are also noted by Philo: 1, 8, 27 and 64[147]. In *De opificio mundi* 92-94.106, Philo deals with raising numbers to the sixth power; the resulting numbers are, of course, both square and cubic. He mentions there especially, as being both square and cubic, 64, 729 and 4096. Nicomachus points out that cubic numbers are sums of successive odd numbers: $1^3 = 1$, $2^3 = 3 + 5$, $3^3 = 7 + 9 + 11$, $4^3 = 13 + 15 + 17 + 19$, etc. (*Arithm. introd.* 2,20).

Another category of special numbers is constituted by the so-called ἀριθμοὶ τέλειοι, 'perfect numbers', i.e., numbers which are equal to the sum of their divisors[148]. The first three are 6 ($=1+2+3$), 28 ($=1+2+4+7+14$) and 496 ($=1+2+4+8+16+31+62+124+248$). To the phenomenon of the perfect numbers attention is paid by, e.g., Euclides, *Elementa* 7 Def. 23; 9,36, and later by Nicomachus, *Arithm. introd.* 1,16, and Theon of Smyrna, *Exp. rer. math.* pp. 45-46 Hiller. Philo also knows about these peculiar numbers; several times he notes that 6 is a perfect number[149], and the number 28 is mentioned by him in the same quality[150].

Two relationships between numbers have to be mentioned, both because of their importance in antiquity and because of their role in numerical arrangements in the Fourth Gospel:

a. The division according to the golden section has already been mentioned (p. 5; see also p. 7). It is found in Euclides' *Elementa*, e.g., 2,11; 6 Def. 3; 6,30; 13,1-6.8-9.

b. The famous 'proposition of Pythagoras', that in a right-angled triangle the sum of the squares of the sides containing the right angle is equal to the square of the hypotenuse, was well-known in antiquity: see, e.g., Euclides, *Elementa* 1,48; 10,28 Lemma 1; Diogenes Laertius, *Vitae philosophorum* 8,12. The lowest natural numbers for which it holds that $a^2 + b^2 = c^2$, are 3, 4 and 5: $3^2 + 4^2 = 5^2$. This combination of numbers was already known to the Babylonians[151]; we find it also in the Greco-Roman world, in such authors as Vitruvius, *De architectura* 9 praef.; Plutarch, *De Is. et Os.* 56; Heron, *Metrica* 1,2. The right-angled triangle with sides 3, 4 and 5 is also mentioned in Philo's works[152].

I omit here the manifold philosophical and religious speculations attached to numbers, speculations which were current in antiquity, not in the least at the beginning of the Christian Era, as, e.g., K. Staehle's collection of Philonic texts[153] illustrates. These speculations, interesting and important though they may be, do not seem very useful for our present purposes. Not only are all numbers from 1 up to 10 inclusive given special meanings in these speculations, but the same is valid for higher numbers in so far as they are divisible by these lower numbers or constitute a sum of them. This means, that at least in principle any number has a special philosophical or religious meaning — which reduces the usefulness of these speculations as a criterion in dealing with the question which numbers should be deemed significant. Simple mathematical considerations which were known in antiquity, seem to be a safer criterion. Besides, much of the speculation is actually based on these simple mathematical truths.

NOTES TO INTRODUCTION

1 See about the methods of literary criticism, form criticism and redaction criticism: H. Zimmermann, *Neutestamentliche Methodenlehre*. Darstellung der historisch-kritischen Methode (7th ed., rev. by K. Kliesch; Stuttgart 1982) 77-266; important studies in these fields are mentioned there (77-78, 125-126, 215-216). See especially about redaction criticism J. Rohde, *Die redaktionsgeschichtliche Methode*. Einführung und Sichtung des Forschungsstandes (Hamburg 1966). About the various kinds of structural analysis, see below.

2 For the sake of clearness and simplicity, I speak about 'author', in the singular; it is not my intention to exclude the possibility that the final redaction of a book should be ascribed to a group.

3 Cfr. J. Gnilka, *Die Verstockung Israels*. Isaias 6,9-10 in der Theologie der Synoptiker (SANT 3; Munich 1961) 19, who broadens the 'framework', in which an evangelist puts the traditional materials, so much that the selection of the materials and the tradition of the Lord's words are also included in it.

4 Of course, this view does not exclude *a priori* the possibility that after the completion of the work secondary additions were made to the text.

5 I mention only a few publications, which introduce into structuralist exegesis and where further references may be found: D. Patte, *What is Structural Exegesis?* (Guides to Biblical Scholarship — New Testament Series; Philadelphia 1976); R. M. Polzin, *Biblical Structuralism*. Method and Subjectivity in the Study of Ancient Texts (Semeia Supplements 5; Philadelphia/Missoula, Mt. 1977); B. van Iersel, 'Exegeet en linguïstiek', *Concilium* 14 (1978) nr. 5, 64-73; W. A. de Pater, 'Strukturele tekstanalyse: enkele achtergronden', *Tijdschrift voor Theologie* 18 (1978) 247-293; D. and A. Patte, *Structural Exegesis: From Theory to Practice*. Exegesis of Mark 15 and 16. Hermeneutical Implications (Philadelphia 1978); A. Fossion, *Lire les Écritures*. Théorie et pratique de la lecture structurale (Collection "écritures" 2; Brussels 1980); W. S. Vorster, 'De Structuuranalyse', in: A. F. J. Klijn, ed., *Inleiding tot de studie van het Nieuwe Testament* (Kampen 1982) 127-152.

6 Patte, *What is Structural Exegesis?*, 22 and 23.

7 See Patte, *What is Structural Exegesis?*, 41-43. The scheme derives from A. J. Greimas, *Sémantique structurale*. Recherche de méthode (Paris 1966) 176-180.

8 B. van Iersel, 'Terug van Emmaüs. Bijdragen tot een structurele tekstanalyse van Lc. 24,13-35', *Tijdschrift voor Theologie* 18 (1978) 294-323; 297.

9 S. Bar-Efrat, 'Some Observations on the Analysis of Structure in Biblical Narrative', *VT* 30 (1980) 154-173; 170. I adapted his coding somewhat.

10 E. Galbiati, *La struttura letteraria dell'Esodo* (Rome 1956).

11 J. Ch. Exum, *Literary Patterns in the Samson Saga*. An Investigation of Rhetorical Style in Biblical Prose (diss. Columbia Univ. 1976; Ann Arbor 1981); id., 'Promise and Fulfilment: Narrative Art in Judges 13', *JBL* 99 (1980) 43-59; id., 'Aspects of Symmetry and Balance in the Samson Saga', *Journal for the Study of the Old Testament* 19 (1981) 3-29.

12 S. Bar-Efrat, 'Literary Modes and Methods in the Biblical Narrative in View of 2 Samuel 10-20 and 1 Kings 1-2', *Immanuel* 8 (1978) 19-31 (= abstract of unpublished Hebrew dissertation, Hebrew University of Jerusalem 1975).

13 U. Cassuto, 'The Second Chapter of Hosea', in: id., *Biblical and Oriental Studies*, I: *Bible* (Jerusalem 1973) 101-140 (orig. written in Hebrew and published in *Mem. S. Poznański* [Warsaw 1927] 115-135); E. Galbiati, 'La struttura sintetica [lege: simmetrica] di Osea 2', in: *Studi sull'Oriente e la Bibbia* (Fs. G. Rinaldi; Genoa 1967) 317-328; repr. in id., *Scritti minori* (Brescia 1979) I 169-183; H. Krszyna, 'Literarische Struktur von Os. 2,4-17', *BZ* NF 13 (1969) 41-59; D. J. A. Clines, 'Hosea 2: Structure and Interpretation', in: E. A. Livingstone, ed., *Studia Biblica 1978*, I (Journal for the Study of the Old Testament, Supplement Series 11; Sheffield 1979) 83-103.

14 R. Pesch, 'Zur konzentrischen Struktur von Jona 1', *Bib* 47 (1966) 517-558; G. H.

Cohn, *Das Buch Jona im Lichte der biblischen Erzählkunst* (Studia Semitica Neerlandica 12; Assen 1969); J. Magonet, *Form and Meaning*. Studies in Literary Techniques in the Book of Jonah (Beiträge zur biblischen Exegese und Theologie 2; Bern/Frankfurt M. 1976); G. Vanoni, *Das Buch Jona*. Literar- und formkritische Untersuchung (Arbeiten zu Text und Sprache im Alten Testament 7; St. Ottilien 1978); H. Witzenrath, *Das Buch Jona*. Eine literaturwissenschaftliche Untersuchung (Arbeiten zu Text und Sprache im Alten Testament 6; St. Ottilien 1978).

15 P. Auffret, 'Essai sur la structure littéraire du psaume I', *BZ* NF 22 (1978) 26-45; R. P. Merendino, 'Sprachkunst in Psalm 1', *VT* 29 (1979) 45-60; W. Vogels, 'A Structural Analysis of Ps 1', *Bib* 60 (1979) 410-416.

16 M. Weiss, 'Wege der neuen Dichtungswissenschaft in ihrer Anwendung auf die Psalmenforschung (Methodologische Bemerkungen, dargelegt am Beispiel von Psalm XLVI)', *Bib* 42 (1961) 254-302; repr. in P. H. A. Neumann, ed., *Zur neueren Psalmenforschung* (Wege der Forschung 192; Darmstadt 1976) 400-451; D. T. Tsumura, 'The Literary Structure of Psalm 46,2-8', *Annual of the Japanese Biblical Institute* 6 (1980) 29-55.

17 S. Schreiner, 'Erwägungen zur Struktur des 90. Psalms', *Bib* 59 (1978) 80-90; P. Auffret, 'Essai sur la structure littéraire du Psaume 90', *Bib* 61 (1980) 262-276. P. Auffret has published analyses of structure of several Psalms, as well as of other biblical and extra-biblical texts; I mention here only his *Hymnes d'Égypte et d'Israel*. Études de structures littéraires (OBO 34; Fribourg/Göttingen 1981).

18 S. Bertman, 'Symmetrical Design in the Book of Ruth', *JBL* 84 (1965) 165-168; H. H. Witzenrath, *Das Buch Ruth*. Eine literaturwissenschaftliche Untersuchung (SANT 40; Munich 1975); K. K. Sacon, 'The Book of Ruth. Its Literary Structure and Theme', *Annual of the Japanese Biblical Institute* 4 (1978) 3-22.

19 W. H. Shea, 'The Chiastic Structure of the Song of Songs', *ZAW* 92 (1980) 378-396.

20 A. G. Wright, 'The Riddle of the Sphinx: The Structure of the Book of Qoheleth', *CBQ* 30 (1968) 313-334; J. A. Loader, *Polar Structures in the Book of Qoheleth* (BZAW 152; Berlin 1979); N. Lohfink, *Kohelet* (Die Neue Echter Bibel; Würzburg 1980); F. Rousseau, 'Structure de Qohelet I 4-11 et plan du livre', *VT* 31 (1981) 200-217.

21 A. Lenglet, 'La structure littéraire de Daniel 2-7', *Bib* 53 (1972) 169-190. See for more references to analyses of (chiastic and concentric) structure in OT and later Jewish literature: C. H. Talbert, *Literary Patterns, Theological Themes and the Genre of Luke-Acts* (SBLMS 20; Missoula, Mt. 1974) 71, with nn. 40-49, and Bar-Efrat, *VT* 30, 154 n. 1.

22 J. C. Fenton, 'Inclusio and Chiasmus in Matthew', in: *Studia Evangelica* [1] (TU 73; Berlin 1959) 174-179; C. H. Lohr, 'Oral Techniques in the Gospel of Matthew', *CBQ* 23 (1961) 403-435; P. Gächter, *Die literarische Kunst im Matthäus-Evangelium* (SBS 7; Stuttgart 1965); J. D. Kingsbury, *Matthew: Structure, Christology, Kingdom* (Philadelphia 1975) 1-39.

23 P. Mourlon Beernaert, 'Jésus controversé. Structure et théologie de Marc 2,1-3,6', *NRT* 95 (1973) 129-149; J. Dewey, *Markan Public Debate*. Literary Technique, Concentric Structure and Theology in Mark 2:1-3:6 (SBLDS 48; Chico, Ca. 1980).

24 C. J. den Heyer, *Exegetische methoden in discussie*. Een analyse van Markus 10,46-13,37 (Kampen 1979^2).

25 J. Lambrecht, *Die Redaktion der Markus-Apokalypse*. Literarische Analyse und Strukturuntersuchung (AnBib 28; Rome 1967); F. Rousseau, 'La structure de Marc 13', *Bib* 56 (1975) 157-172.

26 Talbert, *Literary Patterns*.

27 R. Meynet, *Quelle est donc cette parole?* Lecture 'rhétorique' de l'évangile de Luc (1-9, 22-24) (LD 99; Paris 1979).

28 H. J. de Jonge, 'Sonship, Wisdom, Infancy: Luke II.41-51a', *NTS* 24 (1977-78) 317-354; 337-339.

29 Sr. Jeanne d'Arc, 'Un grand jeu d'inclusions dans "Les pèlerins d'Emmaüs"', *NRT* 99 (1977) 62-76; id., *Les pèlerins d'Emmaüs* (Paris 1977); R. Meynet, 'Com-

ment établir un chiasme? À propos des "pèlerins d'Emmaüs"', *NRT* 100 (1978) 233-249; B. van Iersel, 'Terug van Emmaüs', *Tijdschrift voor Theologie* 18, 294-323.

30 J. Willemse, *Het vierde evangelie*. Een onderzoek naar zijn structuur (Hilversum/Antwerpen 1965), who also records previous analyses of the structure of John (24-98); D. Deeks, 'The Structure of the Fourth Gospel', *NTS* 15 (1968-69) 107-129.

31 C. H. Talbert, 'Artistry and Theology: An Analysis of the Architecture of Jn 1,19-5,47', *CBQ* 32 (1970) 341-366.

32 A. Janssens de Varebeke, 'La structure des scènes du récit de la passion en Joh. XVIII-XIX', *ETL* 38 (1962) 504-522.

33 J. Smit Sibinga, 'Symmetrie en samenhang in Romeinen 4,16-18', in: *Ad Interim*. Opstellen over Eschatologie, Apocalyptiek en Ethiek (Fs. R. Schippers; Kampen 1975) 76-79.

34 P. Lamarche-Ch. le Dû, *Épître aux Romains V-VIII*. Structure littéraire et sens (Paris 1980).

35 K. E. Bailey, 'Recovering the Poetic Structure of I Cor i 17-ii 2. A Study in Text and Commentary', *NT* 17 (1975) 265-296.

36 K. Thieme, 'Die Struktur des Ersten Thessalonicher-Briefes', in: *Abraham unser Vater*. Juden und Christen im Gespräch über die Bibel (Fs. O. Michel; AGJU 5; Leiden/Cologne 1963) 450-458.

37 A. Vanhoye, *La structure littéraire de l'épître aux Hébreux* (Paris 1963, 1976[2]). See also id., 'Discussions sur la structure de l'Épître aux Hébreux', *Bib* 55 (1974) 349-380, where other literature concerning the structure of Heb is discussed.

38 G. M. Burge, '"And Threw Them Thus on Paper": Recovering the Poetic Form of James 2:14-26', *Studia Biblica et Theologica* 7 (1977) 31-45.

39 C. E. Donker, 'Der Verfasser des Jak und sein Gegner. Zum Problem des Einwandes in Jak 2,18-19', *ZNW* 72 (1981) 227-240; 235-237.

40 M. Bogaert, 'Structure et message de la Première Épître de saint Jean', *BVC* 83 (1968) 33-45; A. Feuillet, 'Étude structurale de la première épître de saint Jean. Comparaison avec le quatrième évangile. La structure fondamentale de la vie chrétienne selon saint Jean', in: *Neues Testament und Geschichte*. Historisches Geschehen und Deutung im Neuen Testament (Fs. O. Cullmann; Tübingen/Zürich 1972) 307-327; E. Malatesta, *Interiority and Covenant*. A Study of εἶναι ἐν and μένειν ἐν in the First Letter of Saint John (AnBib 69; Rome 1978).

41 U. Vanni, *La struttura letteraria dell'Apocalisse* (Brescia 1980[2], orig. Rome 1971); E. Schüssler Fiorenza, 'Composition and Structure of the Book of Revelation', *CBQ* 39 (1977) 344-366; F. Hahn, 'Zum Aufbau der Johannesoffenbarung', in: *Kirche und Bibel* (Fs. E. Schick; Paderborn etc. 1979) 145-154; J. Lambrecht, 'A Structuration of Revelation 4,1-22,5', in: id., ed., *L'Apocalypse johannique et l'Apocalyptique dans le Nouveau Testament* (BETL 53; Gembloux/Louvain 1980) 77-104. Further references to analyses of (chiastic and concentric) structure in NT texts can be found in Talbert, *Literary Patterns*, 75, with nn. 73-82, and in R. A. Culpepper, 'The Pivot of John's Prologue', *NTS* 27 (1980-81) 1-31; 3 n. 11 (concerning John) and 7 n. 29 (concerning the rest of the NT).

42 N. W. Lund, *Chiasmus in the New Testament* (Chapel Hill 1942), who discusses many OT passages as well; see also his earlier article 'Chiasmus in the Psalms', *AJSL* 49 (1932-33) 281-312; J. Jeremias, 'Chiasmus in den Paulusbriefen', *ZNW* 49 (1958) 145-156, reprinted in somewhat enlarged form in id., *Abba*. Studien zur neutestamentlichen Theologie und Zeitgeschichte (Göttingen 1966) 276-290 (this article contains J.'s judgment about the work of Lund: 'Leider erwies sich aber die Arbeit als völlig unbrauchbar. Lund analysiert viel zu grosse Einheiten [z.B. Mt. 5-7; 1. Kor. 12-14] und sucht in ihnen einen bis ins kleinste durchgefeilten, streng schematischen Aufbau nachzuweisen, was nur mit Hilfe von Gewaltsamkeiten möglich ist', *ZNW* 49, 145); A. di Marco, 'Der Chiasmus in der Bibel. Ein Beitrag zur strukturellen Linguistik', *Linguistica Biblica* 36 (1975) 21-97; 37 (1976) 49-68; 39 (1976) 37-85; 44 (1979) 3-70, where the older literature on this topic is summarized.

43 Concerning OT literature, I refer to three recent studies: T. Collins, *Line-Forms in*

Hebrew Poetry. A Grammatical Approach to the Stylistic Study of the Hebrew Prophets (Studia Pohl, Series Maior 7; Rome 1978); S. A. Geller, *Parallelism in Early Biblical Poetry* (HSM 20; Missoula, Mt. 1979); J. L. Kugel, *The Idea of Biblical Poetry*. Parallelism and Its History (London 1981). Parallelism in the NT was studied by R. Schütz, *Der parallele Bau der Satzglieder im Neuen Testament und seine Verwertung für die Textkritik und Exegese* (FRLANT NF 11; Göttingen 1920); C. F. Burney, *The Poetry of Our Lord*. An Examination of the Formal Elements of Hebrew Poetry in the Discourses of Jesus Christ (Oxford 1925); O. Linton, 'Le *parallelismus membrorum* dans le Nouveau Testament', in: *Mélanges Bibliques* en hommage au R. P. Béda Rigaux (Gembloux 1970) 489-507; see also id., 'Coordinated Sayings and Parables in the Synoptic Gospels: Analysis versus Theories', *NTS* 26 (1979-80) 139-163.

44 A number of them, concerning inclusion, repetition, chiastic and concentric patterns in Homer, Hesiod, Aeschylus, Sophocles, Euripides, Pindar, Herodotus, Thucydides, Plato, Apollonius, Plutarch, Catullus, Horace, Vergil and Propertius, are listed in Lohr, *CBQ* 23, 409 n. 19, 410 n. 25, 412 nn. 27-28, 414 n. 32, 425 n. 47, 425-426 nn. 49-59, and Talbert, *Literary Patterns*, 67, with nn. 1-14. Some additions to these lists: L. Richardson, *Poetical Theory in Republican Rome*. An Analytical Discussion of the Shorter Narrative Hexameter Poems Written in Latin During the First Century Before Christ (Undergraduate Prize Essays: Yale University 5; New Haven 1944); S. Bertman, 'The *Telemachy* and Structural Symmetry', *TAPA* 97 (1966) 15-27; C. P. Segal, 'The "Electra" of Sophocles', *TAPA* 97 (1966) 473-545. Talbert, *Literary Patterns*, 68sqq, points out interesting parallels between symmetry and balance in literature and in other forms of art.

45 See for chiasm the collection of texts in H. Lausberg, *Handbuch der literarischen Rhetorik*. Eine Grundlegung der Literaturwissenschaft (Munich 1973²) parr. 800-803 (the term χιασμός is used by Hermogenes, *De inventione* 4,3, who indicates with it 'den [ohne Bedeutungsänderung der Gesamtperiode] überkreuzweise durchführbaren Austausch der ganzen Kola in einer aus vier Kola bestehenden Periode [...], nicht auf die Stellung der Satzglieder innerhalb der Kola', Lausberg, *Handbuch*, par. 723 n. 1; for this latter phenomenon the ancient term is ἀντιμεταβολή or *commutatio*); for parallelism or isocolon the materials collected in Lausberg, *Handbuch*, parr. 719-754; for *inclusio* (or *redditio*) the materials in Lausberg, *Handbuch*, parr. 625-627.

46 Cfr. also *Contra Sophistas* 13. See F. Blass, *Die attische Beredsamkeit*, II: *Isokrates und Isaios* (Leipzig 1874) 102, 104; F. Pfister, 'Der Begriff des Schönen und das Ebenmass', *Würzburger Jahrbücher für die Altertumswissenschaft* 1 (1946) 341-358; 346-347. In these things, Isocrates followed his teacher Gorgias, see Pfister, *Würzburger Jahrbücher* 1, 346, and the literature mentioned there.

47 In *The Works of Aristotle* Translated into English under the Editorship of W. D. Ross, XI (Oxford 1924).

48 See n. 47.

49 See about these theories and their application Blass, *Die attische Beredsamkeit* II, 142-160; Pfister, *Würzburger Jahrbücher* 1, 345-355 and 358, where other publications of P. on the same topic are mentioned; cfr. also his 'Der Begriff des Schönen und das Ebenmass', in: J. Burian-L. Vidman, eds., *Antiquitas Graeco-Romana ac tempora nostra* (Prague 1968) 340-343.

50 F. Seck, 'Die Komposition des "Panegyrikos"', in: id., ed., *Isokrates* (Wege der Forschung 351; Darmstadt 1976) 353-370, esp. 364-370. I changed his way of coding in the following scheme; S. uses successive letters: a, b, c, etc., thereby suggesting a succession which is, in fact, absent.

51 Seck refers to S. Heller, 'Die Entdeckung der stetigen Teilung durch die Pythagoräer', *Abhandlungen der Deutschen Akademie der Wissenschaften zu Berlin*, Klasse für Mathematik, Physik und Technik (1958) nr. 6, 5-28; 20; reprinted in: O. Becker, ed., *Zur Geschichte der Griechischen Mathematik* (Wege der Forschung 33; Darmstadt 1965) 319-354. — The numbers in the proportions mentioned in what follows are, of course, rounded off.

52 F. Pfister, 'Ein Kompositionsgesetz der antiken Kunstprosa', *Philologische Wochenschrift* (1922) 1195-1200; 1195-1197; id., *Würzburger Jahrbücher* 1, 347-348. The author does not inform the reader about the text-edition used for his count of lines; the figures given by P. are more or less in agreement with the numbers of lines in the edition of Plato's *Phaedrus* by C. F. Hermann (Teubner; Leipzig 1851; I consulted the *editio stereotypa* of 1922), when one takes into account the diversity in length of the lines and uses the whole line as unit of count. P. has found numerically symmetric compositions, similar to the one described here, in Herodotus' *Historiae*, Gorgias' *Helena* and *Palamedes*, Ps.-Xenophon's *Respublica Atheniensium*, the first book of Thucydides, Plato's *Protagoras*, Xenophon's *Historia Graeca*, Plutarch's *De Pythiae oraculis*, Lucian's *De dea Syria*, Ps.-Callisthenes, Sallust's *Catilinae coniuratio* and *Bellum Iugurthinum*, Tacitus' *Germania*, *Agricola* and *Dialogus de oratoribus*, Apuleius' *Metamorphoses*, see *Phil. Wochenschrift* (1922) 1197-1200, and *Würzburger Jahrbücher* 1, 349-354, with the literature on p. 358.

53 K. Vretska, 'Platonica. I. Zum Kompositionsprinzip der Mitte bei Platon', *Gymnasium* 63 (1956) 406-414; see also *Platon: Der Staat*, eingeleitet, übersetzt und erklärt von K. Vretska (Stuttgart 1958) 40-47.

54 *Platons Staat* ... neu übersetzt und erläutert ... von O. Apelt (Philoscphische Bibliothek 80; Leipzig 1916[4]) 488 n. 85. As for his unit of counting, he speaks only generally of 'eine Zählung der Seitenzahlen rückwärts und vorwärts'.

55 F. G. Lang, 'Kompositionsanalyse des Markusevangeliums', *ZTK* 74 (1977) 1-24; see esp. 11-13.

56 Lang, *ZTK* 74, 17-18.

57 F. Blass, *Die attische Beredsamkeit*, III/1: *Demosthenes* (Leipzig 1877) 560-562 (cfr. 105-114) gives an analysis by means of a count of cola of three orations of Demosthenes (*De corona*, *Olynthiacus* I, *Contra Philippum* III). This seems a more natural and exact way of counting, as a colon may be a unit used by an author himself.

58 P. Maury, 'Le secret de Virgile et l'architecture des Bucoliques', *Lettres d'humanité* 3 (1944) 71-147. M.'s analysis was accepted by J. Perret, *Virgile.* L'homme et l'oeuvre (Connaissance des lettres 33; Paris 1952) 14-18 (see also P.'s own numerical analyses, pp. 24-27 — concerning various *Eclogae* — and pp. 60-61 — concerning *Georgica* 3-4), and by G. Qvarnström, *Poetry and Numbers.* On the Structural Use of Symbolic Numbers (Scripta minora ... 1964-1965:2, Lund 1966) 34-35.

59 O. Skutsch, 'Symmetry and Sense in the Eclogues', *Harvard Studies in Classical Philology* 73 (1969) 153-169.

60 J. Van Sickle, *The Design of Vergil's Bucolics* (Filologia e Critica 24; Rome 1978), esp. 22-24, 210 (his earlier studies in this field are taken into account in this publication). Verse count is applied incidentally to Vergil's works by Richardson, *Poetical Theory*, 101-163, and B. Otis, *Virgil.* A Study in Civilized Poetry (Oxford 1963) 151, 190 sqq *et alibi*. — Numerical patterns in Theocritus' *Idyllia* are pointed out by J. Irigoin, 'Les bucoliques de Théocrite. La composition du receuil', *Quaderni Urbinati di Cultura Classica* 19 (1975) 27-44, and by Van Sickle, *Design of Bucolics*, 180 n. 71 (where other publications of Van S. concerning this subject are mentioned).

61 Van Sickle, *Design of Bucolics*, 23.

62 Van Sickle, *Design of Bucolics*, 22.

63 O. Skutsch, 'The Structure of the Propertian *Monobiblos*', *Classical Philology* 58 (1963) 238-239.

64 See the recent study of P. van der Lugt, *Strofische structuren in de Bijbels-Hebreeuwse poëzie*. De geschiedenis van het onderzoek en een bijdrage tot de theorievorming omtrent de strofenbouw van de Psalmen (Dissertationes Neerlandicae, Series Theologica; Kampen 1980).

65 Exceptions are Lam 1,7 and 2,19; according to H.-J. Kraus, *Klagelieder (Threni)* (BKAT 20; Neukirchen 1968[3]) 6, 22, 38, these strophes originally had three members as well.

66 Numerical composition techniques using the verse line as basic unit have been detected in the book of Proverbs by P. W. Skehan, but not without considerable rearrangement of the text; see his articles 'The Seven Columns of Wisdom's House in Pro-

verbs 1-9', *CBQ* 9 (1947) 190-198; 'A Single Editor for the Whole Book of Proverbs', *CBQ* 10 (1948) 115-130; 'Wisdom's House', *CBQ* 29 (1967) 468-486; all three articles in revised form in id., *Studies in Israelite Poetry and Wisdom* (CBQMS 1; Washington 1971) 9-16, 17-26 and 27-45 respectively. In Prov 2-7, S. detects seven poems of 22 verse lines each (22 being the number of letters of the Hebrew alphabet), which constitute the 'seven columns' of the house which Wisdom built according to Prov 9,1. In fact, 'the Book of Proverbs is the house of Wisdom. That is to say, its author — compiler — designer (for he was all three) wrote the Hebrew text of his composition in such a way that its layout in the columns of his scroll visibly showed forth the design of a house, which he himself identified (Prov 9:1) as Wisdom's House' (*CBQ* 29, 468). The vertical dimensions of this house (i.e., the numbers of lines of the columns) come from the numbers of cubits of Solomon's temple in 1 Kgs 6. A detailed exposition of S.'s theory would lead us too far; I mention only a few more interesting details. Prov 10,1-22,16, entitled 'Proverbs of Solomon' in 10,1, has a size of 375 lines; 375 is the numerical value of *šlmh* (see below n. 71, for the computation of the numerical value of names). The entire book of Prov has, according to S., a size of 930 lines; 930 is the numerical value of the three names occurring in the title (1,1): 'Proverbs of Solomon, son of David, king of Israel'; *šlmh* = 375, *dwd* = 14, *yśrʾl* = 541, their sum is 930. For other poetic texts from the OT, S. has proposed similar numerical analyses (be it less spectacular than the above one): Moses' song in Deut 32 is made up of 3 × 23 verse lines, see 'The Structure of the Song of Moses in Deuteronomy (32:1-43)', *CBQ* 13 (1951) 153-163, also in *Studies*, 67-77. In Job, the standard length of speeches is 22 or 23 lines; longer discourses are multiples of this length, see 'Strophic Patterns in the Book of Job', *CBQ* 23 (1961) 125-142, and 'Job's Final Plea (Job 29-31) and the Lord's Reply (Job 38-41)', *Bib* 45 (1964) 51-61; both articles also in *Studies*, 96-113 and 114-123 respectively. See also his 'The Text and Structure of the Book of Wisdom', *Traditio* 3 (1945) 1-13, where S. deals with the relationship between logical divisions and numerical divisions in Wis.

67 See A. Lauha, *Kohelet* (BKAT 19; Neukirchen 1978) 9-10.

68 A. G. Wright, 'The Riddle of the Sphinx Revisited: Numerical Patterns in the Book of Qoheleth', *CBQ* 42 (1980) 38-51; see now also id., 'Additional Numerical Patterns in Qoheleth', *CBQ* 45 (1983) 32-43. Cfr. also id., 'Numerical Patterns in the Book of Wisdom', *CBQ* 29 (1967) 524-538, where it is set forth how the parts of Wis are proportioned to each other according to the golden section.

69 Wright, *CBQ* 30, 313-334 (see above, p. 3 with n. 20).

70 Wright, *CBQ* 42, 43.

71 The computation of the numerical value of words or names (in Greek, according to the current numerical value of the letters: $\alpha = 1$, $\beta = 2$, ... $\iota = 10$, ... $\rho = 100$ etc.) was a well-known practice in antiquity. In Jewish literature, it is called *gematria* (*gymṭryʾ*, see, e.g., b. Ber. 8a; Lev. Rab. 21,4); in Greek, we find the word ἰσόψηφος, 'equal in numerical value' (see e.g., *Anthologia Palatina* 11,334). See about these phenomena: F. Dornseiff, *Das Alphabet in Mystik und Magie* (ΣΤΟΙΧΕΙΑ 7; Leipzig/Berlin 1925²) 91-118 (older literature mentioned there, 92 n. 2); O. Rühle, art. ἀριθμέω etc., *TWNT* I, 461-464; R. Weisskopf, *Gematria, Buchstabenberechnung, Tora und Schöpfung im rabbinischen Judentum* (diss. Tübingen 1978), a résumé of which appeared in *TLZ* 105 (1980) 636-637.

72 See K. Ohly, *Stichometrische Untersuchungen* (Zentralblatt für Bibliothekswesen, Beiheft 61; Leipzig 1928). Cfr. also T. Birt, *Das antike Buchwesen in seinem Verhältnis zur Literatur*. Mit Beiträgen zur Textgeschichte des Theokrit, Catull, Properz und anderen Autoren (Berlin 1882), who supposed the length of a standard line to be determined by the number of letters; Ohly makes it quite clear that the syllable was the basic unit in stichometry (22-30).

73 See Ohly, *Stichometrische Untersuchungen*, 31-71.

74 See F. G. Kenyon, *The Chester Beatty Biblical Papyri*. Descriptions and Texts of Twelve Manuscripts on Papyrus of the Greek Bible, III Supplement: Pauline Epistles. Text (London 1936). Stichometric indications have survived in P⁴⁶ for

Rom, Heb, 2 Cor (not quite legible), Eph, Gal, Phil, Col (not quite legible). The indications have been added, according to the editor (p. xii), by a cursive hand, apparently of the early 3rd century.

75 See about *f*[13]: Eb. Nestle, *Einführung in das Griechische Neue Testament* (Göttingen 1909[3]) 95; cfr. E. von Dobschütz's 4th edition of this work (Göttingen 1923) 52, 35. These manuscripts contain information not only about the number of στίχοι, but also about the number of ῥήματα of the gospels; the latter numbers do not differ very much from the former (Matt: 2522 ῥήματα, 2560 στίχοι; for Mark the numbers are 1675 and 1604 respectively, for Luke 3803, to be corrected probably into 3083, and 2750, for John 1938 ῥήματα). N. presumes that the ῥήματα are meant as 'lines', and remarks: 'Die Angaben über die ῥήματα scheinen irgendwie mit Angaben syrischer Handschriften über die Zahl der *ptgm*ʾ [transcr.] (Worte) zusammenzuhängen' (1909[3], p. 95). In fact, both Syriac *ptgm* and Greek ῥῆμα can mean 'line' (of poetry), see for the former R. Payne Smith, *Thesaurus Syriacus* (Oxford 1879-1901; repr. Hildesheim 1981) s.v. *ptgm* 6): '*comma, membrum versus, sententia brevior quam versus*, στίχος'; for the latter Liddell-Scott, s.v. ῥῆμα 2b: '*verse, line*', referring to Aristophanes, *Ranae* 1379, cfr. 97. We meet, then, in *f*[13] two kinds of stichometric indications next to each other. Ohly, *Stichometrische Untersuchungen*, 4-9, points out that, next to στίχος, 'sich ἔπος als Terminus für die Hexameterzeile bei Abmessung von Prosawerken vom 4. Jahrhundert bis zum Ausgang des Altertums gehalten hat' (9).

76 See B. M. Metzger, *The Text of the New Testament*. Its Transmission, Corruption, and Restoration (Oxford 1968[2]) 15-16.

77 Stichometric indications are supplied in the canon list in the *Codex Claromontanus* and the canon list of Nicephorus (patriarch of Constantinople 806-818), both in E. Preuschen, *Analecta*. Kürzere Texte zur Geschichte der alten Kirche und des Kanons (Sammlung ausgewählter kirchen- und dogmengeschichtlicher Quellenschriften 8; Freiburg/Leipzig 1893) 142-144 and 156-158 respectively. The redactor of the *Mommsen Canon* (dating from ± 360) informs us that the numbers of lines he gives for each biblical book are the result of a count of syllables per book; the sum total of a count was divided by 16, the number of syllables of the στίχος (see the text in Preuschen, *Analecta*, 139-140). It is evident here that the syllable is the basic unit in stichometry.

78 See C. D. Ginsburg, *Introduction to the Massoretico-Critical Edition of the Hebrew Bible* (London 1897; reprint New York 1966) 68-113, and the recent article of G. E. Weil, 'Les décomptes de versets, mots et lettres du Pentateuque selon le manuscrit B 19a de Leningrad. Un essai d'arithmétique sommaire des scribes et des massorètes', in: *Mélanges Dominique Barthélemy* (OBO 38; Fribourg/Göttingen 1981) 651-703.

79 Weil, in: *Mélanges Barthélemy*, 652-655, seems to do so.

80 There are, in fact, different traditions concerning numbers of letters, words and verses of the Hebrew OT; their relationship to the actual MT is not always clear. See about this problem Weil's article in *Mélanges Barthélemy*, and esp. his remark on pp. 678-679: 'Les décomptes qui se voulaient précis lorsqu'ils ont été donnés par les maîtres de la *Massorah*, autant que la notation du mot médian, choisis comme un frein à toute variation de la structure du texte canonique, selon l'un ou l'autre des traditions orthographiques, ont fini par être recopiés par un souci religieux de la tradition scribale, sans rapport avec leur objet premier. La forme des textes, le nombre de leur mots et leur orthographe différaient de plus en plus par rapport au nombre des sommes témoins qui devaient en garantir la conservation traditionnellement acceptée'.

81 J. Smit Sibinga, *Literair handwerk in Handelingen* (Leiden 1970) 12-13 (with n. 5) points to the count of verses, words and syllables in the text-transmission of the Veda, the holy scriptures of the classical Indian religion, which counts seem to date from ± 600 B.C.; he refers to F. Max Müller, *Selected Essays on Language, Mythology and Religion* II (London 1881) 119; cfr. H. H. Gowen, *A History of Indian Literature from Vedic Times to the Present Day* (repr. New York 1968; orig. 1931) 47. J. Vendryes,

Le langage. Introduction linguistique à l'histoire (L'évolution de l'humanité — Synthèse collective I/3; Paris 1950) 63-64, deals with the division into syllables as a natural division of language, esp. with metre as resting upon the number of syllables, and remarks in this connection: 'Ainsi dans l'Inde et en Grèce, aux débuts de la littérature, on composait de longs poèmes où il était tenu un compte rigoureux du nombre des syllabes, si nous en jugeons du moins par les héritiers directs des richis védiques ou des fondateurs de la lyrique lesbienne' (64). For this Lesbian lyric poetry, in which verses have a fixed number of syllables, V. refers to L. Havet, *Métrique grecque et latine* (Paris 1893[3]) 166; cfr. now also D. Korzeniewski, *Griechische Metrik* (Die Altertumswissenschaft; Darmstadt 1968) 128-140.

82 I derive the reference to Clearchus from Smit Sibinga, *Literair handwerk*, 14-15.

83 See Lausberg, *Handbuch der lit. Rhetorik*, parr. 719-754. Hermogenes, *De inventione* 4,4 (ed. Rabe, p. 183 l. 17-p. 184 l. 6), determines the size of colon, comma and σχοινοτενές (a long colon) in numbers of syllables.

84 In the second part of the quotation, 'τ' (rather than τε) should perhaps be read in order to obtain an exact equality of syllables' (W. Rhys Roberts, in his edition of Demetrius' *De elocutione*, 285).

85 The phenomenon of the isocolon as it occurs in Greek and Latin literature, has a parallel in OT poetry, in what Geller, *Parallelism in Early Biblical Poetry*, terms 'syllable symmetry': 'lines are syllabically symmetrical when A and B lines contain the same number of syllables, or when either line exceeds the other by one syllable' (45). G. adduces numerous examples.

86 U. Cassuto, *A Commentary on the Book of Genesis*, I: *From Adam to Noah, Genesis I-VI 8* (ET Jerusalem 1961; orig. in Hebrew, Jerusalem 1944) 14-15.

87 P. Beauchamp, *Création et séparation*. Étude exégétique du chapitre premier de la Genèse (Bibliothèque de Sciences religieuses; Paris etc. 1969) 68, 74.

88 F. Langlamet, 'David et la maison de Saül. Les épisodes "benjaminites" de II Sam., IX; XVI,1-14; XIX,17-31; I Rois, II,36-46', *RB* 86 (1979) 194-213, 385-436, 481-513; 87 (1980) 161-210; 88 (1981) 421-428 (to be continued); see esp. *RB* 87, 179-205. Earlier publications of L. are mentioned *RB* 86, 194-195; see also his reviews of F. Crüsemann, *Der Widerstand gegen das Königtum*, *RB* 87 (1980) 408-425; of C. Conroy, *Absalom Absalom!*, *RB* 88 (1981) 70-79, and of D. M. Gunn, *The Story of King David*, *RB* 88 (1981) 79-92. Recently, L. applied the same method to passages from Gen, in his review of P. Weimar, *Untersuchungen zur Redaktionsgeschichte des Pentateuchs*, *RB* 88 (1981) 402-415. The same method of counting is applied to Num 22,21-35 by L.'s pupil H. Rouillard; see her 'L'ânesse de Balaam. Analyse littéraire de Nomb., XXII,21-35', *RB* 87 (1980) 5-37, 211-241; 220-223. She observes among other things that the episode has a size of 248 words, = 8 × 31; the narrative takes 155 words, = 5 × 31, and the discourse 93, = 3 × 31.

89 J. Smit Sibinga, 'Text and Literary Art in Mark 3:1-6', in: *Studies in New Testament Language and Text* (Fs. G. D. Kilpatrick; NTS 44; Leiden 1976) 357-365; 365 n. 32.

90 J. Smit Sibinga, 'Matthew 14:22-33 — Text and Composition', in: *New Testament Textual Criticism*. Its Significance for Exegesis (Fs. B. M. Metzger; Oxford 1981) 15-33; 31 n. 43.

91 Most of his contributions in this field can be found in D. N. Freedman, *Pottery, Poetry and Prophecy*. Collected Essays on Hebrew Poetry (Winona Lake 1980). For a critical discussion of the method of syllable-count as applied by Freedman and others, esp. by D. K. Stuart, *Studies in Early Hebrew Meter* (HSM 13; Missoula, Mt. 1976), see T. Longman, 'A Critique of Two Recent Metrical Systems', *Bib* 63 (1982) 230-254. F.'s method of syllable-count was recently followed by M. D. Coogan, 'A Structural and Literary Analysis of the Song of Deborah', *CBQ* 40 (1978) 143-166, esp. 157-158.

92 D. N. Freedman, 'The Structure of Psalm 137', in: *Near Eastern Studies* (Fs. W. F. Albright; Baltimore 1971) 187-205; 188-189 (also in id., *Pottery, Poetry and Prophecy*, 303-321).

93 D. N. Freedman, in: *Near Eastern Studies*, 187-205. F. follows the consonantal text

of the MT, with one exception; in 137,1 he reads *bbbl* instead of *bbl*, with 11QPs[a]. He counts according to the vocalization of the MT, except on a few points: a) in 137,6 he reads *ʾeʿleh* instead of *ʾaʿăleh*; b) segolates are counted as monosyllabic words; c) *yᵉrûšālēm* is read instead of the *Qere perpetuum yᵉrûšālaim*; d) half-open syllables are ignored; e) in 137,5, *ʾeškᵉḥēkī* is read, instead of MT's *ʾeškāḥēk*, supposing that the *yōd* at the beginning of the following word marks also the end of the word under consideration. Cfr. also M. Halle-J. J. McCarthy, 'The Metrical Structure of Psalm 137', *JBL* 100 (1981) 161-167, where an analysis is given of the metrical structure of Ps 137 based on a count of syllables, in which count, however, the syllables following the last stress of a line are omitted (besides, the text is emendated on a few points).

94 See for specimina of word-count in the analysis of the structure of Psalms L. Kunz, 'Zur Liedgestalt der ersten fünf Psalmen', *BZ* NF 7 (1963) 261-270; 264, about Ps 1; Langlamet, *RB* 87, 203-205, about Pss 111-112.

95 L. Sabottka, *Zephanja*. Versuch einer Neuübersetzung mit philologischem Kommentar (BibOr 25; Rome 1972).

96 Sabottka, *Zephanja*, 26-27. He counts the tetragrammaton at 2 syllables, and reads in 1,4 *yᵉrûšālēm*.

97 Sabottka, *Zephanja*, 55. — In passing, I mention the fact that in Christian Syriac poetry the syllable is the basic metrical unit, see L. Costaz, *Grammaire syriaque* (Beyrouth 1955) 228. According to L. Zunz, *Die gottesdienstlichen Vorträge der Juden historisch entwickelt*. Ein Beitrag zur Altertumskunde und biblischen Kritik, zur Literatur- und Religionsgeschichte (Frankfurt/M 1892[2], repr. Hildesheim 1966) 382-383, the three benedictions accompanying the *šᵉmaʿ* in the Jewish morning prayer have a size, in their original form, of 45, 63 and 45 words respectively. I found the reference to Zunz' book in Smit Sibinga, in: *Studies in NT Language and Text*, 365 n. 2.

98 J. Schniewind, *Das Evangelium nach Matthäus* (NTD 2; Göttingen 1936, 1962[10]) 40, referring to a certain Wilh. Weber; cfr. J. Dupont, *Les Béatitudes*, III: Les évangelistes (EB; new edition, Paris 1973) 309 n. 4, who refers to the same remark of Schniewind, and adds: 'L'auteur emprunte la remarque à un certain Wilhelm Weber, qui nous est inconnu'. It is possible that Schn. refers to the German 'Althistoriker' Wilh. Weber (1882-1948), who was his colleague as a professor in Halle in the years 1925-1927. Weber published, among other works, *Josephus und Vespasian*. Untersuchungen zu dem jüdischen Krieg des Flavius Josephus (1921), and *Der Prophet und sein Gott*. Eine Studie zur vierten Ekloge Vergils (1925).

99 E. Bammel, 'Herkunft und Funktion der Traditionselemente in 1. Kor. 15,1-11', *TZ* 11 (1955) 401-419; 402.

100 H. J. de Jonge, *NTS* 24, 338 n. 5. — G. Bouwman, *Paulus aan de Romeinen*. Een retorische analyse van Rom 1-8 (Cahiers voor levensverdieping 32; Averbode 1980) points out several isocola, made up of two members with an equal number of syllables, in Rom: 1,14-15 (p. 136), 2,12 (p. 162), 6,3bc (p. 224), 6,23 (without the concluding formula 'in Christ Jesus our Lord', p. 231).

101 J. Schattenmann, *Studien zum neutestamentlichen Prosahymnus* (Munich 1965). S. discusses also texts from Wis (7,21-8,1), from contemporary paganism, from Philo, and from early Christian and gnostic literature.

102 Schattenmann, *Studien*, 3 n. 1: 'Im Verlauf des Hellenismus wird die metrische Dichtung in Ost und West allmählich verdrängt durch die rhythmische, die ohne Rücksicht auf Quantität nur die Silbenzahl berücksichtigt', with a reference to C. Schneider, *Geistesgeschichte des antiken Christentums* (Munich 1954) II 51, who quotes as the oldest religious example of this kind of 'Dichtung' a hymn to Demeter, transmitted by Aristophanes, *Ranae* 386-389, a fragment made up of 4 lines of 8 syllables each (other poems with a similar structure are mentioned by Schattenmann, *Studien*, 46-47); then Schneider remarks: 'Sowohl griechisch wie syrisch als auch lateinisch wird das die Form christlicher Dichtung, die sich durchsetzt'. As a well-known instance of Greek syllable-counting poetry, I adduce the *kontakia* of the

sixth-century Byzantine poet Romanus: 'La métrique du kontakion ... est purement tonique et syllabique.... Pour que chaque strophe d'un kontakion puisse être chantée sur le même air, il faut que les éléments dont elle se compose, les *kôla*, aient le même nombre de syllabes et les accents principaux placés aux mêmes endroits que les kôla qui leur correspondent dans le modèle ou à peu près' (J. Grosdidier de Matons, in his edition of Romanus' hymns: Romanos le Mélode, *Hymnes*, 1: *Ancien Testament* [SC 99; Paris 1964] 17).

103 Schattenmann, *Studien*, 12.

104 Schattenmann, *Studien*, 14.

105 Schattenmann, *Studien*, 16-18.

106 J. Irigoin, 'La composition rythmique du prologue de Jean (I,1-18)', *RB* 78 (1971) 501-514.

107 For his method of counting stressed syllables, see *RB* 78, 502 n. 10: 'Pour le décompte des syllabes toniques, on a tenu compte à la fois des règles de l'accentuation grecque (existence de mots qui ne portent pas d'accent, proclitiques ou enclitiques) et des réalités phonétiques parfois dissimulées sous ces règles, c'est-à-dire l'existence de groupes de mots, constitués de prépositifs et de postpositifs encadrant un mot vraiment accentué, par exemple καὶ - τὸν - πατέρα - μου ou ὁ - πατὴρ - γάρ', with a reference to P. Maas, *Greek Metre* (Oxford 1962) par. 135.

108 Irigoin adopts the conclusion of P. Lamarche, 'Le Prologue de Jean', *RSR* 52 (1964) 497-537; 514-523 (reprinted, somewhat modified, in his *Christ vivant*. Essai sur la christologie du Nouveau Testament [LD 43; Paris 1966] 87-138), and K. Aland, 'Eine Untersuchung zu Joh 1,3.4. Über die Bedeutung eines Punktes', *ZNW* 59 (1968) 174-209 (reprinted, somewhat enlarged, as 'Über die Bedeutung eines Punktes. Eine Untersuchung zu Joh. 1,3.4', in: id., *Neutestamentliche Entwürfe* [Theologische Bücherei 63; Munich 1979] 351-391), that the division behind οὐδὲ ἕν was preferred (so Lamarche) or accepted unanimously (so Aland) in the first centuries; see *RB* 78, 503, with n. 11.

109 Cfr. Talbert, *CBQ* 32, 362-363, esp. 363: 'Ancient authors often used more than one structural principle in the same literary work'.

110 See Blass-Debrunner-Rehkopf, par. 39.1; E. Schwyzer, *Griechische Grammatik*, I: Allgemeiner Teil. Lautlehre. Wortbildung. Flexion (Handbuch der Altertumswissenschaft, 2. Abt., 1. Teil, 1. Band; Munich 1968[4]) 313. Cfr. below, pp. 43-44.

111 The triangular number of a natural number *n* is the sum of all successive natural numbers from 1 up to and including *n*: 1 + 2 + 3 ... + *n*. These numbers are called 'triangular numbers', because the units which make them up can be arranged in parallel lines and constitute, in that case, an equilateral triangle, the side of which is equal to the last number of the series. Take, for instance, 10, as the triangular number of 4; this can be arranged as follows:

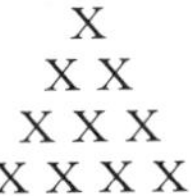

See also below, pp. 27-28. A perfect number is a number which is equal to the sum of its divisors, see below p. 29.

112 The qualification μονογενής is in John very closely related to 'the Son of God' or 'the Son', cfr. 3,16-18; 1 John 4,9-10; see F. Büchsel, art. μονογενής, *TWNT* IV, 745-750; 747-750; Th. C. de Kruijf, 'The Glory of the Only Son (John i 14)', in: *Studies in John* (Fs. J. N. Sevenster; NTS 24; Leiden 1970) 111-123.

113 J. Irigoin, 'La composition rythmique du Magnificat (Luc I 46-55)', in: *Zetesis* (Fs. E. de Strycker; Antwerpen/Utrecht 1973) 618-628.

114 J. Smit Sibinga, 'Eine literarische Technik im Matthäusevangelium', in: M. Didier, ed., *L'Évangile selon Matthieu*. Rédaction et théologie (BETL 29; Gembloux 1972) 99-105. Cfr. B. Gerhardsson, *The Mighty Acts of Jesus according to Matthew* (Scripta minora ... 1978-1979:5; Lund 1979) 41 *et alibi*.

115 Smit Sibinga, in: *L'Évangile selon Matthieu*, 99.
116 Smit Sibinga, in: *L'Évangile selon Matthieu*, 103.
117 J. Smit Sibinga, 'The Structure of the Apocalyptic Discourse, Matthew 24 and 25', *ST* 29 (1975) 71-79.
118 Smit Sibinga, in: *NT Textual Criticism*, 15-33.
119 Smit Sibinga, in: *NT Textual Criticism*, 30-33. The words which are put between square brackets in *NA*[25], in 14,22.27, are included in the count.
120 Smit Sibinga, in: *Studies in NT Language and Text*, 360-365.
121 Smit Sibinga, *Literair handwerk in Handelingen*.
122 Smit Sibinga, *Literair handwerk in Handelingen*, 17-18.
123 J. Smit Sibinga, 'A Study in I John', in: *Studies in John* (Fs. J. N. Sevenster; NTS 24; Leiden 1970) 194-208.
124 Smit Sibinga, in: *Studies in John*, 197-201.
125 Smit Sibinga, in: *Studies in John*, 200.
126 Smit Sibinga, in: *Studies in John*, 204-205. The name Καιν is considered to be a monosyllable.
127 Smit Sibinga, in: *Studies in John*, 205-208. This observation is mentioned in W. G. Kümmel, *Einleitung in das Neue Testament* (Heidelberg 1973[17]) 384 n. 5.
128 J. Smit Sibinga, 'Melito of Sardis. The Artist and His Text', *VC* 24 (1970) 81-104. In fact, the investigation of Melito's homily was the starting point for his research into NT texts, see *Studies in John*, 196.
129 Smit Sibinga, *VC* 24, 85.
130 An example of the use of word-count in Greek literature is the proem of Ps.-Hippocrates' *De decentia* (the date of this writing is unclear; it may even be as late as the 1st cent. C.E.), made up of 33 + 40 + 27 = 100 words; so, first and third part together are one and a half times the size of the second part; see J. Wittenzellner, *Untersuchungen zu der Pseudohippokratischen Schrift Περὶ Παθῶν* (diss. Erlangen/Nürnberg 1969) 41, whose count has to be corrected, however. For the use of these techniques in later times, one may point to *Codex Bezae*, where 'numerical verbal equality between the Greek and the Latin' has been observed by J. Rendel Harris, *Codex Bezae* (Cambridge 1891) 53-61, and to Bernard of Clairvaux' *Sermo* 74 as analysed by J. P. Th. Deroy, *Bernardus en Origenes*. Enkele opmerkingen over de invloed van Origenes op Sint Bernardus' Sermones super Cantica Canticorum (Haarlem 1963) 150-154. I derive these examples from Smit Sibinga, *VC* 24, 84 n. 12, and id., in: *Studies in NT Language and Text*, 365 n. 32.
131 Cfr. H. Windisch, 'Der johanneische Erzählungsstil', in: *ΕΥΧΑΡΙΣΤΗΡΙΟΝ* (Fs. H. Gunkel; FRLANT 36; Göttingen 1923) II 174-213.
132 *NA*[26], 40*.
133 I mention a few reviews from one language area: T. Baarda, 'Op weg naar een standaardtekst van het Nieuwe Testament? Enkele opmerkingen bij de verschijning van de 26ste druk van "Nestle"', *Gereformeerd Theologisch Tijdschrift* 80 (1980) 83-137; J. Delobel, 'Een nieuwe standaardtekst van het Nieuwe Testament', *Bijdragen* 41 (1980) 34-46; H. J. de Jonge, 'De nieuwe Nestle: N[26]', *NedTTs* 34 (1980) 307-322. One quotation (from de Jonge's article, p. 312): 'De belangrijkste kritiek is m.i., dat (1.) te weinig rekening is gehouden met taaleigen en stijl van individuele schrijvers van in het N.T. vervatte geschriften en in verband hiermee met het niveauverschil tussen stilistisch betere en slechtere lezingen, waarvan de eerste in veel gevallen te verwerpen zijn als correcties; en voorts (2.) dat er te veel rekening is gehouden met het getuigenis van bepaalde, van oudsher hooggeschatte tekstgetuigen, vooral de Vaticanus'.
134 Including the words between square brackets. Only occasionally, I depart from both editions. I shall argue such decisions in the appropriate place. In matters of orthography and of differences between *NA*[25] and *NA*[26] which do not affect numbers of syllables and words, I follow *NA*[26].
135 For these theories, I refer to the description and discussion of them in Kümmel, *Einleitung in das NT*, 170-177. As recent advocates of far-reaching theories in the

field of literary criticism of the Fourth Gospel, I mention M.-É. Boismard-A. Lamouille, avec la collaboration de G. Rochais, *L'évangile de Jean* (Synopse des quatre évangiles en français, III; Paris 1977), discussed critically by F. Neirynck a.o., *Jean et les synoptiques*. Examen critique de l'exégèse de M.-É. Boismard (BETL 49; Louvain 1979); W. Langbrandtner, *Weltferner Gott oder Gott der Liebe*. Der Ketzerstreit in der johanneischen Kirche. Eine exegetisch-religionsgeschichtliche Untersuchung mit Berücksichtigung der koptisch-gnostischen Texte aus Nag-Hammadi (Beiträge zur biblischen Exegese und Theologie 6; Bern/Frankfurt M. 1977), and J. Becker, in his commentary on John.

136 C. H. Dodd, *The Interpretation of the Fourth Gospel* (Cambridge 1953) 290.

137 Computer-counting has been used only to test my own counts. Counting 'by hand' was necessary, because — if the hypothesis holds true — the author of the Fourth Gospel did so, too. The computer-count was carried out by Dr. A. Ollongren and his collaborators of the *Centraal Reken Instituut* of the *Rijksuniversiteit* at Leiden. The method used in counting words and syllables by means of a computer is described by Smit Sibinga, *Literair handwerk in Handelingen*, 20-21. In order to facilitate verification, the counts are given in detail at the end of the book.

138 Both 'narrative' and 'discourse' are used here very strictly: 'discourse' comprises all which is presented as literally spoken by a character; the rest is 'narrative'.

139 See K. Menninger, *Zahlwort und Ziffer*. Eine Kulturgeschichte der Zahl (Göttingen $1958^2 = 1979^3$) II 73-80.

140 Philo's scattered passages about numbers have been collected, by way of reconstruction of his lost writing Περὶ ἀριθμῶν, by K. Staehle, *Die Zahlenmystik bei Philon von Alexandreia* (Leipzig/Berlin 1931). See also the index of R. Marcus in the Loeb-edition of Philo's works, Supplement II (Cambridge, Mass./London 1961) s.v. Number-symbolism.

141 Just as it is the case with the name 'triangular numbers' (see n. 111 above), so the names 'square numbers' and 'rectangular numbers' have to do with geometrical presentations of numbers. The units which make up a square number can be arranged in a square; 9, $= 3^2$, can be presented in this way:

X X X
X X X
X X X

Likewise, the rectangular number 12, $= 3 \times 4$, can be presented as:

X X X X
X X X X
X X X X

142 See O. Becker, 'Geschichte der antiken Mathematik', in: O. Becker-J. E. Hoffmann, *Geschichte der Mathematik* (Bonn 1951) 13-113; 50; B. L. van der Waerden, *Erwachende Wissenschaft*. Ägyptische, babylonische und griechische Mathematik (Wissenschaft und Kultur 8; Basel/Stuttgart 1956; orig. Dutch, Groningen 1950) 158-164; W. Burkert, *Weisheit und Wissenschaft*. Studien zu Pythagoras, Philolaos und Platon (Erlanger Beiträge zur Sprach- und Kunstwissenschaft 10; Nuremberg 1962) 404-410.

143 See about Aristotle's rendering of Pythagoraean teachings: Burkert, *Weisheit und Wissenschaft*, 26-46.

144 *10*: *De decalogo* 26; *De opificio mundi* 47; *De plantatione* 124-125; *28*: *De opif. m.* 101; *Quaestiones et solutiones in exodum* 2,87; *De specialibus legibus* 2,40; *36*: *Quaestiones et solutiones in genesin* 3,49; *55*: *Quaest. et sol. in gen.* 1,83; *De vita Mosis* 2,79; *120*: *Quaest. et sol. in gen.* 1,91; *300*: *Quaest. et sol. in gen.* 2,5. See further the register of Staehle, *Zahlenmystik*, s.v. τρίγωνος.

145 *4*: *De opif. m.* 51.106; *De plantat.* 121-122; *Quaest. et sol. in gen.* 3,61; *9*: *Quaest. et sol. in gen.* 3,61; *36*: *Quaest. et sol. in gen.* 3,49; *49*: *Quaest. et sol. in gen.* 3,39; *64*: *Quaest.*

et sol. in gen. 1,91; 3,49; *100*: *Quaest. et sol. in gen.* 3,56. See further the register of Staehle, *Zahlenmystik*, s.v. τετράγωνος.

146 *6*: *Legum allegoria* 1,3; *De spec. leg.* 2,58; *De opif. m.* 13; *56*: *Quaest. et sol. in gen.* 1,91; *90*: *Quaest. et sol. in gen.* 3,56; *110*: *Quaest. et sol. in gen.* 1,83.

147 *Quaest. et sol. in gen.* 2,5; 3,56; about *8*: *De opif. m.* 106; *Quaest. et sol. in gen.* 2,5; 3,49; about *64*: *Quaest. et sol. in gen.* 1,91; 3,49.

148 See Van der Waerden, *Erwachende Wissenschaft*, 160-161; Burkert, *Weisheit und Wissenschaft*, 408, with nn. 31-32.

149 *De decal.* 28; *Leg. alleg.* 1,3.15; *De opif. m.* 13.89; *Quaest. et sol. in exod.* 2,87; *Quaest. et sol. in gen.* 3,38; *De spec. leg.* 2,177.

150 *De opif. m.* 101; *Quaest. et sol. in exod.* 2,87; *De spec. leg.* 2,40; *De vita Mos.* 2,84.

151 See Van der Waerden, *Erwachende Wissenschaft*, 122-128; Becker, in: *Geschichte der Mathematik*, 33.

152 *De opif. m.* 97; *Quaest. et sol. in exod.* 2,93; *Quaest. et sol. in gen.* 2,5; 4,27; *De spec. leg.* 2,177; *De vita contemplativa* 65; *De vita Mos.* 2,80.

153 See n. 140.

CHAPTER ONE

JOHN 1,19-2,11: THE TESTIMONY OF THE BAPTIST AND THE BEGINNING OF JESUS' PUBLIC MINISTRY

Before discussing the composition of John 1,19-2,11, some preliminary problems have to be dealt with, concerning the division of certain words into syllables, and concerning a few problems of textual criticism.

In Greek transcriptions of Semitic words beginning with *iōta*, the *iōta* functions as a semivocal[1]. So, Ἰωάννης is counted at three syllables, as are also Ἰουδαῖος and Ἰορδάνης; Ἰησοῦς and Ἰωσήφ are counted at two syllables. The names Ἠσαΐας and Βηθσαϊδά are considered as tetrasyllabic; such a pronunciation is strongly suggested by the diaeresis and the spelling βηθσαειδα present in mss.[2]. The name Μωϋσῆς is counted at three syllables; the Latin transliteration helps to show that it was pronounced as a trisyllable[3].

Another problem is the division into syllables of words of the radix ἱερ-. To these belong ἱερεύς in 1,19, and ἱερόν which occurs in another passage to be discussed later (5,14). The solution of this problem affects also the division into syllables of Ἱεροσόλυμα. This Greek version of the name Jerusalem was apparently associated with the word ἱερός/ν, as is evident from Josephus, *Contra Apionem* 1,310-311. Josephus quotes the account of Lysimachus (2nd or 1st century B.C.) about the exodus from Egypt and the entry into the new country of the Jewish people (*C. Ap.* 1,305-311). At the end of this account, Lysimachus narrates that after having traversed the desert and reached inhabited country, the Jews plundered the temples which they found there (τὰ ἱερὰ συλῶντας); and the city which they built was called Ἱερόσυλα, because of their propensity to do this. Later on, they changed the name into Ἱεροσόλυμα. In his *Bellum Judaicum* 6,438, Josephus tells that Melchizedek, being the first to build τὸ ἱερόν, gave the city which was previously called Σόλυμα the name of Ἱεροσόλυμα (cfr. *Ant.* 7,67; 12,136). The presence of the shorter form Σόλυμα (Josephus, *Bell.* 6,438; *Ant.* 1,180; 7,67; cfr. *C. Ap.* 1,248, where Manetho, 3rd century B.C., is quoted, who calls the inhabitants of Jerusalem Σολυμῖται; cfr. also *C. Ap.* 1,173-174; Tacitus, *Historiae* 5,2) suggests that the name was split up into ἱερο-σόλυμα, which makes the association with ἱερός/ν rather obvious. The connection with ἱερός/ν is also made in Eusebius, *Praeparatio Evangelica* 9,34,13, where the Jewish historian Eupolemus (2nd century B.C.) is quoted. It is evident too from the Latin transcription *Hierosolyma* (and the like), and the Coptic *thierosolyma*, mostly contracted to *thilēm* (feminine definite article + nomen). So it can be assumed that Ἱεροσόλυμα was associated with ἱερός/ν[4].

As historical Greek knows the consonantal *iōta* only as the second element of diphthongs[5], we may safely consider ἱερός as a trisyllable. This view is indubitably confirmed by the use of the word in instances such as Homer, *Iliad* 1,147; 8,66; 11,194.631; 16,407, and Theocritus, *Idyllia* 5,22, where the first syllable of the various forms of ἱερός is an *elementum longum*, and the last syllable is an *elementum breve*, followed in turn by a *longum*; consequently, we have to do with *dactyli*, made up of three syllables[6]. It is true that contracted forms of ἱερός are found as well: ἱρός in Ionic dialect, and ἶρος in Aeolic[7], but when the non-contracted form is used, it is a trisyllable[8]. Ἱεροσόλυμα has, then, six syllables.

There are two instances of difference between the text of John 1,19-2,11 as printed in *NA*^{25} and that in *NA*^{26} which affect numbers of S and W:

1. In 1,26, *NA*^{25} reads στήκει with B L 083 *f*1 *pc*, whereas *NA*^{26} has ἕστηκεν, with P^{66} A C W^{s} ΘΨ 063 *f*13 *Mehrheitstext* Or[9]. Between the two forms, there is no difference of meaning; both the perfect with present meaning ἕστηκα and the derivative Hellenistic present form στήκω mean 'I stand'[10]. Precisely the circumstance that στήκει is a Hellenistic form, while ἕστηκεν is the classic form, makes it probable that an original στήκει has been replaced, for stylistic reasons, by ἕστηκεν[11]. An additional argument in favour of the reading στήκει is the proximity of the form εἱστήκει in John 1,35.

2. In 1,47, *NA*^{26} reads ὁ Ἰησοῦς, with P$^{66.75}$ Sin A L W^{s} Θ Ψ *f*1.13 *Mehrheitstext*; the article is omitted in *NA*^{25}, with B H S Γ 234 399 1071[12]. G. D. Fee observes about the 45 instances in John, where the name Ἰησοῦς immediately follows the verb (and where no apposition follows the name and the verb used is not ἀπεκρίθη), that there is no instance where all mss. omit the article; there are, however, 9 instances among the 45 of all mss. having the articular reading, and 7 where only one ms. has the anarthrous one. So Fee can state: 'In general the Johannine pattern is ... clear: to read the article'[13]. He observes a somewhat stronger tendency to omit the article in instances such as 1,47, where the name follows a verb of the mental processes (saying, thinking, etc.), particularly in the Neutral tradition, although in such cases, too, several instances of an articular text without textual variation are found (2,22; 5,6; 6,10; 9,39[14]; 13,1; 19,28[15]; 21,21)[16]. In the present case, the anarthrous reading is found in one representative of the Neutral tradition (B), as well

as in a few representatives of the Byzantine and Caesarean text-type. In his conclusions, Fee mentions among the instances in which personal names in John tend to be anarthrous: 'Perhaps in the nominative when it immediately follows a verb of the mental processes (*saying*, *thinking*, etc.)'[17]. He inclines to considering the tendencies of the Neutral tradition to omit the article with personal names in certain idioms (not only the one in question) more as a matter of preservation than of recension: these tendencies are early and belong to an entire textual tradition, and anarthrous readings are supported by other early mss. from all traditions. Moreover, the tendency to conform to the more common articular text becomes stronger, the later one goes in the manuscript tradition, and in similar constructions in the Synoptic Gospels even the Neutral tradition lacks the tendencies it has in John. Fee sees, however, one difficulty with such a conclusion: in certain idioms, the anarthrous readings have broader manuscript support in the Neutral tradition than in other idioms. As an example of the latter, Fee adduces the personal names immediately after verbs of the mental processes[18].

So, we are left at a deadlock concerning the presence of the article before the name Ἰησοῦς in 1,47. Neither the internal nor the external evidence is conclusive. The best thing to do, then, is to assume provisionally the anarthrous reading as being most in agreement with Fee's conclusions, and to await whether the numerical features of the text yield a clear confirmation or negation of this choice. I readily admit that this is a circular reasoning, as the textual decision is made to a certain extent dependent upon the hypothesis to be proved. Such a reasoning is, however, unavoidable in the present case, as the other evidence is inconclusive. Moreover, the numerical data will only be accepted as evidence when *several* observations concerning size and proportion converge in supporting one reading.

1. *John 1,19-2,11: a series of short scenes*

The Johannine description of the testimony of John the Baptist and of the beginning of Jesus' public ministry is divided into short pericopes, which are situated on a series of successive days. After the Prologue (1,1-18), we read in 1,19-28 about the testimony of John the Baptist which he bears in front of an embassy from Jerusalem asking him who he is. After a few negative answers he identifies himself with the 'voice' from Isa 40,3 (1,19-23). When the envoys ask for the meaning of his baptism, he answers by pointing to the unknown one who is standing among them (1,24-27). The pericope is concluded by an indication of place (1,28).

The testimony of the Baptist is continued on the next day, when he sees Jesus coming to him. He witnesses to Jesus as the Lamb of God, as the one who came after John but ranks ahead of him because he was before John, as the one on whom the Spirit is resting, as the Son of God (1,29-34).

The next day, John indicates Jesus once again as the Lamb of God, this time in the presence of two of his disciples who thereupon join Jesus (1,35-39). Andrew, one of these two, then brings his brother Simon to Jesus, the Messiah (1,40-42).

The next day, Jesus calls Philip (1,43-44), and Philip brings Nathanael to Jesus. Nathanael confesses Jesus as the Son of God and the King of Israel, and he receives from Jesus the promise that he will see 'greater things' (1,45-51).

'On the third day' (2,1), Jesus and his disciples are present at a wedding at Cana in Galilee; Jesus' mother is also there. She applies to Jesus, when the wine has run out, and he changes a large quantity of water into wine (2,1-10). This miracle is qualified by the evangelist as the 'beginning of the signs', in which Jesus 'revealed his glory, and his disciples believed in him' (2,11).

With the distribution of events over five days we already have a strong suggestion that we have to do here with five successive short scenes. The changes of *dramatis personae*, of action and of place strengthen this suggestion:

1. In 1,19-28, John the Baptist and the envoys from Jerusalem are the acting characters[19]: they are discussing the Baptist's identity and his baptism. The place of action is 'Bethany beyond Jordan' (1,28). The last verse of the pericope (1,28) is an obvious conclusion[20]; the sentence structure, constituted by a form of the demonstrative pronoun οὗτος by way of a résumé of the preceding, a verb and an indication of place, occurs in John more often in closing sentences:

1,28 ταῦτα ἐν Βηθανίᾳ ἐγένετο πέραν τοῦ Ἰορδάνου
2,11 ταύτην ἐποίησεν ... ἐν Κανὰ τῆς Γαλιλαίας
4,54 τοῦτο ... ἐποίησεν ... ἐλθὼν ἐκ τῆς Ἰουδαίας εἰς τὴν Γαλιλαίαν
6,59 ταῦτα εἶπεν ἐν συναγωγῇ ... ἐν Καφαρναούμ
8,20 ταῦτα ... ἐλάλησεν ἐν τῷ γαζοφυλακίῳ ... ἐν τῷ ἱερῷ

2. In 1,29-34, the Baptist and Jesus are on the stage. The latter's role is a purely passive one: the Baptist testifies on his behalf.

3. At the beginning of the next scene (1,35-42), the Baptist, two of his disciples and Jesus are on the stage. After 1,37, the Baptist disappears, and his two disciples follow Jesus to his abode (1,39). Thereafter Andrew, one of the two, finds his brother Simon and brings him to Jesus

(1,42). It is true that in this scene the unity of persons, action and place is somewhat less strict than in the two preceding scenes; nevertheless, the events narrated are logically connected (two people come into contact with Jesus through the Baptist, one of them brings his brother into contact with Jesus), and they are situated by the evangelist on one day (cfr. p. 81 below, with n. 87).

4. The fourth scene (1,43-51) begins with Jesus and Philip on the stage, at the moment when Jesus decides to leave for Galilee (1,43; I suppose that in the text as we have it Jesus is meant to be the subject of ἠθέλησεν and εὑρίσκει[21]). Then Philip finds Nathanael (1,45), and brings him to Jesus (1,46-47). This scene displays more or less the same pattern of action as the preceding one: a person enters into contact with Jesus, and brings then another person to him[22].

5. The fifth scene (2,1-11) is situated 'on the third day' (2,1), at a wedding-feast at Cana in Galilee. In 2,1-2 Jesus' mother, Jesus himself and his disciples are introduced as *dramatis personae*. In the course of the scene a few other characters appear to be present, whose assisting at a wedding is self-evident[23]: servants (2,5), steward and bridegroom (2,9). The unity of the scene is marked by the inclusion constituted by the mention of the place of action and of the disciples' presence both in 2,1-2 and in 2,11[24].

John 1,19-2,11 is made up, then, of five short scenes — short, at least, according to Johannine standards[25]. I shall deal firstly with these scenes separately, and only afterwards with the connections between them. This procedure is somewhat different from the one followed in the other chapters of this thesis, where firstly the entire passage in question (e.g., John 5 or 6) is dealt with, and only then are its various parts discussed. The reason for this difference is that in the other instances it can be established rather easily that the entire passage in question constitutes a literary unit, whereas it is hardly self-evident that 1,19-2,11 is a literary unit. As we shall see, one can at best speak here of a series of small literary units which are connected in various ways.

2. *John 1,19-28 and 1,29-34: the testimony of the Baptist*

a) *John 1,19-28*

John 1,19-28 is obviously made up of two parts:

1. In 1,19-23 questions are asked — after the introduction of the *dramatis personae* — about John the Baptist's role in salvation history. After a few negative answers, the Baptist answers positively in 1,23: he is the 'voice' from Isa 40,3. With this statement the question 'who are you?' (1,19) has been answered.

2. In 1,24-27 a new question is asked, after the inquiring party has been introduced anew: now the meaning of John's baptism is asked for, and John answers to this question.

Finally, 1,28 closes the scene[26].

The two halves of the scene display some similarity: both begin with a reference to the mission of the interrogators by means of the verb ἀποστέλλειν[27]. This is followed by one or more questions asked by the envoys and answered by John (cfr. τί οὖν in 1,21.25). In the question which occurs in the second half (1,25), the questions and answers of the first half are referred to (1,19-21); even the titles from the first half are found again in the second half in the same order (the Christ, Elijah, the prophet).

Two features in the literary composition of this passage suggest that, in addition to the bipartition of the scene, the OT quotation in 1,23 constitutes its centre:

a. The three decisive answers of the Baptist begin with an emphatic ἐγώ:

1,20 ἐγὼ οὐκ εἰμὶ ὁ χριστός
23 ἐγὼ φωνὴ βοῶντος ...
26 ἐγὼ βαπτίζω ἐν ὕδατι ...[28]

(The Baptist's negative answers in 1,21, becoming gradually shorter, are parallel to his answer in 1,20.)
The answer 1,23 is the middle one of this series.

b. The answer 1,23 is not introduced by ἀπεκρίθη, λέγει or some such thing (as it is currently done in the present pericope and elsewhere in John), but by ἔφη, which occurs in John, apart from 1,23, only in 9,36 *v.l.*; 9,38 (cfr. 18,29)[29].

The literary structure of John 1,19-28 having been analysed, the second and decisive step of the investigation will be taken. We shall transpose this structure into numbers of S and W, to see whether it is also discernible in these numbers. A series of observations strongly suggest an affirmative answer to this question.

First of all, the direct discourse put in the mouth of John the Baptist amounts to the round number of 50 W (on a sum total of 157 W for the entire passage)[30]. Out of these 50 W, 10 W are used for the OT quotation 1,23bc. In the number of S, the surplus-technique has been applied: the OT quotation 1,23bc has a size of 22 S, on a sum total of 322 S for the entire passage 1,19-28.

As for the numbers of S and W, the middle of the pericope lies unmistakably in 1,23. Both the number of W and of S of this verse are square numbers: 16 W, $= 4^2$, or 36 S, $= 6^2$; 36 is, moreover, triangular number of 8. The verse is preceded by 71 W, and followed by 70 W. In numbers of S, the Baptist's words in 1,23b-d (made up of 12 + 10 + 12 S) constitute exactly the middle of the passage: they are preceded and followed by 144 S, = 12^2. Both groups of 144 S begin with a clause of 14 S (1,19a.24), and are made up of two parts, which contain each a number of S which is a multiple of 9: 1,19-20 (introduction, first question and answer) has a size of 81 S, = 9^2, 1,21-23a (questions and answers, followed by introduction to direct discourse) amounts to 63 S, = 7 × 9[31]; 1,24-27 (presentation of interrogators, question and answer) contains 117 S, = 13 × 9, and the conclusion 1,28 has a size of 27 S, = 3 × 9. This obvious preference for multiples of 9 (other instances will be adduced below) may have to do with the circumstance that the numerical value of Βηθανία, the place where the scene is located (1,28), is 81, = 9^2 (2 + 8 + 9 + 1 + 50 + 10 + 1 = 81). The closing sentence in which this name is mentioned (1,28) has a size of 27 S, = 1/3 × 81, and the beginning of the pericope 1,19-20 has a size of exactly 81 S.

In Table I, the above observations concerning numbers of S are rendered schematically.

Table I. John 1,19-28 syllables

1,19a	14	
19b-20	67/ 81	
21-23a		63/144
23b		12
23c		10
23d		12/ 34
24	14	
25-27	103/117	
28		27/144/322

The middle of the pericope, 1,23b-d, contains exactly 1/3 of the number of S spoken by the Baptist in the entire passage: 34 S, on a sum total of 102 S for the Baptist's discourse. Moreover, the quantities of discourse ascribed to the Baptist (measured in numbers of S) are divided over the pericope so as to constitute an arithmetical series: his answers in 1,20-21 amount together to 12 S, his answer in 1,23 to 34 S, and the one in 1,26-27 to 56 S. The difference both between 12 and 34, and between 34 and 56, is 22.

The pericope contains another arithmetical series: after the heading 1,19a, of 7 W, it contains 30 W for 1,19b-20, 50 W for 1,21-23, and 70 W for 1,24-28; together 7 + 150 W.

In addition to the division into narrative and discourse, there is another division of the text which the author of the Fourth Gospel seems to have used in construing his text in numerical patterns, viz., a division according to the actors. Several scholars have pointed out that the author of John constructs his stories as a kind of stage-plays with successive scenes, with dialogue and monologue, with protagonists and antagonists[32]. Within a given passage, the numbers of S and W of all sentences in which the same person or group is the actor, are counted together. In this procedure, subordinate clauses are counted with the main clause on which they are dependent, and direct discourse is ascribed to its speaker. Normally, the actor in a narrative sentence coincides with the subject of the main clause. In the present pericope, the envoys from Jerusalem are the actor in 1,21a-c.f.22.24-25. These sentences, in which they are the actor, are evenly divided over the two parts: those in the first part (1,21a-c.f.22) as well as the one in the second part (1,24-25) amount to 49 S, $= 7^2$; the numbers of W are 27 and 26 respectively (cfr. Table V below). The first group of 49 S begins with 7 + 7 S (1,21a.b-c) and contains a clause of 14 S in 1,22c; the second group is made up of 14 + 35 S (1,24.25). The factor 7 dominates here.

In the first part (1,19-23), the general question asked in 1,19: 'who are you?', is answered only in 1,23[33]. What is in between (1,20-22), comprises only negative answers and repetitions of the question. This construction of the text is also discernible in numbers of S: both 1,19.23 and 1,20-22 have a size of 89 S.

Some details in 1,19-28 require our attention:

1. The long sentence 1,19, with which the scene opens, is made up of 50 S of narrative followed by 3 S of discourse. The long subordinate clause 1,19b, of 36 S ($= 6^2$, and triangular number of 8), is made up of 27 ($= 3 \times 9$) + 9 S (for ὅτε ... Λευίτας and ἵνα ... αὐτόν respectively). Again, the factor 9 appears.

2. The emphatically negative answer of John the Baptist, together with its circumstantial and solemn introduction (1,20), has a size of 28 S; 28 is both the triangular number of 7, and a perfect number. The introduction is made up of 3×6 S (6 is the triangular number of 3, a rectangular number in its quality of being the product of 2 and 3, and a perfect number), together 18 S, $= 2 \times 9$:

καὶ ὡμολόγησεν	6 S
καὶ οὐκ ἠρνήσατο	6
καὶ ὡμολόγησεν	6/18

3. 1,21 contains: a) introduction to direct discourse and questions, both of 7 S; b) introduction and answer, both of 3 S, together 6 S; c) a question of 6 S; d) an introduction of 5 S followed by an answer of 1 S; again together 6 S:

καὶ ἠρώτησαν αὐτόν·	7 S
τί οὖν; σὺ Ἠλίας εἶ;	7/14
καὶ λέγει·	3
οὐκ εἰμί.	3/ 6
ὁ προφήτης εἶ σύ;	6
καὶ ἀπεκρίθη·	5
οὔ.	1/ 6/32

Again, we meet a sequence of 3 × 6 S.

4. In 1,26b-27, the Baptist says:

		syll.	words
a	ἐγὼ βαπτίζω ἐν ὕδατι	9	4
b	μέσος ὑμῶν στήκει ὃν ὑμεῖς οὐκ οἴδατε	13	7/11
c	ὁ ὀπίσω μου ἐρχόμενος	9	4
d	οὗ οὐκ εἰμὶ ἐγὼ ἄξιος	9	5
e	ἵνα λύσω αὐτοῦ τὸν ἱμάντα τοῦ ὑποδήματος	16/56	7/12/27

Measured in numbers of W, element *c* is the centre of the Baptist's saying: this christological qualification (cfr. 1,15.30; Matt 3,11; Mark 1,7) is preceded by 11 W and followed by 12 W. Three elements (*a*, *c* and *d*) have a size of 9 S. The sum totals for this saying are interesting: 56 is a rectangular number (7 × 8), and 27 is a cubic number (3^3), and a multiple of 9.

b) *John 1,29-34*

By means of the new introduction to direct discourse in 1,32 ('and John testified saying'), the testimony of the Baptist 1,29-34 is divided into two parts: 1,29-31 and 1,32-34[34].

The determination of the literary structure of 1,29-34 seems to be a difficult task (apart from the observation of the obvious bipartition), to judge from the various different proposals made in this field. This lack of unanimity may be caused by the circumstance that, on the one side, literal or almost literal repetitions and other evident similarities are numerous in this passage, whereas, on the other hand, no clear pattern seems to be present in them. It is useful to list the evident repetitions and similarities, before rendering a few proposals concerning the literary composition of John 1,29-34:

a. Sayings concerning Jesus introduced by οὗτός ἐστιν are found in 1,30.33.34[35].

b. Quotations are found in 1,30.33.34; twice, the Baptist quotes what he has previously said (1,30.34), and once he quotes what God has said to him (1,33).

c. The words κἀγὼ οὐκ ᾔδειν αὐτόν at the beginning of 1,31 are repeated literally at the beginning of 1,33. Moreover, κἀγώ is found at the beginning of 1,34.

d. Both in 1,31 and in 1,33, we meet a reference to John's baptism in water, with which God charged him:

1,31 ἦλθον ἐγὼ ἐν ὕδατι βαπτίζων
33 ὁ πέμψας με βαπτίζειν ἐν ὕδατι

John's baptism in water is contrasted with Jesus' baptism in Holy Spirit, mentioned at the end of 1,33: οὗτός ἐστιν ὁ βαπτίζων ἐν πνεύματι ἁγίῳ.

e. Both in 1,32 and in 1,33, it is mentioned that John sees the Spirit descending and resting upon Jesus:

1,32 τεθέαμαι τὸ πνεῦμα καταβαῖνον ... καὶ ἔμεινεν ἐπ'αὐτόν
33 ἐφ'ὃν ἂν ἴδῃς τὸ πνεῦμα καταβαῖνον καὶ μένον ἐπ'αὐτόν[36]

J. Howton[37] distinguishes three parts in John 1,29b-34, and each one of these three parts is, in turn, tripartite:

A	a	1,29b*a*	B	a	31a	C	a	33a
	b	29b*b*		b	31b		b	33b-d
	c	30		c	32		c	34

Within each of the parts A, B and C, the smaller parts a, b and c are of increasing length (except Cc, by way of climax). Bc and Cc are about John's testimony. All three c-parts (1,30.32.34) deal with the Messiah; Bb and Cb deal with the Baptist, Bb with his baptism in water, Cb with the baptism in Holy Spirit. Ba, Ca and Cc begin with κἀγώ.

Howton's scheme integrates some of the repetitions noted above (nrs. c and d), but on the whole his scheme is too arbitrary to be correct. The division into parts is insufficiently argued. The new beginning in 1,32 is not given a function in the scheme. The narrative introduction 1,29a is left aside, whereas the introduction 1,32a*a* is not. That all three c-parts are about the Messiah is true but not relevant as 1,29 and 1,33cd are also about him. Part Bb is indeed about the Baptist, but Cb says more about Jesus than about the Baptist. Howton's proposal does not offer a solution for the problem of the structure of John 1,29-34.

A chiastic pattern is proposed for John 1,29-34 by Ch. Exum[38]:

A 1,29-30 A' 34
B 31-32 B' 33

Parts A and A' are corresponding in so far as both relate John's witness: to Jesus as the Lamb of God and as pre-existent in 1,29-30, as the Son of God in 1,34. Parts B and B' are corresponding on account of repetitions c, d and e of the above series; elements of part B are repeated in the same order in part B'.

The correspondences detected by Exum are real; against his scheme is, nevertheless, the fact that repetitions a and b, and the bipartition by means of the new introduction 1,32a*a*, do not find a place in it.

According to M. Roberge[39], John 1,29-34 displays concentric symmetry:

A 1,29ab*a* A' 34
B 29b*b* B' 33d
C 31 C' 33a-c
D 32

Parts A and A' contain both a title for Jesus. B and B' are about the mission of Jesus: to take away the sin of the world (1,29), to baptize in Holy Spirit (1,33). C and C' deal with the manifestation of the Messiah, which was the goal of John's baptism (1,31) and concerning which God gave his revelation to the Baptist (1,33). The central part D contains John's testimony: he saw the Spirit rest upon Jesus, which manifested him as the Messiah. Roberge considers 1,30 as an addition, about Jesus' preexistence.

Roberge's scheme is, mostly, based on real correspondences; it has, moreover, the advantage that the new introduction at the beginning of 1,32 can be integrated in it: it marks the central position of 1,32. His scheme has also its weaknesses:

1. Repetitions a and b from the above series are not integrated in it.
2. When 1,30 is left aside as an addition, Roberge does not describe the structure of John 1,29-34, but of a supposed earlier version of this passage.
3. It is strange that 1,29b, being one clause, is divided over two parts, its first half corresponding to 1,34, and its second half corresponding to 1,33d. Likewise, the one sentence 1,33 is divided over two elements.

In Roberge's scheme, repetition e from the above list has a function, not in the correspondence of parts, but in their sequence: C' follows and explains D. This draws attention to the circumstance that repetitions or other obvious similarities between parts of a text can have various functions: they need not always indicate a correspondence within a chiastic or concentric pattern[40].

To me it seems that the first observation to be made concerning the structure of John 1,29-34 is very simple: the discourse in the passage contains two different kinds of assertions. On the one side, there are sentences giving statements of fact about the Baptist's activity, about what he did and saw: in 1,31, John says that he came baptizing in water in order that Jesus might be manifested to Israel, and in 1,32 he testifies that he saw the Spirit descending like a dove from heaven and resting upon Jesus. Both statements concern the event of Jesus' being baptized by John. On the other side, there are sentences in which qualifications of Jesus are given, by means of titles or otherwise; sentences which contain John's witness concerning Jesus. In 1,29, Jesus is called 'the Lamb of God, who takes away the sin of the world'. In 1,30, he is qualified as the one about whom the Baptist said: 'After me comes a man who ranks ahead of me, because he was before me'. Another qualification of Jesus is given in 1,33, where God's words to the Baptist are quoted: 'The one on whom you will see the Spirit descending and resting, he is the one who is to baptize in Holy Spirit'; the οὗτός ἐστιν-formula 1,33d constitutes the main point of the verse, the rest summing up what has been said earlier. Both kinds of assertions together are found in the closing sentence 1,34, which makes, for that reason, the impression of being a conclusion: 'And I have seen (statement of fact about the Baptist) and I have testified that this is the Son of God (qualification of Jesus)'.

In the sequence of the two kinds of assertions, a scheme becomes visible:

A	1,29b-30	qualifications of Jesus
B	31b	statement of fact about the Baptist
B'	32*bc*	statement of fact about the Baptist
A'	33b-d	qualification of Jesus
b	34*a*	statement of fact about the Baptist
a	34*bc*	qualification of Jesus

The function of most repetitions observed at the beginning of this section now becomes clear:

a. The οὗτός ἐστιν-sayings are found in parts A, A' and a.

b. The quotations are also found in A, A' and a.

c. The clause κἀγὼ οὐκ ᾔδειν αὐτόν separates A from B, and B' from A'. The third κἀγώ is found at the beginning of the concluding sentence 1,34, which contains both kinds of assertions in a much shorter form (for that reason, the two parts of 1,34 are indicated in the above scheme by small type).

The function of the new introduction at the beginning of 1,32 becomes also visible now: it marks the transition from A and B to B' and A'.

A correspondence which is not literal but anyhow evident, and which is noted in Roberge's scheme reproduced above, is that between 1,29 and 1,33: in both verses, Jesus' mission is indicated by means of a substantival participle of the present (ὁ αἴρων τὴν ἁμαρτίαν τοῦ κόσμου, ὁ βαπτίζων ἐν πνεύματι ἁγίῳ). The first participle occurs in A, the second one in A'[41].

Repetitions d and e of the above series do not have a function within the proposed scheme. They have, nevertheless, their own place. The repetition of words from B and B' in A' serves to indicate that the qualification of Jesus given at the end of A' is based upon the event of Jesus' baptism and on what happened on that occasion, the significance of which was revealed to John by God. The Baptist's witness concerning Jesus is based on the fact he reports, as expressed in 1,31-32. The repetitions in question have their function more in the logic of the Baptist's words than in their structure. It should be noted, moreover, that the main point of 1,33 is made in 1,33d.

The clause ἵνα φανερωθῇ τῷ 'Ισραήλ (1,31) has a function similar to that of the repetitions in 1,33. In part A, the Baptist reveals Jesus to Israel. This revelation was the goal of the fact of his baptism, dealt with in part B. The phrase κἀγὼ οὐκ ᾔδειν αὐτόν indicates that the Baptist himself was not able to take the step, from what he did and saw to the interpretation of Jesus to be derived from it; the phrase is, in that way, very appropriate to mark the transition from A to B, and from B' to A'[42].

It now has to be examined whether the literary unity of 1,29-34 and the structure just described are also discernible in numbers of S and W.

The direct discourse of the passage amounts to the round number of 100 W, the narrative amounts to 15 W. The distribution of W over the two halves of the pericope, 1,29-31 and 1,32-34, is given in Table II.

Table II. John 1,29-34		words		
1,29a	narrative	10		
29b-31	discourse		45	
32*a*	narrative (up to and including ὅτι)	5/		15
32*b*-34	discourse		55/100/115	

The first half is made up of 10 W of narrative and 45 W of discourse, together 55; the second half is made up of 5 W of narrative and 55 W of discourse, together 60. So, the name 'Ιωάννης in 1,32 is the middle word of the pericope (this is also the case in numbers of S: the name is preceded by 112 S and followed by 113 S). The division of the 100 W of discourse into 45 and 55 W is interesting: 45 and 55 are triangular numbers, of 9 and 10 respectively, and their sum is a square number ($100 = 10^2$; see above, p. 28).

The passage contains three quotations. Twice, the Baptist quotes his own words (1,30.34). The first one of these two quotations, 1,30bc, has a size of 12 W; the second one, 1,34*c* (from οὗτος onward) has half that size, 6 W. The quotation of God's words 1,33cd is as long as the two other quotations together: 18 W. The three quotations together amount to 36 W. So, out of 100 W of discourse, 36 W are quotations and 64 are not; to put it otherwise, $6^2 + 8^2 = 10^2$, or $(2 \times 3)^2 + (2 \times 4)^2 = (2 \times 5)^2$. We find here the lowest natural numbers for which Pythagoras' proposition holds, that $a^2 + b^2 = c^2$ (see above, p. 29).

In the numbers of S, 33 appears several times. John 1,29-34 contains 33 S of narrative (over against 195 S of discourse). The quotation of God's words 1,33cd has a length of 33 S; the two other quotations (1,30bc.34*c*) amount together to 23 + 10 = 33 S. The verse 1,31 has a size of 33 S. In addition, it should be mentioned that 1,29b-31 amounts to 33 W without the quotation 1,30bc.

In Table III, the numbers of S and W are given for 1,29-34, in accordance with the literary structure of the passage described above (the transitions 1,31a.33a are counted separately).

Table III. John 1,29-34

					syll.				words	
	1,29a	narrative introduction		20				10		
A	29b-30	qualification of Jesus			53				29	
	31a	'I myself did not know him'	(86)		7		(45)		4	
B	31b	statement of fact about Baptist			26				12	
	32*a*	narrative introduction		13/		33		5/		15
B'	32*bc*	statement of fact about Baptist			27/	53			12/24	
	33a	'I myself did not know him'	(85)		7/	14	(44)		4/	8
A'	33b-d	qualification of Jesus			51/	104			28/	57
a + b	34	conclusion				24/228				11/115

The chiastic pattern A-B-B'-A' is recognizable in numbers of both S and W. In numbers of S, there is a difference of 2 S between A and A', and of 1 S between B and B', but the sum totals for (A + B) and (A' + B') are almost equal: 86 and 85 S. Their sum is 171, triangular number of 18, and 3/4 of the sum total of 228 S. In numbers of W, the symmetry is almost perfect: there is a difference of only 1 W between A and A', and B and B' are of equal size. It appears now that the 55 W of the second half 1,32*b*-34 are made up of 44 W, = 4 × 11, for (B' + A'), and 11 W for the conclusion. Of equal length to the conclusion is the first sentence of the discourse of 1,29-34: 1,29b contains also 11 W. Both sentences contain a christological title: 'the Lamb of God' in 1,29b, 'the Son of God' in 1,34.

The transitions between A and B, and between B' and A', are marked by short clauses, of 6 or 7 S, or 4 W. Not only has the clause κἀγὼ οὐκ ᾔδειν αὐτόν (1,31a.33a) this size, but the same is valid for the last clause of A (1,30c: ὅτι πρῶτός μου ἦν, 6 S or 4 W) and the last clause of B' (1,32*c*: καὶ ἔμεινεν ἐπ'αὐτόν, 7 S or 4 W).

It should be noted — also in view of what will follow in the next section — that multiples of 11 are found frequently in the numbers of S and W of 1,29-34: the figure 33 appeared several times; units of 55, 44 and 11 W were observed.

Another figure which has a certain importance in the numbers of S of 1,29-34 is 53. The first half (1,29-31) has a size of 106 S, = 2 × 53; half of these, 53, are used in 1,29b-30 (= A). B and B' (1,31b.32*bc*) amount together to 26 + 27 = 53 S (see Table III).

Finally, a few details from this passage have to be discussed:

1. 1,30bc, the Baptist's quotation of his own previous words, is made up of 3 × 4 W:

ὀπίσω μου ἔρχεται ἀνήρ	4 W
ὃς ἔμπροσθέν μου γέγονεν	4
ὅτι πρῶτός μου ἦν	4/12

2. The Baptist's saying 1,32*bc* is made up of 8 + 4 W:

τεθέαμαι τὸ πνεῦμα καταβαῖνον ὡς περιστερὰν ἐξ οὐρανοῦ	8 W
καὶ ἔμεινεν ἐπ'αὐτόν	4/12

3. The final sentences of the pericope, starting from 1,33b, are made up of elements, the size of which is a multiple of 3 when measured in numbers of S, and whose sum total amounts to 75 S:

33 ἀλλ'ὁ πέμψας με βαπτίζειν ἐν ὕδατι	12 S	
ἐκεῖνός μοι εἶπεν	6/18	
ἐφ'ὃν ἂν ἴδῃς τὸ πνεῦμα καταβαῖνον	12	
καὶ μένον ἐπ'αὐτόν	6	
οὗτός ἐστιν ὁ βαπτίζων ἐν πνεύματι ἁγίῳ	15/33	
34 κἀγὼ ἑώρακα		6
καὶ μεμαρτύρηκα		6/12
ὅτι		2
οὗτός ἐστιν ὁ υἱὸς τοῦ θεοῦ		10/12/24/75

The conclusion of the passage on John's testimony is marked by an isocolon of 12 + 12 S.

c) *John 1,19-34*

Now that the structure of John 1,19-28 and 1,29-34 has been investigated, both by conventional literary analysis and by numerical analysis as far as numbers of S and W are concerned, attention has to be focussed on the two pericopes together, because there are several reasons to consider them as coherent. They share a common theme: the testimony of John the Baptist. He is the protagonist in both pericopes; he testifies on behalf of Jesus, in the first pericope negatively by assigning to himself only a modest role in comparison with the one who comes after him, in the second pericope positively by indicating Jesus as the bearer of salvation. The coherence of the two scenes is marked by the inclusion constituted by μαρτυρία in 1,19 and μεμαρτύρηκα in 1,34 (cfr. ἐμαρτύρησεν in 1,32). With the perfect μεμαρτύρηκα in 1,34 the testimony of the Baptist is closed[43]. In the next scenes, the theme will be the call of the disciples, and Jesus and his first disciples will be the main characters.

Both scenes are further connected by means of a series of references:

a. In 1,30, the Baptist quotes his own previous words. These are found (as far as they can be found at all in John) in 1,27, although not literally[44]. The words ὀπίσω μου ἔρχεται in 1,30 take up ὁ ὀπίσω μου ἐρχόμενος from 1,27, and the difference in rank which is described in 1,30, is present in 1,27 in the image of not being worthy to unfasten the sandals. It is true that the words of the Baptist in 1,15 agree much more literally with those in 1,30, but there he refers also to what he *has* said, probably to be understood as an anticipation within the hymn 1,1-18 of what follows in 1,27.30.

b. Κἀγὼ οὐκ ᾔδειν αὐτόν (1,31.33) refers to ὃν ὑμεῖς οὐκ οἴδατε (1,26).

c. Διὰ τοῦτο ἦλθον ἐγὼ ἐν ὕδατι βαπτίζων (1,31) and ὁ πέμψας με βαπτίζειν ἐν ὕδατι (1,33) refer to ἐγὼ βαπτίζω ἐν ὕδατι (1,26; cfr. 1,25.28).

d. A reader who is acquainted with sayings such as Mark 1,8 parr; Acts 1,5; 11,16, which sayings are to be situated in the same tradition as John 1,26b.33d[45], would expect that the Baptist's words 'I baptize in water' (1,26) were followed by its antithetic parallel 'he will baptize you in Holy Spirit', or some such thing. Such words are only heard from the Baptist in the next scene (in 1,33); they are there in a less direct opposition to 'baptizing in water', so that it may be presumed that this opposition was known to the author of the Fourth Gospel. The question which is evoked in 1,26 (also by the emphatic ἐγώ), wherein the unknown one will baptize, is only answered in 1,33[46].

The coherence of 1,19-28 and 1,29-34 is also evident from numbers of W and S. The discourse of the Baptist amounts to 50 W in 1,19-28; in 1,29-34 it is twice that size, 100 W. The number of W for 1,19-34 is 272, which is a rectangular number (16 × 17), and a figure of a symmetrical structure: first and third digit are identical[47].

Many multiples of 11 occur in the numbers of S of 1,19-34. The sum total of S is 550, = 50 × 11. The discourse put in the mouth of the Baptist (quotations included) amounts to 297 S, = 27 × 11; the rest amounts to 253 S, = 23 × 11. John's discourse contains an OT quotation (1,23bc) of

22 S, = 2 × 11, a quotation of God's words (1,33cd) of 33 S, = 3 × 11, and two quotations of his own words (1,30bc.34*c*), of together again 33 S. The discourse of the Baptist without the quotations of words said by others (OT and God) amounts to 242 S, = 2 × 11²; 242 is, moreover, a symmetrical number. The two quotations of others' words amount together to 55 S, which is exactly 1/10 of the sum total of 550 S.

Within this framework, a few data concerning 1,19-28 which were not yet mentioned, become relevant. This passage contains 165 S, = 15 × 11, of discourse (and 1,29-34 contains, as was observed earlier, 33 S, = 3 × 11, of narrative). Apart from the 102 S spoken by the Baptist (quotation included), the pericope contains 220 S, = 20 × 11.

1,19-34 contains 360 S of discourse (360 = 10 × 36; 36 is both a square and a triangular number, of 6 and 8 respectively), and 190 S (triangular number of 19) of narrative.

A schematic arrangement of most of the above is given, as far as numbers of S are concerned, in Table IV.

Table IV. John 1,19-34 syllables

	1,19-28	1,29-34	1,19-34		
narrative	157 +	33 =			190
discourse of Baptist (without quotations)	80 +	129 =	209		
quotations by Baptist:					
own words		33 =	33/242		
words of others	22 +	33 =		55/297	
discourse of envoys	63/165	=			63/360
	322 +	228 =			550

A division of the sentences of 1,19-34 according to the actors is given in Table V, first in numbers of S (Va), then in numbers of W (Vb). Sentences listed in the column 'impersonal' are sentences without a personal subject. 1,19 is listed in the column 'Baptist', because the Baptist is the logical subject of the main clause 1,19a.

Table Va. syll. divided acc. to actors John 1,19-34

	Baptist		envoys		impersonal	
1,19-20	81					
21a-c			14			
21de	6					
21f			6			
21gh	6					
22			29			
23	36					
24-25			49			
26-27	68					
28					27	
29-34	228					
total	425	+	98	+	27 =	550

Table Vb. words divided acc. to actors John 1,19-34

	Baptist		envoys		impersonal	
1,19-20	37					
21a-c			8			
21de	4					
21f			4			
21gh	3					
22			15			
23	16					
24-25			26			
26-27	32 (/92)					
28					12	
29-34	115					
total	207	+	53	+	12 =	272

The sentences with the Baptist as actor in 1,19-34 amount to 425 S, = 17 × 25; the other sentences have together a length of 125 S, = 5 × 25. In numbers of W, there is a proportion of 4:5 between the sentences with the Baptist as actor in 1,19-28 and those in 1,29-34: 92 = 4 × 23, 115 = 5 × 23.

d) *John 1,19-28.29-34 and the passages about John the Baptist in the Prologue John 1,1-18*

Up to now, it has been tacitly supposed that John 1,19 constitutes the beginning of the Johannine narration about Jesus' ministry, to which the Baptist's testimony is the introduction. And, indeed, 1,19 is the beginning of a chain of episodes, of descriptions of events (whether they are fictional or not), a chain that continues through practically the entire gospel. The Prologue 1,1-18, however, does not belong to this chain. It is not a story about events which happened or are supposed to have happened, and it differs in this respect from what follows.

Other arguments may be advanced as well for considering the Prologue and the ensuing stories as more or less separate units. There is an evident difference of style between the Prologue and what follows it. It is a widespread conviction that the Prologue is a kind of hymn, written in a poetic style (about the exact nature of this style, opinions differ), whereas the following stories are written in narrative prose[48].

Scholars who have tried to analyse the literary structure of the Prologue, do not agree in their results; generally, however, they consider John 1,1-18 as a coherent and well-structured unit[49]. One literary datum especially makes this clear, viz., the inclusion constituted by 1,1-2 and 1,18[50]: in 1,1-2 it is said that the Word is πρὸς τὸν θεόν, and is himself θεός, and in 1,18 we hear about the μονογενὴς θεός, who is εἰς τὸν κόλπον τοῦ πατρός. Only these two parts of the Prologue deal with the Word's being with God and his being God. The unity and consistency of the Prologue appeared also from a count of syllables (see above, pp. 19-21, concerning Irigoin's analysis, and my proposal of correction).

Despite these arguments for the mutual independence of 1,1-18 and 1,19sqq, there is the fact that 1,19 starts with the conjunction καί. This is most naturally understood as a connecting link with 1,15[51], where the testimony of John the Baptist was already the topic. The verse 1,15, in turn, is a continuation of 1,6-8, where John the Baptist and his testimony are mentioned for the first time. The connection between 1,19sqq and (parts of) the preceding Prologue does not, of course, exclude the relative independence of both (cfr. the repeated use of the conjunction καί at the beginning of a narration, both in John and elsewhere in the NT[52]), but it does suggest that the two parts of the gospel cannot be considered as totally disconnected. John 1,19 is both a new beginning and a continuation of 1,15[53].

A few observations concerning numbers of W and S also suggest that there is a relationship between the parts of the Prologue about John the Baptist (1,6-8.15) and the two ensuing scenes in which the Baptist is the protagonist. The factor 11, prominent in numbers of W and S in 1,19-28.29-34, is already present in 1,6-8.15. The first passage about the Baptist (1,6-8) has a size of 33 W, = 3 × 11; its last sentence (1,8) contains 11 W. The two final clauses in 1,7 have both a length of 11 S. The second passage about the Baptist (1,15) has a size of 22 W, = 2 × 11, or 44 S, = 4 × 11. The quotation of the Baptist's own words present in it (1,15cd) takes up exactly half of these: it contains 11 W or 22 S. An addition of the numbers of S for 1,6-8.15.19-28 results in 74 + 44 + 322 = 440, = 40 × 11.

An addition of the numbers of S for the direct discourse of the Baptist in 1,15.19-28.29-34 results in a sum total of 28 + 102 + 195 = 325, triangular number of 25. Out of these, 195 or exactly 3/5, occur in the pericope 1,29-34. The Baptist's discourse in 1,15 has a size of 28 S; 28 is triangular number of 7, and a perfect number.

Interesting too, are the quotations which are put in the Baptist's mouth. The quotation 1,15cd has a size of 22 S, the quotation in 1, 19-28 (1,23bc) is of equal length, and the three quotations in 1,29-34 (1,30bc.33cd.34*c*) amount together to 66 S, = 3 × 22. The sum total for all five quotations is the rectangular number of 110 S (10 × 11).

A characteristic of a rectangular number is that the half of it is a triangular number (see above, p. 28). Table VI shows how the 110 S of the five quotations are made up of 55 S for the quotations of the Baptist's own words, and 55 for the quotations of others' words; 55 is the triangular number of 10. The table shows, moreover, that in numbers of W both groups of quotations are of almost equal length, and that the two quotations of others amount together to 28 W, triangular number of 7 and a perfect number.

Table VI. quotations by Baptist in John 1,1-34		syll.		words	
1,15cd	quotation of Baptist's own words	22		11	
23bc	OT quotation		22		10
30bc	quotation of own words	23		12	
33cd	quotation of God's words		33/55		18/28
34*c*	quotation of own words	10/	55/110	6/	29/57

3. *John 1,35-42 and 1,43-51: the call of the first disciples*

a) *John 1,35-42*

Just as 1,19-28 and 1,29-34, the scene 1,35-42 is made up of two parts. In the first part (1,35-39), John the Baptist calls the attention of two of his disciples to Jesus; these two follow Jesus, converse with him, and stay with him the rest of the day. In the second part (1,40-42), Andrew, one of these two (he is introduced in 1,40), finds his brother Simon and brings him to Jesus, who gives Simon a new name.

Within the first part, there is a small change at 1,37/38, when the Baptist disappears quietly from the stage, and Jesus starts to play the most important role. In 1,35-37, the Baptist directs his disciples to Jesus, and in 1,38-39 these are with Jesus. A similar change seems present in the second part, where it occurs at 1,41/42: firstly, Andrew meets his brother Simon and tells him about Jesus, then Jesus and Simon meet[54]. Actually, both halves of the scene display the same pattern: by means of a statement which contains a christological title, somebody calls the attention of others to Jesus; thereafter, these others enter into direct contact with Jesus[55].

The passage 1,35-42 contains 136 W, triangular number of 16, while 1,19-34 is twice that length: 272 W, which is a rectangular number (see above, p. 28). The 136 W are made up of 111 W of narrative and 25 W of discourse; 111 is a number which consists of three identical digits, and 25 is square number of 5 (see below, Table IX). Among the 111 W of narrative, 11 W are used for the explanation of Aramaic titles occurring in the discourse (1,38e.41c.42e). Without these, we have 100 W of narrative, while the preceding pericope 1,29-34 contains 100 W of discourse.

A division of the sentences of the pericope according to the actors is given in numbers of S in Table VIIa, and in numbers of W in Table VIIb. In 1,35, the first part of the verse is attributed to John the Baptist, the second part (from καί onward) to his disciples.

Table VIIa. syll. divided acc. to actors John 1,35-42

	Baptist		B.'s disciples		Jesus		impersonal		Andrew	
1,35*a*	14									
35*b*			10							
36	22									
37			24							
38ab					27					
38c-f			26							
39ab					11					
39c			23							
39d							7			
40-42a									89	
42b-e					34					
total	36	+	83	+	72	+	7	+	89	= 287

Table VIIb. words divided acc. to actors John 1,35-42

	Baptist		B.'s disciples		Jesus		impersonal		Andrew	
1,35*a*	6									
35*b*			6							
36	11									
37			11							
38ab					12					
38c-f			11							
39ab					5					
39c			13							
39d							4			
40-42a									40	
42b-e					17					
total	17	+	41	+	34	+	4	+	40	= 136

Table VIIa shows that the sentences with John the Baptist as actor in 1,35-42 amount to 36 S, $= 6^2$, while the sentences with Jesus as actor have together twice that length: 72 S. As 36 is a triangular number (of 8), 72 is a rectangular number (8×9; see above, p. 28). The 287 S of the entire pericope are divided into 72 S for the sentences with Jesus as actor, and 215 S for the other sentences; that means, that they have been divided as well as possible according to a proportion of 1:3.

In the numbers of W, given in Table VIIb, the factor 17 is prominent. The sentences with the Baptist as actor amount together to 17 W; those with Jesus as actor have together twice that length, 34 W. These are evenly divided over the two parts of the pericope: 17 in 1,38ab.39ab, again 17 in 1,42b-e. 1,35-37 (the part of the pericope which ends with the quiet disappearance from the stage of the Baptist) has a size of 34 W: 17 W (made up of 6 + 11 W) for the sentences with the Baptist as actor, again 17 W (also made up of 6 + 11 W) for the sentences in which his disciples are actor. To these observations should be added that the entire pericope contains 136 W, $= 8 \times 17$, and that the verse 1,40 has a length of 17 W.

The bipartition of the pericope is recognizable in the distribution of S: 1,35-39 contains 164 S, = 4 × 41, and 1,40-42 contains 123 S, = 3 × 41. Both parts contain 24 S of discourse, and in both cases these are divided in more or less the same way according to a proportion of 1:2. The discourse begins both times with a statement of 8 S which contains a christological title and which directs the attention of others to Jesus (1,36b.41b). Thereafter, 16 S are used for the discourse in the description of Jesus' meeting with these others (a conversation in 1,38-39, a saying of Jesus in 1,42).

The verse 1,39 describes Jesus' invitation to his new disciples to come and see where he is staying, and their positive reaction to this invitation: they even stay with him; it ends with an indication of time. This verse constitutes exactly the middle of the pericope: 1,35-38.39.40-42 is made up of 57 + 22 + 57 W, or 123 + 41 + 123 S. As the central verse contains 41 S, its size is exactly 1/3 of the number of S of the preceding and following verses.

The centre of the pericope has been indicated more precisely: the words ἦλθαν ... ἐκείνην (1,39c) constitute the central sentence of 1,35-42. The numbers of W for 1,35-39b.39c.39d-42 are 62 + 13 + 61. As this central sentence is made up of 6 + 7 W, the pericope divides into two equal halves between the words μένει and καί in 1,39c (cfr. the comma between these two words in, e.g., *NA*[25] and *UBSGNT*). So, the disciples' reaction to Jesus' invitation has been marked as the central element of the pericope.

The entire first part (1,35-39) consists of units of 11 or 12 W:

1,35	12 W	(made up of 6 + 6 W)
36	11	(made up of 6 + 5)
37	11	
38ab	12	
38c-f	11	
39a-*ca* (up to and including μένει)	11	(made up of 5 + 6)
39*cb*-d	11	

Finally, a few details from this passage:

1. 1,35-37 is made up of 24 + 22 + 24 = 70 S:

1,35	the Baptist is standing with two of his disciples	24 S
36	he sees Jesus walking by and indicates him as 'the Lamb of God'	22
37	his disciples hear him and follow Jesus	24/70

2. 1,38-39, the conversation between Jesus and his new disciples and their stay with Jesus, has a size of 45 W, triangular number of 9. As the

entire pericope has a size of 136 W, triangular number of 16, there remain 91 W, triangular number of 13, for the rest of it (= 1,35-37.40-42).

3. The second part of the scene begins with an introductory explanation about Andrew (1,40); then follow a meeting of Andrew and Simon (1,41), and a meeting of Jesus and Simon, arranged by Andrew (1,42). The descriptions of both meetings are of equal length: 43 S.

b) *John 1,43-51*

Just as the three pericopes dealt with above, the pericope 1,43-51 is made up of two parts: 1,43-44 and 1,45-51. In the first part the call of Philip is related, and in the second part it is narrated how Philip brings Nathanael to Jesus and how Nathanael and Jesus meet. The second part displays, in turn, a bipartition: it begins with a conversation between Philip and Nathanael (1,45-46); then follows the conversation between Jesus and Nathanael (1,47-51). The dialogue 1,45-46 evidently leads up to what follows (cfr. 1,45 with 1,41, and 1,46cd with 1,39ab), and should be considered as an introduction to the dialogue of Jesus and Nathanael, not as the conclusion of the call of Philip[56].

Within the passage 1,43-51, the final verse 1,51 has a relatively independent position: although Jesus was speaking in 1,50, 1,51 starts anew with the introduction καὶ λέγει αὐτῷ. Also remarkable is the fact that although Jesus' words in 1,51 are addressed only to Nathanael according to the introduction 1,51a, the saying itself is addressed to several persons, witness the plurals ὑμῖν and ὄψεσθε.

The importance of Jesus' saying in 1,51 appears from its being introduced by the formula ἀμὴν ἀμὴν λέγω ὑμῖν. It is, moreover, the first time that this formula is used in John (24 more instances will follow).

From the point of view of contents, the saying constitutes the climax of the entire narration from 1,19 onward. In the series of scenes 1,19-51, christological titles and predicates abound. By means of these, John the Baptist and the first disciples witness on behalf of Jesus in various ways, by attributing them to Jesus or — in the case of the Baptist — by denying them for himself. The following titles and predicates are mentioned: 'the Christ' or 'the Messiah' (1,20.25.41), 'Elijah' (1,21.25), 'the Prophet' (1,21.25), 'the Lamb of God' (1,29.36), 'the Son of God' (1,34.49), 'Rabbi' (1,38.49), 'of whom Moses wrote in the Law, and the prophets' (1,45), 'the King of Israel' (1,49); possibly also 'the one who comes after me' (1,27) and 'he who baptizes in Holy Spirit' (1,33) have to be included in this series. After all these confessions by others, Jesus reveals himself in the saying 1,51 as 'the Son of Man' (John 9 is comparable, where a similar series of confessions by the man born blind finds its climax in Jesus' self-revelation as the Son of Man 9,35-37, see below, p. 198)[57]. He promises his audience, that they will be witnesses of his continuing communication with God, his Father. This seems to be, at least, the general meaning of Jesus' saying in 1,51 — which is sufficient in this connection[58]. A literal fulfilment of Jesus' promise is not to be found in John; the saying has to be interpreted, then, as a *Bildwort*, indicating that Jesus, the Son of Man, is in lasting communication with heaven, with God, and that he is the place of God's revelation, just as Bethel was for Jacob (cfr. Gen 28,10-19; the allusion to Gen 28,12 in John 1,51 is unmistakable). The idea which is expressed here in an image is found elsewhere in John without image: 5,19-30; 8,16.28-29; 10,30.38; 14,9-11[59].

In dealing with the quantitative aspects of the structure of John 1,43-51, it will be supposed that in 1,47a the anarthrous reading is the correct one (see above, pp. 44-45).

In numbers of S, the surplus-technique has been applied to 1,43-51: the passage has a size of 348 S; 48 out of these are used for Jesus' saying 1,51bc.

As for the numbers of W, there is a proportion of 3:4 between narrative and discourse. The narrative has a size of 72 W, = 3 × 24 (and, moreover, a rectangular number, being 8 × 9); the discourse contains 96 W, = 4 × 24. The first and last sentence of 1,45-51, viz., 1,45.51, have both a length of 24 W. The 72 W of narrative are divided into 27 W, = 3 × 9, in the first part of the passage (1,43-44), and 45 W, = 5 × 9, in the second part (1,45-51). The discourse of Jesus amounts to 55 W, triangular number of 10; 5 out of these are used in Jesus' quotation of his own words in 1,50b (εἶδον ... συκῆς). See below, Table IX.

A division of the quantity of S according to the actors is given in Table VIIIa (the ensuing Table VIIIb gives the same division of the quantity of W, in view of what follows under c.).

Table VIIIa. syll. divided acc. to actors John 1,43-51

	Jesus		Philip		Nathanael	
1,43	38					
44-45			72			
46ab					22	
46cd			13			
47	40					
48ab					14	
48cd	30					
49					29	
50-51	90					
total	198	+	85	+	65	= 348

Table VIIIb. words divided acc. to actors John 1,43-51

	Jesus		Philip		Nathanael	
1,43	17					
44-45			36			
46ab					10	
46cd			7			
47	19					
48ab					6	
48cd	16					
49					15	
50-51	42					
total	94	+	43	+	31	= 168

The sentences with Philip and Nathanael as actors amount together to 85 + 65 = 150 S. Those with Jesus as actor amount to 198 S; 48 of these are used for his saying 1,51bc, so there remain 150 S for the rest of these sentences. The successive (combinations of) sentences with Jesus as actor 1,47.48cd.50-51 have a size of 40, 30 and 90 S respectively.

The factor 19 has a certain prominence in numbers of S in 1,43-51. Philip speaks in 1,45bc.46d in 33 + 5 = 38 S, = 2 × 19; Nathanael also speaks in 38 S, in 1,46b.48b.49b-d: 13 + 6 + 19 = 38. Nathanael's final saying, the confession 1,49b-d, uses 19 S, which is half of the sum total of 38 S. With this confession, he answers to Jesus' proof of omniscience in 1,48d, also expressed in 19 S. The first verse of the pericope (1,43), describing the call of Philip, has a length of 38 S, = 2 × 19.

The second part of the pericope, 1,45-51, is made up of an introductory conversation between Philip and Nathanael (1,45-46), of 84 S, = 12 × 7, and a dialogue of Jesus and Nathanael (1,47-51), of 203 S, = 29 × 7. These 203 S are made up of 150 S for 1,47-50 (150 is the numerical value of the name Ναθαναήλ: 50 + 1 + 9 + 1 + 50 + 1 + 8 + 30 = 150), and 53 S for the last verse, the detached saying of Jesus and its introduction. In the dialogue 1,47-51, Jesus' discourse amounts to 110 S, a rectangular number (10 × 11); 10 of these are used in Jesus' quotation of his own words in 1,50b. Nathanael speaks in 25 S, = 5^2, in 1,47-51.

There is a progression in the successive pieces of discourse in 1,48-50: Jesus' proof of omniscience 1,48d has a size of 11 W; it is answered by Nathanael's confession 1,49b-d, of 12 W, which is followed by Jesus' words in 1,50b-d, of 13 W.

The position of the words Ἰσραηλίτης (1,47) and Ἰσραήλ (1,49) is at least striking: Ἰσραηλίτης is word nr. 84 of the pericope, and Ἰσραήλ is word nr. 126. So the former word completes the first half of the sum total of 168 W, and the latter completes 3/4 of 168.

So far, the numerical data do not suggest that the text has to be changed. On the contrary: the articular reading in 1,47a would spoil many of the quantitative aspects of the pericope's structure. More of these aspects, concerning 1,35-51 and 1,35-2,11, will be dealt with below.

c) *John 1,35-51*

The two pericopes 1,35-42 and 1,43-51 are coherent — just as it was the case with the two preceding pericopes, 1,19-28 and 1,29-34. Both pericopes relate the call of disciples. All call stories told here display — with one exception — more or less the same pattern: somebody (John the Baptist, Andrew, Philip) draws the attention of others (two disciples of the Baptist, Simon, Nathanael) to Jesus (as the Lamb of God, as the Messiah, as the fulfilment of the OT), and thereafter these others enter into immediate contact with Jesus. This pattern is recognizable in 1,35-39.40-42.45-51[60]. An exception is 1,43, where the call of Philip is described in a way reminiscent of the synoptic call stories (Mark 1,16-18.19-20; 2,14 and parallels): Jesus himself calls with the words 'follow me'[61]. The two pericopes 1,35-42.43-51 each contain two call stories which are connected in each case because the one who brings someone into contact with Jesus in the second story (Andrew, Philip) has himself become a disciple of Jesus in the first story. There is a comparable link between the two pericopes: we are informed in the second pericope that Philip is 'from Bethsaida, from the town of Andrew and Peter' (1,44). Within the narration, this information is intended to make a connection with the preceding pericope: Philip is related to those who became earlier disciples of Jesus[62].

The two pericopes 1,35-42 and 1,43-51 display also several minor similarities:

1,35-42	1,43-51
1,37.38.40 ἀκολουθεῖν (scil. Jesus)	1,43 ἀκολουθεῖν (scil. Jesus)
38 ῥαββί (to Jesus)	49 ῥαββί (to Jesus)
39 ἔρχεσθε καὶ ὄψεσθε	46 ἔρχου καὶ ἴδε
40 ἦν Ἀνδρέας ...	44 ἦν δὲ ὁ Φίλιππος
41 εὑρίσκει οὗτος τὸν ... Σίμωνα καὶ λέγει αὐτῷ· εὑρήκαμεν τὸν Μεσσίαν	45 εὑρίσκει Φίλιππος τὸν Ναθαναὴλ καὶ λέγει αὐτῷ· ὃν ἔγραψεν Μωϋσῆς ... εὑρήκαμεν
41 τὸν Μεσσίαν	49 βασιλεὺς ... τοῦ Ἰσραήλ[63]
42 proof of Jesus' omniscience	47-48 proof of Jesus' omniscience
42 Jesus characterizes Simon as Cephas, 'the rock'	47 Jesus characterizes Nathanael as 'true Israelite'
42 σὺ εἶ ... σὺ ...	49 σὺ εἶ ... σὺ ...

Apparently, the two pericopes 1,35-42 and 1,43-51 are coherent[64].

The coherence of the two pericopes is also discernible in numbers of S and W. John the Baptist and Jesus, the two 'revealers' in 1,35-51, speak together in 8 + 142 = 150 S. The narrative in 1,35-51 has a size of 396 S, = 11 × 36.

The discourse of John the Baptist and Jesus together in 1,35-51 amounts to 74 W, that of the disciples to 47 W. Both numbers are made up of the same digits, and — as it is always the case with two natural numbers below 100 which contain the same digits but in reversed order — their sum, 121, is divisible by 11[65]; it is, moreover, the square number of 11. A schematic arrangement of the above is given in Table IX.

Table IX. John 1,35-51

	syllables				
	1,35-42		1,43-51		1,35-51
narrative in John 1,35-51	239	+	157	=	396
discourse of Baptist	8			=	8
of Jesus	27	+	115	=	142/150
of disciples	13	+	76	=	89
(individuals included)	287	+	348	=	635
	words				
	1,35-42		1,43-51		1,35-51
narrative in John 1,35-51	111	+	72	=	183
discourse of Baptist	5			=	5
of Jesus	14	+	55	=	69/74
of disciples	6	+	41	=	47/121
(individuals included)	136	+	168	=	304

The results of a division of 1,35-51 according to the actors are given, in numbers of both S and W, in Table X (cfr. Tables VII and VIII).

Table X. syll. and words divided acc. to actors John 1,35-51

	syllables			words		
Baptist actor	36			17		
Jesus	270/306			128/145		
disciples		322			155/300	
impersonal			7/635			4/304

The sentences with the Baptist as actor have together a size of 36 S, = 4 × 9; those with Jesus as actor have together a size of 270 S, = 30 × 9. The sum total for the sentences with Jesus and the Baptist as actors is, then, 306 S, which is a rectangular number (17 × 18); it contains, moreover, the same digits as 36 (the zero left aside; see n. 65 above).

The sentences with Jesus as actor amount to 128 W, = 2^7. Together with the sentences with the Baptist as actor, they amount to 145 W, while the sentences with the disciples as actor have an overall size of 155 W; the sum of these two numbers is 300, triangular number of 24.

Above, the similarities between 1,35-42 and 1,43-51 were pointed out. The call story 1,43, being more of the synoptic type, was observed to fall largely outside these similarities. This story constitutes, together with the appended explanation 1,44, the exact middle of 1,35-51 when measured in numbers of S: it is preceded and followed by 287 S. In numbers of W, Jesus' command 'follow me' in 1,43 (cfr. p. 68 above) is the exact middle of 1,35-51: for 1,35-43b.43c.44-51, the numbers of W are 151 + 2 + 151.

The verse 1,43 contains 17 W; so the factor 17, prominent in the numbers of W of the preceding pericope 1,35-42 (see above, p. 63), occurs here once more.

It should be noted again, that the numerical data do not suggest a change in the text of 1,47a adopted so far.

4. *John 1,19-51: the testimony of the Baptist and the call of the first disciples*

It has been observed up to this point that 1,19-51 is made up of four scenes, grouped two by two: in the first two scenes the testimony of the Baptist is related, in the last two the call of the disciples. The two groups of two scenes are connected because it is the Baptist who directs two of his disciples to Jesus, so that they become his first followers. The connection is stressed by means of πάλιν in 1,35, referring back to the beginning of the preceding scene, and by the literal repetition of the Baptist's words: 'Behold the Lamb of God' from 1,29 in 1,36; now, these words invite two of his disciples to follow Jesus[66].

There are other features of these four scenes as well which suggest that 1,19-51 should be considered as a unit in its own right[67]:

a. They are situated by the evangelist on four successive days (1,29.35.43: 'the next day'), whereas the ensuing scene 2,1-11 is situated 'on the third day'.

b. They are located at or in the neighbourhood of the place where John was baptizing, whereas 2,1-11 is located in Galilee.

c. Christological titles and predicates abound in this series of scenes, see above, p. 65.

d. Each one of the four scenes displays a bipartition, as was already observed in the discussion of the separate scenes (1,19-23.24-28; 1,29-31.32-34; 1,35-39.40-42; 1,43-44.45-51)[68].

In the numbers of W of 1,19-51, the factor 16 (a square number) is dominating. The size of the entire passage is 576 W, or 36 × 16, or 24^2; it begins and ends with sentences of 24 W or 53 S (1,19.51). The two scenes in which the testimony of the Baptist is narrated (1,19-34) have together a length of 272 W, = 17 × 16 (a rectangular number; 272 is, moreover, a symmetrical number). The two scenes in which the vocation of the disciples is told (1,35-51) have together a size of 304 W, = 19 × 16.

A division into narrative and discourse (of the various characters) is given, for numbers of W, in Table XI.

Table XI. John 1,19-51

	words		
narrative in 1,19-51	267		
discourse of Baptist		155	
of Jesus		69/224	
of disciples (individuals included)	47		
of envoys	38/		352/576

The discourse of Jesus and John the Baptist, the two main speakers, together amounts to 224 W, = 14 × 16; the rest (including the narrative) amounts to 352 W, = 22 × 16.

Multiples of 16 also appear in a division of W according to the actors, as is shown in Table XII (cfr. Tables Vb, VIIb and VIIIb).

Table XII. words divided acc. to actors John 1,19-51

Baptist actor		224
Jesus		128
envoys	53	
disciples	155	
impersonal	16/224/576	

Again, the Baptist and Jesus stand out: the sentences with them as actors amount to 224 W, = 14 × 16, and 128 W, = 8 × 16, respectively. The remaining sentences also amount to 224 W; among these, 16 W are used for the sentences without a personal subject.

In Table XIII, the numbers of S are given for the four scenes of 1,19-51 separately, with a division into narrative and discourse.

Table XIII. John 1,19-51 syllables

	narrative	discourse
1,19-28	157	165
29-34	33	195
35-42	239	48
43-51	157/586	191/599

The first and last scene of the series contain the same quantity of narrative: 157 S. The sum total for the discourse is 599 S. One might be inclined to suppose that the text is too short by one syllable, and that this number has to be 600. However, the other numerical data found so far do not support this supposition. A choice for the articular reading in

1,47a would only result in the addition of 1 S to the narrative, but it would leave the discourse at 599 S.

A division of the number of S according to the actors is given in Table XIV (cfr. Tables Va, VIIa and VIIIa).

Table XIV. syll. divided acc. to actors John 1,19-51

A	Baptist actor	461
	Jesus	270/731
B	envoys	98
	disciples	322
	impersonal	34/454/1185

Again, the sentences with the Baptist and Jesus as actors are taken together (indicated as A) over against the rest (indicated as B). Now, B:A = A:(A + B) = 454:731 = 731:1185 = 0,62, which is a proportion according to the golden section (see above, p. 29).

As we saw earlier, there is within 1,19-51 a change of protagonist at the beginning of the third scene. It occurs because of the words of the Baptist ἴδε ὁ ἀμνὸς τοῦ θεοῦ (1,36b): his two disciples hear these words and follow Jesus (1,37). The Baptist's saying 1,36b is the middle of 1,19-51 when measured in numbers of S: it is preceded by 588 and followed by 589 S.

Again, a series of numerical data confirm the anarthrous reading in 1,47a. From the point of view of the text's size, there is no reason to propose corrections in the *NA*[25]-text.

5. *John 2,1-11: the wedding-feast at Cana*

A preliminary remark has to be made concerning the count of W in John 2,1-11: the relative pronoun ὅτι (2,5b) is printed in modern editions as two words, to distinguish it from the conjunction ὅτι but it is in fact one word, just as ὅστις and ἥτις[69].

The story about the 'sign' at Cana is built according to a pattern which is often present in miracle stories[70]. It begins with an introduction (2,1-2), in which the setting for what will be told is given, and in which the characters are introduced, in so far as their presence at a wedding-feast is not self-evident. The essential word γάμος is found at the beginning and at the end of this introduction.

The exposition follows in 2,3-4: there is a shortage of wine, and Jesus' mother draws her son's attention to it. He answers her[71] with what seems to be a refusal. Nevertheless, she says to the servants — as we are told in 2,5 — to do whatever Jesus will command them.

The command of Jesus' mother marks the transition to the next stage of the story: the preparation of the miracle (2,6-8). This part begins with information which is necessary to understand what follows, about six big jars standing near. Then we are told that Jesus commands the servants to fill the jars with water, which they do. After that, he orders them to draw water and to bring it to the steward, which order they also execute.

The preparation of the miracle is followed by its demonstration (the miracle itself is not described): the steward tastes the water which has become wine, and praises the bridegroom for having kept it till now (2,9-10).

The story proper is followed in 2,11 by an interpretative comment: the sign at Cana was the 'beginning' of Jesus' signs, he revealed his glory in it, and his disciples believed in him. This comment constititutes the conclusion of the miracle story; its concluding character becomes even more evident from a comparison with similar passages from John[72]:

a. 20,30-31 is the conclusion of John 1-20. Both this passage and 2,11 are determined by the combination of the performance of signs by Jesus and belief in him.

b. The same combination is found in 12,37-43, the conclusion of the Johannine account of Jesus' public ministry, although there attention is focussed upon the refusal to believe in him[73].

So, the miracle story 2,1-11 displays a succession of five elements: introduction (2,1-2), exposition (2,3-4), preparation of the miracle (2,6-8), demonstration (2,9-10) and conclusion (2,11). The words directed by Jesus' mother to the servants (2,5) have, as it seems, a connecting function: they bring Jesus and the servants together, and mark in that way the transition from exposition to preparation. For that reason, they can be considered either as the end of the exposition (the servants are only told to be ready) or as the beginning of the preparation (the readiness of the servants will be used by Jesus)[74].

There are indications which suggest some kind of concentric symmetry in the pericope:

1. First and last element constitute together an inclusion: the indication of place 'at Cana of Galilee' from 2,1 is repeated in 2,11, and Jesus' disciples are mentioned explicitly only in 2,2.11 (see already above, p. 47 with n. 24).

2. The exposition (2,3-4) corresponds to the demonstration (2,9-10). In 2,3-4, a tension is evoked, because the shortage of wine is mentioned, both by the narrator and by Jesus' mother (2,3a.3b). The need is stressed by Jesus' apparent refusal to do something about it in 2,4. The tension is resolved in 2,9-10, when the removal of the need is described: there is wine again, even of a better quality than before[75]. Next to this main correspondence, it is striking that in 2,1-11 the important word οἶνος is used only in these two elements.

The position of 2,5 is perhaps best defined in this way: in the *sequence* of elements it belongs with what precedes, as it creates a suspense for the reader after which the actual preparation for the miracle begins in 2,6; in the *concentric disposition* of elements it belongs with what follows, because the tension evoked in 2,3-4 is resolved in 2,9-10, and the command in 2,5, together with its execution in 2,7-8, constitutes the way in which the need of 2,3-4 is removed. Apparently, the story displays both a linear and a concentric structure.

Schematically, the concentric structure of 2,1-11 can be rendered as follows[76]:

A 2,1-2 A' 11
B 3-4 B' 9-10
C 5-8

It should be noted, however, that the correspondence of A and A' is weakened because the two elements are not on the same level from the point of view of narrative technique. Element A' is not a part of the story, but an interpretative comment on it, integrating the story into the Fourth Gospel as a whole[77].

The composition of John 2,1-11 also displays numerical features. Table XVa gives a division of 2,1-11 according to the actors in numbers of S (in view of Tables XX and XXIII below, the same division is given in numbers of W in Table XVb). In 2,2, 12 S or 8 W are attributed to Jesus, and 7 S or 4 W to his disciples, because the words εἰς τὸν γάμον belong logically to ἐκλήθη, of which Jesus is the subject, at least primarily. The parenthetic main clause 2,9b is attributed to the servants.

Table XVa. syll. divided acc. to actors John 2,1-11

	impersonal		mother		Jesus		disciples		servants		steward	
2,1a	22											
1b			10									
2					12		7					
3			25									
4					23							
5			23									
6	38											
7ab					18							
7c									11			
8ab					20							
8c									5			
9a											30	
9b									17			
9c-10											56	
11a					34							
11b							14					
total	60	+	58	+	107	+	21	+	33	+	86	= 365

Table XVb. words divided acc. to actors John 2,1-11

	impersonal		mother		Jesus		disciples		servants		steward	
2,1a	11											
1b			7									
2					8		4					
3			13									
4					15							
5			11									
6	18											
7ab					8							
7c									5			
8ab					9							
8c									3			
9a											14	
9b									8			
9c-10											27	
11a					16							
11b	—		—		—		7		—		—	
total	29	+	31	+	56	+	11	+	16	+	41	= 184

The above Table XVa shows that the sentences with Jesus and his mother as actors amount together to 58 + 107 = 165 S, over against 60 + 21 + 33 + 86 = 200 S for the rest of the pericope.

It was observed above that in the sequence of elements of 2,1-11, the verse 2,5 is best considered as the end of the exposition. Table XVI gives the numbers of W for the various elements of 2,1-11 according to the linear structure of the text, with 2,3-5 as exposition.

Table XVI. John 2,1-11

		words
2,1-2	introduction	30
3-5	exposition	39/69
6-8	preparation	43
9-10	demonstration	49/92
11	conclusion	23/184

The first two elements, leading up to Jesus' action, have together a size of 69 W, = 3 × 23. The next two elements, in which Jesus' action and its results are narrated, contain together 92 W, = 4 × 23. The conclusion has a length of 23 W. This structure is apparently determined by the factor 23. The ensuing verse 2,12, which makes the transition to the next narration, has a size of 23 W in the *NA*[25]-text (reading οἱ ἀδελφοί), and of 46 S, = 2 × 23, in the *NA*[26]-text (reading οἱ ἀδελφοὶ [αὐτοῦ]).

The factor 23 is also present in 2,1-11 in the numbers of S. Both 2,4 and 2,5 have a size of 23 S; so does the summary of the story in 2,11a*a* (ταύτην ... Γαλιλαίας). As 2,6-8 has a size of 92 S, = 4 × 23, the middle element of the story contains a number of S which is divisible by 23, whether 2,5-8 (115 S, = 5 × 23) or 2,6-8 (92 S, = 4 × 23) is considered as middle element.

In Table XVII, the numbers of S and W are given for the concentric structure of 2,1-11. The verse 2,5 is considered now as the beginning of the middle element C.

Table XVII. John 2,1-11		syllables			words	
2,1-2	A	51			30	
3-4	B		48		28	
5-8	C			115		54
9-10	B'		103/151		49/77	
11	A'	48/		99/250/365	23/	53/184

As for the numbers of S: 115 and 151, the sum totals of S for elements C and (B + B') respectively, are made up of the same digits. The digits 1 and 5 return in the number of S for element A, which is 51. As the middle element C has a size of 115 S, out of a sum total of 365 S for the entire pericope, there remain 250 S for the other elements. These are made up of two symmetrical numbers: 151 S for elements B + B', and 99 S for elements A + A'.

As for the numbers of W: the corresponding elements B and B' contain both a number of W which is a multiple of 7, and in which the factor 7 is also present in another way, as the (perfect) number 28 is triangular number of 7, and 49 is square number of 7. The middle element C is almost as long as the two outer elements A and A' together: 54 and 53 W respectively.

Out of the 54 W of element C, 18 W or exactly 1/3 are used for the information about the six jars (2,6), and 36 W, or 2/3, for the command of Jesus' mother (2,5) and its execution (2,7-8).

The division of the discourse over the pericope comes close to symmetry: 18 W in the exposition 2,3-5, 10 W in the preparation of the miracle 2,6-8, and 19 W in the demonstration 2,9-10. The discourse in the preparation amounts to 26 S, = 2 × 13, that in the demonstration to 39 S, = 3 × 13.

A number of details from 2,1-11 have to be discussed from the point of view of numerical composition:

1. In 2,4, the vocative γύναι belongs to the preceding question (cfr. Mark 1,24; 5,7; Matt 8,29; Luke 4,34; 8,28)[78]. Jesus' saying in 2,4 is made up, then, of two clauses which contain the same number of W and almost the same number of S:

τί ἐμοὶ καὶ σοί, γύναι;	5 W	7 S
οὔπω ἥκει ἡ ὥρα μου	5/10	8/15

2. In 2,6, three numerals are used: *six* jars, containing each *two* or *three* measures, are mentioned there. The verse is made up of 12 + 6 = 18 W.

Each one of these three numbers can be separated into the factors 2 and 3, whose product is 6: $12 = 2 \times 2 \times 3 = 2 \times 6$; $6 = 2 \times 3$; $18 = 2 \times 3 \times 3 = 3 \times 6$. Here, there is a connection between the text's numbers of W and the numbers mentioned in the text. The number 23, important in the numerical composition of the pericope, is made up of the digits 2 and 3.

3. In 2,5, Jesus' mother says to the servants: ὅτι ἂν λέγῃ ὑμῖν ποιήσατε. This command is executed in 2,7-8; there, the servants' obedience to Jesus is made discernible in the parallelism between order (λέγει, 2,7a.8a; cfr. λέγῃ 2,5b) and execution[79]:

2,7b	γεμίσατε	τὰς ὑδρίας ὕδατος		
7c	καὶ ἐγέμισαν	αὐτὰς		ἕως ἄνω
8b	ἀντλήσατε νῦν καὶ		φέρετε	τῷ ἀρχιτρικλίνῳ
8c			οἱ δὲ ἤνεγκαν	

The command in 2,5b has a size of 11 S; Jesus' order in 2,7b and its execution in 2,7c are of the same size. The order in 2,8b is made up of 5 + 10 S; its execution is told (2,8c) in 5 S. Both parallelism and numerical equality or proportion illustrate the promptness of the execution (see for a parallel p. 111 below).

4. The long sentence 2,9-10 is made up of: (a) 2,9ab, a subordinate clause, followed by a parenthesis which belongs together with it (cfr. οὐκ ᾔδει — ᾔδεισαν); (b) 2,9c, a main clause, relating the main action, and (c) 2,10, the direct discourse of the steward with its introduction. The three parts have a length of 22, 5 and 22 W respectively.

The words of the steward 2,10bc display a similar structure:

πᾶς ἄνθρωπος πρῶτον τὸν καλὸν οἶνον τίθησιν	7 W	14 S
καὶ ὅταν μεθυσθῶσιν τὸν ἐλάσσω	5	11
σὺ τετήρηκας τὸν καλὸν οἶνον ἕως ἄρτι	7/19	14/39

First and third colon, which are of equal length, are opposed to each other, both in content and in form. The expectation of what 'everyone' does with good wine is opposed to what 'you' did with it. As for the form, the contrast is brought out by the fact that, apart from the subject at the beginning of the cola, the sequence of corresponding elements is reversed in the two cola when compared with each other, as the different types of underlining make evident[80].

6. *John 1,35-2,11: the call of the disciples, and their belief*

The story about Jesus changing water into wine at Cana is not disconnected from what precedes. As it stands, it constitutes the first fulfilment of the promises made by Jesus in 1,50-51: 'You will see things greater than these', and 'you will see the heaven opened and the angels of God ascending and descending upon the Son of Man'. The 'greater things' of 1,50 are greater in comparison with the proof of omniscience given by Jesus when he saw Nathanael under the fig tree (1,47-48). The change of water into wine is easily conceived of as 'greater' than this proof of omniscience. Nathanael is witness of both: to him Jesus demonstrates his omniscience, to him are addressed Jesus' words in 1,50, and he is among the disciples present at Cana (2,2.11; according to 21,2, Nathanael was from Cana). Moreover, Jesus says in 1,50 that Nathanael *believes* because of his proof of omniscience; it is to be expected, then, that the seeing of 'greater things' will even more evoke faith. And indeed, in 2,11 the evangelist remarks that the disciples *believe* in Jesus, who revealed his glory in the miracle.

It was observed above (p. 66) that the *Bildwort* 1,51 expresses that Jesus is in permanent communication with God, and that he is the place of God's revelation. This communication and revelation concern, among other things, Jesus' works; consequently, these are in John often called 'the work(s) of God', and the like (4,34; 9,3.4; 10,37; 14,10; cfr. 5,20.36; 10,25.32; 17,4). In particular the story about the raising of Lazarus (11,1-44) shows that this miracle of Jesus is based upon his exceptional communication with God ('I knew that you hear me always', 11,42), and that in this act of Jesus God's glory is revealed (11,40), which implies Jesus' glorification (11,4). We may consider, then, Jesus' miracle at Cana, in which he revealed his glory (2,11), as the first illustration (cfr. 2,11: 'the *beginning* of the signs') of his permanent communication with God and his being God's revelation, which are described in images in 1,51[81].

In addition to this connection on the level of content, there is a geographical link between 2,1-11 and what precedes. In 1,43, the reader is told that Jesus decides to leave for Galilee; in 2,1, the goal of the journey has been reached[82].

Finally, it seems that 2,11 is the conclusion not only of the Cana-pericope, but also of the entire series of pericopes 1,35-2,11: the disciples' belief in Jesus, mentioned at the end of 2,11, is the conclusion of a process which is going on from 1,35 onwards (cfr. 1,37.39.41.45.49). The last clause of 2,11 makes the impression of concluding a larger section than only 2,1-11[83]. It suggests that the first Cana-miracle should be conceived of as a 'private' miracle[84], reaching its goal only in the disciples.

So, we have in John 1,35-2,11 a series of three connected scenes, having as its theme the call and the belief of the disciples[85]. The first two scenes, situated on 'the next day' (1,35.43) and set in the neighbourhood of the place where John was baptizing, relate the call of individual disciples; in the third scene, situated 'on the third day' and set in Galilee (2,1), the disciples are spoken of as a group, which comes to belief in Jesus.

That the three scenes 1,35-2,11 belong together, appears also from numbers of S, and, to a less extent, from numbers of W. The three pericopes amount together to exactly 1000 S (cfr. Tables IX and XVa). These are made up of 635 S for the first two pericopes about the call of the disciples (1,35-51), and 365 S for the pericope about the miracle at Cana (2,1-11); the figures 635 and 365 are made up of the same digits.

The results of a separation of narrative and discourse (of the various characters) are given — in numbers of S — in Table XVIII.

Table XVIII. John 1,35-2,11

	syllables		
narrative in John 1,35-2,11			664
discourse of the Baptist	8		
of Jesus		183	
of the disciples	89		
of Jesus' mother		17/200	
of the steward	39/	136/336/1000	

The discourse of Jesus and his blood-relative, his mother, together, amounts to 200 S, being exactly 1/5 of the sum total of 1000 S. The rest of the discourse amounts to 136 S, which is the triangular number of 16. At the same time, another division of the quantity of discourse presents itself (which is not immediately visible in the table): the discourse of all speaking characters apart from Jesus uses 136 (= 8 × 17) + 17 = 153 S, triangular number of 17, well-known from John 21,11.

The series of scenes 1,35-2,11 has a length of 488 W (cfr. Tables IX and XVb), out of which 89 W are put in the mouth of Jesus, and 399 are used for the rest. Here, a choice for the articular reading in 1,47a would result in a change of the number 399 into 400. An extensive series of numerical observations offers, however, resistance to this change.

Table XIX gives the results of a division of the sentences according to the actors for John 1,35-2,11 in numbers of S (cfr. the above Tables VIIa, VIIIa and XVa).

Table XIX. syll. divided acc. to actors John 1,35-2,11

Baptist actor	36	
disciples		343
Jesus		377/720
impersonal	67	
Jesus' mother	58	
servants	33	
steward	86/	280/1000

For the sentences with the two main characters, Jesus and the disciples, as actors together, 720 S are used, or 18 × 40; for the other sentences, 280 S are used, or 7 × 40.

The same division of the text is given in numbers of W in Table XX (cfr. the above Tables VIIb, VIIIb and XVb).

Table XX. words divided acc. to actors John 1,35-2,11

Baptist actor	17		
disciples		166	
Jesus		184/350	
impersonal			33
Jesus' mother	31		
servants	16		
steward	41/		105/488

The sentences with the two main characters as actors (Jesus and his disciples) amount together to 350 W, = 10 × 35. The sentences with other persons as actors amount together to 105 W, = 3 × 35 (105 is, moreover, triangular number of 14).

7. *John 1,19-2,11: a series of coherent scenes*

Finally, the question has to be asked whether John 1,19-2,11 is to be considered as a series of *coherent* scenes. An affirmative answer to this question is already suggested by the circumstance that both John 1,19-51 and John 1,35-2,11 are series of coherent scenes (see sections 4. and 6. of this chapter).

On the level of contents, the five scenes are linked together. John the Baptist bears testimony, at first negatively, by saying what he himself is not and by pointing to the one who comes after him (1,19-28), then positively, by witnessing to Jesus as the Lamb of God etc. (1,29-34). It is the Baptist who directs two of his disciples to Jesus, and one of these, Andrew, brings his brother Simon to Jesus (1,35-42). Then two others become his followers; one of these is from the town of Andrew and Peter (1,43-51). With his first followers, Jesus is present at a wedding-feast; he performs his first sign by changing water into wine, and his disciples believe in him (2,1-11).

The five scenes are also linked together by chronological indications. The first and second scene are connected by means of the expression τῇ ἐπαύριον; so are the second and third, and the third and fourth scene. The fifth scene is connected with what precedes by means of the words καὶ τῇ ἡμέρᾳ τῇ τρίτῃ. The first four scenes are, then, situated on four successive days, and the fifth scene takes place on the third day after the fourth scene[86]. This kind of chronological connection, by counting (almost) successive days, stops after 2,11: 2,12 begins with the vague indication of time μετὰ τοῦτο, followed in 2,13 by the remark that the Jewish Festival of Passover was near.

Some scholars are of the opinion that this succession of days should represent a week; in this connection, it is often supposed that 1,35-39 and 1,40-42 have to be situated on two successive days[87], and sometimes this week is considered as the week of the 'new creation', parallel to the seven days of creation in Gen 1,1-2,4a[88]. However, the evangelist nowhere indicates that it is his intention to mark an exact week; he marks five separate days, which occupy together a space of time of six or seven days (depending upon whether 'the third day' of 2,1 is counted inclusively or not). A reference to the story of the creation of Gen 1,1-2,4a is present in the Prologue (1,1sqq compared with Gen 1,1sqq), but not, or at most by means of a very far-fetched exegesis, in 1,19-2,11[89].

More seriously should be taken the parallel between the count of days in John 1,19-2,11 and that in the description of the theophany on Mount Sinai of Exod 19 as found in intertestamentary and rabbinic literature[90]. In its most elaborate form, it is found in Mek. Exod 19 (Bachodesh, 1-3) and in Tg. Ps.-J. Exod 19. There, the events at Mount Sinai are distributed over six days; the sixth day is at the same time 'the third day' of Exod 19,11.16. The distribution over six or seven days is found in a less elaborate form in other writings as well[91], and it goes back at least to the end of the first or the beginning of the second century C.E.[92]. In all these texts, a series of six or seven successive days is counted; not all days need to be mentioned explicitly; the final day of the series is 'the third day' of Exod 19,11.16. Exactly this happens also in John 1,19-2,11; there also, we find a series of six or seven days, the last one of which is called 'the third day'.

There are, moreover, parallels of content between the days of the theophany on Mount Sinai and those of John 1,19-2,11. God reveals his glory on the third day, that Israel may believe in Moses forever (Exod 19,9; see esp. the version of this verse in Tg. Ps.-J., where God's coming in the cloud is interpreted as his self-revelation 'in the density of the cloud of the glory'); Jesus reveals his glory at Cana, so that his disciples believe in him. The call of the disciples may be understood as the constitution of the new people of God; this interpretation is suggested by the words 'that he might be revealed to Israel' in 1,31, by the qualification of Nathanael as 'a true Israelite' in 1,47, and by his confession of Jesus as 'the king of Israel' in 1,49. The theme of purification from Exod 19,10.14-15 is recognizable in John's baptism, and in the Jewish rites of purification mentioned in John 2,6. In the OT, the image of the wedding is used as an image for the making of the covenant between God and

Israel (see Isa 54,4-8; 62,4-5; Jer 2; Ezek 16; Hos 1-3); the wedding at Cana can be understood, then, as the making of the 'new covenant' (cfr. Matt 22,1-14; Mark 2,19 parr; Rev 19,7.9; 21,2.9)[93]. The gift of a large quantity of excellent wine fits in very well with the making of the new covenant (cfr., e.g., Deut 8,1-10; Jer 31,10-12; Hos 14,5-8; Joel 2,18-27; 4,18; Amos 9,11-15)[94].

If the count of days in the story of the theophany on Mount Sinai is indeed the basis for the count of days in John 1,19-2,11, the coherence of this series of scenes is made even more evident[95].

It should be noted that the pericope John 2,1-11 does not only conclude the series of scenes 1,19-2,11, but that at the same time it opens the series of scenes constituted by John 2-4. There is at least an evident inclusion, made up by the two miracle stories 2,1-11 and 4,46-54. Between these two stories, there are the following correspondences:

a. Both are situated at Cana of Galilee (2,1.11; 4,46).

b. The first one is characterized as ἀρχὴ τῶν σημείων (2,11), the second one as δεύτερον σημεῖον (4,54).

c. In the second story, there is an explicit reference to the first one: 'So he came *again* to Cana of Galilee, *where he had made the water wine*' (4,46; cfr. also 'again' in 4,54).

d. There is some degree of similarity in the construction of both stories. Somebody asks for a miracle; this request is refused by Jesus, but the petitioner persists, and in the end Jesus performs a sign, which evokes faith. In both stories, an inclusion is constituted by the mentioning of the place of action both at the beginning and at the end of the story (2,1.11; 4,46.54). In both episodes, the interpreting dialogue and monologue, which are characteristic of most other Johannine miracle stories (5; 6; 9,1-10,21; 11,1-44), are all but missing[96].

The section which is included within the two miracle stories displays, moreover, geographical coherence: Jesus goes from Cana to Capernaum (2,12), and from there to Jerusalem (2,13). In 3,22, he begins his journey back: via the Judean territory (3,22) and Samaria (4,4) to Galilee (4,43), then to Cana (4,46). Such an itinerary is not found elsewhere in John. It is not surprising, then, that several scholars consider John 2-4 as a separate section, after 1,19-51[97].

We may conclude, then, that John 2,1-11 has a double function: it is the conclusion of the series of scenes 1,19-2,11, and the beginning of the section 2-4[98]. Within the latter section, the isolated verse 2,12 makes the transition to what follows in 2,13sqq[99]. In view of the inclusion constituted by 2,1.11, and the concluding function of 2,11, it seems unjustified to consider 2,12 as part of the Cana-story 2,1-11[100].

John 2,1-11 fulfils then *mutatis mutandis* the requirement formulated by Lucian in his *Quomodo historia conscribenda sit* 55: two parts of a narration — in this case the part nearing its completion in 1,51 and the story which in 2,12 is on its way — should μὴ γειτνιᾶν μόνον, ἀλλὰ καὶ κοινωνεῖν καὶ ἀνακεκρᾶσθαι κατὰ τὰ ἄκρα, 'not only be adjacent, but also have something in common and mingle at the extremes'.

Now the question has to be asked whether the coherence of 1,19-2,11 is also apparent from numbers of S and W. From the above observations concerning the size of 1,19-34 (see Table IV) and of 1,35-2,11 (see Table XVIII) it will be evident that 1,19-2,11 has a size of 550 + 1000 = 1550 S. This number is significant, not so much as being a round number (i.e., a number divisible by 50), but mainly because it is the numerical value of ὁ χριστός (70 + 600 + 100 + 10 + 200 + 300 + 70 + 200 = 1550). This important qualification of Jesus' status occurs within John 1,19-2,11 in 1,20.25; the equivalent ὁ Μεσσίας is found in 1,41, followed by its Greek translation. The title 'King of Israel' in 1,49 has the same tenor (see above, p. 68 with n. 63). That the performance of signs such as the one described in 2,1-11 displays Jesus' dignity as the Christ is suggested by other passages from John (see 7,31; 10,24-25; 20,31).

The title χριστός is also found several times elsewhere in John, normally with the article (3,28; 4,29; 7,26.27.31.41*bis*.42; 10,24; 11,27; 12,34; 20,31), a few times without it (1,17 and 17,3 in the combination Ἰησοῦς Χριστός; 9,22; anarthrous Μεσσίας 4,25). In 1 and 2 John, we find ὁ χριστός three times (1 John 2,22; 5,1; 2 John 9; the combination Ἰησοῦς Χριστός in 1 John 1,3; 2,1; 3,23; 4,2.15; 5,6.20; 2 John 3.7). It seems to make no difference whether the title is used with or without the article (cfr. John 1,41 with 4,25, or 4,25 with 4,29)[101]. The Fourth Gospel shows, anyhow, a clear preference for the use with the article, which may explain why the numerical value of the article is added to that of the title in the strict sense[102]. The importance of the title in John is most evident from the conclusion of the gospel, where it is stated that 'these (signs) have been written down in order that you may believe that Jesus is the Christ, the Son of God' (20,31). We meet, then, at the beginning of the Fourth Gospel two sections whose number of S is equivalent to the numerical value of an important christological title: 1,1-18 has a size of 496 S, which is the numerical value of μονογενής (see above, p. 21); 1,19-2,11 has a size of 1550 S, which is the numerical value of ὁ χριστός[103].

In this connection, it is important to note that the passage 1,40-42 is the centre of the entire episode 1,19-2,11. In that passage, Andrew says to his brother Simon: 'We have found the Messiah', and the evangelist adds: 'which is translated: Christ' (1,41). For 1,19-39; 1,40-42; 1,43-2,11 the numbers of S are 714 + 123 + 713, and the numbers of W are 351 + 57 + 352. The centre can be determined more precisely: the words καὶ λέγει αὐτῷ· εὑρήκαμεν τὸν Μεσσίαν in 1,41 are the nucleus of 1,19-2,11, as is evident from Table XXI.

Table XXI. John 1,19-2,11	syllables	words
1,19-39	714	351
40-41*aa*	55/769	25/376
41*ab*-b καὶ λέγει ... Μεσσίαν	13	6
41c-42	55	26
43-2,11	713/768/1550	352/378/760

Significant numbers and proportions appear also when the text of 1,19-2,11 is divided into narrative and discourse (of the various characters). Table XXII gives such a division in numbers of both S and W (cfr. Tables IV and XVIII above).

Table XXII. John 1,19-2,11	syllables			words		
narrative in John 1,19-2,11			854			404
discourse of the envoys		63		38		
of the Baptist		305		155		
of Jesus	183				89	
of the disciples		89		47		
of Jesus' mother	17/	200		8		
of the steward		39/496/696/1550		19/267/356/760		

The discourse amounts to 696 S, which is a symmetrical number. These are made up of 200 S of discourse put in the mouth of Jesus and his mother (see Table XVI and the commentary accompanying it), and 496 S for the discourse of the other characters. The latter number is triangular number of 31, and a perfect number. It shares, moreover, with the sum total of 1550 S for the entire section the factor 31 (496 = 16 × 31; 1550 = 50 × 31). In the 305 S of discourse put in the mouth of the Baptist, two quotations of others' words are comprised: an OT quotation (1,23bc) and a quotation of God's words (1,33cd). These have together a size of 22 + 33 = 55 S. That means that the Baptist's own words amount to 305–55 = 250 S. The numbers of S for the narrative, for the discourse of the Baptist and for the discourse of Jesus are, all of them, multiples of 61: 854 = 14 × 61, 305 = 5 × 61, and 183 = 3 × 61.

In the numbers of W, a symmetrical number is found in the size of the narrative, which is 404 W. There is a proportion of 1:3 between the number of W put in the mouth of Jesus and that put in the mouth of the other characters: 89:267 = 1:3. The envoys from the Jews, who interrogate the Baptist without understanding the meaning of his words (cfr.

5,33-35), speak in 38 W; the steward, ignorant of the origin of the wine and praising the wrong person for it (2,9-10), speaks in exactly half that number: 19 W. The factor 19 returns in the sum total for the entire section: 760 = 40 × 19. The factor 31 is present in the 155 W put in the Baptist's mouth (155 = 5 × 31).

A division of the numbers of W according to the actors has, as it seems, also been applied to John 1,19-2,11; it is shown in Table XXIII (cfr. the above Tables Vb, VIIb, VIIIb and XVb).

Table XXIII. words divided acc. to actors John 1,19-2,11

Baptist actor	224		
envoys		53	
impersonal			45
disciples	166		
Jesus	184		
Jesus' mother	31/ 605		
servants		16	
steward		41/110/760	

The sentences in which Jesus and those who believe in him, who 'are on his side', are actors, are distinguished from the sentences in which others are actor. The sentences without a personal subject are taken as a separate category.

In numbers of W, the sum totals for the two main categories of sentences, those with 'believing' actors and those with other actors, are both divisible by 55: 605 = 11 × 55 (or 5×11^2), and 110 = 2 × 55. Together with the 45 W for the sentences without a personal subject (45 is triangular number of 9), the sum total of 760 W is reached.

There is, finally, a division in John 1,19-2,11, which breaks, in some degree, through the distribution over five days, but which is nevertheless obvious when the *dramatis personae* are considered. At first, John the Baptist is the principal character; afterwards, Jesus takes over that function. The change occurs between 1,37 and 1,38: the final words of the Baptist are recorded in 1,36 (they have a size of 8 S or 5 W, as do his first words in 1,20); when his two disciples hear these words of his — so we are told in 1,37 — they start following Jesus. The Baptist disappears from the scene until 3,23 (only in 1,40 there is a reference to 1,35-37), and in 1,38 Jesus is, for the first time, acting and speaking subject[104].

The bipartition into 1,19-37 and 1,38-2,11 corresponds to a division of the 1550 S of 1,19-2,11 into two parts having a proportion between them of exactly 2:3. The first part has a size of 620 S, = 2 × 310, and the second part amounts to 930 S, = 3 × 310.

We may conclude, that the author of the Fourth Gospel used in 1,19-2,11 — in addition to other means — numbers of S and W to shape his text. He did so both on a larger and on a smaller scale. A general description of the various applications of this technique will be given in the Conclusion.

NOTES TO CHAPTER ONE

1 See above, p. 20 with n. 110.

2 See Blass-Debrunner-Rehkopf, par. 37_2; J. H. Moulton-W. F. Howard, *A Grammar of New Testament Greek*, II: *Accidence and Word-Formation* (Edinburgh 1920) 50, 84.

3 So Moulton-Howard, *Accidence*, 86; see also Bauer, *Wörterbuch*, s.v. Μωϋσῆς. Differently Blass-Debrunner-Rehkopf, par. 38_4; J. Jeremias, art. Μωυσῆς, *TWNT* IV, 852-878; 853 n. 1. According to Smit Sibinga, Μωυσῆς is a trisyllable in Melito of Sardis' Lent Homily, see *VC* 24, 103.

4 The association was, of course, a popular etymology, but as such 'it may well be quite real', so Moulton-Howard, *Accidence*, 101 (cfr. 148), rejecting Westcott's and Hort's refusal of the *spiritus asper* to Ἱεροσόλυμα as coming from a 'false association with ἱερός' (Introduction to their Greek NT, par. 408). The association is also acknowledged by Blass-Debrunner-Rehkopf, par. 39.1; 56.1; E. Lohse, in: G. Fohrer-E. Lohse, art. Σιών etc., *TWNT* VII, 291-338; 318 n. 131; M. Hengel, *Judentum und Hellenismus*. Studien zu ihrer Begegnung unter besonderer Berücksichtigung Palästinas bis zur Mitte des 2. Jh.s. v. Chr. (WUNT 10; Tübingen 1973) 45; id., *Juden, Griechen und Barbaren*. Aspekte der Hellenisierung des Judentums in vorchristlicher Zeit (SB 76; Stuttgart 1976) 165-166.

5 See Schwyzer, *Griechische Grammatik* I, 312.

6 See Liddell-Scott, s.v. ἱερός *in fine*, from where I derive most of the examples.

7 In Homer, both the non-contracted and the contracted form are used; see for ἱρός e.g. *Iliad* 2,420; 5,648; 10,571; 23,207; *Odyssey* 3,278; 6,322; 13,104; 16,184; see Liddell-Scott, s.v. ἱερός.

8 Ἱερός is divided into three syllables also by E. Norden, *Die antike Kunstprosa* vom VI. Jahrhundert v. Chr. bis in die Zeit der Renaissance (Leipzig/Berlin 1915[3]; repr. Darmstadt 1974) 136. — In modern vulgar Greek, it is not necessary to indicate the consonantal value of the *iōta*, 'da die consonantische Aussprache in der reinen Volkssprache Regel ist', so A. Thumb, *Handbuch der neugriechischen Volkssprache*. Grammatik. Texte. Glossar (Strassbourg 1910[2]) par. 11. An earlier stage of the development in the pronunciation of the *iōta* between old and modern Greek is indicated by L. Radermacher, *Neutestamentliche Grammatik*. Das Griechisch des Neuen Testaments im Zusammenhang mit der Volkssprache (HNT 1; Tübingen 1925[2]) 44, who writes about *Koinè*-Greek: 'Vor folgendem Vokal konnte das Iota schon früh spirantisch werden und hat in sorgloser Aussprache etwa unserm j entsprochen'; he adduces examples of 'vulgärer Schreibung', where the *iōta* is omitted, or added at the wrong place. There is no reason to assume that these phenomena of vulgar language should be valid for the Fourth Gospel — without denying, of course, the apparent affinities of the Greek of John with the vulgar language of the period. In the *kontakia* of Romanus, *iōta* followed by a vowel normally constitutes a separate syllable; occasionally, *iōta* is contracted with the following vowel into one syllable (e.g., ταμίειοις counted at three syllables in the hymn on Noah 9,7, SC 99, 114). In considering the freedom which Romanus could permit himself, one should not forget that his *kontakia* are bound to very strict rules concerning their size, measured in numbers of syllables.

9 There are two more variant readings: ἑστήκει (Sin Or) and εἱστήκει (P^{75} 1071 1365 Eus); these, 'besides being inappropriate in the context, are insufficiently sup-

ported', so B. M. Metzger, *A Textual Commentary on the Greek New Testament* (London/New York 1971) 199.

10 See Blass-Debrunner-Rehkopf, parr. 73_4; 341; J. H. Moulton, *A Grammar of New Testament Greek*, I: *Prolegomena* (Edinburgh 1908[3]) 238; Schwyzer, *Griechische Grammatik* I, 767; II: Syntax und syntaktische Stilistik, ed. by A. Debrunner (Handbuch der Altertumswissenschaft, 2. Abt., 1. Teil, 2. Band; Munich 1950) 286-287. Metzger remarks in defence of the reading ἕστηκεν: 'the perfect tense, so frequently employed with theological overtones by the Fourth Evangelist, conveys a special force here' (*Textual Commentary*, 199); in view of the identical meaning of both forms, this remark seems out of place.

11 A similar avoiding of στήκειν is found in *vv. ll.* at Mark 3,31; LXX Exod 14,13; Judg 16,26; 3 Reg 8,11; also *Acta Thomae*, ed. Bonnet, p. 116 l. 2.

12 I derive this information from G. D. Fee, 'The Use of the Definite Article with Personal Names in the Gospel of John', *NTS* 17 (1970-71) 168-183; 181.

13 Fee, *NTS* 17, 180.

14 John 9,38-39a is considered by Fee, following C. L. Porter, 'John ix.38,39a: A Liturgical Addition to the Text', *NTS* 13 (1966-67) 387-394, as not belonging to the original text of John; for a similar hypothesis, see Boismard-Lamouille, *Jean*, 246. We shall see later on that the composition of John 9 in numbers of S and W does not give any indication to support Porter's hypothesis.

15 Fee mentions (p. 181) 19,29 — erroneously, it seems.

16 Fee, *NTS* 17, 180-181.

17 Fee, *NTS* 17, 182.

18 Fee, *NTS* 17, 183. Cfr. also Bernard, 42-43; R. C. Nevius, 'The Use of the Definite Article with "Jesus" in the Fourth Gospel', *NTS* 12 (1965-66) 81-85; Neirynck, *Jean et les synoptiques*, 236-239.

19 Despite the historical improbability of the (partial) identification of 'priests and Levites' (1,19) and 'Pharisees' (1,24; οἱ om.), it is evident from the reference in the question 1,25 to the preceding conversation (1,19-21), that that conversation continues, and that the dialogue partners of the Baptist are, at least partly, the same people. Cfr. Bauer, 34; Bernard, 35; M.-É. Boismard, *Du Baptême à Cana (Jean 1,19-2,11)* (LD 18; Paris 1956) 33-34.

20 Cfr. Lagrange, 38; Bultmann, 64; Strathmann, 46; Boismard, *Du Baptême à Cana*, 25; Schnackenburg, I 283; Brown, 54; Haenchen, 160. A. Serra, *Contributi dell'antica letteratura giudaica per l'esegesi di Giovanni 2,1-12 e 19,25-27* (Scripta Pont. Fac. Theol. 'Marianum' 31; Rome 1977) 93, discerns a kind of inclusion in 1,19-28, constituted by the mention of the name 'John' in 1,19.28.

21 This does not exclude the possibility that at an earlier stage of the text Andrew, Simon, or the other of the two disciples of 1,35 was the subject of εὑρίσκει; so, e.g., Bultmann, 68; R. T. Fortna, *The Gospel of Signs*. A Reconstruction of the Narrative Source Underlying the Fourth Gospel (SNTSMS 11; Cambridge 1970) 184-185; J. L. Martyn, 'We have found Elijah', in: *Jews, Greeks and Christians*. Religious Cultures in Late Antiquity (Fs. W. D. Davies; SJLA 21; Leiden 1976) 181-219; 202-208; see for a full discussion with more references: Neirynck, *Jean et les synoptiques*, 196-198.

22 Cfr. for this pattern in these two scenes: A. B. Hulen, 'The Call of the Four Disciples in John 1', *JBL* 67 (1948) 153-157; 155-156; Boismard, *Du Baptême à Cana*, 17; F. Bovon, 'Le structuralisme français et l'exégèse biblique', in: R. Barthes a.o., *Analyse structurale et exégèse biblique*. Essai d'interprétation (Neuchâtel 1971) 9-25; 23; F. Hahn, 'Die Jüngerberufung Joh 1:35-51', in: *Neues Testament und Kirche* (Fs. R. Schnackenburg; Freiburg etc. 1974) 172-190; 174-175.

23 Cfr. B. Olsson, *Structure and Meaning in the Fourth Gospel*. A Text-Linguistic Analysis of John 2:1-11 and 4:1-42 (ConB, NT Series 6; Lund 1974) 78, 89.

24 So also G. Ferraro, *L'"ora" di Cristo nel quarto vangelo* (Aloisiana 10; Rome 1974) 101-103; Olsson, *Structure and Meaning*, 78-79; J. Breuss, *Das Kanawunder*. Hermeneutische und pastorale Überlegungen aufgrund einer phänomenologischen Analyse von Joh 2,1-12 (BibB 12; Fribourg 1976) 23.

25 This division of John 1,19-2,11 is found (with 2,12 appended to 2,1-11) in the text-editions of Tischendorf^{8} and *UBSGNT*^{3}. It coincides with the chapter division in the *Codex Vaticanus*, with the restriction that there 1,18-28 is considered as a separate chapter. The division is also supported, although not always explicitly, by the authors who notice the series of successive days in 1,19-2,11; see below, n. 86. The 'dramatic' character of the division into scenes is worked out by H. Windisch, 'Joh. Erzählungsstil', in: *ΕΥΧΑΡΙΣΤΗΡΙΟΝ*, II 191-195 (for 1,19-51), 208-209 (for 2,1-11); C. P. Bowen, 'The Fourth Gospel as Dramatic Material', *JBL* 49 (1930) 292-305, esp. 298-303; J. Muilenburg, 'Literary Form in the Fourth Gospel', *JBL* 51 (1932) 40-53 (for 1,19-51); cfr. also C. M. Connick, 'The Dramatic Character of the Fourth Gospel', *JBL* 67 (1948) 159-169; B. Noack, *Zur johanneischen Tradition.* Beiträge zur Kritik an der literarkritischen Analyse des vierten Evangeliums (Teologiske Skrifter 3; Copenhagen 1954) 114-119. Windisch, however, makes the changes of person prevail too much over the conspicuous indications of days, and arrives in that way at a division of 1,19-51 into two acts (1,19-34.35-51) containing together nine scenes.

26 For this bipartition, cfr. Westcott, I 32; Windisch, in: *ΕΥΧΑΡΙΣΤΗΡΙΟΝ*, II 191-192; Muilenburg, *JBL* 51, 42-45 (divides into 1,19-24.25-28); Strathmann, 44; Boismard, *Du Baptême à Cana*, 25; W. Grundmann, 'Verkündigung und Geschichte in dem Bericht vom Eingang der Geschichte Jesu im Johannes-Evangelium', in: H. Ristow-K. Matthiae, eds., *Der historische Jesus und der kerygmatische Christus.* Beiträge zum Christusverständnis in Forschung und Verkündigung (Berlin 1961^{2}) 289-309; 292-293; B. M. F. van Iersel, 'Tradition und Redaktion in Joh i 19-36', *NT* 5 (1962) 245-267; 257; Schnackenburg, I 274; Willemse, *Het vierde evangelie*, 235; Brown, 41, 46, 70; Schneider, 66; G. Richter, 'Zur Frage von Tradition und Redaktion in Joh 1,19-34', in: id., *Studien zum Johannesevangelium* (Biblische Untersuchungen 13; Regensburg 1977) 288-314; 296; G. Gaeta, 'Battesimo come testimonianza. Le pericopi sul Battista nell'evangelo di Giovanni', *Cristianesimo nella storia* 1 (1980) 279-314; 300; Haenchen, 158. The text-editions of Westcott-Hort (followed by Nestle's editions, up to and including the 25th), Von Soden and *UBSGNT*^{3} divide into 1,19-23.24-27.28 (in Von Soden's edition as parts of 1,19-34); *NA*^{26} divides into 1,19-23.24-28.

27 Cfr. Van Iersel, *NT* 5, 257-258; Richter, *Studien*, 303.

28 Cfr. S. Sabugal, *ΧΡΙΣΤΟΣ*. Investigación exegética sobre la cristología joannea (Barcelona 1972) 175; Gaeta, *Crist. n. storia*, 1, 300.

29 E. Galbiati, 'La testimonianza di Giovanni Battista (Giov. 1,19-28)', *BeO* 4 (1962) 227-233; 227-228, also considers 1,23 as the centre of 1,19-28. According to G., the passage displays concentric symmetry: 1,21 and 25 are corresponding (dealing with the attitude, of the Baptist and the Jews respectively, to the messianic reality which is now present), and so are 1,20 and 26-27 (about the testimony of the Baptist), and 1,19 and 28 (giving the historical and topographical circumstances). In my view, these correspondences of content are too vague to be used in analysing the composition of the text: 'attitude to the messianic reality' and 'testimony of the Baptist' are present throughout the pericope. G. neglects the literary correspondences, so much that 1,24 is omitted from his scheme. The central position of 1,23 is also stressed by J. Cazeaux, '"C'est Moïse qui vous condamnera ..."', *Lumière et Vie* 29 (1980) nr. 149, 75-88; 80.

30 I suppose 1,23d (καθὼς εἶπεν ...) to belong to the Baptist's direct discourse, just as in the parallel cases 6,31.45; 7,38.42; 10,34; 13,18; 15,25, the formula of quotation is part of the direct discourse.

31 This division also in Brown, 41, 46, 50.

32 See n. 25 above, and below, pp. 197-198, with n. 27.

33 So also Richter, *Studien*, 298.

34 So also the text-editions of Westcott-Hort (followed by Nestle's editions, up to and including the 25th), Von Soden (as parts of 1,19-34), *UBSGNT*^{3} and *NA*^{26}, as well as Westcott, I 32; Muilenburg, *JBL* 51, 46; Bultmann, 58; Van Iersel, *NT* 5, 258;

Schnackenburg, I 284; Willemse, *Het vierde evangelie*, 236; Brown, 41, 58, 70; Schneider, 71; Richter, *Studien*, 296. The bipartition in question is mentioned but not judged to be essential by Gaeta, *Crist. n. storia* 1, 292.

35 See about such formulas E. Norden, *Agnostos Theos*. Untersuchungen zur Formengeschichte religiöser Rede (Leipzig/Berlin 1913; repr. Darmstadt 1974[6]) 177sqq.

36 Cfr., e.g., for nrs. c, d and e: Becker, 89; Gaeta, *Crist. n. storia* 1, 293; for nrs. c and d: Richter, *Studien*, 296; for nrs. c and e: Haenchen, 168. These and other repetitions, also in 1,19-34 as a whole, give often rise to literary-critical hypotheses about an original text which has been edited by a redactor, or about a combination of two parallel versions of the same story; so, e.g., Bultmann, 58; H. Sahlin, 'Zwei Abschriften aus Joh 1 rekonstruiert', *ZNW* 51 (1960) 64-69; Van Iersel, *NT* 5, 245-267; M.-É. Boismard, 'Les traditions johanniques concernant le Baptiste', *RB* 70 (1963) 5-25 (cfr. already id., *Du Baptême à Cana*, 18-21); Boismard-Lamouille, *Jean*, 83; Becker, 89sqq. See about such theories Brown, 67-71, and Richter, *Studien*, 292-293. R. himself considers 1,19-34 as a unit (in which older materials were worked up) which does not derive from the evangelist (he added only 1,30c) but from a 'Grundschrift' (293-297). Anyhow, in the present state of the text these repetitions have their own function, as I shall try to show.

37 J. Howton, '"Son of God" in the Fourth Gospel', *NTS* 10 (1963-64) 227-237; 231-232.

38 Ch. Exum's proposal, dating from 1966, is mentioned by his teacher C. H. Talbert, *CBQ* 32, 364-365 n. 102.

39 M. Roberge, 'Structures littéraires et christologie dans le IVe évangile. Jean 1,29-34', in: R. Laflamme-M. Gervais, eds., *Le Christ hier, aujourd'hui et demain* (Québec 1976) 467-477; 468-470.

40 Gaeta, *Crist. n. storia* 1, 294, makes the threefold κἀγώ (1,31.33.34) decisive for the structure of 1,29-34: the saying about Jesus' pre-existence 1,30 evokes a series of statements beginning with κἀγώ, about the position of the Baptist over against Jesus and in view of the manifestation of the pre-existent one.

41 See about these participial sayings, mostly used of God but also applied to Christ: Norden, *Agnostos Theos*, 166-168, 201sqq; G. Delling, 'Partizipiale Gottesprädikationen in den Briefen des Neuen Testaments', *ST* 17 (1963) 1-59; in abridged form under the title 'Geprägte partizipiale Gottesaussagen in der urchristlichen Verkündigung' in id., *Studien zum Neuen Testament und zum hellenistischen Judentum*. Gesammelte Aufsätze 1950-1968 (Göttingen 1970) 401-416.

42 See below, chapter IV, for another instance of a passage (viz., John 9,13-34) in the structure of which the alternation of 'statement of fact' and 'interpretation' is of importance.

43 1,19-28 and 29-34 are taken together in the text-editions of Westcott-Hort (followed by Nestle's editions, up to and including the 25th) and Von Soden, and by Westcott, I lxxxviii, 31; Windisch, in: *ΕΥΧΑΡΙΣΤΗΡΙΟΝ*, II 191-193; Bauer, 31; Lagrange, 34; Bultmann, 57; Barrett, 170; Grundmann, in: *Der historische Jesus*, 292; C. H. Dodd, *Historical Tradition in the Fourth Gospel* (Cambridge 1963) 251; Willemse, *Het vierde evangelie*, 233-235; Brown, 41, 45, 58 (67: inclusion 1,19.34); P. van Diemen, *La semaine inaugurale et la semaine terminale de l'évangile de Jean*. Message et structures (Diss. Pontifical Biblical Commission; Rome 1972) 137 (inclusion); Sabugal, *ΧΡΙΣΤΟΣ*, 155-157 (156: inclusion); Schulz, 35; Olsson, *Structure and Meaning*, 24 (with n. 16); Martyn, in: *Jews, Greeks and Christians*, 185; Schneider, 65; I. de la Potterie, *La vérité dans Saint Jean*, I: Le Christ et la vérité. L'Esprit et la vérité (AnBib 73; Rome 1977) 95 (inclusion); Richter, *Studien*, 296-297 (296: inclusion); Becker, 89; Cazeaux, *Lumière et Vie* 29 nr. 149, 78 (inclusion).

44 So also Bauer, 36; Boismard, *Du Baptême à Cana*, 19, 60-61; Grundmann, in: *Der historische Jesus*, 293; Schnackenburg, I 289; Haenchen, 167.

45 According to Dodd, *Historical Tradition*, 253-256, John 1,26-27.33d is a version of the tradition which is found also in Mark 1,8 parr; Acts 1,5; 11,16; 13,25, but it

is independent from the version of the synoptic gospels and Acts. Only in that way can it be explained that John displays agreements with and differences from all parallel texts.

46 Cfr. Barrett, 174; Boismard, *Du Baptême à Cana*, 20; Richter, *Studien*, 297; Haenchen, 169.

47 For similar figures in the numbers of S of Melito of Sardis' Περὶ Πασχα, see Smit Sibinga, *VC* 24, 95-96, who refers (95 n. 31) concerning this category of figures to W. Schultz, *Rätsel aus dem hellenischen Kulturkreise*, I: Die Rätselüberlieferung (Mythologische Bibliothek III/1; Leipzig 1909) XVI. See also P. Friesenhahn, *Hellenistische Wortzahlenmystik im Neuen Testament* (Leipzig/Bern 1935) 26.

48 See the survey of opinions in S. A. Panimolle, *Il dono della Legge e la grazia della Verità (Gv 1,17)* (Teologia oggi 21; Rome 1973) 65-71. Cfr. Willemse, *Het vierde evangelie*, 222: 'De stijl van de proloog is zeer poëtisch; zo poëtisch dat men er vaak een hymne in wil herkennen en terugvinden.... Dit in tegenstelling met het op de proloog volgende, dat duidelijk in verhalend proza geschreven is'.

49 I refer to the surveys in A. Feuillet, *Le prologue du quatrième évangile* (Bruges/Paris 1968) 137-149; Panimolle, *Dono della Legge*, 71-77 (see also his own analysis, 77-105); Culpepper, *NTS* 27, 2-6 (see also his own analysis, 9-17).

50 So, e.g., M.-É. Boismard, *Le Prologue de saint Jean* (LD 11; Paris 1953) 107; Willemse, *Het vierde evangelie*, 223; Feuillet, *Le prologue*, 160; Panimolle, *Dono della Legge*, 85-86; Boismard-Lamouille, *Jean*, 76; Culpepper, *NTS* 27, 9-10. See further the surveys mentioned in the preceding note.

51 So Westcott, I 33; Lagrange, 34; Bernard, 34; Muilenburg, *JBL* 51, 43 n. 17; Bultmann, 58 n. 2; Hoskyns-Davey, 172; Barrett, 171; Van den Bussche, *Boek der tekens*, 156-157; Grundmann, in: *Der historische Jesus*, 292; Schnackenburg, I 274; Willemse, *Het vierde evangelie*, 234; Brown, 42; Schneider, 66; Becker, 89.

52 John 2,1.13; 4,27; 7,1; 9,1; 10,40; 11,28; 18,38c; Matt 4,23; 8,14.23.28; 9,1.9.27.35; 10,1 etc.; Luke 2,22.41; 4,14.16.31; 5,12.17.27; 6,17 etc.; Acts 2,1; 14,8; 15,1; 28,1. In Mark and Rev, a strong tendency can be observed to begin stories or sections with καί. There are, e.g., among the 91 sections into which the Greek text of Mark is divided in *UBSGNT*[3], no less than 78 sections beginning with καί.

53 Cfr., e.g., Bauer, 31: '19 nimmt der Verf. endgültig den Erzählerton auf'; Lagrange, 34, about 1,19: 'Ce n'est pas ici un nouveau témoignage, c'est l'exposé historique de ce qui avait figuré dans le prologue à l'état absolu'; Schulz, 36 (as Bauer).

54 The division into 1,35-39 and 40-42 is found in the text-editions of Westcott-Hort (followed by Nestle, up to and including the 25th edition), Von Soden (as parts of 1,35-51), and *UBSGNT*[3], and in Westcott, I 46 (with a subdivision into 1,35-37.38-39 and 1,40-41.42); Muilenburg, *JBL* 51, 47-48; Hoskyns-Davey, 179-181; Brown, 41, 76; Hahn, in: *NT und Kirche*, 174; Schneider, 73. Strathmann, 51, considers 1,35-39.40-42 as parts of 1,35-51; Bultmann, 68, and Schulz, 41, do so with 1,35-37.38-39.40-42, and Windisch, in: *ΕΥΧΑΡΙΣΤΗΡΙΟΝ*, II 193, does so with 1,35-39.40-41.42. *NA*[26] has a capital letter at the beginning of 1,40, and prints 1,35-40 and 41-42 as separate paragraphs. E. Leidig, *Jesu Gespräch mit der Samaritanerin und weitere Gespräche Jesu im Johannesevangelium* (Theologische Dissertationen 15; Basel 1981[2]) 175-179, makes 1,35-42a into a unit, on the basis of a supposed succession of 'Heilsbegegnen', 'Heilsangebot', 'Heilserleben' and 'Bekenntnis', which she discerns in other conversations in John as well. The bipartition of the scene is also supported by those scholars who hold that 1,35-39 and 1,40-42 are situated on two successive days; see below, p. 81, with nn. 87 and 88.

55 M. De Goedt, 'Un schème de révélation dans le 4e Évangile', *NTS* 8 (1961-62) 142-150, discerns the same 'scheme of revelation' in John 1,29-34.35-39.47-51; 19,24b-27: 'Un envoyé de Dieu *voit* un personnage (le nom en est indiqué) et *dit*: "*Voici* (suit une appellation par laquelle le 'voyant' dévoile le mystère d'une mission, ou d'une destinée)"' (142). To this series, John 1,42 may be added; only is

there the 'behold', followed by an appellation, replaced by 'you shall be called Cephas'. De Goedt's scheme of revelation is used both at the beginning and at the end of the scene 1,35-42, be it with a different function: at the beginning Jesus is the object, at the end Peter.

56 The bipartition into 1,43-44.45sqq also in Hoskyns-Davey, 181-184; Brown, 41, 76, 84-85; Hahn, in: *NT und Kirche*, 174; Schneider, 73. 1,43-44 and 45sqq are considered as parts of 1,35-51 by Bultmann, 68; Strathmann, 51; Schulz, 42. The pericope is divided into 1,43-46.47sqq by Muilenburg, *JBL* 51, 50, and Willemse, *Het vierde evangelie*, 238; this division also in *NA*[26]. 1,43-46 and 47sqq are considered to be parts of 1,35-51 by Westcott, I 46 (cfr. my n. 54); Windisch, in: *ΕΥΧΑΡΙΣΤΗΡΙΟΝ*, II 193-194, does so with 1,43-44.45-46.47sqq. Leidig, *Jesu Gespräch*, 179-181, considers 1,45-51 as a unit: the conversation between Jesus and Nathanael. Boismard, *Du Baptême à Cana*, 15, situates 1,43-46 and 1,47-51 on two successive days; similarly T. Barrosse, 'The Seven Days of the New Creation in St. John's Gospel', *CBQ* 21 (1959) 507-516; 512-513; this supposition does not, however, find support in the text itself. — According to Hahn, in: *NT und Kirche*, 187, 1,45-51 is built in the following way: after an indication of the situation and a confession of faith (1,45) comes a short dialogue (1,46); this is followed by a 'doppelter Gesprächsgang' (1,47-48b.48c-49), which ends in a confession of faith, to which Jesus answers with a promise in 1,50-51. Hahn's description of the text's structure does not take into account that 1,45-46 constitutes one conversation, and that 1,48 contains both question and answer.

57 See esp. Bultmann, 75-76; Dodd, *Interpretation*, 228, 292-294; Boismard, *Du Baptême à Cana*, 22-23 (earlier authors mentioned there, 22 n. 10); Lightfoot, 99-100; Schnackenburg, I 273, 321-328; Willemse, *Het vierde evangelie*, 243-246; Boismard-Lamouille, *Jean*, 99; C. B. Cousar, 'John 1:29-42', *Int* 31 (1977) 401-406; 402.

58 I refer to three recent studies about this text and its problems: S. S. Smalley, 'Johannes 1,51 und die Einleitung zum vierten Evangelium', in: *Jesus und der Menschensohn* (Fs. A. Vögtle; Freiburg etc. 1975) 300-313; F. J. Moloney, *The Johannine Son of Man* (Biblioteca di Scienze Religiose 14; Rome 1976, 1978[2]) 23-41; Serra, *Contributi*, 259-301.

59 The relatively independent position and the importance of 1,51 in its context are noticed by several scholars; it is pointed out often, that 1,51 is a saying which does not originally belong to its present context (the image it contains is unique in John, and it has parallels elsewhere: Mark 14,62 // Matt 26,64; Acts 7,56; it may have been added here because of the *Stichwort* ὄψῃ-ὄψεσθε). See Dodd, *Interpretation*, 293-294; Noack, *Zur joh. Tradition*, 19, 154; Boismard, *Du Baptême à Cana*, 105-108, 119-122; Van den Bussche, *Boek der tekens*, 184; W. Grundmann, *Zeugnis und Gestalt des Johannes-Evangeliums*. Eine Studie zur denkerischen und gestalterischen Leistung des vierten Evangelisten (Arbeiten zur Theologie 7; Stuttgart s.a. [1961]) 32; Schnackenburg, I 318-321; Brown, 88-91; Sabugal, *ΧΡΙΣΤΟΣ*, 157; Schulz, 43-44; Hahn, in: *NT und Kirche*, 180, 189; Olsson, *Structure and Meaning*, 74, with n. 64; Smalley, in: *Jesus und der Menschensohn*, 307-313; Becker, 99-100.

60 In these three stories, the 'scheme of revelation' detected by De Goedt, *NTS* 8, 142-150, is found (see n. 55 above), although with different objects (in the first story Jesus, in the two other stories disciples). The parallelism between 1,41-42 and 1,45-47 is observed from a literary-critical point of view by Martyn, in: *Jews, Greeks and Christians*, 205-208, and Boismard-Lamouille, *Jean*, 87-88 (cfr. Neirynck, *Jean et les synoptiques*, 189-191).

61 See A. Schulz, *Nachfolgen und Nachahmen*. Studien über das Verhältnis der neutestamentlichen Jüngerschaft zur urchristlichen Vorbildethik (SANT 6; Munich 1962) 97sqq. Cfr. also Lightfoot, 98; Dodd, *Historical Tradition*, 303; Schnackenburg, I 312; Hahn, in: *NT und Kirche*, 177-178; Schneider, 75-76; Becker, 102-103; Haenchen, 179, 181.

62 Cfr. for these 'personal connections' in 1,35-51: Bultmann, 72; Strathmann, 53; Schnackenburg, I 313; Willemse, *Het vierde evangelie*, 238.

63 The two titles have the same tenor, cfr., e.g., PsSal 17,32; Mark 15,32; see Bultmann, 74 n. 1.

64 Similarities between 1,35-42 and 1,43-51 are noticed by Muilenburg, *JBL* 51, 51; Boismard, *Du Baptême à Cana*, 17, 21-22; Lightfoot, 100; Willemse, *Het vierde evangelie*, 238; Brown, 84-85; Sabugal, *ΧΡΙΣΤΟΣ*, 196; Cousar, *Int* 31, 405; Becker, 99-104. Cazeaux, *Lumière et Vie* 29 nr. 149, 84-85, discerns a concentric pattern in 1,35-51: 1,35-39 corresponds to 47-51, 40-41 to 44-46, and 42 to 43; most of these correspondences, however, are by no means obvious. Several scholars consider 1,35-51 as a unit: Westcott, I lxxxviii, 23; Bauer, 39; Windisch, in: *ΕΥΧΑΡΙΣΤΗΡΙΟΝ*, II 193-194; Lagrange, 44; Bultmann, 57; Hulen, *JBL* 67, 153-157; Strathmann, 50; Barrett, 179; Grundmann, in: *Der historische Jesus*, 294; Dodd, *Historical Tradition*, 302; Schnackenburg, I 306; Willemse, *Het vierde evangelie*, 237-238; Brown, 41; Bovon, in: *Analyse structurale*, 23-24; Sabugal, *ΧΡΙΣΤΟΣ*, 155-157; Schulz, 40; Hahn, in: *NT und Kirche*, 172-190; Martyn, in: *Jews, Greeks and Christians*, 185 (1,35-50 as a unit); Schneider, 73; Becker, 89, 99; so also the text-editions of Westcott-Hort (followed by Nestle, up to and including the 25th edition) and Von Soden.

65 Cfr. Friesenhahn, *Hellenistische Wortzahlenmystik*, 26. Greek-speaking people in antiquity used the decimal system in their pronunciation of numbers, cfr. above, p. 27. For them, the similarity between 74 and 47 was at least audible.

66 Cfr. Barrett, 180; Boismard, *Du Baptême à Cana*, 19, 71; Van den Bussche, *Boek der tekens*, 178; Willemse, *Het vierde evangelie*, 241; Brown, 76; Hahn, in: *NT und Kirche*, 173-174; Gaeta, *Crist. n. storia* 1, 293.

67 They are considered as constituting a unit by Windisch, in: *ΕΥΧΑΡΙΣΤΗΡΙΟΝ*, II 191-195; Bernard, xxxi; Muilenburg, *JBL* 51, 51-52; Bultmann, 57; Hoskyns-Davey, 167; Strathmann, 43; Dodd, *Interpretation*, 292; Van den Bussche, *Boek der tekens*, 66; Schnackenburg, I 273; Willemse, *Het vierde evangelie*, 241-253; Schulz, 35; Schneider, 65; Becker, 89; F. J. Moloney, 'From Cana to Cana (John 2:1-4:54) and the Fourth Evangelist's Concept of Correct (and Incorrect) Faith', in: E. A. Livingstone, ed., *Studia Biblica 1978*, II (Journal for the Study of the New Testament, Supplement Series 2; Sheffield 1980) 185-213; 185-186.

68 Cfr. Muilenburg, *JBL* 51, 40-53; Willemse, *Het vierde evangelie*, 238; Brown, 41.

69 See G. B. Winer's *Grammatik des neutestamentlichen Sprachidioms*, 8th edition by P. W. Schmiedel, I (Göttingen 1894) par. 5,6. In the Introduction to their Greek NT, par. 411, Westcott and Hort consider it better to print ὅ τι as one word.

70 See G. Theissen, *Urchristliche Wundergeschichten*. Ein Beitrag zur formgeschichtlichen Erforschung der synoptischen Evangelien (SNT 8; Gütersloh 1974) 57-89, esp. 81-83.

71 Cfr. J. P. Michaud, 'Le signe de Cana dans son contexte johannique', *Laval Théologique et Philosophique* 18 (1962) 239-285 and 19 (1963) 253-283; 18 (1962) 246: 'Le dialogue entamé au verset 3 par les brèves paroles de Marie se poursuit immédiatement au verset 4, sans aucune séparation'.

72 About these conclusions, see M. de Jonge, 'Signs and Works in the Fourth Gospel', in: T. Baarda a.o., eds., *Miscellanea Neotestamentica* II (NTS 48; Leiden 1978) 107-125; 108-112; also in id., *Jesus: Stranger from Heaven and Son of God*. Jesus Christ and the Christians in Johannine Perspective (SBLSBS 11; Missoula, Mt. 1977) 117-140; cfr. also Willemse, *Het vierde evangelie*, 125.

73 One could also compare 10,40-42, a passage which constitutes an inclusion with 1,19sqq and concludes 1,19-10,42, according to Van den Bussche, *Boek der Werken*, 238. There, belief in Jesus is mentioned next to the fact that John the Baptist did no miracle.

74 The same division as proposed here with a caesura at 2,5/6 is given by Westcott, I 80; Bultmann, 79; Strathmann, 56; Schulz, 45; Becker, 106; with a caesura at 2,4/5 by Olsson, *Structure and Meaning*, 22, 98, and *passim* in his analysis of the text on pp. 21-94 (see esp. 30, 85-86). It is given with 2,5 as a transition by L. Dequeker, 'De bruiloft te Kana (Jo., II,1-11)', *Collectanea Mechliniensia* 52 (1967) 177-193; 178,

and, as it seems, also by Schnackenburg, I 338. With a caesura at 2,5/6, it is also found in A. Smitmans, *Das Weinwunder von Kana.* Die Auslegung von Jo 2,1-11 bei den Vätern und heute (BGBE 6; Tübingen 1966) 25, who, however, makes 2,6-10 into one element, and in M. Rissi, 'Die Hochzeit in Kana (Joh 2,1-11)', in: *Oikonomia.* Heilsgeschichte als Thema der Theologie (Fs. O. Cullmann; Hamburg-Bergstedt 1967) 76-92; 88, who, however, makes 2,6-11 into one element (R. mentions on p. 84 2,3-*6* as preceding unit; witness p. 88, this has to be corrected into 2,3-*5*). With a caesura at 2,4/5, it is also found in R. Pesch, 'Das Weinwunder bei der Hochzeit zu Kana (Joh 2,1-12). Zur Herkunft der Wundererzählung', *Theologie der Gegenwart* 24 (1981) 219-225; 221, who, however, makes 2,9-11 into one element. The various authors just mentioned differ considerably in the way in which they characterize the elements. Bultmann, Strathmann, Schulz and Becker consider 2,3-5 as preparation of the miracle, and 2,6-8 as the miracle itself. This seems wrong, as the miracle itself is not told, and is prepared only in 2,5-8. — In the text-editions of Westcott-Hort (followed by Nestle, up to and including the 25th edition), Von Soden, *UBSGNT*[3] and *NA*[26], the concluding verse 2,11 is distinguished from the preceding story.

75 So also P. Geoltrain, 'Les noces à Cana, Jean 2,1-12. Analyse des structures narratives', in: A. Jaubert a.o., *Lecture de textes johanniques.* Introduction à l'analyse structurale (Cahiers Bibliques 13; Paris 1974) 83-90; 86; Olsson, *Structure and Meaning*, 87, 90.

76 So also (with caesura at 2,4/5) Van Diemen, *Semaine*, 593-596.

77 Cfr. Olsson, *Structure and Meaning*, 63, 78-79.

78 So Schnackenburg, I 333.

79 These parallelisms are also noticed by Van Diemen, *Semaine*, 594, 625; J. A. Grassi, 'The Wedding at Cana (John II 1-11): A Pentecostal Meditation', *NT* 14 (1972) 131-136; 134; Olsson, *Structure and Meaning*, 46, 54, 83; Serra, *Contributi*, 221. Cfr. Schnackenburg, I 337, about 2,7: 'Die Diener, durch Maria schon vorbereitet, kommen der Anordnung ohne weiteres nach'.

80 Cfr. about this contrast P. W. Meyer, 'John 2,10', *JBL* 86 (1967) 191-197; 194; Olsson, *Structure and Meaning*, 61-63 (with n. 95).

81 Cfr. for the exegesis of 1,50-51 given here, and the relationship of these verses with 2,1-11: Westcott, I 80; Bauer, 44; K. L. Schmidt, 'Der johanneische Charakter der Erzählung vom Hochzeitswunder in Kana', in: *Harnack-Ehrung.* Beiträge zur Kirchengeschichte ... A. von Harnack ... dargebracht (Leipzig 1921) 32-43; 33; Bultmann, 74-75; Hoskyns-Davey, 182-183; R. Schnackenburg, *Das erste Wunder Jesu (Joh. 2,1-11)* (Freiburg 1951) 4, 25-26 (also his commentary on John, I 317-321); Boismard, *Du Baptême à Cana*, 105-108, 133-136 (also Boismard-Lamouille, *Jean*, 98-99); Lightfoot, 93, 99; Grundmann, in: *Der historische Jesus*, 294-295; Brown, 83, 88, 91, 105; Dequeker, *Coll. Mechl.* 52, 179; Rissi, in: *Oikonomia*, 82; A. M. Serra, 'Le tradizioni della teofania sinaitica nel Targum dello pseudo-Jonathan Es. 19.24 e in Giov. 1,19-2,12', *Marianum* 33 (1971) 1-39; 25 (also id., *Contributi*, 291-301); Van Diemen, *Semaine*, 35-38, 42, 433-442, 639-641; W. Nicol, *The Sēmeia in the Fourth Gospel.* Tradition and Redaction (NTS 32; Leiden 1972) 39 (for John's source); Hahn, in: *NT und Kirche*, 173; Olsson, *Structure and Meaning*, 32, 76; S. Pancaro, *The Law in the Fourth Gospel.* The Torah and the Gospel, Moses and Jesus, Judaism and Christianity according to John (NTS 42; Leiden 1975) 303-304, cfr. 292; Martyn, in: *Jews, Greeks and Christians*, 184; Schneider, 78, 79; Becker, 97, 104, 110-112; Cazeaux, *Lumière et Vie* 29 nr. 149, 79; Haenchen, 182; Moloney, in: *Studia Biblica 1978*, II 188.

82 So Becker, 100; Haenchen, 181; cfr. Lagrange, 48.

83 So also Olsson, *Structure and Meaning*, 77; M. de Jonge, in: *Miscellanea Neotestamentica* II, 113.

84 So Barrett, 189, cfr. 188; cfr. Lightfoot, 94; Becker, 87, 112.

85 The pericope 2,1-11 is considered as belonging closely together with 1,35-51 by Brown, 41, 77, 79, 105; Rissi, in: *Oikonomia*, 81-82; cfr. Olsson, *Structure and Mean-*

ing, 24 (with n. 16). — In addition, I mention the circumstance that throughout 1,35-2,11 motifs from wisdom literature are found, whereby Jesus is depicted as God's Wisdom. Wisdom teaches people (Prov 1,23; Wis 7,22; 9,18); Jesus is called 'Rabbi', 'teacher' (John 1,38.49). 'Searching for Wisdom' and 'finding Wisdom' occur in Prov 1,28; 3,13; 4,22; 8,35; Wis 1,1-2; 6,12; the disciples search for (cfr. John 1,38) and find Jesus as the Messiah and as the one about whom Moses and the prophets wrote (John 1,41.45). Wisdom searches for people who are worthy of her (Wis 6,16); Jesus finds Philip (John 1,43). Prov 8,34; Wis 7,28; 8,9.16 speak about staying with Wisdom; the disciples stay with Jesus (John 1,38-39). Wisdom offers to man her bread and wine (Prov 9,5), her water (Sir 15,3), herself as food and drink (Sir 24,21; cfr. Isa 55,1-3); Jesus changes water into wine and offers thereby drink to the wedding-guests (John 2,1-11). See more amply about these parallels: Boismard, *Du Baptême à Cana*, 78-80, 139-143; R. J. Dillon, 'Wisdom Tradition and Sacramental Retrospect in the Cana Account (Jn 2,1-11)', *CBQ* 24 (1962) 268-296; Brown, 79, 106-107.

86 So already Origen, *In Joannem* 6,258-259 (SC 157, pp. 324 and 326); also J. A. Bengel, *Gnomon Novi Testamenti* ... (Tübingen 1759^{2}) 322, and among modern authors B. W. Bacon, 'After Six Days: A New Clue for Gospel Critics', *HTR* 8 (1915) 94-121; 106-118; Schmidt, in: *Harnack-Ehrung*, 33; Strathmann, 43, 56; Barrett, 13, 189; Lightfoot, 92-93; Brown, 105-106; Dequeker, *Coll. Mechl.* 52, 179-180; Rissi, in: *Oikonomia*, 81-82; W. Wink, *John the Baptist in the Gospel Tradition* (SNTSMS 7; Cambridge 1968) 92; Geoltrain, in: *Lecture de textes johanniques*, 84; Hahn, in: *NT und Kirche*, 173; Olsson, *Structure and Meaning*, 23; Schneider, 69; Becker, 87. Cfr. also Neirynck, *Jean et les synoptiques*, 194-195.

87 Which is thought to be supported by the variant reading πρωΐ for πρῶτον in 1,41, implied in *mane*, found in a series of Old Latin mss. (it$^{b,e,j^{vid},r^{1\ vid}}$). This reading, poorly attested, 'avoids the ambiguities of πρῶτος/πρῶτον and carries on the narrative from ver. 39', so Metzger, *Textual Commentary*, 200; cfr. Hoskyns-Davey, 181.

88 A week is counted by Westcott, I 31; Bernard, 33-34; cautiously by Bultmann, 79 n. 3 (referring to others); further by P. W. Skehan, 'The Date of the Supper', *CBQ* 20 (1958) 192-199; 197 n. 3 (cont. on p. 198; S. makes a separate day out of the disciples' staying with Jesus in 1,39); Grundmann, *Zeugnis und Gestalt*, 33; Schnackenburg, I 285, 330-331; M. Weise, 'Passionswoche und Epiphaniewoche im Johannes-Evangelium. Ihre Bedeutung für Komposition und Konzeption des vierten Evangeliums', *KD* 12 (1966) 48-62; Ferraro, *L'"ora" di Cristo*, 93-94; G. Voss, 'Kosmische Bildwirklichkeit in der neutestamentlichen Verkündigung. Ein Versuch zu Joh 1-2', *US* 32 (1977) 13-38; 36. The week of John 1,19-2,11 is supposed to be parallel to the week of Gen 1,1-2,4a by Boismard, *Du Baptême à Cana*, 14-15 (somewhat modified as to the exact count of days in Boismard-Lamouille, *Jean*, 99, cfr. Neirynck, *Jean et les synoptiques*, 194-195); Barrosse, *CBQ* 21, 507-516; Van Diemen, *Semaine*, 57-99 (he counts 8 days, by making 'that day' of 1,39 into a separate day) ; L. P. Trudinger, 'The Seven Days of the New Creation in St. John's Gospel: Some Further Reflections', *EvQ* 44 (1972) 154-158. Parallelism between John 1,*1*-2,11 and Gen 1,1-2,4a is defended by F. Quiévreux, 'La structure symbolique de l'Évangile de Saint Jean', *RHPR* 33 (1953) 123-165; 131-132; Willemse, *Het vierde evangelie*, 154-157 (who sees 8 days in John 1,1-2,11); idem with John 1,*1*-2,*12*: W. F. Hambly, 'Creation and Gospel. A Brief Comparison of Gen 1,1-2,4 and Jo 1,1-2,12', *SE* V (TU 103; Berlin 1968) 69-74. A survey of these theories is given by Serra, *Contributi*, 29-44.

89 Cfr. for criticism of these week-theories H. Van den Bussche, 'La structure de Jean 1-12', in: M. É. Boismard a.o., *L'Évangile de Jean.* Études et problèmes (RechBib 3; Bruges 1958) 61-109; 67-69; id., *Boek der tekens*, 169; F.-M. Braun, *Jean le Théologien et son évangile dans l'église ancienne* (EB; Paris 1959) 15; J. P. Charlier, *Het teken van Kana* (De christen in de tijd 9; Antwerpen 1961) 42 (orig. French: *Le signe de Cana.* Essai de théologie johannique [Brussels 1959]); Schnackenburg, I 330-331; Willemse, *Het vierde evangelie*, 151-154; Brown, 105-106; Rissi, in: *Oikonomia*, 81; Olsson, *Structure and Meaning*, 23-24; Becker, 107.

90 See esp. Serra, *Marianum* 33, 1-39, and id., *Contributi*, 29-138; further J. Potin, *La fête juive de la Pentecôte*. Étude des textes liturgiques (LD 65; Paris 1971) I 314-317; Olsson, *Structure and Meaning*, 24-25, 102-109; cfr. also Grassi, *NT* 14, 131-136. See for criticism of this theory, warning against too much eisegesis: B. Lindars, in: B. Lindars-P. Borgen, 'The Place of the Old Testament in the Formation of New Testament Theology. Prolegomena and Response', *NTS* 23 (1976-77) 59-75; 64-65.

91 See b. Šabb. 86b-87a; b. Yoma 4b; b. Ta^can. 28b; Mek. de R. Simon b. Yochai on Exod 19,1-6 (Yithro); Sipra Lev 9,1; Pirqe R. El. 46; S. ^cOlam Rab. 5. In an indirect way, it is found also in Pseudo-Philo, *Liber Antiquitatum Biblicarum* 19,7; m. Ta^can. 4,6, where Moses is said to have smashed to pieces the tables of the Law on the 17th of Tammuz, i.e., 40 days after the 7th of Siwan.

92 As is evident from its being mentioned in Ps.-Philo's *Lib. Ant. Bibl.*, the Mekilta, Sipra, and is confirmed by the names of the authorities mentioned: the Tanna^ʾim, R. Aqiba (died 135), R. Yose the Galilean (± 110), R. Eleazar b. Azariah (± 100).

93 In rabbinic literature, the making of the covenant at Mount Sinai is considered as the wedding of the Lord and Israel, see, e.g., Mek. Exod 19,17 (Bachodesh, 3); see further E. Stauffer, art. γαμέω etc., *TWNT* I, 646-655; 652.

94 See Serra, *Contributi*, 230-232; about wine as symbolizing the Torah, *ibd.*, 234-250.

95 John 1,19-2,11 is obviously considered as one coherent series of scenes by Westcott, I lxxxviii, 31; P. Defourny, 'Au sujet de la composition du quatrième évangile', *Collectanea Mechliniensia* 11 (1937) 359-367; Barrett, 13; Boismard, *Du Baptême à Cana*, 14-15; Lightfoot, 93-94; Barrosse, *CBQ* 21, 507-516; Dequeker, *Coll. Mechl.* 52, 179-180; Talbert, *CBQ* 32, 342-345; Hahn, in: *NT und Kirche*, 173; Becker, 87. Other scholars consider 2,1-11 both as the closing scene of 1,19-2,11 and as the opening scene of the following section, see below n. 98.

96 Cfr. for the relationship between the two Cana-pericopes: Bauer, 74; Boismard, *Du Baptême à Cana*, 107 (also Boismard-Lamouille, *Jean*, 105); S. Temple, 'The Two Signs in the Fourth Gospel', *JBL* 81 (1962) 169-174 (with literary-critical consequences); Brown, 194; Van Diemen, *Semaine*, 8-29; E. Galbiati, 'Nota sulla struttura del "libro dei segni" (Giov. 2-4)', *Euntes Docete* 25 (1972) 139-144; 140, 142 (repr. in id., *Scritti minori*, I 185-191); Olsson, *Structure and Meaning*, 64-65; Breuss, *Kanawunder*, 27-28; Martyn, in: *Jews, Greeks and Christians*, 191-192; M. de Jonge, in: *Misc. Neotestamentica* II, 112-113; Moloney, in: *Studia Biblica 1978* II, 189-191.

97 So Van den Bussche, in: *L'Évangile de Jean*, 76-77, who is followed by: Charlier, *Het teken van Kana*, 67; J. Riedl, 'Der "Anfang" der Wunder Jesu (Jo 2,11a) und die johanneische Geschichtsschreibung', in: *In Verbo Tuo* (Fs. zum 50-jähr. Bestehen des Missionspriesterseminars St. Augustin; St. Augustin 1963) 259-275; 263-264; Willemse, *Het vierde evangelie*, 123; I. de la Potterie, 'Structura primae partis Evangelii Johannis (capita III et IV)', *VD* 47 (1969) 130-140; 133-137; Galbiati, *Euntes Docete* 25, 139-144. See further Schulz, 44; Moloney, in: *Studia Biblica 1978*, II 185-213.

98 This double function is also noticed by Windisch, in: *ΕΥΧΑΡΙΣΤΗΡΙΟΝ*, II 208; F.-M. Braun, 'Le don de Dieu et l'initiation chrétienne (Jn 2-4)', *NRT* 86 (1964) 1025-1048; 1047; Schnackenburg, I 328-329; Brown, 41, 105; Olsson, *Structure and Meaning*, 18 n. 2: 'At the same time as the Cana narrative ends the "second prologue" in Jn (1:19-2:11), it is the introduction to chs. 2-4'. It is interesting to see how Willemse, *Het vierde evangelie*, inclines very strongly to considering John 2,1-11 exclusively as a beginning of what follows (105, 145, 154, 237), but is nevertheless compelled by the literary reality to relate 2,1-11 to what precedes (151-157, 248, 251).

99 The same view concerning 2,12 in Westcott, I 87; Bowen, *JBL* 49, 303; Strathmann, 56; Dodd, *Historical Tradition*, 235; Schnackenburg, I 356, 358; Brown, 95, 112.

100 Olsson's remark (*Structure and Meaning*, 23 n. 12) that the verse 2,12 belongs especially together with what precedes, as to the indications of persons and of place found in it, is true, but it does not remove the obviously concluding character of 2,11. Bar-

rett, 13, considers 1,19-2,11 as the first paragraph of the section 1,19-12,50, and on pp. 188-194 he discusses 2,1-12 as one pericope. The chapter division of the *Codex Alexandrinus* and the text-editions of Tischendorf[8] and *UBSGNT*[3] make 2,12 belong to what precedes; the chapter division of the *Codex Vaticanus* and the editions of Westcott-Hort and Von Soden take the verse together with what follows. Other editions (Souter, *NA*[25], *NA*[26]) print 2,12 as a separate paragraph — which might be the best solution.

101 See F. Hahn, *Christologische Hoheitstitel.* Ihre Geschichte im frühen Christentum (FRLANT 83; Göttingen 1974[4]) 208-209; W. Grundmann, in: W. Grundmann-F. Hesse-M. de Jonge-A. S. van der Woude, art. χρίω etc., *TWNT* IX, 482-576; 533 (with the literature referred to in n. 319); cfr. also A. S. van der Woude, *ibd.*, 500.

102 A parallel for the use of the article with a name in the computation of the numerical value of that name is afforded by an inscription from Meharrakah, Nubia (*CIG* III, 5113), where ὁ Σ]άραπις and Ἶσ(ις) πάνκαλος are put on a level: of both, the numerical value is 662. The completion of the first name not only with Σ, but also with the article ὁ is necessary to reach a numerical value of 662.

103 One could compare the view of J. Willemse, *Het vierde evangelie*, 264-274, that John 1,1-18 constitutes a kind of compendium of 'Son'-christology, in which Jesus is viewed in his immediate relation with God, and that John 1,19-51 constitutes a kind of compendium of 'Messiah'-christology, in which Jesus is viewed in continuity with the OT history of salvation.

104 A certain caesura at 1,37/38 is noticed by Westcott, I 46; Muilenburg, *JBL* 51, 48; Bultmann, 68; Van Diemen, *Semaine*, 189-193; Schulz, 41. Willemse, *Het vierde evangelie*, 241-242, considers 1, 35-37 as a connection between 1,19-34 and 1,35-51. Dodd, *Historical Tradition*, 248-249, 251, considers 1,19-37 as the elaboration of the three parts of the statement about John the Baptist in 1,6-8: a) 'he was not the light'; b) 'he came to a testimony, to testify to the light'; c) 'that all might believe through him'. Part a) is elaborated in 1,19-28, part b) in 1,29-34, and part c) in 1,35-37.

CHAPTER TWO

JOHN 5: HEALING, CONTROVERSY AND DEFENCE

Preliminary remarks have to be made concerning problems of syllable- and word-count and of textual criticism.

For the syllable-count of the word ἰαθείς in John 5,13, the considerations put forward at the beginning of the preceding chapter concerning the *iōta* of ἱερός and cognate words are valid: the *iōta* with which ἰαθείς begins, is a vocal, and therefore a separate syllable; so, the word is to be counted at three syllables (cfr. instances such as Homer, *Iliad* 5,899; 12,2; *Odyssey* 9,520.525).

In the count of words we meet the question whether τριάκοντα καὶ ὀκτώ in 5,5 should be counted at three words or at one word. In his work Περὶ Ἰλιακῆς προσῳδίας, the grammarian Herodianus (2nd century C.E.) discusses the numeral δυοκαίδεκα in *Iliad* 2,557. He refers to his predecessor Pamphilus (second half of 1st century C.E.), who τρία ποιεῖ καὶ κατὰ παράθεσιν ἀναγινώσκει, 'makes three (words) and reads according to juxtaposition'; ἡ κατὰ σύνθεσιν ἀνάγνωσις, 'the reading according to composition', has the poetic use as its origin (*Herodiani Technici Reliquiae*, ed. Lentz, II p. 35). Later on, Herodianus discusses δυωκαιεικοσίπηχυ from *Iliad* 15,678, and considers it ὑφ'ἓν ἀναγνωστέον, 'to be read as one word'; he adds: τινὲς δὲ καὶ κατὰ παράθεσιν, 'but some (read it) also according to juxtaposition' (ed. Lentz, II p. 97). So we may conclude that composed numerals can be written and counted in two ways: as one word, or as two or more separate words[1]. I shall assume provisionally, in agreement with the common modern way of printing, the latter possibility, and return to the question in the course of the numerical analysis.

Between the text of John 5 in *NA*[25] and that in *NA*[26], there are five differences which affect numbers of W and S. These have to be discussed briefly:

1. In 5,10c, *NA*[25] omits σου after τὸν κράβατον (with A B C[3] *f*[1] *Mehrheitstext* e); *NA*[26] reads τὸν κράβαττόν σου (with P[66.75] Sin C* D L N W[s] Θ Ψ *f*[13] 892 1010 1241 *al* lat sy). Two considerations in favour of the *NA*[25]-text are: a) the addition of σου could seem to have been made for the sake of completeness or clarity; b) the addition of σου may be an adaptation to the context, where τὸν κράβαττόν σου is found twice (5,8.11; cfr. 5,9 τὸν κράβαττον αὐτοῦ). On the other hand, supposing the longer

reading to be original, the omission of σου might be an attempt to improve the text stylistically: according to the standards of classical Greek, the genitive of the personal pronoun is only used in its possessive function when necessary in the interest of clarity, and not when the person indicated by the pronoun coincides with the subject of the clause[2]. As in our case a 'you' is the logical subject of the infinitive ἆραι, the genitive σου may have been omitted by a corrector. The reading with σου is not contrary to Johannine style (cfr. 4,35: ὑμῶν; 11,2; 12,3: αὐτῆς; 13,12.18; 17,1: αὐτοῦ; 20,25.27: μου/σου; also 21,18: σου; in all these texts the person indicated by the pronoun is the subject of the clause). However, when assuming that the reading with σου is the original one, one has to answer the question why σου was deleted in 5,10 only, and not also in 5,8.11. As far as we see, there is no answer to this question. So it seems best to retain the shorter *NA*25-reading[3].

2. In 5,15, *NA*25 reads εἶπεν (with Sin C L *pc* it sys.c.p), and *NA*26 ἀνήγγειλεν (with P66.75 A B W Θ Ψ 063 *f*1 *Mehrheitstext* f syh). There are also mss. reading ἀπήγγειλεν (D K Δ *f*13 33 1010 1241 1424 *al*), but this reading is probably only a variant of ἀνήγγειλεν[4]. Has ἀνήγγειλεν been changed into εἶπεν, or are there reasons why εἶπεν might have been changed into ἀνήγγειλεν? Other occurrences of ἀναγγέλλειν and ἀπαγγέλλειν in John (4,25; 16,13.14.15.25; 20,18 *l.v.*), and in other NT writings (Matt 11,4; 12,18; 28,8.10; Mark 16,10.13; Luke 7,22; 9,36; 24,9; Acts 14,27; 15,4.27; 17,30 *l.v.*; 20,20.27; 26,20; Rom 15,21; 1 Cor 14,25; 1 Thess 1,9; Heb 2,12; 1 Pet 1,12; 1 John 1,2.3.5) suggest the meaning 'to proclaim', with a strong religious connotation[5]. This is especially evident in the use of the verbs in miracle stories, where the proclamation of what happened is found frequently: Matt 8,33; Mark 5,14.19; Luke 7,18; 8,34.36.47; Acts 11,13; 12,14.17[6], and this is clearly the meaning of ἀνήγγειλεν in John 5,15, within the miracle story 5,1sqq. A change of an original but rather trivial εἶπεν — similar to expressions used in, e.g., John 9,11.15.17 — into a significant ἀνήγγειλεν (or ἀπήγγειλεν), with its appropriate meaning of 'religious proclamation', a verb occurring many times in the NT, can be understood more easily than the reverse movement[7]. Therefore, the *NA*25-text has to be preferred here.

3. At the beginning of 5,17, *NA*25 reads ὁ δέ, with P75 Sin B W 892 1241 *pc* pbo, whereas *NA*26 has ὁ δὲ ['Ιησοῦς] (the square brackets indicate the doubt of the editors as to the presence of 'Ιησοῦς in the original text); the longer text is read by P66 A D L Θ Ψ 063 *f*1.13 *Mehrheitstext* latt sy(s) co (see *UBSGNT*3 for a fuller enumeration of witnesses[8]). Here, too, the *NA*25-reading seems to be the preferable one: an original ὁ δέ has been amplified, 'to provide a subject for ἀπεκρίνατο'[9], to ὁ δὲ 'Ιησοῦς. The combination of substantival article and δέ more often occurs in John

(1,38; 2,8; 4,32; 6,20; 7,41; 9,15.17.38; 18,7; 20,25; also 21,6), so the use of this combination in 5,17 is in accordance with Johannine style. That the absence of the name might be 'an Alexandrian deletion prompted by stylistic considerations'[10], does not seem very obvious; at least, in other instances in John, where such a deletion would be appropriate because of the very close sequence of two occurrences of the name Ἰησοῦς, it has not been carried out (see esp. 12,22-23, and also 1,37-38; 1,42; 13,23; 18,19-20; 19,38; 20,14-15, and 21,4-5).

4. In 5,19c, *NA*^{25} reads conditional ἄν, with only Sin B, whereas *NA*^{26} reads ἐάν, which reading is supported by all other known Greek mss. Conditional ἄν (= ἐάν) is used very rarely in the NT; the only writing in which it can be established with some certainty is John (13,20; 16,23; 20,23*bis*; as *v.l.* John 12,32, and Acts 9,2). In pagan and Jewish Greek literature of the period it is also rare[11], and in papyri (where ἐάν is the dominant form) it is 'decidedly a symptom of illiteracy'[12]. Though it is not quite clear whether ἄν is an Ionic[13] or an Attic[14] form, it is anyhow the more uncommon one, and scribes never fail to correct it (see the texts referred to above). For that reason it seems preferable to read it in John 5,19c.

5. In 5,29b, *NA*^{25} reads οἱ τὰ φαῦλα πράξαντες (with P^{66c} B a e ff^{2}), whereas in *NA*^{26} δέ is added after οἱ (with P^{75} Sin A D L Θ Ψ 063 0124 *f*$^{1.13}$ *Mehrheitstext* lat sy^{h}). Here, a third reading also exists: καὶ οἱ (P^{66*} W). The most probable explanation is in this case that an original asyndeton has been eliminated in two different ways. This elimination may have been favoured by the parallel texts Dan 12,2 (LXX: οἱ μὲν εἰς ζωὴν αἰώνιον, οἱ δὲ εἰς ὀνειδισμόν, οἱ δὲ εἰς διασπορὰν καὶ αἰσχύνην αἰώνιον; Theod: οὗτοι εἰς ζωὴν αἰώνιον καὶ οὗτοι εἰς ὀνειδισμὸν καὶ εἰς αἰσχύνην αἰώνιον) and Matt 25,46 (οὗτοι εἰς κόλασιν αἰώνιον, οἱ δὲ δίκαιοι εἰς ζωὴν αἰώνιον). In an antithetic parallelism such as the present one, John more often uses an asyndeton (see, e.g., 1,17; 3,31; 4,22; 5,23.43.45; 6,53-54.63; 7,8; 8,15.23)[15].

So, in all five instances of difference between *NA*^{25} and *NA*^{26}, *NA*^{25} seems to give the preferable reading.

1. *John 5 as a literary unit*

In John 5,1-9 it is described how Jesus, while staying in Jerusalem, heals a man who has been ill for 38 years. On Jesus' word: 'Stand up, take up your bed, and walk' (5,8), the man takes up his bed and walks, but this happens to take place on a Sabbath (5,9). The Jews establish his breach of the Law, but the man appeals to what his healer said to him (5,10-11). On enquiry, he does not know the name of his healer, who has disappeared in the meantime (5,12-13). Later on, Jesus and the man meet in the temple, and the man tells the Jews that Jesus is the one who cured him (5,14-15). The Jews persecute Jesus because he has broken the Sabbath; he answers them: 'My Father is at work till now, and I am at work' (5,17). These words are understood by the Jews as an attempt to make himself equal with God, and therefore they seek to kill him (5,16-18). Jesus answers them in a long monologue, in which he speaks about the total dependence of the Son on the Father in his acting, *and* about their total unity. The Son does not act by himself, he can only do what he sees the Father doing; the Father shows to the Son everything he does, and he has given the power to give life and to judge, now and in the future, to the Son (5,19-30). To justify these claims, a series of witnesses on behalf of Jesus is produced; among these are the Scriptures, which were not capable of bringing the Jews to faith, though they testify about Jesus. The Jews accept praise from one another, but they do not seek the glory that comes from the one God. Moses is their accuser before the Father, for if they would believe Moses, who wrote about Jesus, they would believe Jesus. But if they do not believe what Moses wrote, how can they believe what Jesus says? (5,31-47)

This description of the contents of John 5 already suggests a certain dramatic and thematic coherence within the chapter. There are also reasons of a more formal nature to consider John 5 as a unit. First of all, John 5 constitutes a unity of place: miracle story and discourse are located in Jerusalem, whereas the preceding and following stories (4,46-54; 6) are located in Galilee. Moreover, John 5 constitutes a unity of time: the episode is dated to a 'Festival of the Jews' (not indicated more precisely), whereas the preceding story is dated apparently not too long after a Festival of Passover (4,45; cfr. 2,13), and the following one in the proximity of a Festival of Passover (6,4). Besides, the temporal relationship of the events of John 5 to what precedes and to what follows is indicated by the vague expression μετὰ ταῦτα (5,1; 6,1). This expression occurs, it is true, also within John 5, in 5,14, but there we find it without the indication of a festival, without an important change of *dramatis personae*, with a change of place only within Jerusalem (from the pool of 5,2 to the temple), and in a direct dramatic connection with what precedes[16].

On the level of acting characters, John 5 constitutes a unity as well: in the healing story Jesus and the crippled man are on the stage (5,1-9); after this the latter, now cured, and the Jews are in discussion (5,10-13), Jesus and the healed man meet once again (5,14), the latter informs the Jews that Jesus cured him (5,15), and the Jews and Jesus are in conflict about Jesus' violation of the Sabbath (5,16sqq). Only here in John —

and in 7,23, where the present story is referred to — do we meet the man who has been ill for 38 years and is healed — although in John 5 his physical presence is confined to 5,1-15 —, and the Jews of Jerusalem are on the stage neither in what directly precedes, nor in what directly follows.

A few scholars consider 4,43 (or 46)-5,47 as a unit[17], because in the sign of 4,46-54 as well as in the healing of 5,1-9 Jesus gives life by his word, which illustrates 5,21.24. Moreover, in this way a sequence appears which is comparable to the sequence in John 2-3: an action of Jesus in Cana of Galilee is followed by an action of Jesus in Jerusalem and a discourse of Jesus. From the above it will be clear, however, that there is a break between 4,54 and 5,1, whereas 5,1-47 is one continuous episode — though, of course, a certain thematic similarity between 4,43-54 and 5,1-47 is evident. Besides, it is by no means certain that John 2-3 is a unit; dramatically, it is no more so than 4,43-5,47.

Is the unity of John 5 also discernible in numbers of S and W? The entire chapter has a size of 1619 S or 789 W; neither number is a round one, or seems otherwise significant. The results of a division into narrative and discourse are given in Table I.

Table I. John 5

	syllables		words	
narrative in John 5		418		197
	a)	b)	a)	b)
discourse of Jesus	1095	1114	537	546
of the healed man	71	59	36	30
of the Jews	35	28/1201/1619	19	16/592/789

N.B. In the a)-columns the quotations of Jesus' words in 5,11.12 are counted as discourse of the healed man and the Jews respectively; in the b)-columns they are counted as discourse of Jesus.

In the numbers of S, the 1201 S of discourse attract attention. One might conjecture that the discourse is too long by one S in the *NA*[25]-text, and that the number should be 1200. However, we did not find other indications for the text being too long; on the contrary, the *NA*[25]-text appears to be correct as far as its size is concerned — to anticipate further analysis.

The numbers of S display an interesting feature. The number of S of the narrative, 418, is the product of 11 and 38; the number 38, and its half, 19, will appear to be very important in the composition of John 5 in numbers of S and W. The importance of the number 38 is evident from the text itself: the crippled man has been ill for 38 years (5,5).

As for the numbers of W, it might be noteworthy that in the b)-column of discourse there are *546* W of discourse of Jesus, and 30 + 16 = *46* W of discourse of the man and the Jews together. More important is, that the sum total of 789 W has been divided as well as possible according to a proportion of 1:3 into 197 W of narrative and 592 W of discourse.

The same proportion returns in a division of the number of W according to the actors as is given in Table II.

Table II. words divided acc. to actors John 5

	Jesus	man	Jews	other subjects	
5,1a				6	
1b	5				
2-3				25	
5		14			
6	17				
7		27			
8	11				
9a		13			
9b				7	
10			15		
11		17			
12			12		
13a		7			
13b-14	32				
15		14			
16			13		
17	12				
18			27		
19-47	515				
total	592 +	92 +	67 +	38	= 789

The sentences with Jesus as actor amount to 592 W; the rest to 1/3 of this number, 197 (= 92 + 67 + 38). The sentences with Jesus as actor have together a size of 5*92* W; those with the man as actor have together a size of *92* W.

So, the unity of John 5 is evidently discernible in the arrangement of numbers of W. In the chapter in its entirety, rational proportions are visible; these have been realized in two ways, with the word as unit of count. Counting the numeral in 5,5 at one word would spoil these proportions.

2. *The sections of John 5 and their connections*

Roughly speaking, John 5 is made up of two sections: a miracle story, and a monologue of Jesus. The monologue is connected with the miracle story by means of a short quasi-dialogue between Jesus and the Jews, 5,16-18. It is true that in this passage the Jews do not *say* anything in the strict sense of the word, but this circumstance is no argument against the dialogue-character of these verses. Both διώκειν[18] and ζητεῖν ἀποκτεῖναι

(5,16.18) describe a juridical action against Jesus, and the ὅτι-clauses in 5,16.18 contain the accusation put forward by the Jews: Jesus breaks the Sabbath law, and he does so with an appeal to God as his Father. It also suits the dialogue-character that Jesus 'answers' to their accusations, in 5,17.19. The aor. med. ἀπεκρίνατο, rare in the NT and occurring only here in John, suggests a solemn, formal answer[19], which confirms the juridical atmosphere of this quasi-dialogue.

The passage 5,16-18 is hardly an independent unit, as it leads up to the monologue on the one hand, and arises from the preceding story on the other. The latter circumstance is especially important for 5,16: this sentence is not only the beginning of the confrontation, in which Jesus and the Jews are opposed to each other, but also the conclusion of the preceding story. In their conversation with the healed man the Jews have discovered that it was Jesus who cured him and who, for that reason, infringed upon the Sabbath law. As soon as they know that (5,15), they attack Jesus (5,16). A slight inclusion can be discerned, constituted by 5,9b and 5,16b; in both clauses, the Sabbath is mentioned. In fact, 5,9b lays the basis for the accusation of 5,16b[20].

The miracle story contains several elements, as will be set forth in detail under 3.a. Anyhow, the presence of the man who is healed by Jesus makes it into a unit. He appears in 5,5, and nothing is heard of him after 5,15. The use of the adjective ὑγιής in John is confined to this episode (and 7,23); it occurs in 5,6.9.11.14.15[21]. There is a slight break at 5,15/16, because there the man disappears and the Jews and Jesus enter into discussion.

It will be evident from the above that miracle story and quasi-dialogue are rather tightly connected. The same is valid for the relationship of the latter passage and the monologue. The monologue is (at least in its first part, 5,19-30) a reaction of Jesus to the accusation of the Jews in 5,18, that he is making himself equal with God. He defends himself by saying that the Son, in the work of giving life and judging, which the Father delegated to him, does not act of his own accord, but merely does what he sees the Father doing[22]. So there is a clear coherence of quasi-dialogue and monologue. Besides, the monologue is addressed to the Jews, with whom Jesus is already engaged in a dispute.

Yet the monologue is relatively independent from what immediately precedes it, not only because of the difference of literary genre, but also because of a change in terminology[23]. The expressions 'his own Father' and 'making himself equal with God', as well as the verb ἐργάζεσθαι are found in the quasi-dialogue but not in the monologue, where we meet the substantive ἔργα (5,20.36). The combination 'the Father'-'I' occurs in the quasi-dialogue (5,17) and in the second part of the monologue

(5,36.37.43.45), but not in its first part, where we meet the combinations 'the Father'-'the Son' (5,19-23.26) and 'I'-'the one who sent me' (5,24.30).

The monologue itself is made up of two parts (as was indicated above): 5,19-30 and 5,31-47. 5,30 makes up an inclusion with 5,19:

5,19c οὐ δύναται ὁ υἱὸς ποιεῖν ἀφ'ἑαυτοῦ οὐδέν
30a οὐ δύναμαι ἐγὼ ποιεῖν ἀπ'ἐμαυτοῦ οὐδέν

In both instances, the entire verse is about the dependence of the Son upon the Father, in 5,19 in what he *sees*, in 5,30 in what he *hears*[24]. A comparison of the vocabulary used in 5,30 with that used in 5,19-29 and in 5,31-47 makes it obvious that we are dealing here with an *inclusio* and not with a *responsio*[25]: κρίνειν and κρίσις occur only in what precedes, whereas μαρτυρεῖν and μαρτυρία are characteristic of 5,31sqq but do not occur in 5,30. The preposition περί occurs 7 × in 5,31-47; it does not occur in 5,30, where ἀπό is found, as in 5,19. The verb ποιεῖν connects 5,30 with what precedes: it occurs 7 × in 5,19-29, once in 5,31-47 (5,36). Over against all these obvious links is only the use of the 1st pers. sg. in verbal forms and personal pronouns (esp. ἐμαυτοῦ; within John 5, only found in 5,30.31): in 5,19-29, the 1st pers. sg. occurs only in 5,24 (and in the Amen-formulae 5,19.24.25), but it is used very frequently in 5,31-47.

A second argument for the unity of 5,19-30 is the coherence of the vocabulary used in this part[26], about which a few things have been noted above. Within John 5, the combinations 'the Father'-'the Son' and 'I'-'the one who sent me' occur only in this part (in 5,23b, a transition is made from one combination to the other). The word υἱός is not found in John 5 outside this section; it occurs not only in the combination just mentioned, but also in ὁ υἱὸς τοῦ θεοῦ (5,25) and υἱὸς ἀνθρώπου (5,27). Two other combinations, related to each other, which are characteristic of the passage under consideration and which do not occur elsewhere in John 5, are 'life' over against 'judgment' (5,21-22.24.26-27.29), and 'life' over against 'death' (5,21.24.25.28-29). Strikingly, we meet the substantive κρίσις 5 × in 5,19-30 (5,22.24.27.29.30), and the verb κρίνειν twice (5,22.30); these 7 mentions of 'judgment' are balanced by 7 mentions of the gift of life, distributed in exactly the same way: 5 × the substantive ζωή (5,24*bis*.26*bis*.29), twice the verb ζῳοποιεῖν (5,21*bis*; the verb ζῆν occurs in 5,25, and the substantive ζωή further on, in 5,39.40). In 5,19-30, Jesus speaks about himself in the 3rd pers. sg., with the exception of 5,24.30 and the Amen-formulae. He hardly addresses his public directly (only in 5,20.28, and in the Amen-formulae).

The second part of the monologue is 5,31-47[27]. Several features make it into a unit. Jesus refers to himself almost exclusively by verbal forms and personal and possessive pronouns of the 1st pers. sg. (the only exception is found in 5,38bc), and frequently he addresses his public directly in the 2nd pers. pl. Both features distinguish this part from the preceding one. The words μαρτυρεῖν and μαρτυρία frequently occur in 5,31-39 (7 × and 4 × respectively); after these, the *Stichwort* δόξα appears (5,41-44), about which Jesus speaks in a way which makes one think of the way he spoke earlier about μαρτυρία (cfr. 5,41 with 5,34a). The words περὶ ἐμοῦ, occurring 6 × in 5,31-39 in the combination μαρτυρεῖν περὶ ἐμοῦ, return in 5,46. From 5,38 onward, πιστεύειν with its equivalents ἔρχεσθαι πρός (5,40; cfr. 6,35; 7,37-38) and λαμβάνειν with a personal object (5,43; cfr. 1,12 and 17,8) serves as a *Stichwort*[28]. The series of witnesses 5,31-40 ends with the Scriptures as witnessing on behalf of Jesus; this theme recurs in 5,45-47, where Moses and his writings are adduced as pointing to Jesus[29]. Although 5,31-47 seems to be somewhat less homogeneous than 5,19-30, there is much to make it into a unit.

We meet, then, in John 5 the typically Johannine sequence of narration, dialogue and monologue, which has been detected by Dodd in the episodes which, according to him, make up the first part of the Fourth Gospel (as far as ch. 12 inclusive): 2,1-4,42; 4,46-5,47; 6; 7-8; 9,1-10,39; 11,1-53; 12,1-36; Dodd detects it in John 13-20 as well, where, however, the sequence of narration and discourse has been reversed[30]. He describes this pattern as follows: 'The unit of structure is the single episode composed of narrative and discourse, both related to a single dominant theme. The incidents narrated receive an interpretation of their evangelical significance in the discourses; or, to put it otherwise, the truths enunciated in the discourses are given dramatic expression in the actions described.... The episodes are constructed upon a common pattern, subject to endless variations. Each of them tends to move from narrative, through dialogue, to monologue, or at least to a form of dialogue in which comparatively long speeches are allotted to the chief Speaker. Most of them have an epilogue or appendix...'[31]. It is evident in John 5 that quasi-dialogue and monologue give an interpretation of the narration. In the narration Jesus heals a man, he restores him to life[32], and by that action (not only because of the command 5,8; cfr. 5,16; 7,23) he violates the Sabbath law[33]. In quasi-dialogue and monologue, his work of healing on the Sabbath turns out to be a work such as his Father performs; it is a sign of the work of making alive which the Son performs in dependence upon and in unity with the Father. These pretensions are legitimated by adducing witnesses who, however, do not convince the Jews[34].

From the above, it will be clear that both the healing and Jesus' infraction of the Sabbath law are the materials to be interpreted. Dodd's view that the dialogue starts as early as 5,10[35] does not seem correct. The interpreting dialogue, which reveals the 'evangelical significance' of the previous action, takes place only in the confrontation of Jesus and the Jews from 5,16 onward. As the interpreting monologue is a monologue of Jesus in all Johannine instances of the sequence of narration, dialogue and monologue adduced by Dodd, one might expect that the dialogue leading up to it is a dialogue of Jesus with others; such a dialogue is obviously found in 3,1sqq; 4,7sqq; 6,25sqq; 7-8; 11; 13-16.

John 5 is, then, made up of a narration and a monologue which are connected by means of a short quasi-dialogue. A sharp separation between narration and quasi-dialogue cannot be made: 5,16 seems to belong to both. The monologue has two parts: 5,19-30 and 5,31-47[36].

In Table III, the numbers of S and W are given for the sections of John 5. In this table, 5,16-18 is considered to constitute the quasi-dialogue.

Table III.	John 5	syllables	words
5,1-15	narration	464	222
16-18	quasi-dialogue	111	52
19a	introduction to monologue	15	7
19b-30	monologue — 1st part	474	247
31-47	monologue — 2nd part	555/1029/1155/1619	261/515/567/789

The above table contains several numbers of a symmetrical structure: 464 S or 222 W for 5,1-15, 111 S for 5,16-18, 474 S for 5,19b-30, 555 S for 5,31-47, 515 W for 5,19-47.

In numbers of S, the second part of the monologue (5,31-47) is five times as long as the quasi-dialogue (5,16-18; cfr. Jesus' speaking about himself in the 1st pers. sg. in these two sections): 111 and 555 S respectively. Quasi-dialogue and first part of the monologue together (5,16-30) amount to 600 S. The sum total of 1155 for the number of S of the entire interpreting part (5,16-47) is interesting: it is the product of the successive prime numbers 3, 5, 7 and 11. 1029, the number of S of the monologue 5,19b-47, is 3×7^3.

As for the numbers of W: it is striking that both the sum total of the interpreting part (5,16-47) and the sum total of the entire episode, 567 and 789 respectively, display an ascending sequence of figures: 5-6-7 and 7-8-9[37].

So far, the division of John 5 into narration, quasi-dialogue and (bipartite) discourse appears to be discernible also in numbers of S and W. It should be noted that the numbers in Table III suggest that the dialogue 5,16-18 should be connected mainly with the ensuing monologue; it will be shown below, however, that numerical arrangements within 5,1-18 suggest that 5,16-18, or at least 5,16, belongs to what precedes as well. In this way, the connecting function of these verses is at least compatible with numbers of S and W.

The above numbers of W strongly suggest that the numeral in 5,5 has to be counted at three words — which is confirmed by the numerical analysis which follows.

3. *The sections of John 5 separately and their details*

a) *John 5,1-18: healing and controversy*

As the quasi-dialogue 5,16-18 is hardly an independent unit, and as, on the other hand, the monologue 5,19-47 is easily distinguished from the quasi-dialogue, I shall here treat 5,1-18 as a unit — a unit which is made up, of course, of various elements.

The story begins with a description of the situation in which the following scene takes place (5,1-5): Jesus goes up to Jerusalem on the occasion of a 'Festival of the Jews', and in Jerusalem there is a pool where a multitude of invalids is gathered. Among these is a man who has been ill for 38 years. Within this introduction, the first and last verses (5,1.5) are corresponding in so far as there the principal characters of the following story are introduced: Jesus is introduced in 5,1, the crippled man in 5,5. Even the third party, the Jews, is introduced in 5,1, though indirectly: 'there was a Festival of the *Jews*'. In the other two verses (5,2-3), the local setting is described. From a topographical point of view, the first verse stands somewhat apart from what follows, because it describes Jesus' journey *to* Jerusalem — the indication of time 5,1a: 'after these things, there was a Festival of the Jews', serves only as an explanation for his coming —, whereas the following three verses describe a situation *in* Jerusalem[38].

The healing of the crippled man is described in 5,6-9a; it ends with the demonstration of the cure in 5,9a.

In 5,9b, important information is given concerning the healing: it took place on a Sabbath. This information provides the reason for the ensuing scene: the conversation between the Jews and the healed man (5,10-13). The Jews tell the man who is carrying his bed that he is not allowed to do so on a Sabbath, but he refers to the order his healer gave him. The Jews ask him who his healer is; the man is not able to answer to this question, because Jesus has meanwhile disappeared[39].

A new, very brief scene is constituted by 5,14; it is introduced by the indication of time μετὰ ταῦτα, and it distinguishes itself from what precedes by a change of actors (Jesus and the man meet again) and of place (their meeting takes place in the temple). After Jesus' command not to sin any more, we are told in 5,15 that the man goes away and tells the Jews that it was Jesus who cured him. In itself, this verse again consitutes a new scene. However, both the second meeting of Jesus and the man, and the ensuing scene between the man and the Jews, are told most succinctly, so that it seems advisable not to insist too much on the independence of these small scenes. The first one of them merges very smoothly into the second one, by means of the clause: 'the man went away' (5,15). Their main function seems to be to bring Jesus into contact with the Jews and to connect, in this way, the miracle story with the ensuing quasi-dialogue and monologue.

About the quasi-dialogue 5,16-18 and its relationship to what precedes, the necessary comments have been made (see pp. 102-103), in the analysis of the composition of John 5 as a whole[40].

In Table IV, the numbers of S are given for the various parts of 5,1-18 according to the division described above; the first column contains the numbers of the entire text, the second column those of the narrative only, and the third one those of the discourse only.

Table IV. John 5,1-18 syllables

	entire text	narrative	discourse
5,1-5	115	115	
6-9a	143	75	68
9b-13	130	69/144	61/129
14-15	76	51	25
16-18	111/460/575	93/144/403	18/ 43/172

The introduction 5,1-5 has, in numbers of S, a size which is exactly 1/5 of the sum total of 575 S. This proportion of 1:5 may have to do with the mention of 5 porticoes in 5,2. The two main scenes of the story, 5,6-9a and 5,9b-13, have a length of 143 S, = 11 × 13, and 130 S, = 10 × 13, respectively. 5,14-15 contains 76 S, = 2 × 38, which last number occurs in the story itself: the crippled man has been ill for 38 years (5,5)[41].

The quantity of narrative is evenly divided over the story: 144 S, = 12^2, for the narrative in the two main parts (5,6-13), and again 144 S for the narrative in the ensuing brief scenes and the quasi-dialogue (5,14-18). A multiple of 13 appears again in the sum total of S for the narrative: 403 is 31 × 13. As 5,16-18 has 93 S, = 3 × 31, of narrative, there is a proportion of 10:3 between the numbers of S of narrative in 5,1-15 and those in 5,16-18.

Between the size of the discourse in 5,6-13 and that in 5,14-18, there is a proportion of 3:1, as 129 is 3 × 43. The factor 43 can be explained by the addition of the numbers mentioned in the text: 5 porticoes (5,2) and 38 years (5,5).

The factor 43 returns in the sum total of S for 5,1-9a (introduction and miracle story): it has a size of 258 S, = 6 × 43. These are made up of 68 S of discourse, and 190 S of narrative, in which number the factor 19, present in the 38 years of 5,5, returns (190 is also triangular number of 19). 5,10-18 contains 200 S of narrative (not perceptible in Table IV).

In the above, the factor 13 has appeared a few times. From 5,6 onward, the text is made up (up to 5,30 inclusive) of units which measure (multiples of) 13 S:

5,6-7	91 S, =	7 × 13
8-9a	52	4 × 13
9b	13	1 × 13
10-13	117	9 × 13
14-17	130	10 × 13
18-30	546	42 × 13

Table V contains an arrangement of the numbers of W of 5,1-18, in accordance with the division set out earlier, and also in three columns, for the entire text, the narrative only and the discourse only, respectively.

Table V. John 5,1-18 words

	entire text	narrative	discourse
5,1-3	36	36	
5	14/ 50	14/50	
6-9a	68	35	33
9b-13	67/135	35/70	32/65
14-15	37	26	11 (/76)
16	13/ 50	13	
17-18	39/274	31/70/190	8/19

Measured in numbers of W, 5,1-16 displays a well balanced composition. The two main parts (5,6-9a.9b-13) are of almost equal size, 68 and 67 W respectively. The introduction (5,1-5) has a length of 36 + 14 = 50 W, the concluding scenes (5,14-16) measure 37 + 13 = 50 W. 5,1-9 has a size of 125 W, = 5^3 (cfr. the 5 porticoes of 5,2; not perceptible in Table V).

The narrative in 5,1-18 amounts to 190 W; again, the factor 19 appears. Both 5,6-9a and 5,9b-13 contain 35 W of narrative. The 70 W of narrative in 5,6-13 are followed by again 70 W of narrative in 5,14-18.

The corpus of the story (5,6-13) contains 65 W, = 5 × 13, of discourse, divided into 33 W for 5,6-9a, and 32 W for 5,9b-13. Up to 5,15 inclusive, the discourse amounts to 76 W, = 2 × 38; in 5,14-18 there are 19 W of discourse. The discourse of Jesus, the quotations of his words in 5,11.12 included, amounts to 38 W, divided into 19 W in 5,6-13, and again 19 W in 5,14-18 (not perceptible in Table V).

5,9-18 is made up of units containing (multiples of) 13 W:

5,9a	13 W,	= 1 × 13
9b-11	39	3 × 13
12-15	65	5 × 13
16	13	1 × 13
17-18	39	3 × 13

So the entire passage has a size of 169 W, = 13^2. 5,14-15 contains 26 W, = 2 × 13, of narrative.

A division of the sentences of 5,1-18 according to the actors in numbers of W has been given in Table II. It can be observed there that the sentences with other subjects occurring in 5,1-9 amount to 38 W, a number with which the reader will have become conversant in the meantime. In 5,1-18 the sentences with Jesus as actor amount to 77 W, divided according to a proportion of 3:4; 33 W in 5,1-9, and 44 in 5,13-18. The factor 11 appears here. The sentences with the man as actor amount in 5,1-9a to 14 + 27 + 13 = 54 or 2 × 27 W; in 5,9b-15, they amount to again 38 W.

After these remarks concerning 5,1-18 (or 5,1-15 or 5,1-16) as a whole, several details of the text have to be dealt with.

1. In the introduction 5,1-5, the first and last verses are corresponding (see p. 107 above). This leads to an arrangement of numbers of S and W as given in Table VI.

Table VI. John 5,1-5	syllables		words	
5,1	25		11	
2	43		16	
3	20/63		9/25	
5	27/	52/115	14/	25/50

The factor 5, occurring in the narration itself in the 5 porticoes mentioned in 5,2, is fairly conspicuous here: 25 S, = 5^2, in 5,1; 25 W both for 5,1.5 and 5,2-3, 50 W, = 10 × 5, for 5,1-5. The 25 W of 5,2-3 are made up of 16 + 9 W; to put it otherwise, $3^2 + 4^2 = 5^2$. The first and last verses together amount to 52 S, = 4 × 13; apparently, the factor 13 plays its role from the beginning of the story. 5,2 has a size of 43 S, which number is the sum of 5 (porticoes, 5,2) and 38 (years, 5,5; see p. 109 above). The factor 19, prominent in this story, is already found in 5,5, exactly in the part where the number 38 is mentioned:

ἦν δέ τις ἄνθρωπος ἐκεῖ	8 S
τριάκοντα καὶ ὀκτὼ ἔτη ἔχων ἐν τῇ ἀσθενείᾳ αὐτοῦ	19/27

It was observed above (p. 107) that 5,1 stands somewhat apart from what follows. Without this verse, narration and quasi-dialogue (comprising, then, 5,2-18) have a size of 550 S or 263 W. This last number is significant as it is exactly 1/3 of the sum total of 789 W for John 5.

2. In the miracle story itself, we meet several multiples of 9 in the numbers of S. The final sentence of the introduction (5,5) has a length of 27 S, = 3 × 9. 5,6 contains 36 S, = 4 × 9, and the words of the crippled man in 5,7 amount to 45 S, = 5 × 9 (and triangular number of 9). Jesus' powerful word in 5,8 and its effect in 5,9 amount together to 45 S as well. This is also the size of 5,9b-10, the beginning of the next part. 5,6-8, the conversation between Jesus and the man, contains 45 S of narrative.

In this conversation, the factor 11 is prominent. 5,7 has a size of 55 S, 5,8 of 22 S. The three verses amount to 55 W, made up of 22 W of narrative and 33 W of discourse. 5,6-7 contains 44 W, 5,8 contains 11 W.

In 5,6, three actions of Jesus (seeing, knowing, speaking) are described in three successive cola of equal length:

τοῦτον ἰδὼν ὁ Ἰησοῦς κατακείμενον	12 S
καὶ γνοὺς ὅτι πολὺν ἤδη χρόνον ἔχει,	12
λέγει αὐτῷ· θέλεις ὑγιὴς γενέσθαι;	12/36

Jesus' powerful word and its effect (5,8b-9a) are rendered in three cola of 15 S; the wording of 5,9a*b* resembles very much the wording of Jesus' saying in 5,8b[42]:

ἔγειρε ἆρον τὸν κράβαττόν σου καὶ περιπάτει.	15 S
καὶ εὐθέως ἐγένετο ὑγιὴς ὁ ἄνθρωπος	15
καὶ ἦρεν τὸν κράβαττον αὐτοῦ καὶ περιεπάτει.	15/45

3. In 5,9b-13, words of Jesus are quoted by others in 5,11c.12c. These two quotations measure together 12 + 7 = 19 S. Without these quotations, 14 S are put in the mouth of the man (5,11), and twice that quantity, 28 S, in the mouth of the Jews (5,10.12). Including the quotation, the Jews speak in 19 W in 5,10.12 (cfr. Table I).

In this scene, the man's statement in 5,11bc ('the one who cured me, he said to me: Take up your bed and walk') is the centre: it is the middle one of three utterances (in 5,10.11.12), and the main point of the scene is made here, because in these words Jesus' violation of the Sabbath is established. Both numbers of S and of W confirm that this statement is the centre of 5,9b-13. It is preceded by 53 S or 26 W (= 2 × 13) and followed by 51 S or 28 W. When only the discourse is counted, 17 S or 9 W precede, and 18 S or 10 W follow. The statement itself has a size of 13 W or 26 S, = 2 × 13, or exactly 1/5 of the sum total of 130 S for 5,9b-13.

The final sentence of this scene, 5,13, has a size of 27 S, = 3^3; so did the final sentence of the introduction, 5,5.

4. Units of 27 S are also found in 5,16-18. This short quasi-dialogue begins with the information that the Jews were prosecuting Jesus because of his violation of the Sabbath (5,16); then follows Jesus' answer (5,17), in which he legitimates his action: as his Father is at work on the Sabbath, so is he. Both accusation (5,16) and defence (5,17) have a length of 27 S.

In 5,18, two charges are brought against Jesus. The first one (5,18b) takes up the violation of the Sabbath from 5,16. The second one is, that he calls God his own Father (5,18c*a*), whereby 5,17 is taken up. From the point of view of the Jews, his crime is not only that he breaks the Sabbath, but also that he does so with an appeal to God as his Father. In that way, he claims for himself the same prerogatives as the Father possesses, as is made evident in 5,18c*b*: 'making himself equal with God'. He who breaks the Sabbath and does so with the argument that he is at work as his Father is, makes himself equal with God[43]. So, 5,18bc*a* combines 5,16 and 5,17; it also has a size of 27 S, which are preceded by 20 S in 5,18a and are followed by 10 S in 5,18c*b*. The entire verse 5,18 has, moreover, a length of 27 W, or 57 S, = 3 × 19.

Out of the 27 S of 5,17, 2/3 or 18 S are used for Jesus' statement 5,17b. They are arranged as follows:

ὁ πατήρ μου ἕως ἄρτι ἐργάζεται	12 S
κἀγὼ ἐργάζομαι	6/18

The proportion of 2:1 between the two clauses, about the work of the Father and that of Jesus respectively, may be a way to convey or to confirm both the unity of Father and Son (5,21-23; 10,30) and the dependence of the Son upon the Father (5,19; 14,28).

Jesus' saying in 5,17 states very succinctly the theme of at least the first part of the ensuing discourse: in his work, the Son is one with the Father and at the same time dependent upon him. In this way, it serves more or less as a title for the monologue which follows[44]. This saying is preceded by 500 S (= 5,1-17a), and followed by 1101 S (= 5,18-47).

b) *John 5,19-30: Jesus' defence, first part*

The best way to investigate the composition of John 5,19-30 is to start with noting the evident similarities which are present in the text[45]:

1. The formula ἀμὴν ἀμὴν λέγω ὑμῖν occurs three times: 5,19.24.25.
2. There is close similarity between 5,19 and 5,30 (see above, p. 104).
3. The verb θαυμάζειν occurs twice in the 2nd pers. pl. pres.: in 5,20 at the end, and in 5,28 at the beginning, the first time connected with 'greater works', in which 'raising the dead' is comprised (cfr. 5,21), the second time in a direct connection with the rising of the dead[46].
4. 5,21 and 5,26 display remarkable similarity:

21	ὥσπερ γὰρ ὁ πατήρ ...	26	ὥσπερ γὰρ ὁ πατήρ
	ζῳοποιεῖ		ἔχει ζωήν ...
	οὕτως καὶ ὁ υἱός ...		οὕτως καὶ τῷ υἱῷ ...
	ζῳοποιεῖ		ζωὴν ἔχειν ...

The similarity becomes even more striking as soon as it is seen that ὥσπερ occurs in John only in 5,21.26; elsewhere he uses καθώς (31 × ; combined with οὕτως 3,14; 12,50; 14,31; 15,4) or ὡς (13 × ; combined with οὕτως 7,46 *l.v.*).

5. There is also similarity between 5,22 and 5,27:

22 ἀλλὰ τὴν κρίσιν πᾶσαν δέδωκεν τῷ υἱῷ
27 καὶ ἐξουσίαν ἔδωκεν αὐτῷ κρίσιν ποιεῖν

6. Because of similarities 4. and 5., the larger units 5,21-23 and 5,26-27 are similar[47]: in both passages, the granting of life or possession of life in themselves of Father and Son, and their judgment are dealt with successively. In 5,23, a final clause (completed by an antithetically parallel main clause) follows, to motivate the delegation of the power to judge, and in 5,27 a causal clause follows (cfr. for the combination of 'life' and 'judgment' 3,16.17; 5,24.29; 12,47).
7. 5,24 and 5,25 are similar (apart from the Amen-formula)[48]:

24	(cfr. ἐκ τοῦ θανάτου)	25	οἱ νεκροί
	ὁ τὸν λόγον μου ἀκούων ...		ἀκούσουσιν τῆς φωνῆς τοῦ υἱοῦ τοῦ θεοῦ
			καὶ οἱ ἀκούσαντες
	ἔχει ζωὴν αἰώνιον ...		ζήσουσιν
	μεταβέβηκεν ... εἰς τὴν ζωήν		

8. 5,25 and 5,28-29 display similarity[49]:

25	ἔρχεται ὥρα ...	28-29	ἔρχεται ὥρα
	ὅτε οἱ νεκροί		ἐν ᾗ πάντες οἱ ἐν τοῖς μνημείοις
	ἀκούσουσιν τῆς φωνῆς τοῦ υἱοῦ τοῦ θεοῦ		ἀκούσουσιν τῆς φωνῆς αὐτοῦ (i.e., of the Son of Man) ...
	καὶ οἱ ἀκούσαντες		
	ζήσουσιν		εἰς ἀνάστασιν ζωῆς ...

X. Léon-Dufour[50] arrives at a description of the composition of 5,19-30 using observations 2., 4. and 8. from the above series, and combining with these two other observations:

a. 5,26 and 5,27 belong together, as do 5,28 and 5,29 — an observation which is in itself correct.

b. 5,20 corresponds to 5,22-23, because of the identity of subject and the ἵνα-clauses in both parts — an observation which is less correct, as the identity of subject does not apply to 5,23, and the same subject also occurs in 5,21a.26.27a, and as the presence of the conjunction ἵνα both in 5,20 and 5,23 is not in itself significant.

According to Léon-Dufour, the literary structure of John 5,19-30 is as follows:

a. 5,24 is, between 5,19.30, the centre of a chiasm.

b. Within this chiasm, there are two smaller chiasms: 5,20-23, with 5,21 as its centre, and 5,25-29, with 5,26-27 as its centre; moreover, the two centres 5,21 and 5,26-27 are corresponding.

There are two major objections against this plan. Firstly, similarities 1., 3., 6. and 7. from the above series are not integrated in it. Secondly, it is rather strange that 5,21, dealing only with raising the dead and giving them life, corresponds to 5,26-27, dealing with having life and judging, whereas in the case of 5,21, too, the next sentence (5,22) is about judging. Moreover, the term 'chiasm' is not appropriate here, as there is no a-b-b'-a'-structure; one should speak here of 'concentric symmetry'.

A. Vanhoye arrives at a simpler scheme for John 5,19-30, integrating all of the above similarities, except 8.; the passage displays a pattern of concentric symmetry[51]:

a 5,19							a' 30	(2.)
	b 20					b' 28-29		(3.)
		c 21-23			c' 26-27			(4., 5., 6.)
			d 24	d' 25				(1., 7.)

The figures between brackets indicate the similarities on which the correspondences are based. The Amen-formula in 5,24 does not only correspond to the one in 5,25, but also to the one in 5,19, marking in that way the end of the first half of the concentric structure[52].

The concentric symmetry is tempered here and there by parallel symmetry[53]: both halves (5,19-24 and 5,25-30) end with a sentence in which Jesus speaks about himself in the 1st pers. sg., after having done so in the 3rd pers. sg. (except in the Amen-formulae, of course). 5,21-23 and 5,26-27 deal both successively with life and judgment, and with the Father and the Son.

In Table VII, the numbers of S are given for the elements of John 5,19-30, according to the structure described above.

Table VII. John 5, 19b-30 syllables

5,19b-e	a	54				
20	b		42			
21-23	c			93		
24	d				59	
25	d'				46/105	
26-27	c'			54/		147/252
28-29	b'		70/			112
30	a'	56/				110/222/474

The sum totals of elements b + b', c + c' and d + d' are, all of them, multiples of 7; so is element a' alone (56 is also a rectangular number: 8 × 7). Moreover, the sum total of elements b + b', 112 (= 16 × 7), is made up of two multiples of 7 (42 and 70; 42 is a rectangular number: 6 × 7); the sum total of elements c + c', 147 (= 21 × 7), is 3×7^2, and the sum total of elements d + d', 105 (= 15 × 7), is triangular number of 14, = 2 × 7. So, in all three sum totals the number 7 plays a role in two ways. The two exterior elements, a and a', amount together to 110 S (a rectangular number: 10 × 11; cfr. the role of the number 11 in the numbers of W of this passage, described below).

The number of S of the four exterior elements together (a, b, b' and a') as well as that of the four interior elements together (c, d, d' and c') are numbers of a symmetrical structure: 222 and 252 S respectively. Such a division seems justified by the remarkable correspondence between ἵνα ὑμεῖς θαυμάζητε in 5,20, at the end of element b, and μὴ θαυμάζετε τοῦτο in 5,28, at the beginning of the corresponding element b'; here only, we meet in this passage the verb θαυμάζειν and (outside the Amen-formulae) the 2nd. pers. pl.

Syllable-count has been applied to smaller sections of 5,19-30 as well, also in connection with the preceding quasi-dialogue:

1. In 5,19b-23 (= a + b + c), Jesus is speaking about himself in the 3rd pers., and no asyndeta are found within the passage (with the exception of 5,23b; this sentence, however, is connected with the preceding one by means of *Stichwörter* and a relationship of antithetic parallelism). The connection of 5,23 and 5,24 is asyndetic, and in 5,24 Jesus is speaking about himself in the 1st pers. sg.[54]; moreover, the Amen-formula marks off this verse from what precedes. 5,19b-23 has a length of 189 S, = 7 × 27, made up of three multiples of 9 S: 54 S for 5,19b-e, 72 for 5,20-21, and 63 for 5,22-23; or, somewhat differently, of 126 S, = 2 × 63, for 5,19-21, and 63 for 5,22-23. The importance of the factor 7 in 5,19-30 has already been pointed out; it is present in 63, = 7 × 9. The number 27 appeared to be

important in 5,1-18 (esp. in 5,16-18, see p. 112 above), and is so in 5,19-30 as well, as will be shown later.

The sum total of S of 5,26-30 (= c' + b' + a') is also a multiple of 9: 180, made up of 54 S, = 6 × 9, in 5,26-27, and once again 126, = 14 × 9, in 5,28-30; these three verses have a size of 63 W.

2. 5,19-23 is the part of the monologue in which Jesus answers the accusation from the dialogue, that he is making himself equal with God (5,18): here, the relationship of the Father and the Son is dealt with directly, whereas this is no more the case in 5,24-25. Together with the preceding quasi-dialogue 5,16-18, this passage has a length of 315 S, = 5 × 7 × 9 (15 S in the clause introducing direct discourse 5,19a; 111 + 189 = 300 S for 5,16-18.19b-23).

5,19-20 is the immediate answer to the accusation, in so far as the sequel, 5,21-23, only states in which respect the Father shows everything he does to the Son, viz., regarding the raising of the dead and the judgment. It is not astonishing, then, that 5,19-20 has the same length as the quasi-dialogue 5,16-18: 111 S.

3. 5,25-27, also a passage within which asyndeta do not occur, whereas they are found between 5,24 and 5,25, and between 5,27 and 5,28, has a length of 100 S[55].

In Table VIII, the same is done as in Table VII, but now in numbers of W.

Table VIII. John 5,19b-30

		words a				b
5,19b-e	a	30				30
20	b		22			22
21-23	c			50		50
24	d				31	31/133
25	d'				24/55	24
26-27	c'			27/	77	27
28-29	b'		33/		55	33
30	a'	30/			60/247	30/114/247

As in the numbers of S, the sum totals of numbers of W for elements b + b', c + c' and d + d' are related: they are multiples of 11. Besides, elements b + b' and d + d' are of equal length: 55 W (55 is triangular number of 10). Elements b and b' are in themselves also multiples of 11. Element c measures a round number of W (50), and in element c' the number 27 appears again. As in the numbers of S, the relationship of elements a and a' is of a different kind: they are of equal size, 30 W (see Table VIIIa).

The first half of the passage (5,19b-24) has a length of 133 W, = 7 × 19, the second half of 114 W, = 6 × 19; together, 13 × 19. Once again, the factors 13 and 19 appear (see Table VIIIb). The passage 5,19b-30 opens with a sentence of 19 W beginning with an Amen-formula (5,19bc); there follow two sections of 114 W, = 6 × 19 (5,19d-24.25-30). The first one of these ends with an Amen-saying (5,24), the second one begins with such a saying (5,25). 5,25 from ἔρχεται onward has a size of 19 W, as does 5,26b-27 (cfr. the punctuation in the edition of B. Weiss, where only a comma is put between 5,26 and 5,27).

The numbers of W for the elements of the second half of the passage are the multiples of 3 from 24 up to 33 inclusive: 24, 27, 33 and 30. The first and third element of these four together (d' + b') are as long as the second and fourth element together (c' + a'): 57 W. This corresponds to the similarity, noted at the beginning of the present section under nr. 8., between 5,25 and 5,28-29. The two other elements, c' and a' (5,26-27.30), deal with the relationship of the Father and the Son.

Several details from John 5,19-30 deserve our attention:

1. 5,19b-e has a length of 54 S, = 2 × 27, 27 out of which are in 5,19c. The number 27 already appeared in the numbers of S of 5,16-18. A numerical *concatenatio* seems present here (cfr. p. 196 below). In numbers of W as well, 5,19c takes up half the number of 5,19b-e as a whole: 15 out of 30 W. 5,19de has a size of 19 S, and 5,19bc uses 19 W. 5,19b-20 amounts to 52 W, = 4 × 13.

2. 5,21-23[56], measuring 50 W, is made up of four disticha. In three of these, the two stichoi are parallel. The second distichon, however, is of a chiastic pattern: the Father — does not judge — the judgment — to the Son. The first and second distichon deal with the relationship of the Father and the Son as to the delegation of the power of granting life and judging, the third and fourth distichon deal with the honour which is due to the Son as it is due to the Father. Here, the verb τιμᾶν occurs in all four stichoi, always followed by its object, in the first two stichoi without negation, in the last two with a negation:

			syll.	words
21	a	ὥσπερ γὰρ ὁ πατὴρ ἐγείρει τοὺς νεκροὺς καὶ ζῳοποιεῖ	17	9
	b	οὕτως καὶ ὁ υἱὸς οὓς θέλει ζῳοποιεῖ	13	7
22	a'	οὐδὲ γὰρ ὁ πατὴρ κρίνει οὐδένα	11	6/ 15
	b'	ἀλλὰ τὴν κρίσιν πᾶσαν δέδωκεν τῷ υἱῷ	13/54	7/14
23	c	ἵνα πάντες τιμῶσι τὸν υἱόν	10	5
	d	καθὼς τιμῶσι τὸν πατέρα	9/19	4
	c'	ὁ μὴ τιμῶν τὸν υἱόν	7	5/10
	d'	οὐ τιμᾷ τὸν πατέρα τὸν πέμψαντα αὐτόν	13/20	7/ 11

The first two disticha together amount to 54 S, = 2 × 27, just as 5,19b-e, and 5,26-27. The last two disticha are of almost equal length: 19 and 20 S.

Besides, Father and Son are mentioned alternately, with a turning point between 5,22 and 5,23:

a Father d' Father
b Son c' Son
a' Father d Father
b' Son - c Son

Stichoi b and b' are of equal length: 7 W or 13 S. The length in numbers of W of stichoi b and b' together is that of stichoi a and a' together, less one: 14 and 15 W respectively. Similarly for stichoi c and c', dealing with the Son as do stichoi b and b': both have a length of 5 W, together 10, whereas stichoi d and d' together have a size of 11 W.

3. 5,24 contains, without the introductory formula ἀμὴν ... ὅτι, 49 S, $= 7^2$, or 26 W. The verse is made up of two halves of 25 and 24 S (17 + 8 and 8 + 16 respectively), or 13 and 13 W:

	syll.	words
ὁ τὸν λόγον μου ἀκούων καὶ πιστεύων τῷ πέμψαντί με	17	10
ἔχει ζωὴν αἰώνιον	8/25	3/13
καὶ εἰς κρίσιν οὐκ ἔρχεται	8	5
ἀλλὰ μεταβέβηκεν ἐκ τοῦ θανάτου εἰς τὴν ζωήν	16/24/49	8/13/26

5,24 is marked off from the text preceding and following it, because in this verse Jesus speaks about himself in the 1st pers. sg., whereas he does so in 5,19-23.25-29 in the 3rd pers. sg.[57]. This probably has to do with the fact that this verse is the centre of John 5, measured in numbers of S: 5,1-23 has a length of 779 S, 5,25-47 of 781 S. It is possible to go even further: the words ἔχει ζωὴν αἰώνιον in 5,24 are the centre of John 5: they are preceded by 806 S and followed by 805 S. This is not astonishing: the Fourth Gospel has been written in order that believers 'may have life' (20,31).

4. 5,25 contains, just as 5,24, a square number of S without the introductory formula ἀμὴν ... ὅτι: 36 S, $= 6^2$ (and triangular number of 8). These are made up of 9 S for the clause ἔρχεται ... ἐστιν, and 27 S (a number more often found in numbers of S and W in John 5) for the ὅτε-clause. This clause displays concentric symmetry: it begins with οἱ νεκροὶ ἀκούσουσιν, and ends with καὶ οἱ ἀκούσαντες ζήσουσιν[58]. So, the words τῆς φωνῆς τοῦ υἱοῦ τοῦ θεοῦ are in the centre. They have a length of 9 S or 6 W, and are preceded and followed by 9 S or 4 W.

5. 5,26-27 has a size of 54 S, $= 2 \times 27$, or 27 W. 5,26 is made up of $14 + 17 = 31$ S; the corresponding verse 5,21 (also about 'life') is made up of $17 + 13 = 30$ S.

6. 5,28-29 starts with a short main clause of 7 S, being 1/10 of a sum total of 70 S. The ὅτι-clause is made up of two parts: firstly, it is said in 32 S that an hour is coming in which all those who are in the tombs will hear the voice of the Son of Man and will come forth, and secondly, in 31 S the good and the wicked are distinguished, together with the resurrection of life or of judgment. This second part is made up of two antithetically parallel clauses[59], of 16 and 15 S, or 7 and 7 W respectively.

It is also possible, of course, to make a break in 5,28-29 at the end of 5,28, and to start the second part with καὶ ἐκπορεύσονται[60]. The numbers of S, however, suggest the former division.

7. 5,30 begins with two clauses which are antithetically parallel as for their content (5,30ab), and then a further specification is given of the second member of the parallelism (5,30cd):

		syll.	words
a	οὐ δύναμαι ἐγὼ ποιεῖν ἀπ'ἐμαυτοῦ οὐδέν	14	7
b	καθὼς ἀκούω κρίνω	7	3/10
c	καὶ ἡ κρίσις ἡ ἐμὴ δικαία ἐστίν	12	7
d	ὅτι οὐ ζητῶ τὸ θέλημα τὸ ἐμόν	12	7
	ἀλλὰ τὸ θέλημα τοῦ πέμψαντός με	11/35/42/56	6/20/30

In numbers of S, 5,30a is twice as long as 5,30b. 5,30b and its specification together are three times as long as 5,30a. The numbers of S of 5,30a.b.c + d are, all of them, multiples of 7: 14, 7 and 35. In numbers of W, we meet three cola of 7 W (5,30a.c.d*a*; cfr. the role of the factor 7 in the numbers of S of 5,19-30, see p. 115 above). The specification 5,30cd (its last two cola are antithetically parallel[61]) is made up of cola of 12, 12 and 11 S, or 7, 7 and 6 W. The specification is, in numbers of W, twice as long as the preceding parallelism: 20 and 10 W respectively.

c) *John 5,31-47: Jesus' defence, second part*

The first part of the passage John 5,31-47, viz., 5,31-40, constitutes a coherent whole because of the *Stichwörter* μαρτυρεῖν (5,31.32*bis*. 33.36.37.39) and μαρτυρία (5,31.32.34.36). To justify the pretensions put forward in 5,19-30, Jesus sums up a number of witnesses testifying on his behalf[62]. Although neither of the *Stichwörter* just mentioned is used in 5,40, this verse belongs to what precedes: the Jews suppose they possess eternal life in the Scriptures, and these Scriptures testify on behalf of Jesus (5,39); and yet[63] they are not willing to come to him in order to have life. The expression ζωὴν ἔχειν refers back to 5,39b, and is not used any more in what follows (5,41-47).

5,31-40 is made up of several smaller units[64]:

a. In 5,31-32, Jesus states the general principle that a testimony of him about himself is not valid, but that another one testifies on his behalf, whose testimony is — as Jesus knows — valid.

b. In 5,33-35, Jesus is directly addressing the Jews; he speaks about John the Baptist's testimony and its (relative) value.

c. In 5,36a, Jesus puts over against John's testimony the 'greater testimony', consisting primarily, according to 5,36bc, in the works the Father has given him.

d. Finally, in 5,37-40 the testimony of the Father in the Scriptures is dealt with. 5,36a probably refers to 5,36bc as well as to 5, 37-40[65].

In the series of specific testimonies 5,33-40, a (weak) inclusion is perceptible, constituted by ἵνα ὑμεῖς σωθῆτε (5,34) in the passage about the first testimony, the Baptist's; and ἵνα ζωὴν ἔχητε (5,40) in the passage about the last one, that of the Father in the Scriptures ('being saved' and 'to have life' are practically equivalent in John, see 3,16-17; 10,9-10). In each of the three testimonies the verb ἀποστέλλειν occurs once, although with different subjects and objects (5,33.36.38).

It is supposed, in the above division of 5,31-40 into units, that not only 5,39-40, but also 5,37-38 concerns the Father's testimony in the Scriptures. This assertion needs some proof.

First of all, the perfect μεμαρτύρηκεν (5,37a) as an expression of the 'continuance of what has been completed'[66], makes one think of God's testimony as recorded in the Scriptures, a testimony which has been completed and is still valid[67]. This interpretation is confirmed by the other texts in John where this perfect is used (1,34; 3,26; 5,33: the testimony of the Baptist; 19,35: the testimony of the eye-witness, on which the evangelist's record about the blood and water flowing from Jesus' side has been based)[68]; the present tense is used, on the other hand, to indicate God's witnessing in or during Jesus' ministry (5,31-32; 8,18).

Moreover, it is important to see that the testimonies on behalf of Jesus, summed up in 5,31-40, are addressed to the Jews, who reject Jesus as the one sent by God, and that all testimonies are, for that reason, perceptible facts (although these can be interpreted differently): John the Baptist, Jesus' works, the Scriptures. In this context, it would be difficult to consider the testimony of the Father as an internal testimony, in the heart of the believer[69], or something to that effect. For the same reason, a reference to God's testimony at the baptism of Jesus (1,33)[70] is probably not meant: in the Fourth Gospel, this testimony is not described as a public event, but as a testimony directed to the Baptist alone.

The solution that 5,37a refers to the testimony of the Father in Jesus' works[71] — in which case καί 5,37a has an epexegetical function —, does not take into account the difference in tense between the present μαρτυρεῖ and the perfect μεμαρτύρηκεν. A present tense would be expected in 5,37a, when the clause refers to the Father's testimony in Jesus' works (cfr. also 8,18, and esp. 14,10: 'The Father, abiding in me, performs his works'). Besides, in this interpretation 5,37a says only somewhat more explicitly what was already said implicitly in 5,36: the works, given to Jesus by the Father, testify that the Father sent him (5,36); the Father has testified in the works (5,37a).

So it seems, that 5,37a is about the testimony of the Father, completed and still valid (cfr. the perfect tense), which reaches the Jews in its written form: the Scriptures; these bear now witness on Jesus' behalf (cfr. the present tense μαρτυροῦσαι 5,39).

The next sentence, 5,37b-38, refers to the Jewish reaction to God's testimony in the Scriptures. It contains three denials: the Jews never heard God's voice or saw his form, and do not have his word abiding in them. The ὅτι-clause 5,38b is either an explanation, or it gives the reason why the preceding statements are known to be true [72]: either 'because you do not believe the one he sent' or 'as appears from the fact that you do not believe the one he sent'. The three denials 5,37b-38a have a reproachful character, in so far as the things that are denied here to the incredulous Jews are said to be valid of believing Christians elsewhere in John and in 1 John (see, e.g., John 8,47; 14,24; 12,45; 14,7.9; 8,31; 1 John 2,14). The three denials refer to at least two and probably three things, on which the Jews could pride themselves on the basis of the Scriptures, things that were concerned with the theophany on Mount Sinai and the gift of the Law. The best parallel in this respect to John 5,37b-38a is, as far as I know, Sir 17,13-14, where it is said about Israel at Mount Sinai:

> 'Their eyes saw his glorious majesty,
> and their ears heard the glory of his voice.
> He said to them, "Guard against all wrongdoing",
> and he taught each man his duty towards his neighbour'.

Parallel texts from the OT and later Jewish literature can be adduced for each one of the three denials separately as well, to show that Jewish prerogatives are denied here. The conviction that Israel heard God's voice at Mount Sinai emerges from, e.g., Exod 19,9; Deut 4,33.36; Neh 9,3; Josephus, *Ant.* 3,90. That Israel saw God's form at Mount Sinai, is denied in Exod 19,21, and emphatically in Deut 4,12.15. Another tradition, however, is present in the OT and in later Jewish literature, according to which Israel saw God at Mount Sinai; it is found in Exod 19,11 (cfr. Deut 5,4), and in the comment on this verse in Mek. Exod 19,11

(Bachodesh, 3): 'This teaches that at that moment the people saw what Isaiah and Ezekiel never saw. For it is said: ''And by the ministry of the prophets have I used similitudes'' (Hos 12,11)'[73]. The same text from Hosea is quoted in Mek. Exod 15,2 (Shirata, 3), in a similar framework: 'Whence you can say that a maid-servant saw at the sea what Isaiah and Ezekiel and all the prophets never saw? It says about them', follows Hos 12,11. Here R. Eliezer, ± 90, is mentioned as authority; it seems, then, that the conviction that Israel saw God at Mount Sinai was alive at the time the Fourth Gospel was composed. The third denial concerns the Jewish claim to possess God's word(s), God's Law; this claim can be illustrated from, e.g., Deut 6,6; 30,14; from the idea, found in wisdom literature, that Wisdom, identified with the Law, chooses herself a dwelling-place in Israel (Sir 24,11-12, cfr. 24,23; Bar 3,37-4,4), and from later texts such as 4 Ezra 5,27; syBar 48,22-24[74].

Apparently, in John 5,37b-38a three things are denied on which the Jews could pride themselves on the basis of the Scriptures (cfr. the denial of their descendance from Abraham in 8,39-41). It is possible, of course, to read 5,37b as a simple statement of fact and not as a denial of claims. 5,38a is, however, an evident denial of a Jewish claim, and the three clauses of 5,37b-38a are obviously parallel; moreover, in the present context 5,37b is hardly functional as a simple statement of fact, but it is so indeed as a denial of prerogatives claimed by the Jews.

These Jews make their claims not only for the Israel of the past, but at least also for themselves: Sinai-theophany and gift of the Law are conceived of as realities, in which the present generation is sharing and which are considered as a permanent possession (cfr. the perfect tenses in 5,37b and τὸν λόγον ... μένοντα in 5,38a). This conception of the Sinai-events as a present reality is to be explained as follows. Those who are present at a liturgical reading of the biblical account of the Exodus can identify themselves with the Israel of former times. This identification is already found in the OT, e.g. in Josh 24,5-7, where, in an account of the Exodus, we find alternately 'your fathers' and 'you'. It is also present in Josephus' rendering of the Passover laws (*Ant* 3,248: 'In this month we were delivered from bondage to the Egyptians', '... the ... sacrifice which ... we offered then on departure from Egypt'[75]). It is most evident in parts of the Passover Haggadah[76]. We meet the identification there in the Father's answer to the question of the youngest child: 'Why does this night differ from all other nights?', in which Deut 6,21 is quoted: 'We were Pharaoh's slaves in Egypt'; we meet it in the passage about the four sons, where Exod 13,8.14 are quoted, and in the midrash on Deut 26,5-8. The identification is especially evident in the *Dayyenu*-hymn:

'Had he given us the Sabbath, but not brought us to Mount Sinai, we should have been content!
Had he brought us to Mount Sinai, but not given us the Torah, we should have been content!
Had he given us the Torah, but not brought us into the Land of Israel, we should have been content!'
The theory behind this identification is stated in the following passage: 'In every generation let each man look on himself as if he came forth out of Egypt. As it is said (follows Exod 13,8). It was not only our Fathers that the Holy One, blessed be he, redeemed, but us as well did he redeem along with them. As it is said (follows Deut 6,23)' (cfr. m. Pesaḥ. 10,5).

In the texts quoted we meet the idea that in the liturgical assembly later generations can share in, be present at the events of the Exodus and the gift of the Law[77]. In this light, John 5,37b-38 is interpreted as follows: because of their liturgy, the Jews imagine to have a share in the Sinai-theophany and the gift of the Law, but Jesus denies them this prerogative, because they do not believe him, or: as appears from the fact that they do not believe him[78].

So there is adequate reason to suppose that not only 5,39-40, but also 5,37-38 refers to God's testimony in the OT.

5,41-47, the second part of 5,31-47, is characterized frequently as an explanation of the Jewish unbelief[79]. Such a characteristic is possible for 5,41-44: the Jews cannot accept Jesus, because they do not have the love of God in themselves and are only interested in human honour, and exactly on that point they are opposed to Jesus, who does not accept human praise, does not come in his own name. It will be evident from the content of the explanation, that it is at the same time an accusation[80]. Formally, 5,41-44 is a unit because of the *Stichwörter* δόξα (5,41.44*bis*) and λαμβάνειν (5,41.43*bis*.44).

5,45-47 is marked off from what precedes, because now Moses appears as the accuser of the Jews. Here, the explanation is even more obviously at the same time an accusation: their unbelief directed against Jesus is reduced to their unbelief towards Moses. The twofold mention of Moses (5,45b.46a), and the references to him in 5,46c.47a by means of pronouns make this passage formally into a unit[81].

The passage 5,45-47 is referring back to 5,37-40, because Moses is presented here as one who wrote about Jesus (5,46); in a comparable way the testimony of the Father, of which the Scriptures are the written form, has been put forward in 5,37-40[82]. The following elements are corresponding in the two passages:

1. 'Εκεῖνος μεμαρτύρηκεν περὶ ἐμοῦ (5,37) and αἱ μαρτυροῦσαι περὶ ἐμοῦ (5,39) to περὶ γὰρ ἐμοῦ ἐκεῖνος ἔγραφεν (5,46).

2. Τὸν λόγον αὐτοῦ (5,38) to τοῖς ἐμοῖς ῥήμασιν (5,47; in 5,38 it is implied that whoever believes Jesus has God's word abiding in himself, and the same is said about Jesus' words in 15,7).

3. Τὰς γραφάς (5,39) to ἔγραψεν (5,46) and τοῖς ἐκείνου γράμμασιν (5,47)[83].

4. Δοκεῖτε (5,39) to μὴ δοκεῖτε (5,45), whereas in the enclosed passage 5,41-44 the cognate word δόξα is of importance.

There seems to be even mirrored symmetry in 5,38-39.46c-47; it concerns the majority of the correspondences:

38	a	τὸν λόγον αὐτοῦ	47	a'	τοῖς ἐμοῖς ῥήμασιν
	b	οὐ πιστεύετε		b'	οὐ πιστεύετε
39	c	τὰς γραφάς		c'	τοῖς ἐκείνου γράμμασιν
	d	ἐκεῖναί εἰσιν αἱ μαρτυροῦσαι	46	d'	ἐκεῖνος ἔγραψεν
	e	περὶ ἐμοῦ		e'	περὶ γὰρ ἐμοῦ

A second reason why 5,37-40 is connected with what follows is that one can see already here the aspect of accusation of Jewish unbelief (5,38.40)[84]. It has been pointed out above (p. 105) that πιστεύειν, and verbs related to it as for their meaning, frequently occur in 5,38-47 (and not in 5,31-36). These verbs always occur within the framework of accusation: in the 2nd pers. pl. (or combined with another verb in the 2nd. pers. pl.) accompanied by a negation (5,38.40.43.47), with an obvious connotation of unreality (5,44.46*bis*.47), or with an object which is opposed to Jesus (5,43). In general, verbs in the 2nd pers. pl., most of them accompanied by negations, are frequent in 5,37-47, when compared with the preceding verses 5,31-36. The accusing tendency of 5,37-47 is manifest.

Another factor contributing to the unity of 5,37-47 is that this passage contains a continuing series of allusions to Deut. References to texts from Deut have been given above in connection with the three denials of 5,37b-38a[85]. Other allusions are:

a. To Deut 30,15-20 and related passages (keeping of the Law as a condition for 'life') in John 5,39-40.

b. To Deut 6,5 and related passages (the commandment 'to love the Lord your God') in John 5,42, when the genitive τοῦ θεοῦ is an objective genitive; in case it is a subjective genitive (the text of John allows of both interpretations), Deut 7,8 and related passages (about God's love for Israel) enter into consideration.

c. To Deut 18,18-20 (about the prophet as Moses, who 'will speak in my name' and to whom Israel has to hear, contrasted with the false prophet, who unjustly speaks 'in my name' or speaks 'in the name of other gods') in John 5,43[86].

d. To Deut 6,4 ('the Lord is one') in John 5,44 ('the one God')[87].

e. To Deut 31,19.21.26; 32,46 (about the Song of Moses and the Book of the Law as witnesses against Israel in case of infidelity) in John 5,45 (Moses as accuser)[88]. At the same time, the Jewish idea of Moses as their intercessor, present in Deut 9,18-29; 33, is reversed: Moses is not their intercessor, but their accuser[89].

f. To Deut 18,15-19 (the prophet as Moses) in John 5,46c (and possibly also in 5,39c)[90].

Apparently, it is possible to consider 5,31-40 as well as 5,37-47 as literary units. The passage 5,37-40 is a transition, belonging to both units: to 5,31-40 because it contains the final one of the series of testimonies, and to 5,37-47 because this testimony is concerned with the Scriptures, and because the accusation of the Jews starts here (cfr. above p. 83, and the words of Lucian quoted there).

5,31-36 and 5,41-47, the parts of 5,31-47 outside the transition 5,37-40, display a few superficial similarities:

1. 5,34a resembles 5,41; both clauses are followed by an ἀλλά-clause[91].

2. In 5,32 Jesus speaks in a positive sense about the 'other' witnessing on his behalf, and in 5,43 he speaks in a negative sense about the 'other' the Jews will accept.

3. In the first part John the Baptist is mentioned by name twice (5,33.36), as is Moses in the second part (5,45.46).

In Table IX, the numbers of S and W are given for John 5,31-47 according to the literary pattern described above.

Table IX. John 5,31-47	syllables	words
5,31-36	210	100
37-40	135	62
41-47	210/555	99/261

In numbers of S, 5,31-36 and 5,41-47 are of equal length, so that 5,31-40 and 5,37-47 are also of equal length: 345 S. In numbers of W there is a difference of 1 W between the size of 5,31-36 and that of 5,41-47, and also, of course, between the size of 5,31-40 and 5,37-47: 162 and 161 W respectively.

Measured in numbers of W, there is a proportion according to the golden section between 5,37-40 and 5,31-36, and also between 5,31-36 and 5,37-47: 62:100 = 100:162/161 = 162/161:261 = 0,62. Slightly less perfect is the proportion between 5,37-40 and 5,41-47, and between 5,41-47 and 5,31-40.

The numbers of S and W are also interesting in themselves. 345, the number of S of 5,31-40 and 5,37-47, is made up of three successive figures in ascending order; 210, the number of S for 5,31-36 and 5,41-47, is made up of successive figures in descending order (210 is, moreover, triangular number of 20). 135, the number of S of 5,37-40, is made up of three successive odd figures (cfr. above under 2. *in fine*, with n. 37).

In the numbers of W, the round number 100 appears for 5,31-36, whereas 5,41-47 has a length of 99 W, a multiple of 11. 162, the sum total for 5,31-40, is 2×9^2; 161, the sum total for 5,37-47, is a symmetrical number.

In Table X, the numbers of S are given for the various parts of 5,31-40.

Table X.	John 5,31-40	syllables			
5,31-32	principle	59			
33-35	testimony of the Baptist			90	
36a	contrast: greater testimony	16/			75
36bc	testimony of the works		45		
37-40	testimony of the Father in the Scriptures		135/180/270/345		

The wording of the general principle 5,31-32 together with 5,36a, serving as a heading for what follows, reaches a size of 75 S. These two parts are connected in so far as the true testimony of the other, who witnesses about Jesus (5,32), is announced in 5,36a: it is the Father, who is behind the testimony of the works and that of the Scriptures.

The descriptions of the three specific testimonies are obviously related in their numbers of S: 5,33-35 has a size of 90 S (a rectangular number: 9×10), 5,36bc has half that size, 45 S (triangular number of 9), and 5,37-40 has one and a half times that size: 135 S. The sum total of these three numbers is 270, in which the factor 27 appears again. Moreover, the numbers suggest that 5,36a functions as a heading for 5,36bc as well as for 5,37-40: these two passages contain the testimony greater than John's in so far also as their length is exactly twice the length of the passage about his testimony (another indication for the belonging together of both passages might be that the heading 5,36a as well as the closing sentence 5,40 have a length of 16 S).

In this way, the testimony of the Baptist, as a human testimony of only relative value, stands somewhat apart between 5,31-32 and 5,36, about God's testimony. Table XI shows the position of 5,33-35 between 5,31-32 and 5,36 in numbers of S and W.

Table XI. John 5,31-36	syllables		words	
5,31-32	59		28	
33-35		90		40
36	61/120/210		32/60/100	

5,31-32 and 5,36 together amount to 120 S (triangular number of 15) or 60 W, over against 90 S or 40 W for 5,33-35. So, the proportion between 5,31-32.36 and 5,33-35 is in numbers of S 4:3, and in numbers of W 3:2.

Several details of 5,31-47 are interesting from the point of view of composition in numbers of S and W:

1. 5,31-32:

		syll.	words
a	ἐὰν ἐγὼ μαρτυρῶ περὶ ἐμαυτοῦ	12	5
b	ἡ μαρτυρία μου οὐκ ἔστιν ἀληθής	12/24	6/11
c	ἄλλος ἐστὶν ὁ μαρτυρῶν περὶ ἐμοῦ	12	6
b'	καὶ οἶδα ὅτι ἀληθής ἐστιν ἡ μαρτυρία	15	7
a'	ἣν μαρτυρεῖ περὶ ἐμοῦ	8/23	4/11/28

In elements a and a' we meet forms of the present indicative of μαρτυρεῖν; in c we find a present participle of this verb. This central element introduces the 'other'. Elements b and b' are connected by the words μαρτυρία and ἀληθής, arranged according to a chiastic pattern[92].

Elements a, b and c have, all of them, a length of 12 S. Elements a and b together and b' and a' together (both combinations are combinations of principal and subordinate clauses) are in numbers of S of almost equal length (24 and 23), and in numbers of W of exactly equal length (11). The sum total of W, 28, is both a triangular and a perfect number.

2. 5,33-35. 5,33 constitutes an isocolon:

ὑμεῖς ἀπεστάλκατε πρὸς Ἰωάννην	11 S	4 W
καὶ μεμαρτύρηκεν τῇ ἀληθείᾳ	11	4

The passage 5,33-35 as a whole is made up of six short main clauses, arranged according to a pattern of concentric symmetry as far as the subjects of the clauses are concerned. Table XII gives the numbers of S and W of these clauses.

Table XII.	John 5,33-35	syllables	words
5,33a	Jews subject	11	4
33b	Baptist	11/22	4
34a	Jesus	17	8
34b	Jesus	13/30	6/14
35a	Baptist	15	8/ 12
35b	Jews	23/38/ 60	10/ 14

In numbers of S, the two central clauses, with Jesus as subject, have half the total length of the other clauses: 30 over against 60 S. In numbers of W, the two clauses with the Jews as subject are as long as those with Jesus as subject: 14 W.

3. 5,37-40 is made up of two parts; both contain three elements, but do so in different order. 5,37a and 5,39c deal with the testimony of the Father and of the Scriptures. In 5,37b-38a the Jewish claim to share in the Sinai-theophany and the gift of the Law is denied, and 5,39ab deals with the unjust Jewish claim to possess life in the Scriptures (see, e.g., Sir 17,11[93]). 5,38bc and 5,40 are about the Jewish refusal to believe Jesus, to come to him. In Table XIII, the numbers of S and W are given for the elements of 5,37-40.

Table XIII.	John 5,37-40		syllables				words			
5,37a	a	testimony of the Father	19				9			
37b-38a	b	denial of Jewish claims		41				18		
38bc	c	unbelief of the Jews			19				8	
39ab	b'	unjust Jewish claim		25/		66		11/		29
39c	a'	testimony of the Scriptures	15/			34/100	7/			16
40	c'	unbelief of the Jews			16/	35				9/17

The first half, 5,37-38, is made up of 19 + 41 + 19 S (the importance of the factor 19 in John 5 has already been shown several times); both elements of 19 S indicate the Father with ἐκεῖνος, and as Sender of Jesus[94]. The elements about the testimony together (a and a') are almost as long as those about the Jewish unbelief together (c and c'): 34 and 35 S, 16 and 17 W. The surplus-technique has been applied to elements c and c' together, in which the unbelief of the Jews is accused: they amount together to 35 S, on a sum total of 135 S.

In the numbers of W, the factor 9 is prominent: elements a and c' have a length of 9 W, element b is made up of 9 + 9 W, and elements b' and a' together amount to 18 W, = 2 × 9. Element c, of 8 W, is the middle of the passage: it is preceded and followed by 27 W, = 3 × 9. Again the number 27 appears.

There is a striking sequence of numbers of S in 5,36-39. 5,36-37a measures 80 S, 5,37b-38 60 S, and 5,39 40 S.

We observed earlier (p. 118) that the words ἔχει ζωὴν αἰώνιον in 5,24 constitute the centre of John 5 in numbers of S. In a comparable way, the words ζωὴν αἰώνιον ἔχειν in 5,39 constitute in numbers of W the centre of 5,33-47, i.e., the entire passage under consideration without the general principle 5,31-32. These words are preceded and followed by 115 W. We met this number in 5,1-18 (see above under 3.a., with Table IV).

4. 5,41-44. There is a correspondence here between 5,41-42 and 5,44: in both elements we meet the expression δόξαν λαμβάνειν παρά. Jesus and the Jews are contrasted in so far as Jesus is not interested in human

honour, whereas the Jews accept honour from one another. A second point of correspondence is, that the Jews do not have the love of God in themselves (5,42), and do not seek the honour from the one God (5,44). The middle element 5,43 is made up of two parallel sentences[95], in its entirety as well as in its parts of (almost) equal length in numbers of S:

ἐγὼ ἐλήλυθα	6 S	ἐὰν ἄλλος ἔλθῃ	6
ἐν τῷ ὀνόματι τοῦ πατρός μου	10	ἐν τῷ ὀνόματι τῷ ἰδίῳ	10
καὶ οὐ λαμβάνετέ με	7	ἐκεῖνον λήμψεσθε	6

In Table XIV, the numbers of S and W are given for the parts of 5,41-44.

Table XIV. John 5,41-44	syllables	words
5,41-42	35	17
43a	23/58	12/29
43b	22	10
44	36/58/116	18/28/57

In numbers of S, the corresponding elements are of equal size with a difference of 1 S, but in such a way that the two halves of the chiastic construction, determined by the correspondence of 5,41-42 to 5,44 and of 5,43a to 5,43b, are of exactly equal length. 5,43 has a length of 23 + 22 = 45 S, a factor prominent in the numbers of S of 5,33-40 (see Table X and its commentary).

In numbers of W, the corresponding elements are of equal length with a difference of 1 and 2 W; the two halves of the chiastic construction measure 29 and 28 W, together 57, = 3 × 19.

5. 5,45-47. This passage, in which the Jews are accused, has a size of 94 S, = 2 × 47[96].

In 5,45 Jesus and Moses are opposed to each other, in an isocolon of two times 20 S (a rectangular number: 4 × 5) or 9 W (a square number: 3^2), within which there is a chiasm:

μὴ δοκεῖτε ὅτι ἐγὼ	×	κατηγορήσω ὑμῶν πρὸς τὸν πατέρα	20 S	9 W
ἔστιν ὁ κατηγορῶν ὑμῶν		Μωϋσῆς, εἰς ὃν ὑμεῖς ἠλπίκατε	20	9

5,46 and 5,47 constitute together an antithetic parallelism[97]: a conditional clause beginning with εἰ, about (not) believing Moses or his writings, is followed by a main clause about believing Jesus or his words (in 5,46, a brief explanation follows in a γάρ-clause). There is a chiasm within this parallelism: in 5,46 the indirect object follows the verb, whereas in 5,47 this order is reversed. The end of 5,46 (ἐκεῖνος ἔγραφεν) is taken up at the beginning of 5,47 (τοῖς ἐκείνου γράμμασιν). Both verses have a length of 12 W.

Finally, it should be noted that 5,44 seems to have a double function: it is evidently part of 5,41-44 (see above), but at the same time it is connected with what follows, because of the correspondence of the beginning of 5,44 (πῶς ... πιστεῦσαι) and the end of 5,47 (πῶς ... πιστεύσετε). The resulting passage 5,44-47 is made up of 18 + 18 + 12 + 12 = 60 W, or 130 S, wherein the factor 13 appears once more.

After the above analysis, we may conclude that the author of John made use of numbers of S and W in the composition of John 5. For a general description of the various ways in which he applies this technique, I refer to the Conclusion. In John 5, several basic numbers are used: the factor 43 is prominent in 5,1-18, and the factors 19 and 13 may safely be said to be constitutive in 5,1-30. The factor 5 plays a role in 5,1-18, and especially at the beginning of the chapter, in 5,1-5. There is a clear connection between three of these basic numbers and the numbers mentioned in the text: the number 5 occurs in 5,2, 19 is half of 38, mentioned in 5,5; 43 is the sum of 5 and 38.

NOTES TO CHAPTER TWO

1 Cfr., e.g., R. Kühner, *Ausführliche Grammatik der griechischen Sprache*, I: Elementar- und Formenlehre, 3rd ed. by F. Blass, vol. 1 (Hannover 1890) 626 n. 1, who points to the fact that both ways of writing occur in mss., and refers to the passages from Herodianus just quoted.

2 See Moulton, *Prolegomena*, 84-85, and Moulton-Howard, *Accidence*, 431-432, with examples from papyri; id., *Grammar*, III: *Syntax*, by N. Turner (Edinburgh 1963) 38; Blass-Debrunner-Rehkopf, par. 278.

3 So the earlier editors, summed up in Appendix II of *NA*[26].

4 Cfr. J. Schniewind, art. ἀγγελία etc., *TWNT* I, 56-71; 61: 'In der handschriftlichen Überlieferung gehen bei vielen Schriftstellern ἀπαγγέλλειν und ἀναγγέλλειν durcheinander.... Attisch wird ἀπαγγέλλειν bevorzugt; daher hat man sich bei nichtattizistischen Koine-Schriften, also auch in LXX und NT, stets für ἀναγγέλλειν zu entscheiden'; see also J. H. Moulton-G. Milligan, *The Vocabulary of the Greek Testament*. Illustrated from the Papyri and Other Non-Literary Sources (London 1914-1929) 30-31; G. D. Kilpatrick, 'Atticism and the Text of the Greek New Testament', in: *Neutestamentliche Aufsätze* (Fs. J. Schmid; Regensburg 1963) 125-137; 134-135.

5 For this meaning in the use of both verbs in pagan Greek literature, in the LXX and in the Apostolic Fathers, see Schniewind, *TWNT* I, 61-66.

6 See Theissen, *Urchristliche Wundergeschichten*, 81, 257, 260-261.

7 Similar corrections in John 4,51; LXX Jdt 8,34; 11,17; Job 15,18; cfr. also Acts 17,19 (D).

8 *UBSGNT*[3] gives two more variant readings: ὁ δὲ κύριος (1253 sy[s]) and ὁ δὲ Ἰησοῦς κύριος (sy[pal]); both are 'clearly secondary' according to Metzger, *Textual Commentary*, 210.

9 Metzger, *Textual Commentary*, 210. The name Jesus is often added in the *Textus Receptus*, see, e.g., in John: 4,16.46; 6,14; 8,20.21; 11,45; 13,3; 18,5.

10 Metzger, *Textual Commentary*, 210. The editors of *UBSGNT*[3] were not able to decide between this solution and the one described above, and found a compromise in the square brackets, as is evident from Metzger's elucidation.

11 See Bauer, *Wörterbuch*, s.v. It occurs more often in Epictetus, so Radermacher, *Grammatik*, 98. See also J. Smit Sibinga, *The Old Testament Text of Justin Martyr*, I: The Pentateuch (Leiden 1963) 119-121, esp. 121 with n. 2.

12 Moulton, *Prolegomena*, 43 n. 2; cfr. Radermacher, *Grammatik*, 198.

13 So Moulton, *Prolegomena*, 43 n. 2 (referring to others).

14 So Liddell-Scott, s.v.

15 Cfr. for this explanation, starting from an original asyndeton, Turner, *Syntax*, 340-341; cfr. Aristotle, *Rhetorica*, 1413b (cfr. 1407a); Ps.-Demetrius, *De elocutione*, 192.

16 Only here in John, this indication of time is used *within* a narration and not at its beginning; comparable is, at best, 19,38; cfr. A. Duprez, *Jésus et les dieux guérisseurs*. A propos de Jean, V (Cahiers de la RB 12; Paris 1970) 145.

17 4,43-5,47: Hoskyns-Davey, 249sqq; J. Bligh, 'Jesus in Jerusalem', *HeyJ* 4 (1963) 115-134, 176; 116; 4,46-5,47: Dodd, *Interpretation*, 318-319; A. Feuillet, 'La signification théologique du second miracle de Cana (Jn IV, 46-54)', *RSR* 48 (1960) 62-75, reprinted in id., *Etudes Johanniques* (Bruges 1962) 34-46. See for a thorough criticism of this opinion Van Diemen, *Semaine*, 4-8. As far as I can see, John 5 is commonly considered to be a separate unit (so also the chapter division in the *Codex Vaticanus*).

18 See Liddell-Scott, s.v. διώκειν IV: 'as law-term, *prosecute*'. John 5,16 is referred to under V: '*persecute*', but the idea of juridical prosecution fits very well here.

19 Cfr. Matt 27,12; Mark 14,61; Luke 3,16; 23,9; Acts 3,12; see E. A. Abbott, *Johannine Grammar* (London 1906) nr. 2537; H. St. J. Thackeray, *A Grammar of the Old Testament in Greek* according to the Septuagint, I: Introduction, Orthography and Accidence (Cambridge 1909) par. 21.6 (p. 239); G. Bonaccorsi, *Primi saggi di filologia neotestamentaria*. Letture scelte dal Nuovo Testamento greco con introduzione e commento, I (Turin 1933) 105.

20 The double function of 5,16 is also observed by J. Bernard, 'La guérison de Bethesda. Harmoniques judéo-hellénistiques d'un récit de miracle un jour de sabbat', *MScRel* 33 (1976) 3-34; 34 (1977) 13-44; see 33 (1976) 11.

21 Cfr. Haenchen, 272, 284.

22 Cfr. — also concerning the background of 5,17 — esp. Dodd, *Interpretation*, 320-328; amply about the background of 5,17: Odeberg, 201-203, and Bernard, *MScRel* 33, 13-34.

23 Cfr. A. Vanhoye, 'La composition de Jn 5,19-30', in: *Mélanges Bibliques* en hommage au R. P. Béda Rigaux (Gembloux 1970) 259-274; 259-260.

24 The correspondence of 5,19 and 5,30 has been noted by several scholars: Bengel, *Gnomon*, 360, 362; Westcott, I 195-196; Abbott, *Joh. Grammar*, nr. 2605; Bauer, 87; Lagrange, 149; Bernard, 246; P. Gächter, 'Strophen im Johannesevangelium', *ZKT* 60 (1936) 99-120, 402-423; 113, and also id., 'Zur Form von Joh 5,19-30', in: *Neutestamentliche Aufsätze* (Fs. J. Schmid; Regensburg 1963) 65-68; 66; Bultmann, 185, 190 n. 3, 197; Hoskyns-Davey, 255; Strathmann, 106; Van den Bussche, *Boek der werken*, 80; X. Léon-Dufour, 'Trois chiasmes johanniques', *NTS* 7 (1960-61) 249-255; 253; J. Blank, *Krisis*. Untersuchungen zur johanneischen Christologie und Eschatologie (Freiburg 1964) 109, 181; Brown, 219; Talbert, *CBQ* 32, 349 n. 32; Vanhoye, in: *Mélanges Rigaux*, 260; Schnackenburg, II 126; J. Riedl, *Das Heilswerk Jesu nach Johannes* (Freiburger theologische Studien 93; Freiburg 1973) 225; Schneider, 129; Boismard-Lamouille, *Jean*, 165; Becker, 235; Haenchen, 281.

25 Cfr. Vanhoye, in: *Mélanges Rigaux*, 260-261.

26 Cfr. Vanhoye, in: *Mélanges Rigaux*, 261-262.

27 The two parts of the monologue are connected by means of the rhetorical figure of πολύπτωτον, i.e., the employment of the same noun or pronoun in various successive cases: τὸν πέμψαντα-τῷ πέμψαντι-τοῦ πέμψαντος-ὁ πέμψας (5,23.24.30.37). The effect of the figure is reinforced in this case by the addition of the substantive πατήρ to the first and the last occurrence of the participle πέμψας; in 5,23 the substantive precedes the participle, in 5,37 the order is reversed. See about this rhetorical figure

Lausberg, *Handbuch der literarischen Rhetorik*, parr. 640-648, where relevant materials are summed up. Another impressive instance of πολύπτωτον is found in John 21,1-14: τοῖς μαθηταῖς-τῶν μαθητῶν-οἱ μαθηταί-ὁ μαθητής-οἱ μαθηταί-τῶν μαθητῶν-τοῖς μαθηταῖς (21,1.2.4.7.8.12.14). The only time the word is used in the singular is exactly in the middle of the series. I owe these observations to J. Smit Sibinga. I found another example in John 18,37-38: τῇ ἀληθείᾳ-τῆς ἀληθείας-ἀλήθεια.

28 Cfr. J. Beutler, *Martyria.* Traditionsgeschichtliche Untersuchungen zum Zeugnisthema bei Johannes (Frankfurter Theologische Studien 10; Frankfurt/M 1972) 263-264 (with n. 236), 265 n. 243; Schneider, 134.

29 Cfr. Gächter, *ZKT* 60, 118; Bultmann, 205; Lightfoot, 146-147; Beutler, *Martyria*, 256, 265.

30 Dodd, *Interpretation*, 290-291, 384-386, 400, and in his treatment of the single episodes, 297-379; in a less elaborated version already in id., 'Le Kerygma apostolique dans le quatrième évangile', *RHPR* 31 (1951) 265-274; 271-274.

31 Dodd, *Interpretation*, 384.

32 In this connection, it is significant that the verb ἐγείρειν is used to indicate both physical healing (in Jesus' command to the crippled man 5,8) and the eschatological raising of the dead (5,21); so E. Haenchen, 'Johanneische Probleme', *ZTK* 56 (1959) 19-54; 50, reprinted in id., *Gott und Mensch.* Gesammelte Aufsätze (Tübingen 1965) 78-113; the same in his commentary on John, 276-277; also Willemse, *Het vierde evangelie*, 280-281; Pancaro, *Law*, 12-13.

33 It was forbidden to heal on a Sabbath, except in instances of danger of life, see esp. Mek. Exod 31,13 (Shabbata, 1); this text with other rabbinic materials in Str-B I, 623-624.

34 The thematic connections of narration and monologue are worked out by Dodd, *Interpretation*, 318-332; S. Hofbeck, *Semeion.* Der Begriff des 'Zeichens' im Johannesevangelium unter Berücksichtigung seiner Vorgeschichte (Münsterschwarzacher Studien 3; Münsterschwarzach 1970[2]) 112-113; Pancaro, *Law*, 13-16.

35 Dodd, *Interpretation*, 320, 400.

36 See the Appendix for the divisions of John 5 as given in commentaries, other literature and text-editions.

37 This phenomenon also occurs in Melito's Paschal Homily, see Smit Sibinga, *VC* 24, 96, on Περὶ Πασχα parr. 9-29.

38 Bultmann, 179; Hofbeck, *Semeion*, 109, and Schulz, 83, consider 5,2-5 as description of the situation. Apparently, they assign a relatively independent position to 5,1, as is also done by J. L. Martyn, *History and Theology in the Fourth Gospel* (Nashville 1979[2]; orig. New York/Evanston 1968) 68-69 (cfr. also the Appendix, where can be seen which scholars consider 5,1 as a separate part). 5,1-3 is considered as an introduction by Noack, *Zur joh. Tradition*, 114; Van den Bussche, *Boek der werken*, 68-71 (cfr. 52); Brown, 209 (cfr. also Boismard-Lamouille, *Jean*, 157). Against this view is the circumstance, that 5,5 introduces the second protagonist of the miracle story, and that the action starts only with 5,6, as is evident from a comparison with Mark 1,16 parr.19 parr; 2,14 parr; John 1,47; 9,1.

39 A division at 5,9a/9b is frequently made in literature and text-editions; somewhat less frequently, a division is made at 5,9/10; see the Appendix, and for the break at 5,9a/9b also Noack, *Zur joh. Tradition*, 114-115; Martyn, *History and Theology*, 68-69; Duprez, *Jésus et les dieux guérisseurs*, 141, 143-144; J. Roloff, *Das Kerygma und der irdische Jesus.* Historische Motive in den Jesus-Erzählungen der Evangelien (Göttingen 1970) 81; Nicol, *Sēmeia*, 31-32; Bernard, *MScRel* 33, 4-11, who tries to point out concentric structures in 5,5-9a and 5,9b-16 — unconvincingly, in my opinion (cfr. Boismard-Lamouille, *Jean*, 162: 5,9bsqq is an addition deriving from 'Jean II-B', i.e. the penultimate stage in the development of the Fourth Gospel as we know it). Haenchen, 282, sees 5,9b as a transition from the miracle story to the following unit.

40 For this division into dramatic scenes, cfr. Windisch, in: *ΕΥΧΑΡΙΣΤΗΡΙΟΝ*, II 189; Noack, *Zur joh. Tradition*, 114-115; Martyn, *History and Theology*, 69; Roloff,

Kerygma, 81 n. 98; Becker, 232. They see breaks at 5,9a/9b; 13/14; 14/15; 15/16 (the last break not in Roloff and Becker; Windisch is not quite clear about the exact divisions he makes). Leidig, *Jesu Gespräch*, 207-211, considers 5,1-16 as Jesus' conversation with the crippled man, with the elements 'Heilsbegegnen' (5,1-7), 'Heilsangebot und -zeichen' (5,8-13) and 'Bekräftigung des Heilsangebots' (5,14-16).

41 It may be worth mentioning that 5,5-13 has a size of exactly 300 S. However, 5,5 belongs together with what precedes — as many observations of a numerical nature will confirm.

42 We seem to have here an arithmetical parallel to the phenomenon of 'Stichwortverbindung innerhalb der Wundergeschichte', as observed by H. J. Held, 'Matthäus als Interpret der Wundergeschichten', in: G. Bornkamm-G. Barth-H. J. Held, *Überlieferung und Auslegung im Matthäusevangelium* (WMANT 1; Neukirchen-Vluyn 1975[7]) 155-287; 224-227. Held writes about it on p. 226: 'In den Wundergeschichten des Matthäusevangeliums werden durch Stichworte folgende Teile der Perikope verbunden: Bitte, Heilungswort und Eintritt des Wunders'. Clear examples are found in Matt 8,1-4; 9,20-22. Of course, this literary 'Stichwortverbindung' is also used in John 5,8b-9a (only the petition is missing).

43 Bligh, *HeyJ* 4, 124-125, discerns three charges in 5,18: the violation of the Sabbath, Jesus' calling God his Father, and his making himself equal to God. Against this view is the construction of the sentence: οὐ μόνον ... ἀλλὰ καί, followed by a participle. Cfr. for the view that 5,18bc contains two accusations, with 5,18c*b* added as an explanation or conclusion: Lagrange, 142; Odeberg, 203; Barrett, 256; Van den Bussche, *Boek der werken*, 78; id., 'Guérison d'un paralytique à Jérusalem le jour du sabbat', *BVC* 61 (1965) 18-28; 28; Grundmann, *Zeugnis und Gestalt*, 45; Blank, *Krisis*, 110; Martyn, *History and Theology*, 70; Roloff, *Kerygma*, 82; Schnackenburg, II 128-129; Schulz, 85; Riedl, *Heilswerk*, 194; Pancaro, *Law*, 55-56; Haenchen, 274.

44 So, e.g., Odeberg, 202-203; Bultmann, 182; Hoskyns-Davey, 255; Strathmann, 102; Barrett, 256; Gächter, in: *Neutestamentliche Aufsätze*, 65; Brown, 213; Vanhoye, in: *Mélanges Rigaux*, 260; Riedl, *Heilswerk*, 190-191, 193.

45 Following Léon-Dufour, *NTS* 7, 253-255, and esp. Vanhoye, in: *Mélanges Rigaux*, 268-274.

46 Cfr. Bernard, 244; Brown, 219.

47 This is observed by several scholars: Bauer, 86; Bernard, 243; Barrett, 218; Van den Bussche, *Boek der werken*, 88; Brown, 214, 219; Schnackenburg, II 142-143; Schulz, 86-87, 90. The similarity of only 5,21 and 5,26 is noted by Bultmann, 195, and Riedl, *Heilswerk*, 217. Boismard-Lamouille, *Jean*, 169, make 5,21 correspond to 5,25-26, on the level of 'Jean II-B'.

48 Cfr. Ferraro, *L'"ora" di Cristo*, 144.

49 Cfr. Barrett, 262-263; Blank, *Krisis*, 172-181; Brown, 219; Schnackenburg, II 148-149; Ferraro, *L'"ora" di Cristo*, 140-150; Bernard, *MScRel* 34, 17.

50 Léon-Dufour, *NTS* 7, 253-255.

51 Vanhoye, in: *Mélanges Rigaux*, 270-272; this structure also (summarily) in Talbert, *CBQ* 32, 349 n. 32, who refers on p. 356 to J. Forbes, *The Symmetrical Structure of Scripture* (Edinburgh 1854) 67sqq, for an a-b-b'-a'-structure in John 5,19-30. Vanhoye's scheme is followed by Ferraro, *L'"ora" di Cristo*, 140, and Bernard, *MScRel* 34, 17-20.

Gächter, *ZKT* 60, 112-115, 119, gives a strophic division into 5,19.20.21.22-23.24.25.26-27.28-29.30, with 5,24 as centre; so, first part, centre and second part start with an Amen-formula, and in first and second part we meet at the end the stem κριν-, and the expression ὁ πέμψας αὐτόν/με. Apart from G.'s hypothetical principles of division (he tries to determine the rhythm of an original Aramaic text; see chapter III, under 4.a., ad 1.), the literary correspondences are not taken into account sufficiently in this analysis (see for criticism of G. also Vanhoye, in: *Mélanges Rigaux*, 268-269). A. J. Simonis, *Die Hirtenrede im Johannes-Evangelium*. Versuch einer Analyse von Johannes 10,1-18 nach Entstehung, Hintergrund und Inhalt (AnBib

29; Rome 1967) 28 n. 52, considers 5,25-30 to be a unit; argument is the triple occurrence of words (ἀκούειν, ζωή, κρίσις, ποιεῖν).

A division based on theological and not on literary principles is given by G. Iber, *Überlieferungsgeschichtliche Studien zum Begriff des Menschensohns im Neuen Testament* (Diss. Heidelberg 1953) 128sqq: in 5,19-20 the idea of revelation is expressed in general terms; in 5,21-23 the 'Dass' is made concrete, and in 5,24-29 the 'Wie', while 5,24-26 corresponds to 5,21, and 5,27-29 to 5,22-23, exceeding it at the same time; 5,30, finally, refers back to 5,19. More or less similar divisions in Westcott, I 188; Lagrange, 145; Bultmann, 185; Bligh, *HeyJ* 4, 126; Hofbeck, *Semeion*, 111; Schnackenburg, II 133; Schulz, 86-87, 91; Schneider, 129-132.

A different division is given by Moloney, *Son of Man*, 76: the theological introduction 5,19-20 corresponds to the theological conclusion 5,30; both deal with the absolute dependence of the Son upon the Father. 5,21.22 are about the *exercising* of the Son's authority to give life, and the *basis* of his authority to judge respectively, whereas in 5,26.27 the *basis* of his authority to give life and the *exercising* of his authority to judge are dealt with respectively. 5,23 is a 'theological reflection'. 5,24-25 is about the Son as giver of life, with judgment as a sub-theme, 5,28-29 is about the Son as judge, with the giving of life as a sub-theme. Though insufficiently based on literary criteria, M.'s observations are no doubt partly correct; problematic are: the distinction between the exercising of authority and its basis, to which the text does not give rise; the correspondence of 5,19-20 to 5,30, where only 5,19 and 5,30 are corresponding (as rightly observed by M. on p. 71); the independent position of 5,23, which verse is, in fact, only appended to 5,22; the description of 5,28-29, where in fact life and judgment are presented as equivalent possibilities.

52 Cfr. also Brown, 214.

53 So Vanhoye, in: *Mélanges Rigaux*, 272, referring to Lund, *Chiasmus in the NT*, 41.

54 See also below, p. 118 with n. 57.

55 5,25-30 is divided into 5,25-27.28-30 by Simonis, *Hirtenrede*, 28 n. 52: in 5,25-27 ζωή is found twice, and ζῆν once; in 5,28-30 κρίσις occurs twice, and κρίνειν once. Cfr. also Gächter, *ZKT* 60, 114.

56 Cfr. for the literary analysis Vanhoye, in: *Mélanges Rigaux*, 264-265; Bernard, *MScRel* 34, 26-27.

57 Cfr. Bultmann, 193; Strathmann, 104; Lightfoot, 141; Van den Bussche, *Boek der werken*, 80; Léon-Dufour, *NTS* 7, 254; Gächter, in: *Neutestamentliche Aufsätze*, 66; Brown, 220; Schulz, 89; Boismard-Lamouille, *Jean*, 166; Becker, 236.

58 So Vanhoye, in: *Mélanges Rigaux*, 266; V. wrongly omits ὅτε in his structured rendering of the text.

59 Cfr. Vanhoye, in: *Mélanges Rigaux*, 267.

60 For the various possibilities of punctuation in 5,28-29, see the punctuation apparatus in *UBSGNT*[3] ad John 5,28-29.

61 Cfr. Vanhoye, in: *Mélanges Rigaux*, 267.

62 Cfr. for this view of John 5,31-40 Bauer, 88; J. Giblet, 'Le témoignage du Père (Jn 5,31-47)', *BVC* 12 (1955) 49-59; 50; Lightfoot, 145; Van den Bussche, *Boek der werken*, 91; Brown, 227; Schnackenburg, II 168; Schulz, 94-95; Pancaro, *Law*, 208-209; Boismard-Lamouille, *Jean*, 175.

63 Adversative καί, see Blass-Debrunner-Rehkopf, par. 442.1; M. Zerwick, *Biblical Greek*, Illustrated by Examples (Scripta Pontificii Instituti Biblici; Rome 1963) par. 455.

64 Gächter, *ZKT* 60, 115-116, 119, gives the division 5,31-32.33-34.35.36.37-38, with 5,35 as the central strophe (5,39-40 is, according to G., part of the next unit 5,39-47, see n. 83 below). Simonis, *Hirtenrede*, 28 n. 52 considers 5,31-35 as a unit, containing 7 × μαρτυρία or μαρτυρεῖν, and 3 × ἀληθής or ἀλήθεια. J. Bernard, 'Témoignage pour Jésus-Christ: Jean 5:31-47', *MScRel* 36 (1979) 3-55; 4-5, gives a strophic division into 5,31-32.33-36a.36bc.37-38.39-40.

65 Cfr., e.g., Bultmann, 201; Barrett, 266.

66 'Die *Dauer* des *Vollendeten*', Blass-Debrunner-Rehkopf, par. 340.

67 So Westcott, I 210; Bauer, 89; Lagrange, 152; Bultmann, 200; Hoskyns-Davey, 273; Strathmann, 108; Giblet, *BVC* 12, 54-55; Van den Bussche, *Boek der werken*, 93; Blank, *Krisis*, 205; Schulz, 95; Riedl, *Heilswerk*, 231. Beutler, *Martyria*, 261-262, distinguishes between 5,37-38, about God's testimony in the OT, God's word, and 5,39, about the testimony of the Scriptures as an external résumé of God's testimony. Pancaro, *Law*, 219, 226-231, wrongly makes these two aspects of the same testimony into two different testimonies. Recently, U. C. von Wahlde, 'The Witnesses to Jesus in John 5:31-40 and Belief in the Fourth Gospel', *CBQ* 43 (1981) 385-404; 385-395, has argued that 'the witness of the Father mentioned in 5:37-38 is precisely the word of the Father which he has given to Jesus and which Jesus gives to the world' (390). He can do so only by neglecting the value of the perfect μεμαρτύρηκεν and the OT references and polemical thrust that are present in 5,37-38 (see below about these).

68 In 1 John 5,9.10 the perfect μεμαρτύρηκεν is used to indicate the testimony God has borne to his Son. Jesus' ministry, viewed as a testimony of the Father, completed and still valid, is meant there, cfr. R. Schnackenburg, *Die Johannesbriefe* (HTKNT XIII/3; Freiburg etc. 1975[5]) 270.

69 So, e.g., Barrett, 266-267; Brown, 227-228.

70 So, e.g., Bengel, *Gnomon*, 363.

71 So, e.g., H. Grotius, *Annotationes in libros evangeliorum*. Cum tribus tractatibus & Appendice eo spectantibus (Amsterdam 1641) 896-897; Schnackenburg, II 174.

72 Cfr. Barrett, 267; Zerwick, *Biblical Greek*, par. 420.

73 I quote the translation of J. Z. Lauterbach, in his edition of the Mekilta de-Rabbi Ishmael (Philadelphia 1933-1935).

74 See for a more extensive enumeration and discussion of parallels to John 5,37b-38a M. J. J. Menken, 'Jezus en de Schriften volgens Johannes 5,37-47', in: *Schrift in veelvoud*. Bijdragen over het gebruik van de Schrift (Fs. J. J. A. Kahmann; Boxtel 1980) 41-61; 45-48.

75 I quote H. St. J. Thackeray's translation, in the Josephus-edition of the Loeb Classical Library, IV (London-Cambridge Mass. 1930, repr. 1967).

76 Ed. N. N. Glatzer (rev. ed. New York 1969; I quote G.'s translation). According to L. Finkelstein, 'The Oldest Midrash', *HTR* 31 (1938) 291-317, and id., 'Pre-Maccabean Documents in the Passover Haggadah', *HTR* 35 (1942) 291-332; 36 (1943) 1-38 (both articles are reprinted in id., *Pharisaism in the Making*. Selected Essays [New York 1972] 13-39 and 41-120), the introduction with Deut 6,21, the passage about the four sons (in its original form, at least), the midrash on Deut 26,5-8 and the *Dayyenu*-hymn belong to the oldest, pre-Maccabean parts of the Passover Haggadah: they fit well into what is known about the political and religious circumstances in Palestine in the 3rd and 2nd century B.C. before the Maccabean Revolt (more specifically, they come from high-priestly circles of that period) and can hardly have come into existence later; there are striking similarities in the scriptural passages quoted between the Passover Haggadah and the LXX, over against the MT. See also chapter III, n. 11.

77 See for a more extensive discussion of this liturgical identification, and of two other ways in which Jews of the 1st century C.E. possibly thought to share in the past events of the theophany at Mount Sinai, viz., mystical experience and study of the Scriptures, Menken, in: *Schrift in veelvoud*, 48-54.

78 Cfr. for this interpretation of John 5,37b-38 Giblet, *BVC* 12, 55-56; Van den Bussche, *Boek der werken*, 93-94; N. A. Dahl, 'The Johannine Church and History', in: *Current Issues in New Testament Interpretation* (Fs. O. A. Piper; New York 1962) 124-142; 133-135; Blank, *Krisis*, 205; W. A. Meeks, *The Prophet-King*. Moses Traditions and Johannine Christology (NTS 14; Leiden 1967) 299-301; Pancaro, *Law*, 216-231; Bernard, *MScRel* 36, 27-34.

79 So Lagrange, 154; Bernard, 253; Strathmann, 108; Giblet, *BVC* 12, 57; Bligh, *HeyJ* 4, 133-134; Beutler, *Martyria*, 264; said only of 5,41-44 by Westcott, I 202; Blank, *Krisis*, 208-209; Pancaro, *Law*, 231-232; Boismard-Lamouille, *Jean*, 176.

80 This is the characteristic of 5,41-47 given by Bauer, 91; Bultmann, 202; Hoskyns-Davey, 274; Van den Bussche, *Boek der werken*, 95; Brown, 228; Schnackenburg, II 178.

81 Cfr. Gächter, *ZKT* 60, 118. On pp. 116-119, G. gives the following division into strophes of 5,39-47 (considered by him as a unit, see n. 83 below): 5,39-40.41-42.43.44.45.46-47, with 5,43 as centre. Bernard, *MScRel* 36, 6, divides 5,41-47 into 5,41-44.45-47.

82 Cfr. Odeberg, 224-225; Gächter, *ZKT* 60, 118 (on p. 112, G. mentions as division of Schanz: 5,31-36.37-47); Bultmann, 205; Lightfoot, 146-147; Beutler, *Martyria*, 256, 265 (with n. 245); Pancaro, *Law*, 232 (P. refers, ibd. n. 126, to *Papyrus Egerton* 2, where John 5,39 is immediately followed by 5,45); Haenchen, 295, 296 (also referring to *Pap. Eg.* 2).

83 Gächter, *ZKT* 60, 118, considers 5,39-47 as a unit because of this correspondence.

84 So also Pancaro, *Law*, 231 n. 125 (cont. 232).

85 Cfr. esp. Deut 4,33 LXX with John 5,37b.

86 Cfr. Van den Bussche, *Boek der werken*, 96 n. 3; T. F. Glasson, *Moses in the Fourth Gospel* (SBT 40; London 1963) 80; Schnackenburg, II 179.

87 Cfr. Schnackenburg, II 180.

88 Cfr. Bernard, 257; Van den Bussche, *Boek der werken*, 97; Brown, 226.

89 See Glasson, *Moses*, 105; Schnackenburg, II 181; Pancaro, *Law*, 256-257.

90 Cfr. Bauer, 91; Lagrange, 156; Bernard, 258; Strathmann, 109; Brown, 226; Schnackenburg, II 182; Pancaro, *Law*, 257. — See for a more extensive list of allusions to Deut in John 5,37-47 and discussion of them Menken, in: *Schrift in veelvoud*, 54-56.

91 Cfr., e.g., Abbott, *Joh. Grammar*, nr. 2605.

92 Cfr. about the literary structure of 5,31-32 Gächter, *ZKT* 60, 116; Pancaro, *Law*, 210; Boismard-Lamouille, *Jean*, 173; Bernard, *MScRel* 36, 6-7.

93 See Str-B, II 467, III 129-132, for a rich collection of materials illustrating this Jewish claim.

94 Cfr. Bernard, *MScRel* 36, 26-27.

95 Cfr. about the literary structure of 5,41-44 Gächter, *ZKT* 60, 118; Pancaro, *Law*, 231-232, 233-234; Bernard, *MScRel* 36, 43; Haenchen, 296.

96 See below, p. 205 with n. 43, about a possible association of the number 47 with 'judgment'. 5,14, a verse in which Jesus warns the healed man to sin no more, 'lest something worse (the judgment?) will happen to you', has a size of 47 S.

97 Cfr. Pancaro, *Law*, 258; Bernard, *MScRel* 36, 48.

APPENDIX

isions of John 5 proposed in literature and text-editions

visions of the monologue 5,31-47 as given by earlier Roman Catholic exegetes can be found in ·hter, *ZKT* 60, 112.)

stcott	[1] [2-9a] [9b - 18] [19-23 24-29] [30] [31 - 40 41-47]
.er	[1 - 18] [19 - 47]
'range	[1 -9a] [9b - 18] [19 - 30 31 - 47]
nard	[1] [2- 9] [10 - 19] [20 - 29] [30 - 40] [41-47]
hter, *ZKT* 60, 11-120	[19 - 30] [31 - 38] [39 - 47]
:mann	[1 -9a 9b - 18] [19 - 30 | 31 - 40 41-47]
kyns-Davey	[1 - 18] [19 - 29] [30 - 40] [41-47]
thmann	[1 -9a] [9b - 18] [19 - 30] [31 - 36] [37 - 40] [41-47]
.d, *Interpretation*, 18-332	[1 - 9] [10 - 18] [19 - 30] [31 - 47]
'ett	[1 - 18] [19 - 30 31 - 40 41-47]
den Bussche, *ek der werken*, 67-97	[1 - 15] [16 - 18 19 - 30 31 - 40 41-47]
ndmann, *Zeugnis d Gestalt*, 44-46	[1 - 18] [19 - 30 31 - 40 41-47]
n, *HeyJ* 4, 7-119	[1 -9a] [9b - 18] [19 - 30] [31 - 47]
vn	[1 - 15] [16 - 18 19 - 25] [31 - 40 41-47] (26-30 is a duplicate of 19-25)
ert, *CBQ* 32, 6	[1] [2-9a] [9b - 16] [17-18] [19 - 30]
noye, *Mélanges gaux*, 259-260	[1 - 9] [10 - 18] [19 - 30]
ackenburg	[1 -9a 9b-15] [16 - 30] [31 - 40 41-47]
.er, *Martyria*, 4-255	[1 -9a] [9b - 18] [19 - 30 31 - 40 41-47]
lz	[1] [2-9a] [9b - 18] [19 - 30] [31 - 40] [41-47]
., *Heilswerk*, 9-190, 230	[1 - 9] [10 - 18] [19 - 30] [31 - 47]
eider	[1 -9a 9b - 18] [19 - 30 31 - 40 41-47]
er	[1 2-9a 9b - 18] [19 - 30] [31-32 33-38 39 - 47]
chen	[1 2-9a 9b - 18 19 - 30] [31 - 47]

editions:

endorf[8]	[1 - 18] [19 - 47]
ott-Hort	[1] [2-9a] [9b-13 14 - 18 19-23 24 25-29 30] [31 - 40 41 - 47]
Soden	[1 2 - 9 10-15 16 17-18 19 - 30] [31 - 40 41 - 47]
	[1 -9a] [9b - 18] [19-23] [24 - 29] [30] [31-35] [36-40] [41 - 47]
NT^{3}	[1 - 9a 9b - 18] [19 - 30] [31 - 40 41 - 47]
	[1] [2-9a] [9b - 16] [17-18] [19-23] [24 - 29] [30] [31-35] [36-40] [41-44] [45-47]

CHAPTER THREE

JOHN 6: THE MULTIPLICATION OF THE LOAVES, JESUS' WALKING ON THE SEA, THE DISCOURSE ON THE BREAD OF LIFE AND THE DIVISION AMONG THE DISCIPLES

The numeral εἴκοσι πέντε in 6,19 is provisionally counted at two words (see above, p. 97).

Between the text of John 6 in *NA*[25] and that in *NA*[26], there are five differences that affect an analysis of numbers of W and S. I will discuss them briefly:

1. In 6,2, *NA*[26] reads ἐθεώρουν, with P[66c.(75)] (A) B D L N (Θ) Ψ (*f*[13]) 33 892 1010 1241 *al*, whereas *NA*[25] reads ἑώρων, with P[66*] Sin 063 0273 *f*[1] *Mehrheitstext*. Transcriptional probability could point in the direction of the reading of *NA*[26]: ὅτι ἐθεώρουν can become, by faulty hearing or seeing, ὅτι ἑώρων. From the point of view of intrinsic probability, no clear results seem possible: in 2,23 the evangelist uses the expression θεωρεῖν σημεῖα (cfr. 7,3: θεωρεῖν ἔργα), and in 4,48; 6,14.26 he is speaking about ἰδεῖν σημεῖα (-ον). Θεωρεῖν as well as ὁρᾶν are used throughout the Fourth Gospel (the former verb 23 ×, the latter 30 ×; in neither number 6,2 is included), without much difference of meaning, it would seem (cfr. 6,36 with 6,40; 7,3 with 15,24; 12,45 with 14,7.9, and see especially 16,16.17.19); more probably, the use of either verb depends on the tense used, θεωρεῖν replacing ὁρᾶν in pres. and impf.[1]. There is, however, besides the unusual character of ἑώρων (this impf. occurs only here in the NT), one aspect of the evidence that legitimates a preference for the reading ἑώρων, viz. the circumstance that 2,23 is clearly parallel to 6,2:

2,23 <u>πολλοὶ</u> ἐπίστευσαν εἰς τὸ ὄνομα αὐτοῦ	6,2 ἠκολούθει δὲ αὐτῷ ὄχλος <u>πολύς</u>
<u>θεωροῦντες</u> αὐτοῦ <u>τὰ σημεῖα</u>	ὅτι ἑώρων/<u>ἐθεώρουν τὰ σημεῖα</u>
<u>ἃ ἐποίει</u>	<u>ἃ ἐποίει</u> ἐπὶ τῶν ἀσθενούντων

The parallelism of the two texts is strengthened by the mention of the Passover Festival in the close proximity of both of them (2,23a; 6,4). From this point of view, it is conceivable that the text of 2,23 — being in the memory of a scribe — caused a change from ἑώρων to ἐθεώρουν in 6,2[2]. I shall assume ἑώρων as the correct reading; it will be clear, however, from what precedes, that in this case a satisfactory textual decision is very difficult. Maybe the analysis of the number of S can give us a clue as to the correct reading.

2. In 6,29, *NA*[26] reads [ὁ] 'Ιησοῦς; *NA*[25] reads anarthrous 'Ιησοῦς. The square brackets of *NA*[26] indicate the doubt of the editors as to the presence of the article in the original text. Articular 'Ιησοῦς is read by A B D K L N T Θ 063 *f*1.13 33 1010 *al* Or; anarthrous 'Ιησοῦς by P75 Sin W Ψ' *Mehrheitstext*. As for the internal evidence: in John, 'ἀπεκρίθη 'Ιησοῦς appears to be a set phrase'[3] — which circumstance would make the textual critic prefer the anarthrous reading. Moreover, the immediate context has an only slightly different formula *with* the article, in 6,26: ἀπεκρίθη αὐτοῖς ὁ 'Ιησοῦς (cfr. 6,32.35). The articular reading in 6,29 is possibly an adaptation to this formula. So, in this case, the reading of *NA*[25] seems to be more correct than that of *NA*[26].

3. In 6,37b, *NA*[26] reads πρὸς ἐμέ, with P66.75 Sin K T Δ Θ *al*, and *NA*[25] reads πρός με, with A B D L W Ψ' *f*1.13 *Mehrheitstext*. Just as in the former cases, so here a decision based on the external evidence only is highly questionable. The internal evidence seems to point in the direction of the reading of *NA*[25]: not so much the general usage in the Fourth Gospel, where — apart from 6,37b — 3 × πρὸς ἐμέ is found (6,35.37a.45), and 4 × πρός με (5,40; 6,44.65; 7,37), in both *NA*[25] and *NA*[26][4], but rather the presence of the same expression in the form πρὸς ἐμέ in the preceding clause (6,37a). The reading πρὸς ἐμέ in 6,37b is under suspicion of being an adaptation to this expression in 6,37a. Therefore, here too, *NA*[25] seems to be correct.

4. In 6,52, *NA*[26] reads τὴν σάρκα [αὐτοῦ], *NA*[25] τὴν σάρκα. In this case, as in the second one, the square brackets indicate the doubt of the editors as to the presence of ἀυτοῦ in the original text. Αὐτοῦ is read by P66 B T 892 1424 *pc* lat sy, and omitted by Sin C D L W Θ Ψ' *f*1.13 *Mehrheitstext* ff2 (see *UBSGNT*3 for a fuller enumeration of witnesses). So far, the remark made by B. M. Metzger is understandable: 'The external evidence for and against the presence of αὐτοῦ is ... evenly balanced'[5]. Then he continues: 'Considerations of internal probabilities are not decisive', thereby indicating the second reason for putting αὐτοῦ between square brackets. On considering carefully the internal probabilities, however, they appear to be more decisive than Metzger supposes. Firstly, the longer text is easily understood as an explanation of the shorter one. The reverse movement is less easy to understand[6]. Secondly, the reading with αὐτοῦ can be explained as an accommodation to the preceding verse, where Jesus is speaking about ἡ σάρξ *μου* (cfr. 6,53sqq). Thirdly, the shorter reading seems to make more sense in the context. In 6,51, Jesus says that he will give *his* flesh. In 6,52, the Jews are misquoting him by asking how he can give them *the* flesh to eat. In the

answer, and later on in 6,63, this question is corrected by Jesus: *the* flesh is of no avail, they have to eat the flesh *of the Son of Man*[7]. The consideration of internal probabilities leads to the conlusion that in 6,52 the shorter text has to be preferred.

5. The last point of difference in the text of John 6 between *NA*26 and *NA*25 to be discussed — where once again square brackets in *NA*26 express the doubt of the editors — is in 6,66. *NA*26 reads πολλοί [ἐκ], the presence of the preposition being supported by P66 B T *f*1 33 565 *pc*; in *NA*25 the preposition is omitted, with Sin C D L W Θ Ψ 0250 *f*13 *Mehrheitstext*. As for the internal probabilities: generally, the fourth evangelist prefers ἐκ *partitivum* to the *genitivus partitivus*. I count in *NA*26 at least 35 instances of ἐκ *part.* in John, over against 6 instances of *gen. part.* This last figure, however, makes it impossible to consider the use of the *gen. part.* non-Johannine. More decisive is this: the same expression as in 6,66 occurs a few verses earlier, in 6,60, there in the form πολλοὶ ... ἐκ τῶν μαθητῶν αὐτοῦ. So the suspicion seems justified that the presence of the preposition ἐκ in 6,66 is due to scribal accommodation to 6,60[8]. Maybe the other instances of ἐκ *part.* in the same passage exerted their influence as well (6,64.70.71).

So in the five instances of difference between *NA*26 and *NA*25 a preference for the readings of *NA*25 can be justified. It should be noted that all instances are more or less of the same type: influence of parallel formulae, in the more remote (6,2) or nearer context (6,29.37b.52.66), appears to be obvious. The numerical analysis will be made, then, on the basis of the *NA*25-text.

1. *John 6 as a literary unit*

John 6 contains the stories of the multiplication of the loaves (6,1-15), of Jesus' walking on the water of the Lake of Galilee (6,16-21), the discourse on the bread of life (6,22-59), and the account of the division among the disciples (6,60-71).

When compared with the preceding and following chapters, John 6 evidently constitutes a unity of place: the scene is the Lake of Galilee and its close surroundings (cfr. 6,1.16-17.22-24.59). The preceding chapter has Jerusalem as its scene (5,1), at the beginning of the next chapter, Jesus is going about in Galilee (7,1, cfr. 7,9), and soon the scene moves, once again, to Jerusalem (7,10).

John 6 constitutes a unity of time as well. The chapter is connected with the preceding and the following chapter by the vague indication of time μετὰ ταῦτα (6,1; 7,1). The events of John 5 take place on the occasion of 'a Festival' (not indicated more precisely) 'of the Jews' (5,1), and at the beginning of John 7 the Jewish Festival of Tabernacles is near (7,2), whereas in 6,4 the temporal setting of the multiplication of the loaves is said to be in the proximity of the Jewish Festival of Passover. The ensuing events are in a narrow temporal relationship with the multiplication of the loaves: the crossing of the lake in the evening of the same day (6,16), the discourse on the bread of life and the division among the disciples on the next day (6,22). In this way, the evangelist is suggesting a considerable lapse of time between the events of John 6, and those preceding and following them.

In addition to the local and temporal unity, a thematic unity can be discerned in John 6. The discourse on the bread of life is connected with the miracle of the loaves: just as the healing of the man born blind (ch. 9) points to Jesus as the light of the world (9,5; cfr. 8,12) and the raising of Lazarus (11,1-44) points to Jesus as the resurrection and the life (11,25), so the miracle of the loaves points to Jesus as the bread of life, which is the great theme of the discourse (6,35.41.48-58). The connection between miracle and discourse is, indeed, quite clear from the reference to the miracle in 6,26-27. The division among the disciples, on the other hand, is the consequence of Jesus' words (6,60). In his answer to the murmuring of the disciples, Jesus is referring to his previous words (6,61.63). His speaking about the ascending of the Son of Man 'to where he was before' (6,62) corresponds to the numerous mentions of his descending from heaven in the discourse (6,33.38.50.51.58, cfr. 6,41.42), and his statement 'the flesh is of no avail' (6,63) corresponds to the numerous mentions of 'flesh' in 6,51c-58[9]: his flesh in itself, without his ascension and the gift of the Spirit, is of no avail, is not able to give life. 6,64 is about the unbelief of some of the disciples; in 6,65, this unbelief is 'explained' by Jesus quoting a previous statement of himself: 'This is why I told you that no one can come to me unless it has been granted to him by the Father'. This statement is to be found — in a somewhat different wording — in 6,44, and, in a larger sense, in 6,37-39.45. So it appears that 6,1-15.22-71 constitute a firm thematic unity. But what about the story of the journey across the lake (6,16-21)? What are its thematic connections with the rest of the chapter?

Apparently, the stories of the multiplication of the loaves and the journey across the lake were already connected with each other in the tradition before John: Mark 6,32-52 and its parallel Matt 14,13-33 contain the same sequence of events; in Mark as well as in Matt, the second multiplication story is also followed by a journey across the lake, though without a miraculous act of Jesus (Mark 8,1-10; Matt 15,32-39). It would be a bit naïve, however, to suppose that for an author such as the fourth evangelist, eager to discover a 'symbolic' meaning in the events, the traditional link between the two stories would be the only reason to include the second one in his gospel[10]. Likewise, a mere geographical necessity for including this story (Jesus and his disciples have to come back to Capernaum from the other side of the lake) is, however true it may be, an insufficient explanation of its presence here.

There are four aspects of the story of the journey across the lake and Jesus' walking on the water that provide thematical links with the rest of the chapter:

1. The discourse suggests the gift of the manna as (part of the) OT background of the multiplication of the loaves and Jesus' self-designation as the bread of life (6,31-32.49.58; cfr. the Passover reference in 6,4). Likewise, the crossing of the Reed Sea can be the OT background for the journey across the lake (cfr. Ps 77,19, in a description of the Exodus: 'Your way was in the sea, your path was on the many waters; yet your footsteps were not seen'). The combination of the crossing of the Reed Sea and the gift of the manna is found in the OT: in Ps 78, the crossing of the Sea is mentioned in *v.* 13, and later on the gift of the manna is recorded (*vv.* 23-25; *v.* 24 is possibly quoted in John 6,31). In more general terms, Ps 107,4-5.9 tell how the Lord fills hungry people, wandering in desert wastes, with good things, while *vv.* 23-30 of the same psalm tell about the Lord raising a storm, calming it and thereby delivering people in ships troubled by the storm, and bringing them to their haven. A direct connection of the crossing of the Reed Sea and the gift of the manna is also found in the Passover Haggadah, in the *Dayyenu*-hymn:

'Had he torn the Sea apart for us, but not brought us through it dry, we should have been content! ...
Had he satisfied our needs in the desert for forty years, but not fed us manna, we should have been content!
Had he fed us manna ...'[11].

In this way, the OT background can explain the inclusion of 6,16-21 within John 6[12].

2. The way of acting of the disciples toward Jesus and his behaviour toward them in 6,16-21 can be contrasted with the reaction of the crowd to the miracle of the loaves and Jesus' behaviour in 6,14-15. The crowd, thinking that Jesus is 'the prophet that is to come into the world', tries to make him king, but Jesus withdraws; apparently, this is not the right way to approach him. The disciples on the other hand, want to take him into their boat, after he has presented himself to them with the formula of revelation ἐγώ εἰμι. The crowd, despite the miracle, refuses to accept Jesus as what he really is; the disciples do so. The same difference of attitude is visible in the ensuing episodes: the Jews and many disciples are

reacting to Jesus' words with unbelief (6,41-42.52.60); the Twelve remain faithful (6,66-69)[13].

3. One of the things that becomes clear in the discourse and the ensuing discussion of Jesus with his disciples, but remains not understood by the crowd at all, is that Jesus will give the bread from heaven, his flesh, to eat as the exalted Son of Man, ascended to heaven (6,53.62-63; cfr. 6,27, and 6,51, with its allusion to Jesus' death). Similarly, 6,1-21 draws a picture, first of Jesus' giving of bread, then of his being misunderstood by the crowd, and finally of his disappearing and revealing himself to the disciples on the lake as a divine being, with the words ἐγώ εἰμι. The sequence of events in 6,1-21 reflects the sequence of thought in the discourse and ensuing discussion[14].

4. A final thematical link between 6,16-21 and the rest of the chapter consists in the use of the formula ἐγώ εἰμι. It is used by Jesus absolutely in 6,20, and with a predicate in 6,35.48.51 (cfr. 6,41). First of all, it should be clear that this formula in 6,20 is more than a mere recognition-formula. 'Walking on the water' evokes several OT texts[15], where God is said to be walking on the water: Ps 77,20; Job 9,8 (LXX ἐπὶ θαλάσσης, cfr. John 6,19); Hab 3,8.15; cfr. also Odae Salomonis 39,8-11; said of Wisdom, Sir 24,5. Against this background, it will be clear that Jesus is acting as God here. Jesus' words 'do not be afraid', in answer to the fear of the disciples, are also an indication that the fourth evangelist conceives of Jesus' appearance here as a theophany, cfr., e.g., LXX Gen 15,1; 26,24; 28,13; Judg 6,23; Tob 12,17; Dan 10,12.19; from the NT Matt 17,7; 28,5.10; cfr. from Greek pagan literature Homer, *Iliad* 20,130; Euripides, *Ion* 1549sqq[16]. The formula ἐγώ εἰμι occurs in the LXX-version of Deutero-Isa as a translation of the Hebrew formula of divine revelation *ʾny hwʾ*: Isa 41,4; 43,10; 46,4; 48,12; 52,6; cfr. 43,25; 45,18.19; 51,12. When these things are taken together, it will be clear that ἐγώ εἰμι in John 6,20 is more than a mere formula of recognition: it is a formula of revelation[17], and as such it is used elsewhere in John (8,24.28.58; 13,19). Now, the Johannine ἐγώ εἰμι-sayings with a predicate contain a revelation of the soteriological meaning Jesus has for men (see 6,35.48-51; 8,12; 10,9; 11,25; 14,6). This meaning is based on his relationship with the Father, his being sent by him (cfr. 5,21; 6,57). In John 6, this is clearly expressed in the statement of 6,51: 'I am the living bread *that has come down from heaven*'. So, the ἐγώ εἰμι-sayings with a predicate in John are a soteriological unfolding of Jesus' being sent by God, his coming from God. As this relationship of Jesus and God is expressed in a most pregnant way in the absolute ἐγώ εἰμι, it may be legitimate to consider the ἐγώ εἰμι-sayings with a predicate as an unfolding of the absolute ἐγώ εἰμι, an unfolding mainly as to its

soteriological value; an OT parallel can be found in the combination, in the LXX-version of Second Isaiah, of the absolute use of ἐγώ εἰμι with its predicative use (48,12; 43,25; 45,19; 51,12)[18]. So there is a link between the ἐγώ εἰμι of Jesus in 6,20 on the one hand, and in 6,35.48.51 on the other[19].

These four aspects of 6,16-21 may elucidate why the fourth evangelist included this story in his account of the multiplication of the loaves and the ensuing discussion and discourse[20]. Our conclusion can be that John 6 as a whole constitutes a literary unit[21].

The next step will be to see whether this literary unity also appears in numbers of W and S.

The number of S of John 6 is 2463. In itself, this is an insignificant figure, but when narrative and discourse are separated (6,41b is considered to be discourse), the chapter turns out to be made up of 1038 S of narrative, and 1425 S of discourse, 25 of which are occupied by OT quotations (6,31c.45b), so that there remain without these 1400 S of discourse. Here, the technique of rounding off one part (narrative, discourse) and the surplus-technique are applied. Out of these 1400 S, 1116 are put in the mouth of Jesus (6,42d*b*: ἐκ τοῦ οὐρανοῦ καταβέβηκα included). We have here again a case of application of surplus-technique: 6,41b is the only statement of Jesus in John 6 that is quoted separately by the evangelist; it is also a statement that formulates in a most pregnant way the scandal for the Jews: how can this man, whose father and mother they know, say that he is the bread which came down from heaven? It is, moreover, a statement that — as will appear later — is in the central part of John 6, viz. 6,41-43. It contains 16 S, so there remain without it 1100 S of discourse of Jesus.

The technique of rounding off one part is applied to the number of W as well: the total number of W of John 6 is 1238; the narrative occupies 500 W, and the discourse 738. Counting the numeral in 6,19 at one word would spoil the 500 W. I shall assume in the rest of the analysis that the author of John intended this numeral to be counted at two words.

In Table I, a schematic arrangement of the above results is given.

Table I. John 6	syllables		words	
narrative in John 6		1038		500
discourse (without OT quotations) of persons other than Jesus	284		137	
discourse of Jesus (except 6,41b)	1100		580	
idem in 6,41b	16/1400		9	
OT quotations		25/2463	12/738/1238	

Another division which has been applied to the text of John 6 is a division of the text according to the actors. The numbers of S resulting from such a division are given in Table II.

Table II. syll. divided acc. to actors John 6

	Jesus	Twelve (incl. individual members)[22]	disciples	crowd	impersonal	
6,1	27					
2				31		
3	25					
4					15	
5-6	73					
7-9		97				
10ab	17					
10c					10	
10d				19		
11-12	78					
13		40				
14				41		
15	43/ 263	/137		/ 91	/ 25	
16-17a		46				
17b*a*					10	
17b*b*	13					
18					19	
19		54				
20	14					
21a		12				
21b	/ 27	/112			20/ 49	
22				69		
23					37	
24-25				76		
26-27	105					
28				23		
29	36					
30-31				67		
32-33	83					
34				20		
35-40	232					
41-42				80		
43-51	274					
52				31		
53-59	230/ 960			/366	/ 37	
60			34			
61-65	186					
66			31			
67	20					
68-69		57				
70-71a	49					
71bc	/ 255	19/ 76	/65			
total	1505 +	325 +	65 +	457 +	111	= 2463

(The subtotals correspond to the division of the chapter into pericopes in *UBSGNT*[3].)

The sum of the sentences, in which Jesus and the Twelve are the actors, amounts to 1505 + 325 (triangular number of 25) = 1830 S (triangular number of 60). The two sentences, in which a larger body of disciples is the actor (6,60.66), amount together to 65 S, = 1/5 of 325.

A final striking observation concerning John 6 as a literary unit: the first predicative ἐγώ εἰμι-saying in John 6 (also the first saying of this kind in the whole gospel), 6,35b, which, in a sense, is the most important saying of the whole chapter[23], constitutes the nucleus of the chapter, when measured in S: 1227 S precede this saying of 10 S, 1226 follow it.

2. *The sections of John 6 and their connections*

A division of John 6 is — to a certain extent — a rather simple task. 6,1-15 constitutes a unity of time and place, and relates the multiplication of the loaves and the fishes. The unity of the story is marked by the movements that are depicted at the beginning and end of it: in 6,1, Jesus goes to the farther shore of the Lake of Galilee, and in 6,15 it is told how he withdraws again from there to the hills by himself.

6,16-21, the story of the journey across the lake, constitutes a unity of time and place as well: in the darkness of the night, the disciples are on the lake. Here, too, the unity of the story is marked by movements at the beginning and end: in 6,16-17a, the disciples go down to the lake, and get into their boat; in 6,21, the boat reaches the land they are making for.

The two stories are connected by 6,14-15. These verses are not only the conclusion of 6,1-15, but they also contain information that is essential for 6,16-21: Jesus is separated from his disciples. As such, the two verses connect with what follows[24].

A new indication of time is given in 6,22: 'the next day'. The scene moves to Capernaum (6,22-24). The crowd and Jesus get engaged in a conversation (6,25-34) that ends in a monologue by Jesus, with a few interruptions by his audience (6,35-58). The indication of place is repeated, by way of inclusion, in 6,59, a typical Johannine closing formula (cfr. 1,28; 2,11; 4,54; 8,20; see above, p. 46).

Thereafter, the evangelist goes on by describing the reaction to Jesus' words on behalf of the disciples (6,60-71). The scheme of question and answer, that dominates the preceding section, is present here too. This does not mean, however, that 6,60-71 is only a subsection of 6,22-71; a few indications make clear that 6,60-71 has to be considered a section in itself:

— 6,59 is a typical closing formula (see above);

— the dialogue-partners of Jesus are no longer the crowd of the Jews, but his disciples;

— the key-words of 6,22-59, 'bread' and 'to eat', do not occur in 6,60-71;
— a negative indication: the scheme of question and answer is in John 6 not confined to 6,22-71; as it also occurs in 6,5-10, it cannot be made the criterion for dividing the chapter into sections.

As a result of this analysis, we can distinguish four sections in John 6: 6,1-15.16-21.22-59.60-71. The next question is: can any relationships be discerned between these sections?

6,1-21 constitutes a rather firm unity over against the following dialogue and monologue because 6,1-15.16-21 are connected by the transitional passage 6,14-15, and because the events depicted in these two pericopes take place one day earlier than the events of 6,22sqq.

6,22-59 includes the bulk of the material of John 6. This section constitutes the central part of the whole chapter: it turns around Jesus' self-revelation as 'the bread of life' (6,35.48.51); 6,1-21 contains two 'signs' pointing to this self-revelation (the multiplication of the loaves pointing to Jesus as bread, cfr. 6,26sqq; the walking on the water pointing to his quality of divine being, see above under 1.), whereas in 6,60-71 the different reactions to this self-revelation are related.

So the whole chapter seems to be composed as a triptych: 6,1-21.22-59.60-71[25]. The two outer parts of this triptych are corresponding because of the active presence of the disciples in them, whereas in the central part, the disciples are only mentioned in passing in 6,22.24.

The division of John 6 given here is that common in text-editions, commentaries and studies[26].

A count of S in John 6 according to this division results in a total number of 704 S for 6,1-21 (516 + 188), 1363 for 6,22-59, and 396 for 6,60-71. So, the sum of the numbers of S for the outer parts of the triptych amounts to exactly 1100 S, made up of 704, $= 16 \times 44$, and 396, $= 9 \times 44$, S. To put it otherwise: $44 \times 4^2 + 44 \times 3^2 = 44 \times 5^2$ (see above, p. 29). See Table III.

Table III. John 6	syllables		
6,1-15	516		
16-21	188/704		
22-59			1363
60-71		396/1100/2463	

The link between the outer parts of the triptych is obvious from other numerical observations. When narrative and discourse are separated in 6,1-21.60-71, the narrative amounts to 737 S, 383 of which are in 6,1-15; the discourse amounts to 363 S, 141 of which are in 6,1-21, and 222 in

6,60-71. All these numbers are of a symmetrical structure. The disciples (the Twelve and the larger group) speak in 110 + 18 = 128, = 2^7, S. Out of this number, 110 S (a rectangular number: 10 × 11), or 1/10 of the total number of 1100, occur in the mouth of the Twelve; together with the 215 S spoken by Jesus, a total of 325, triangular number of 25, is reached for the discourse of Jesus *cum suis* (see Table IV).

Table IV. John 6,1-21.60-71	syllables		
narrative in 6,1-21.60-71		737 (383 in 6,1-15)	
discourse of Jesus	215		
of the Twelve	110/325		
of the disciples	18		
of the crowd		20/363 (141 + 222)/	1100

When the numbers of S for the sentences of 6,1-21.60-71 are divided according to the actors, interesting results appear (see Table II). The sentences with Jesus as actor amount to 263 + 27 + 255 = 545 S; the rest amounts to 325 + 65 + 91 + 74 = 555 S (again two numbers of a symmetrical structure). The number of 555 S includes 325 S (triangular number of 25), = 25 × 13, for the sentences with the Twelve as actor, 65, = 5 × 13, for the sentences with the larger group of disciples as actor, and 91, = 7 × 13, also triangular number of 13, for the sentences with the crowd as actor (see already under 1., *in fine*). So, the factor 13 seems rather prominent in this way of dividing the text. The sentences with an impersonal subject amount to 74 S, over against 37, = ½ × 74, in 6,22-59; so, the total number for these sentences in John 6 is 111.

The numbers of W resulting from a division of John 6 according to the actors are given in Table V.

Table V. words divided acc. to actors John 6
(cfr. the explanation given at the end of Table II)

	Jesus	Twelve	disciples	crowd	impersonal
6,1	12				
2				14	
3	13				
4					9
5-6	34				
7-9		44			
10ab	7				
10c					7
10d				8	
11-12	33				
13		17			
14				19	
15	19/118	/ 61		/ 41	/16
16-17a		21			
17b*a*					4

	Jesus	Twelve	disciples	crowd	impersonal	
17b*b*	7					
18					7	
19		22				
20	8					
21a		7				
21b	/ 15	/ 50			11/22	
22				37		
23					15	
24-25				38		
26-27	52					
28				12		
29	17					
30-31				34		
32-33	47					
34				11		
35-40	125					
41-42				42		
43-51	149					
52				15		
53-59	127/517			/189	/15	
60			17			
61-65	96					
66			15			
67	11					
68-69		24				
70-71a	22					
71bc	/129	9/ 33	/32			
total	779 +	144 +	32 +	230 +	53	= 1238

The number of W for the sentences with Jesus as actor in 6,1-21.60-71 is 118 + 15 + 129 = 262; for the sentences with the Twelve as actor it is 61 + 50 + 33 = 144 (= 12^2), made up of 111 in 6,1-21 and 33 in 6,60-71. So the total number of W of the sentences with Jesus *cum suis* as actors amounts to 406, triangular number of 28. The rest of 6,1-21.60-71 amounts to 32 + 41 + 38 = 111 W. Note, once again, the symmetrical numbers: 262, 111, 33.

So far, then, about the tripartite structure of John 6. In the literary analysis at the beginning of this section the two stories of 6,1-21 appeared to constitute a rather firm unity over against the rest of the chapter, among other things because of their being connected by 6,14-15. This unity is somewhat reflected in numbers of W and S. 6,1-21 has a length of 323 W (a symmetrical number). A division of 6,1-21 according to the actors results in 263 + 27 + 137 + 112 = 539 S, = 49 × 11, for the sentences with Jesus and the Twelve as actors, and 91 + 25 + 49 = 165, = 15 × 11, for the rest (see Table II). Once again, the factor 11 appears (cfr. Table III above).

3. *The sections of John 6,1-21.60-71 separately and their details*

a) *John 6,1-15: the multiplication of the loaves*

At the beginning of the preceding section, the essentials have been said about the literary unity of John 6,1-15. There, a correspondence was noticed between 6,1 and 15: the appearance of Jesus, the protagonist, on the stage, and his disappearing from there, by withdrawing to the mountain. (The mountain mentioned in 6,3 has a function different from that of the mountain mentioned in 6,15: in 6,3, the actors stay on the stage. In the present context, it seems to be implied either that Jesus and the disciples leave the mountain of 6,3 to go to the crowd, cfr. 6,10-11, and that Jesus returns to the mountain in 6,15, cfr. πάλιν 6,15, or that in 6,15 Jesus withdraws farther up the mountain; a combination of both implications is also possible[27].)

The remainder of the story displays a certain unity because of the inclusion made up by 6,2 and 14:

6,2 ὄχλος πολύς ... ἑώρων τὰ σημεῖα ἃ ἐποίει
14 οἱ οὖν ἄνθρωποι ἰδόντες ὃ ἐποίησεν σημεῖον[28]

Another argument in favour of this unity is the 'Chorschluss'-function of 6,14: the reaction of the crowd marks the end of the miracle-story[29].

Nevertheless, this division of the story into entrance, corpus and exit does not preclude a somewhat different division, viz. 6,1-4.5-13.14-15, or — in terms of content — situation, action and consequences of the action. Actually, Jesus takes the initiative to a miraculous act in 6,5, and keeps the initiative up to 6,13[30].

A further division of the corpus of the story is obvious: 5-9 discussion, 10-13 Jesus' miracle[31]. Andrew's question in 6,9 has a central position: it is the climax of human ignorance and helplessness, but at the same time here the material is put forward that makes a solution possible: five barley loaves and two fishes[32].

An analysis of the numbers of S and W[33] in John 6,1-15 gives, first of all, a confirmation of the literary unity of the story: the technique of rounding off one part is applied to the discourse of Jesus, that has a length of 50 S. The discourse of the crowd has a size of 20 S. Between the words of Philip and Andrew (6,7.9), there is a proportion of 3:4: Philip speaks in 27 S, Andrew in 36 (see Table VI).

Table VI. John 6,1-15	syllables
narrative in John 6,1-15	383
discourse of Jesus	50
of the crowd	20
of Philip	27
of Andrew	36/516

A division of the numbers of S and W of the integral text of the story according to the actors is given in Table VII (cfr. Tables II and V).

Table VII. syll. and words divided acc. to actors John 6,1-15

	syll.	words
Jesus actor	263	118
the Twelve	137/400	61
crowd	91	41
impersonal	25/116/516	16/118/236

The sentences in which Jesus *cum suis* is the actor, have a total length of 400 S. The sentences in which Jesus alone is the actor, have a length of 118 W, which is exactly half of the sum total of 236 W. Maybe it is worth mention that without the 16 W of the sentences without a personal subject, the story has a length of 220 W, which is another multiple of 11.

The various divisions of the story are clearly reflected in the numbers of S and W. The framework 6,1.15 amounts to 70 S (43 in 6,15; 6,1-14 contains 473 S, = 11 × 43). In the corpus of the story, Andrew's remark about five loaves and two fishes in 6,9 occupies a central position: 205 S precede it in 6,2-8, and 205 S follow it in 6,10-14. The remark itself has a length of 36 S, triangular number of 8 and square number of 6 (see Table VIII).

Table VIII. John 6,1-15 syllables

6,1	27		
2-8		205	
9		36	
10-14		205/446	
15	43/		70/516

Several of these numbers seem to have a special significance within the present context. The figures 5 and 2, that determine the number 205, play a prominent role in the story: Jesus feeds the multitude from 5 loaves and 2 fishes (ἄρτος occurs 5 × in 6,1-15: vv. 5.7.9.11.13, and ὀψάριον 2 × : vv. 9.11[34]), and 200 *denarii* (6,7) and 5000 men (6,10) are mentioned (2 and 5 are the primary factors of both 200 and 5000). We have already seen that Jesus' discourse in 6,1-15 has a length of 50 S, that of the crowd of 20 S. The framework of the story (6,1.15) has a length of 70 S; 7 is the sum of 5 and 2. The numbers 5 and 2 are presented in the middle of the central verse in 14, or 2 × 7, S:

6,9	ἔστιν παιδάριον ὧδε ὃς ἔχει	11 S
	πέντε ἄρτους κριθίνους καὶ δύο ὀψάρια	14
	ἀλλὰ ταῦτα τί ἐστιν εἰς τοσούτους	11/36

36, the number of S of this verse, is 3 × 12; the story tells about 12 baskets (6,13).

In numbers of W, the central position of 6,9 is brought out once more: 109 W precede this verse of 17 W, 110 W (a rectangular number: 10 × 11) follow it (see Table IXa). The number 205 returns here: without the framework (6,1.15) of 31 W, there remain 205 W for 6,2-14 (Table IXb). The division 6,1-4.5-13.14-15 results in 48 + 150 + 38 W; the first unit is made up of 12 + 36 (= 3 × 12) W, the last unit is made up of 2 × 19 W (Table IXc).

Table IX. John 6,1-15 words	a		b		c	
6,1	12		12		12	
2-4	36			36	36/	48
5-8	61/109			61	61	
9		17		17	17	
10-13	72			72	72/150	
14	19			19/205	19	
15	19/110/236		19/	31/236	19/	38/236

In numbers of both W and S, 6,4 (about the proximity of the Passover Festival) seems to be a surplus within 6,1-4: without this verse, the opening and closing passages (6,1-3.14-15) are of almost equal length (39 and 38 W, 83 and 84 S); together, they amount to (almost) half the length of 6,5-13 (167 and 334 S, 77 and 150 W respectively).

About details of the story, mainly concerning its corpus (6,5-13), some remarks have to be made. Firstly about the numbers of S:

1. The combination of question and answer 6,5-7 has a length of 110 S. The commentary given by the evangelist in 6,6 is an isocolon of 2 × 11 = 22 S. Again, two multiples of 11 appear.

2. Andrew's remark in 6,9 contains 36, = 3 × 12, S; it is introduced by 6,8, made up of 12 + 12 = 24 S.

3. 6,5-9 has a length of 110 + 60 = 170 S, and is continued by 17 S in 6,10ab (see below about the role of 17 in the numbers of W of this passage).

4. 6,10-11, the miracle proper, is made up of 75 S of narrative, and 12 S of discourse.

5. 6,12-13, the gathering of the pieces that were left over, has a length of 77 S, made up of 55 S of narrative, and 22 S of discourse.

About the numbers of W:

1. 6,3, about Jesus and the Twelve, has a length of 13 W, preceded by 26, = 2 × 13, W in 6,1-2.

2. The discussion 6,5-9 contains 44 W of narrative; the commentary in 6,6 has a length of 11 W, as well as Philip's answer in 6,7. The discourse amounts to 34 W, half of which, 17, are in the final sentence, Andrew's remark 6,9; the first two sentences (6,5-6) have together a length of 34 (= 2 × 17) W.

3. 6,10-13 contains 60, = 5 × 12, W of narrative, and 12 W of discourse (cfr. the numbers mentioned in this passage: 5000, 12 and 5, in 6,10.13). The two parts of the passage, 6,10-11 (the miracle proper) and 6,12-13 (the gathering of the fragments), have a length of 40 (= 5 × 8) and 32 (= 4 × 8) W respectively. 6,10-11 contains 36 (= 3 × 12) W of narrative, and 4 W of discourse; 6,12-13 contains 24 W (= 2 × 12) of narrative, and 8 W of discourse.

4. 6,5-13 as a whole contains in its first part 6, and in its second part 12 (= 2 × 6) W of discourse of Jesus (4 in 6,10b; 2 × 4 in 6,12cd). The total quantity of discourse is 46 W (cfr. John 2,20). Three units of 17 W attract the attention: the introduction 6,5a, the final sentence 6,13 (mentioning the numbers 5 and 12, whose sum is 17!), and the central sentence 6,9.

In numbers of both S and W of 6,1-15, the factors 11, 12 and 17 seem to be important.

A final note about the text of 6,2, discussed at the beginning of this chapter: in so far as the quantitative aspect of the text is concerned, there is no reason to depart from the *NA*^{25}-text.

b) *John 6,16-21: Jesus' walking on the sea*

The literary unity of 6,16-21 has been dealt with in the preceding section. There is a caesura at 6,18/19: in 6,16-18 the disciples are on the stage without Jesus; in 6,19, Jesus appears and comes to them[35].

The second part of the story, 6,19-21, is, of course, the more important one: in and by the presence of the divine Jesus the disciples, oppressed by darkness, sea and storm, are saved. This part has a tripartite structure: in 6,19a.21, spatial movements are described. The disciples see Jesus walking on the lake and approaching the boat; they want to take him aboard, and the boat reaches the land they are making for. In the middle part (6,19b-20), on the other hand, we are told about their fear and Jesus' reaction; this part has more of a description of mental movements.

6,16-21 has a length of 188 S; 8 of them (4 + 4) are spoken by Jesus (6,20), and the narrative uses 180 S. The sentences with Jesus as actor amount to 15 W, those with the disciples (protagonists in this story) as actor to 50 W, and the sentences with impersonal subjects amount to 22 W (a multiple of 11; see Table V).

The bipartition of the story (6,16-18.19-21) is reflected in the number of S: 88 (another multiple of 11) in 6,16-18, and 100 (a round and square figure) in 6,19-21. At the beginning and end of the story we meet units of 46 S: 6,16-17a (continued in 6,17b by a sentence of 23, = ½ × 46, S), and 6,20-21 (cfr. John 2,20, and above under 3.a., *in fine*). The remaining part 6,17b-19 is made up of 42 S, = 7 × 6 (a rectangular number), for 6,17b-18, and 54 S, = 9 × 6, for 6,19; it contains exactly the description of the frightening journey of the disciples across the lake (see Table X).

Table X. John 6,16-21 syllables

6,16-17a		46
17b	23	
18	19/42/ 88	
19		54
20-21		46/100/188

In the numbers of W of this passage, it is again the factor 11 that asks for attention. Both the first and the last sentence of the story (6,16.21b) have a length of 11 W. The first part (6,16-18) is made up of 4 sentences of a rather regular structure; two of them have a length of 11 W:

6,16	4 + 7 = 11 W
17a	4 + 6 = 10
17b	4 + 7 = 11
18	7 = 7/39

In the second part, the narrative amounts to 44 W, = 4 × 11; half of this number, 22, in 6,19.

The tripartite structure of 6,19-21 is visible in numbers of S, as Table XI shows. A careful balance has been achieved by the author: 48, = 3 × 16, and 32, = 2 × 16, S, together 80, surround a centre of 20 S, made up of 6 + 6 + 4 + 4 S (2 + 4 + 2 + 2 W).

Table XI. John 6,19-21 syllables

6,19a	48	
19b-20		20
21	32/80/100	

c) *John 6,60-71: the division among the disciples*

It has been set forth above, under 2., in how far the section 6,60-71 can be considered a literary unit. Now the question of its structure has to be dealt with.

There is a caesura at 6,65/66. 6,60-65 tells about the negative reaction of the disciples to Jesus' previous words, and Jesus' answer to their reaction. In 6,66-71, a division among the disciples takes place; the Twelve remain faithful to Jesus and confess him — by the mouth of Simon Peter — as 'the Holy One of God' (but out of this group, Judas will defect). The caesura is marked by ἐκ τούτου, which may either indicate the moment since when or the reason why many of the disciples do not follow Jesus any longer[36]. In both interpretations, the expression refers to the start of the process of separation among the disciples, whereas in 6,60-65 the disciples are confronted with the decision for or against Jesus.

So 6,60-71 seems to be made up of two parts, 6,60-65.66-71, both beginning with a sentence in which the negative attitude of πολλοὶ (ἐκ) τῶν μαθητῶν αὐτοῦ is depicted. Because of the occurrence of these words in both 6,60 and 6,66, one could be tempted to consider these verses to form an inclusion, confining the literary unit 6,60-66, about the larger group of disciples; similarly, 6,67-71 would be a literary unit, about the Twelve, confined by the inclusion τοῖς δώδεκα - ἐκ τῶν δώδεκα[37]. In the present form of the story, however, the intended contrast between the larger group of disciples and the Twelve makes it at least possible that 6,66 is meant to be the starting point for what follows — which is confirmed by οὖν at the beginning of 6,67[38]. The numerical analysis may help to decide this matter[39].

Anyhow, both parts are balanced in so far as each of them contains three utterances in direct discourse (6,60bc.61b-64a.65b.67b.68b-69.70bc); in both cases, the second one of these is the longest one. At the end of both parts, we meet a mention of Judas, the betrayer, covertly in 6,64, openly in 6,70-71[40].

The first part displays a cyclic composition. The central utterance is that of Jesus in 6,61b-64a. In this piece of direct discourse, the first and last sentence are corresponding: 'Do you take offence at this?' and 'But there are some of you that do not believe'. Σκανδαλίζεσθαι and οὐ πιστεύειν are almost identical (as can be seen from a comparison of John 16,1 with 13,19; 14,29, and from Rom 9,33; 1 Pet 2,6-8)[41]. The part enclosed between these two sentences about the reaction of the disciples is of a more 'christological' nature: there, Jesus is speaking about himself and his words. In a wider circle, a correspondence can be seen between 6,61a.64b: both sentences deal with Jesus' knowing (6,61: εἰδὼς δὲ ὁ

'Ιησοῦς; 6,64: ᾔδει γὰρ ... ὁ 'Ιησοῦς) about the unbelief of his disciples (expressed by means of γογγύζειν and μὴ πιστεύειν). In a still wider circle, the remark and question of the disciples in 6,60, and Jesus' statement in 6,65 are corresponding: the question of 6,60, 'Who can listen to it (viz. Jesus' discourse)?', is answered in 6,65, 'No one can come to me unless it has been granted to him by the Father' (note δύναται in both utterances)[42]. Besides, in both cases previous words of Jesus are referred to. So, then, 6,60-65 seems to be arranged as follows:

A	B	C	D	C'	B'	A'
6,60	61a	61b	62-63	64a	64b	65

The composition of 6,66-71 is less intricate: the confession of Simon Peter (6,68-69) is surrounded by two utterances of Jesus, both (at least in part) in the form of a question, and both directed to the Twelve[43].

The discourse in 6,60-71 amounts to 222 S (see above, pp. 147-148). A division according to the actors results in 129 W for the sentences with Jesus as actor, and nearly half of this number, 65, for the sentences with the disciples as actor (cfr. p. 148 above, for other multiples of 13 in John 6, in a similar division of the text). This number is made up of 32 W for the sentences with the larger group of disciples as actor, and 33 W for the sentences with the Twelve as actor (see Table V).

As for the different possibilities of bipartition of the passage: the division 6,60-65.66-71 is clearly confirmed by the numbers of S. 6,60-65 has a length of 220 S, = 20 × 11 or 5 × 44; 6,66-71 has a size of 176 S, = 16 × 11 or 4 × 44. The factor 11 is prominent once more.

6,60-65 is made up of 140 S of discourse and 80 S of narrative. At the end of this passage, Jesus is quoting his own previously spoken words (cfr. 6,44; the reference is clear, though there is no absolute verbal agreement). This is an important statement within the present context: it explains why many withdraw, and only the Twelve remain faithful. To this quotation, the surplus-technique has been applied: it has a length of 13 W, on a total of 113 W for 6,60-65. It contains 23 S, on a total of 122 S for Jesus' discourse in 6,60-65; so there remain 99 S, 88 in 6,61b-64a, and 11 introducing the quotation in 6,65b.

The concentric structure of the passage is reflected in its numbers of S and W, as is made visible in Table XII.

The discourse of Jesus 6,61b-64a has a length of 88 S or 44 W, made up of 22 S or 11 W for the framework (C and C'), and 44 + 22 = 66 S (triangular number of 11) or 22 + 11 = 33 W for D. The corresponding

Table XII. John 6,60-65		syllables				words			
6,60	A				34				17 (8 + 9)
61a	B			30				15	
61b	C		8				3		
62-63b	D	44				22			
63c		22/ 66				11/ 33			
64a	C'		14/22/ 88				8/11/ 44		
64b	B'			30/ 60				17/ 32	
65a	A'				4				2
65b					34/72/220				18/37/113

sentences B and B' are of equal length: 30 S (a rectangular number: 5 × 6). A has a length of 34 S or 17 W, A' is made up of 4 + 34 S or 2 + 18 W. The utterance of the disciples in 6,60 has half the length of Jesus' answer in 6,65: 9 and 18 W respectively.

Parts B' and A', taken together, are made up of 34 S of narrative (6,64b-65a), and 34 S of discourse (6,65b), being equivalent to 19 and 18 W respectively. The author made use of the number 34 in other parts of this passage as well: the double question of Jesus 6,61b-62 has a length of 34 S, as does 6,60 (see above; cfr. the role of the number 17, = ½ × 34, in 6,1-15, see above, under 3.a. *in fine*).

Just as the section 6,60-65, so the final paragraph 6,66-71 is closed by 2 × 34 S: the size of both 6,70 and 6,71 is 34 S. The passage has a length of 81 W, = 9^2; the narrative amounts to 44 W. The first and last sentence (6,66.71) are of equal length: 15 W; 6,70 has a length of 16 W. The central position of the confession of Simon Peter can be illustrated from numbers of W: 30 W precede this confession of 20 W, 31 W follow it.

Within 6,66-71, the passage 6,67-69 deserves our attention. It has a length of 77 S, on a total of 176 S, and is arranged as follows:

6,67a	εἶπεν οὖν ὁ Ἰησοῦς τοῖς δώδεκα	10 S	6 W
b	μὴ καὶ ὑμεῖς θέλετε ὑπάγειν	10	5
68a	ἀπεκρίθη αὐτῷ Σίμων Πέτρος	10	4
bc	κύριε, πρὸς τίνα ἀπελευσόμεθα	12	4
d	ῥήματα ζωῆς αἰωνίου ἔχεις	11	4
69*a*	καὶ ἡμεῖς πεπιστεύκαμεν καὶ ἐγνώκαμεν	13	5
b	ὅτι σὺ εἶ ὁ ἅγιος τοῦ θεοῦ	11/77	7/35

Simon Peter's confession divides into two almost equal parts, of 23 and 24 S, both ending with a line of 11 S, and is preceded by 3 × 10 S. The three sentences 6,67.68.69 are, in W, of almost equal length: 11 + 12 (3 × 4) + 12 W, while the other sentences of 6,66-71 are longer: 15 or 16 W (see above).

A detail worth mentioning is the sequence of decreasing numbers of W in 6,71:

ἔλεγεν δὲ τὸν Ἰούδαν Σίμωνος Ἰσκαριώτου	6 W
οὗτος γὰρ ἔμελλεν παραδιδόναι αὐτόν	5
εἷς ἐκ τῶν δώδεκα	4

A final remark concerning 6,70 is important for the whole of John 6. In 6,70, Jesus is speaking about the election of the Twelve, and he does so in 6 + 6 = 12 W. One of them is a devil, so he says in 6,70c; then, there remain eleven, and the length of 6,70c is 11 S. If the author here makes the form suit the contents so remarkably, this may help to explain the prominent role of the factor 11 in John 6, and especially in its last section. Numerous examples of this role have emerged. It clearly concerns numbers of both S and W. One more example to illustrate this: in 6,63c Jesus says in 11 W, i.e., in 22 S, that the words he has spoken are spirit and life, and in 6,68d Simon Peter says in 11 S that Jesus has words of eternal life. So, an intrinsic relationship seems to exist between syllable-technique and word-technique.

4. *John 6,22-59: the discourse on the bread of life*

An analysis of the literary structure of the discourse on the bread of life (John 6,22-59) is no easy task. Those who set themselves to it, have obtained rather divergent results, dependent upon the principles they suppose the author of the Fourth Gospel to have used in the composition of the discourse[44]. The present analysis will start with a survey and a critical discussion of extant analyses, and especially of the principles of composition that are supposed to be at work in the discourse. This survey will provide a (mainly negative) base for an analysis of the literary structure of the discourse, that takes into account as many indications as possible. This analysis will be confronted with a count of S and W. Finally, a series of details of the discourse will be investigated.

a) *Extant analyses of the literary structure of John 6,22-59*

1. A division of the discourse based on observations of a purely formal nature has been proposed by P. Szczygiel and P. Gächter[45]. They divide the discourse, considered as Semitic rhythmical prose, into stichoi, combined to form strophes; a combination of several strophes results in a group of strophes. In this way, Szczygiel arrives at a division into one 'Doppelstrophe' and four 'Tristrophen', each of them displaying symmetry in the number of stichoi per strophe:

I a	6,25-27,	10 stichoi	I b	28-31,	10			
II a	32-34,	9	II b	35-37,	8	II c	38-40,	9
IIIa	41-44,	10	IIIb	45-47,	8	IIIc	48-51,	10
IVa	52-53,	8	IVb	54-56,	7	IVc	57-59,	8
V a	60-63,	10	V b	64-66,	8	V c	67-70,	10

Gächter's division is restricted to 6,35-58, and is somewhat different: there are two parts, 6,35-47.48-58; both parts are divided into two groups of strophes by means of an interruption of the Jews (6,41-42.52), the first part being made up of first a longer and then a shorter group of strophes, the second one of first a shorter and then a longer group of strophes. Besides, there are in both parts introductory and concluding stichoi (6,35b.47.48), while 6,58 is a concluding strophe to the whole discourse.

Especially Gächter's study contains a series of interesting observations about formal aspects of the text of the discourse. Nevertheless, the main thesis of his study and of Szczygiel's is subject to criticism on three points:

a. The thesis is based on two doubtful hypotheses: firstly, that the Greek text of John is a translation of an Aramaic original, and secondly, that it is possible to determine the (supposed) rhythm of the original Aramaic text via the Greek translation.

b. Because of their purely formal approach, both scholars scarcely take into account the natural division of the text; as in such a division the contents of the text are also of importance, it can be said that they do not pay enough attention to the contents of the text.

c. Basically, only one formal characteristic of the text, viz. the supposed rhythm, is used in the analysis; other formal characteristics are scarcely taken into account.

2. A current way of determining the structure of John 6,22-59 is to make the interruptions of the audience, at least those in 6,41-42.52, the starting points of new sections[46]. This seems a rather obvious principle of division; it has, however, one serious difficulty: the interruptions in 6,41-42.52 do not have a function in the progression of the discourse. The questions asked by the Jews are not answered by Jesus; their interruptions are expressions of misunderstanding, affording him the opportunity to clearer revelation. After their interruptions, he is only repeating on a higher level what he said before the interruption. The questions and remarks of the crowd in the first part of the discourse (6,25.28.30-31.34) are elements of a continuing conversation, and do not serve to mark the beginning of a new section[47]. The caesuras in the discourse, if there are any, do not coincide with the interruptions.

Another way of determining the structure of the discourse by way of the interruptions is the proposal of B. Gärtner and E. J. Kilmartin[48] to parallel the questions in John 6,28.30-31.42.52 with the four questions asked by the four sons in the Passover Haggadah: the halachic question of the wise child, the haggadic instruction to the child too young to ask, the mocking question about the interpretation of Scripture of the wicked child, and the practical question of the sincere child. This is, however, a very weak proposal: not all questions find a place in it, and the parallelisms are rather artificial[49].

3. In a third approach, the structure of the discourse is determined from its contents in the following way: at the beginning of the discourse, a twofold theme is stated, and thereafter the two themes, or the two elements of the theme, are worked out in two parts. According to E. Galbiati[50], two themes are stated in 6,26-29: eucharist (6,26-27) and faith (6,29). Then, 6,32-50 deals with faith and the celestial origin of the bread of life, and 6,48-58 deals with the eucharist and the bread as food. 6,48-50 is a transition between the two parts, and constitutes an inclusion with 6,32-33 on the one side, and 6,58 on the other (in these texts, the bread from heaven and the manna are opposed). According to X. Léon-Dufour[51], the theme is stated in 6,31.33: the celestial origin of the bread, and the necessity to eat this bread. The first subject is dealt with in 6,35-47 (in which part 6,41-42 supposes 6,35-40), the second in 6,48-58 (in which part 6,52 supposes 6,49-51). Then, 6,35 corresponds to 6,48, and 6,47 to 6,58. In a similar way, H. Van den Bussche[52] sees the theme stated in 6,33: celestial origin and life-giving power of the bread, of the Son of Man. 6,32-46 is about the origin, 6,47-59 about the life-giving power. With 6,26-31 as introduction, Van den Bussche obtains three parts, all of them beginning with ἀμὴν ἀμὴν λέγω ὑμῖν. According to J.-N. Aletti[53], the discourse has to be divided into two corresponding parts: 6,35-47.48-58. This division is based on a list of 'corrélats lexématiques', having the same syntactic function: a) Jesus' self-designation in 6,35.48; b) the definitions in 6,39.50; c) the objections of the Jews, asking 'How ...?' in 6,41-42.52; d) the answer of Jesus, with its exclusive character, 6,44 ('no man ... unless').53 ('unless ... not'). A confirmation of this division is found first in the fact that the words 'to come to me', 'to believe', 'all' disappear after 6,47, and 'to eat', 'to die' and 'to live' appear only after 6,48, and then in the fact that the double predicate of 6,33 corresponds to the two parts of the discourse: 'that comes down from heaven' to 6,35-47, and 'and gives life to the world' to 6,48-58.

One could compare the view of P. Borgen[54]. His thesis is that the discourse in John 6 is a midrashic homily. Its starting point is 6,31-33:

a quotation from the OT (Exod 16,15), preceded by a haggadic text, and corrected and paraphrased by Jesus. In 6,31-58, the words from the OT quotation are paraphrased together with fragments from haggadic traditions. The first part (6,32-48) is about 'He gave them bread from heaven', the second part (6,49-58) about 'to eat'. Midrashic method, patterns and terminology are detected by Borgen not only in the discourse as a whole, but also in its various parts. Unlike some other scholars, Borgen arrives at his division by means of a form-critical approach, that is, by comparing the text of John with literary models known from elsewhere, whereas others arrive at their divisions by means of an internal analysis of the text of John, trying to detect internal correlations. This seems at once the strength and the weakness of Borgen's thesis: his detection of midrashic patterns in John 6 is, on the one hand, an important step in Johannine exegesis, but on the other hand it raises questions such as: a) Are these the *only* literary patterns at work in John 6? b) Are these the *main* literary patterns at work in John 6? c) Are they handled by Borgen in the right or in the only possible way? An answer to these three questions can be given only by trying to detect the correlations within the discourse.

U. Wilckens[55] joins Borgen in his conception of the discourse as a midrash on the quotation in 6,31; 'bread from heaven' is explained in 6,32-47, 'given to eat' in 6,48-58. In both sections, the movement of thought is similar: after the opposition between the bread of life and the manna (6,32-33.49-50), Jesus presents himself as the bread of life or the living bread (6,35.51ab). 6,36-40, about faith as access to Jesus, is parallel to 6,51c, about eating Jesus' flesh as realization of eating the bread of life. Then, an intervention of the Jews leads, in both sections, to a repetition of the themes of faith and eating in a rather massive way (6,43-46.53-55). The parallel motives of faith and eucharist are already found in the introduction to the discourse (6,26-31), in 6,27: 'to work' is interpreted as 'to believe' in 6,29, and 'the food that lasts to eternal life, that the Son of Man will give you' is a reference to the eucharistic theme of 6,51c.

A more complicated variant of this way of determining the structure of the discourse on the bread of life has been presented recently by L. Schenke[56]. According to him, the twofold theme is: God and Jesus are acting for the life of man; to obtain life, man has to answer. Both elements are present in the passage 6,26-29, that prepares the discourse. The discourse proper has three parts: 6,32-36.37-47.48-58; in each part, the interruption of the crowd marks the transition from the first to the second theme. The last part is the climax of the whole.

Another variation on the same principle of composition is the proposal of B. Lindars[57]. He considers the OT quotation 6,31 the point of departure for *three* sections: 6,32-40 about the gift of the bread from heaven, 6,41-51 about its nature, and 6,52sqq (in which part 'to eat' from 6,31 is worked out) about the crucified Jesus as the gift of God.

It will be clear from what precedes that the argumentation of the scholars just mentioned has to do — at least to a large extent — with the contents of the text. So a few critical remarks about the way these contents are determined will be appropriate here. (The formal aspects will be dealt with in part b. of this section.)

It seems, indeed, that different themes are present in the discourse. The celestial origin of the bread of life (or, in Schenke's terms, God's acting) is one of them. All authors mentioned above are in agreement on this point. The second theme, however, is described differently: the life-giving power of the bread, or the necessity of eating it (Lindars being the only one who sees three themes resulting from 6,31). Now it seems to me, that both descriptions are valid, so that there are *three* themes working in the discourse: a) the celestial origin of the bread; b) its life-giving power; c) the necessity of eating it. And, what is more, none of these three themes is confined to one part of the discourse, but all three are present *throughout the discourse*.

The celestial origin of the bread, identified with Jesus, is dealt with explicitly in 6,31-33.38.41-42.50-51.57-58 (cfr. also ὁ πέμψας με in 6,38.39.44, and cfr. 6,29). The life-giving power of this bread is put forward explicitly in 6,27.33.35.39-40.44.47-51.53-54.57-58. Apparently, this theme is already present in what is the first part, according to the majority of the divisions mentioned above, whereas the first theme is present in the second part as well. The third theme, the necessity of eating the bread, is clearly present in 6,31.48-58; this seems to justify, in a general way, the divisions in question.

Here, however, one should be careful. It is true that in 6,32-48 nothing explicit is said about eating the bread of life. In 6,35, however, after the identification of Jesus with the bread of life, it is said: 'Whoever comes to me shall never be hungry, and whoever believes in me shall never be thirsty'. The mention of hunger and thirst in this imagery strongly suggests that 'to come to' and 'to believe in' somehow imply eating and drinking (cfr. the parallels to 6,35 in 6,48-50.51ab: from these texts, the parallelism of 'to eat' and 'to come to' or 'to believe in' is clear). The mere fact that Jesus is called 'bread' makes this equivalence obvious indeed. So the third theme is present in the discourse wherever Jesus is talking about believing in him, or coming to him: 6,29-30.35-37.40.44-45.47.

The three themes are present, then, throughout the discourse. They cannot be made, by consequence, the principle of division of the discourse. A more promising way, it seems, is to look for possible different treatments of these themes in the course of the dialogue and monologue. A step in this direction is taken by J. Willemse[58], the last scholar to be discussed here. According to him, 6,26-27.32-33 constitute the twofold beginning of the discourse. In 6,26-27, Jesus is the giver of a gift that still belongs to the future; the corresponding part of the discourse is 6,51c-58. In 6,32-33, the Father is the giver of a gift that is present here and now; the corresponding part is 6,35-51b. Both parts have the same subject: the man Jesus as the bread from heaven. The difference between the two parts is a difference of phase. The first part is about Jesus, the second about Jesus crucified. Here, then, the division of the discourse is based on the way the theme is treated, or — in other words — on the aspect under which Jesus is identified with the subject-matter of the discourse: the bread from heaven. I shall explore this possibility, among others, in my own analysis of John 6,22-59.

4. For the sake of completeness, I mention a few other proposals concerning the literary structure of the discourse in John 6, which have obvious shortcomings and, for that reason, will not detain us very long.

According to J. Bligh[59], two parts, similarly built, can be distinguished in the discourse: 6,26-47.48-65. In both parts, Christ makes an offer, then his audience (in the first part the Jews, in the second part the disciples) reacts incredulously, and finally faith is said to be a gift of God. The apparent weakness of this proposal is that 6,51c-59 has to be eliminated to square things.

Another analysis that is weakened by the elimination of part of the text, is that of G. Segalla[60]: he eliminates 6,36-40, as being inserted by a redactor. The circumstance that there is no other reason for this elimination than the impossibility to assign a position to this passage within the literary structure as analysed by Segalla, makes one doubt about the value of his analysis. It is, indeed, a rather one-sided analysis: the discourse is divided into five sections which display a chiastic-circular structure; the sections are connected because the end of a section is at the same time the beginning of the next section[61]. No wonder that from such a point of view chiasms are discerned where there are really none[62]. Nevertheless, the study of Segalla contains a number of useful observations, which I have tried to work up in my own analysis.

Several scholars try to analyse the composition of the discourse in John 6 from a literary-critical point of view, by distinguishing different strands of material in it[63]. In itself, this distinguishing of strands is a legitimate procedure, but one should beware of confusing the different materials used by an author and the literary structure of his work. An author may use different materials to create his own composition out of them. Determining these materials is one thing; determining the literary structure of the composition is another.

5. A large number of scholars try to divide the discourse on the bread of life into units of thought[64]. In the characterization of these units, the misapprehensions pointed out above under group 3. are found sometimes, albeit less clearly than there. Generally, hardly any arguments are given for the divisions proposed, which differ considerably with one another.

b) *An analysis of the structure of John 6,22-59*

The following analysis of the structure of the discourse on the bread of life is based on the presupposition, that the discourse in its present state, whatever may be its pre-history, constitutes a meaningful unit. The analysis will start from a series of observations of a formal nature. Observations dealing with the content of the discourse may have to be called in, but the formal aspects of the text have to come in the first place, lest one's own interpretation determine the analysis of the literary structure.

1. It should be noted, first of all, that within the scheme of question and answer, that is present throughout John 6,22-59, there is a change after 6,34:

a. In 6,22-34, the discourse of the crowd is introduced by εἶπον αὐτῷ/πρὸς αὐτόν (6,25.28.30.34); in 6,41-42.52, however, their reactions are introduced by ἐγόγγυζον ... περὶ αὐτοῦ ... καὶ ἔλεγον, and ἐμάχοντο ... πρὸς ἀλλήλους ... λέγοντες. Apparently, in 6,41-42.52 the audience is speaking rather negatively *about* Jesus, whereas in 6,22-34 they are speaking in a more or less neutral way *to* him.

b. Accordingly, when referring to Jesus, the audience uses the 2nd pers. sg. in 6,22-34, and the 3rd pers. sg. in 6,42.52. Jesus uses the 2nd pers. pl. frequently in 6,22-34, when he is referring to the crowd; from 6,35 onward, the audience is referred to by Jesus in this fashion only a few times: in Amen-formulae in 6,47.53b, and in 6,36.43.49.53cd[65].

c. There is an obvious difference in the quantities of uninterrupted discourse put in the mouth of Jesus. In 6,22-34, these cover two verses at most, after 6,34 they cover at least six verses.

d. Jesus' audience is indicated in 6,22-34 by ὁ ὄχλος (6,22.24) or not at all, whereas in 6,41.52 they are called οἱ Ἰουδαῖοι[66].

e. I refer to what has been said before (4.a., nr. 2.) about the function of the questions and remarks of the crowd: in 6,22-34 they are elements of a continuing conversation, in 6,41-42.52 they are expressions of misunderstanding.

f. There is a clear parallelism between John 4,7-15, the first part of Jesus' conversation with the Samaritan woman, about the 'living water', and John 6,22-34. R. E. Brown, for example, parallels the surprised questions 4,9 and 6,25; Jesus' words in 4,13 and 6,27, about the earthly water and food; the questions in 4,11-12 and 6,30-31, in which Jesus and the OT figures of Jacob and Moses are matched; Jesus' words in 4,14 and 6,32-33, announcing the celestial life-giving water and bread respectively; and finally the approving (though misunderstanding) exclamations: 'Sir, give me this water so that I won't get thirsty' (4,15) and 'Sir, give us this bread all the time' (6,34)[67]. In John 4, the conversation moves to another topic after this exclamation; this circumstance strongly suggests that John 6,22-34 is to be considered a separate unit within 6,22-59. (For similar instances of an imperative at the end of a conversation, see John 7,24.52; 9,23; 10,38; 11,44; 12,36; 14,31; cfr. also 1 John 5,21).

The conclusion from this series of observations will be clear: 6,22-34 is a separate unit within 6,22-59; it is a dialogue of Jesus and the crowd, whereas from 6,35 onward Jesus is delivering a monologue (with a few dialogue-features: 6,36.43.47.49.53)[68].

2. It seems, however, that this separate unit can be divided into an introduction and the dialogue proper; this, at least, is done by a number of scholars, in divergent ways: the caesura can be laid after 6,24, after 6,25 or after 6,26[69]. Now, a caesura after 6,25 seems to be out of place: in 6,26, Jesus reacts to the question asked by the crowd in 6,25. A ceasura at 6,24/25 is easier to defend, because it separates the events that have taken place on the other side of the lake from those at Capernaum. Also possible is a caesura at 6,26/27, because it is only in 6,27 that the motives appear that are prominent in what follows (the giving of 'food that lasts for eternal life', 'to work'). In this case it might be preferable to consider 6,27 as a new start and not so much 6,22-26 as an introduction, because of the heterogeneity of the materials in 6,22-26. A count of S and W may be helpful in a choice between these alternatives.

3. Within the discourse, a series of correspondences can be discerned, on a larger and a smaller scale:

a. 6,35 contains Jesus' statement 'I am the bread of life', followed by a double combination of condition ('whoever comes to me', 'whoever believes in me') and promise of salvation ('shall never be hungry', 'shall never be thirsty'). This ἐγώ εἰμι-saying is repeated by Jesus in 6,48, followed, there too, by condition and promise of salvation (6,50), after the drawing of a negative parallel in the fate of the fathers in the wilderness (6,49); it is repeated once more in 6,51a, in slightly different words, followed, as in the former cases, by condition and promise (6,51b). So, there seems to exist a correspondence between 6,35 and 6,48-51b[70]. Meanwhile, the first ἐγώ εἰμι-saying is quoted in 6,41, with the omission of 'of life' and of the condition and promise, and with the addition of elements from 6,38. The closing sentence of the discourse (6,58) constitutes a variation on the ἐγώ εἰμι-sayings: the first person is replaced by the third person (οὗτός ἐστιν)[71].

b. Three times we meet a contrast between the manna eaten by the fathers in the wilderness, and the bread of life now present in Jesus: 6,31-32.49-50.58[72].

c. Three sentences spoken by Jesus display a remarkable similarity:

6,33 ὁ γὰρ ἄρτος τοῦ θεοῦ ἐστιν ὁ καταβαίνων ἐκ τοῦ οὐρανοῦ
καὶ ζωὴν διδοὺς τῷ κόσμῳ
51ab ἐγώ εἰμι ὁ ἄρτος ὁ ζῶν ὁ ἐκ τοῦ οὐρανοῦ καταβάς
ἐάν τις φάγῃ ἐκ τούτου τοῦ ἄρτου ζήσει εἰς τὸν αἰῶνα (cfr. 50)
58 οὗτός ἐστιν ὁ ἄρτος ὁ ἐξ οὐρανοῦ καταβάς
ὁ τρώγων τοῦτον τὸν ἄρτον ζήσει εἰς τὸν αἰῶνα

All three sentences are about the bread that has descended from heaven and has the capacity to give life[73].

d. Twice, the κόσμος is mentioned in connection with ἄρτος and (especially) ζωή: 6,33.51c[74]. These are the only occurrences of κόσμος in the discourse.

e. There is similarity between 6,34: δὸς ἡμῖν τὸν ἄρτον τοῦτον, and 6,51c*a*: ὁ ἄρτος δὲ ὃν ἐγὼ δώσω (cfr. also 6,27; only in these three places in John 6,22-59, is Jesus presented as the giver of food).

f. There is similarity between 6,36-40 and 6,44-47. The possibility of belief is dealt with in both sections. This possibility is dependent on the will of the Father: men that he gives to the Son, that hear and learn from him, come to Jesus, believe in Jesus — who gives them life, according to his Father's will (6,37-40.44-47); the motive to pronounce these statements is the auditors' seeing Jesus without believing (6,36). The thoughts about the possibility of belief are an answer to the question provoked by the unbelief of the auditors.

The correspondence of 6,36-40.44-47 can be sustained by a series of similarities in details:

6,36	ἑωράκατε	46	ἑώρακεν *bis*
40	(θεωρῶν)		
36	πιστεύετε	47	πιστεύων
40	πιστεύων		
37	πᾶν ὃ δίδωσίν μοι ὁ πατήρ	45	πᾶς ὁ ἀκούσας παρὰ τοῦ πατρός
39	(πᾶν ὃ δέδωκέν μοι)		
37	πρὸς ἐμὲ ἥξει	44	ἐλθεῖν πρός με
	τὸν ἐρχόμενον πρός με		
39 +	ἀναστήσω αὐτὸ(ν) (...) ἐν τῇ	44	ἀναστήσω αὐτὸν ἐν τῇ ἐσχάτῃ ἡμέρᾳ
40	ἐσχάτῃ ἡμέρᾳ		
40	ἔχῃ ζωὴν αἰώνιον	47	ἔχει ζωὴν αἰώνιον

These similarities give a certain impression of reflected symmetry, tempered, however, by the similarity between the closing parts of the two sections (6,40.46-47). Negatively, the two sections are similar in so far as in either of them the terminology of 'bread' and 'eating', so characteristic of the rest of the discourse, is absent[75].

By combining this last observation with observation a. of the present series, we may discern a concentric construction in 6,35-51b[76]:

A 6,35 — 'I am the bread of life' — A' 6,48-51b
B 6,36-40 — possibility of belief — B' 6,44-47
C 6,41-43 interruption
(with quotation 'I am the bread')

Another observation strengthens this view:

g. The small unit 6,41-43 is built according to a perfectly concentric pattern[77]:

6,41	ἐγόγγυζον οὖν οἱ Ἰουδαῖοι		μὴ γογγύζετε μετ᾽ἀλλήλων
	περὶ αὐτοῦ		αὐτοῖς
	ὅτι εἶπεν	43	ἀπεκρίθη Ἰησοῦς καὶ εἶπεν
	ἐγώ εἰμι ὁ ἄρτος ὁ καταβάς		καταβέβηκα
	ἐκ τοῦ οὐρανοῦ		ἐκ τοῦ οὐρανοῦ
42	καὶ ἔλεγον		πῶς νῦν λέγει

οὐχ οὗτος ... μητέρα

Not all elements in this pattern have the same strength; but it is striking to see how even the 'weak' elements (such as εἶπεν) fall into their places.

The combination of observations a., f. and g. of this series makes it clear that 6,35-51b is built concentrically, with 6,42bc as its centre[78].

So far, then, we have two parts: 6,22-34, a dialogue, and 6,35-51b, a monologue. It becomes likely that 6,51c-59 is also a separate section. I continue the series of observations with two observations concerning 6,51c-59:

4. a. In 6,51c, a new element is introduced into the discourse: the word σάρξ, that dominates the discourse from that point onward, in 6,53sqq in combination with αἷμα[79]. The bread that Jesus will give is his flesh, and his life-giving function becomes effective for whoever eats his flesh and drinks his blood. In 6,57, 'eating my flesh' and 'drinking my blood' are even replaced by 'eating *me*', while in 6,58 it is stated once more, that this person, this flesh and blood is 'the bread that came down from heaven', the οὗτός ἐστιν-saying referring back to the ἐγώ εἰμι-sayings of the preceding section.

b. At the beginning of 6,51c-59, a connection is made with the preceding by means of the expression καί ... δέ (δέ being in an exceptional position, viz. as the fourth word in the clause), marking the following as a new and important addition to what has been said before[80], and, in that way, indicating a caesura at 6,51b/51c[81].

These two observations, taken together, make it probable that 6,51c-59 is to be considered a separate section within 6,22-59. It seems, then, that 6,22-59 is made up of three parts: 6,22-34.35-51b.51c-59[82]. The indication of place found at the beginning (Capernaum, 6,24) is repeated at the end (6,59).

Now, this result has to be tested in two ways:

1. Up to this point, the correspondences b., c., d. and e. mentioned in the third series of observations above, have not yet been connected with the division of the text. Can they be connected now?

2. Is it possible to translate the formal division into a division of contents?

Ad 1: Each part of the discourse contains towards its end a reference to the manna eaten by the fathers in the wilderness, contrasted with the bread of life (6,31-32.49-50.58). Likewise, the three similar sentences 6,33.51ab.58 are the final words said by Jesus in each part. The two mentions of κόσμος are at the end of Jesus' words in the first part (6,33) and at the beginning of his words in the final part (6,51c). The final words in the first part (6,34) are similar to the first words in the third part (6,51c*a*)[83].

Ad 2: From the discussion of extant analyses of the literary structure of John 6,22-59, I concluded that it is impossible to divide the discourse on the basis of themes: the celestial origin of the bread, its life-giving power, and the necessity of eating it are present throughout the discourse. However, it seemed that sections might be distinguished according to the way these themes are treated (see pp. 162-163 above). Now it appears that the division found by means of observations of a formal nature can, indeed, be translated into a division based upon different treatments of the themes. The difference of treatment has to do with the measure of identification of Jesus with the bread of life. In 6,22-34, this identification remains implicit. In this section, Jesus speaks about 'the food that lasts for eternal life, which the Son of Man will give you' (6,27), also about 'to believe in him whom he (= God) sent' (6,29), and his last words in this section are 'for the bread of God is he who/that which comes down from heaven and gives life to the world' (6,33), ambiguous words, clear for the reader who knows what is going to follow, but not clear witness 6,34, for the Jews.

From 6,35 onwards, Jesus explicitly identifies himself with the bread of life, in the ἐγώ εἰμι-sayings in 6,35.48.51[84]. He is, in person, the bread of life that came down from heaven. Only from 6,35 onwards, Jesus speaks preponderantly in the 1st pers. about himself[85].

From 6,51c onwards, the line of increasing unambiguousness is brought to its end: the bread of life is Jesus crucified, as is indicated by the new elements σάρξ and αἷμα appearing in this section. Just as in John the incarnation finds its culminating point in the death on the cross (3,16; cfr. 1 John 4,9-10), so the coming down of the bread from heaven ends in its being given as flesh and blood[86]. In 6,58, finally, the identification of Jesus crucified and the bread from heaven is made once more, but, significantly, not in an ἐγώ εἰμι-saying, but in a (related) οὗτός ἐστιν-saying. The ἐγώ εἰμι-sayings are confined to the second section.

So, the discourse on the bread of life passes from implicit to explicit identification of Jesus with the bread of life at 6,34/35, and from identification of Jesus to identification of Jesus crucified at 6,51b/51c. The formal tripartition turns out to correspond to a tripartition of contents[87].

The next question, then, is: what are the relationships between these three parts? Three observations seem to be of interest here:

a. Within the first part, 6,27 contains several words and expressions which are taken up in the third part: τὴν βρῶσιν (cfr. 6,55) τὴν μένουσαν (cfr. 6,56) ... ἣν ὁ υἱὸς τοῦ ἀνθρώπου (cfr. 6,53) ὑμῖν δώσει (cfr. 6,51c)[88]. Moreover, 6,33 corresponds to 6,51c, and 6,34 to 6,51c*a* (see above, pp. 166, 168). It should be noted that βρῶσις, μένειν, ὁ υἱὸς τοῦ ἀνθρώπου, διδόναι with food as its object, and κόσμος occur only in the first and third part of John 6,22-59.

b. The second part is built according to a concentric pattern (see above, pp. 166-167). Such a pattern is not present in such a clear fashion in the first and third part.

c. As for its contents, the second part seems to be the most important one. The implicit revelation of the first part leads to the 'revelatory discourse' of the second part, while the third part does no more than draw the consequences of what has been said in the second part.

So it seems justified to consider 6,22-34 and 6,51c-59 as belonging together, and 6,35-51b as a separate part.

That 6,42bc is the middle not only of 6,41-43 and of 6,35-51b, but also of the entire discourse, may be derived from the following observation. Two of the elements standing on either side of the central sentence 6,42bc and corresponding according to a chiastic pattern, are ὁ καταβὰς ἐκ τοῦ οὐρανοῦ (6,41) and ἐκ τοῦ οὐρανοῦ καταβέβηκα (6,42; see above, observation 3.g.). Now, the expression καταβαίνειν ἐκ τοῦ οὐρανοῦ occurs (with minor variations) seven times in 6,22-59; before 6,42bc always in the order καταβαίνειν-ἐκ τοῦ οὐρανοῦ (6,33.38.41), after 6,42bc always in the order ἐκ τοῦ οὐρανοῦ-καταβαίνειν (6,42.50.51.58)[89]. This might suggest a central position of 6,42bc in the whole of the discourse.

A count of S confirms the presumption that 6,35-51b is a separate part within 6,22-59, and that 6,22-34 and 6,51c-59 belong together. It confirms, moreover, the concentric composition of 6,35-51b, and it confirms that 6,27 is a new start (see above, observation 2.). All this is shown schematically in Table XIII.

Table XIII. John 6,22-59 syllables

6,22-26	232			
27-34	284/516			
35a			7	
35b-d			39	
36-40			186/232	
41-42a			37	
42bc			27	
42d-43			36/100	
44-47			132	
48-51b			99/231/563	
51c-59		284/		800/1363

Framing-technique has been applied here: the two outer parts together amount to 800 S. The corresponding parts 6,35-40 and 6,44-51b are of almost equal length: 232 and 231 S (232 is a symmetrical number; 231 is triangular number of 21). The same is valid of 6,41-42a and 6,42d-43: 37 and 36 S (36 is triangular number of 8). The central part 6,41-43 has a length of exactly 100 S; the central sentence of it, 6,42bc, has a length of 27 S, = 3^3. The chiastic construction of 6,35b-40.44-51b is reflected in the fact that the sum of S for the parts about the bread of life (6,35b-d.48-51b) is 138, and for the parts about the possibility of belief

(6,36-40.44-47) it is 318: two numbers made up of the same figures (318 being well-known from Barn 9,7-8), whose sum is 456, a number made up of three figures in a climbing sequence. The 231 S of 6,44-51b are made up of 132 S, = 12 × 11 (a rectangular number; the OT quotation in 6,45b has a length of 11 S), and 99 S, = 9 × 11, for 6,44-47 and 6,48-51b respectively. 6,35-40.44-51b is exactly what John 6 contains more than 2000 S, viz. 232 + 231 = 463 S.

6,27-34 and 6,51c-59 are of equal length, and the introduction 6,22-26 is as long as 6,35-40. Interestingly, 6,22-34 is as long as 6,1-15: 516 S. This is not so strange, when one takes into account the fact that this part of the discourse has clear connections with the story of the multiplication of the loaves, see the back-references in 6,23.26-27.

The central position and concentric composition of 6,35-51b, as well as the introductory character of 6,22-26 and closing character of 6,59, are confirmed by a count of W, as shown in Table XIV.

Table XIV. John 6,22-59 words

6,22-26	114				
27-34		149			
35a				4	
35b-d			22		
36-40			99/121/125		
41			17		
42a-c			17		
42d-43			17/	51	
44-47			68		
48-51b			56/	124/300	
51c-58		151/			300
59	7/				121/721

The framework 6,22-26.59 has a length of 121 W, = 11^2 (and a symmetrical number). The two parts 6,27-34 and 6,51c-58 are of almost equal length: 149 and 151 W (the latter number being a symmetrical one); their sum is 300 (triangular number of 24). 300 W is also the length of the central part 6,35-51b. Its centre (6,41-43) is made up of 3 × 17 = 51 W. 6,35-40 has a length of 125 W, = 5^3, and 6,44-51b of 124 W. The corresponding parts 6,35b-d and 6,48-51b amount together to 22 + 56 (= 7 × 8: a rectangular number) = 78 W (triangular number of 12). The discourse 6,35b-40, the first half of the chiasm formed by 6,35b-40 and 6,44-51b, has a length of 121 W, = 11^2 (a symmetrical number), made up of 22 and 99 W (remarkably, it was the second half of the chiasm that turned out to consist of two multiples of 11 S). The first and last sentences of these corresponding parts, the ἐγώ εἰμι-statements with condition and promise 6,35b-d and 6,51ab, are of equal length: 22 W.

A case might be made out for the view that 6,22-24 is an introduction, on the basis of the fact that 6,25-34 has a length of 185 W, and 6,51c-59 of 158 W: two numbers made up of the same figures, whose sum is the symmetrical number of 343 W.

In Table XV a combination is made of numbers of W divided according to the tripartite structure of 6,22-59 and according to a division into narrative and discourse (of different speakers). 6,41b.42d*b* are considered to be discourse of Jesus.

Table XV. John 6,22-59 words

	narrative	discourse Jesus	OT quot.	discourse crowd	total
6,22-34	113	100	7	43	263
35-51b	19	257	5	19	300
51c-59	19/151	131/488	-/12	8/70	158/721

First of all, the sum totals on the bottom line are interesting: 151 W (a symmetrical number) of narrative, 500 for Jesus' discourse together with the OT quotations, 70 for the discourse of the crowd. The OT quotation of 7 W in the first part (6,31c) is also put in the mouth of the crowd; together, then, 77 W. Three times the number 19 appears: for the discourse of the crowd in the second part, and for the narrative in the second and third part. Jesus' discourse in the second part, augmented with the words of the OT quotation in this part (occurring actually in Jesus' mouth), has twice the length of Jesus' discourse in the third part: 262 and 131 W (two numbers of a symmetrical structure).

In Table XVI, the same thing is done as in Table XV, but this time the numbers of S are given, and the tripartite division has been refined by putting apart 6,22-26 and 6,59.

Table XVI. John 6,22-59 syllables

	narr.	discourse Jesus	discourse crowd	OT
6,22-26	185	38	9	
27-34	36	155	79	14
35-51b	39	480	33	11/25
51c-58	24/60/ 99	228/383/863/901	15/94/127/136	
59	17/ 202/301			

The narrative in 6,27-34 and 6,51c-58 has a length of 36 S, = 3 × 12, and 24 S, = 2 × 12, respectively; together with the narrative of the central part 6,35-51b, it amounts to 99 S, = 9 × 11, while the narrative portions of the framework 6,22-26.59 amount to 202 S (a symmetrical number). The discourse of Jesus in 6,27-34.51c-58 has a length of 383 S (another symmetrical number). Together with what Jesus says in the central part, it has a length of 863 S, remarkable because the sum total of S for 6,22-59 is 1363, and for John 6 in its entirety it is 2463. The total numbers of S for narrative and discourse of Jesus are 301 and 901 respectively. The discourse of the crowd has a total length of 136 S, triangular number of 16. The factor 16 returns in the total of 160 S spoken by the crowd, when 6,31c (OT quotation).42d*b* (quotation of Jesus' words) are included. The 10 S of the quotation of Jesus' words in 6,42 are then exactly the surplus above 150. Two multiples of 11 occur in the numbers of S of the crowd's discourse: 88 in the first part (including 6,22-26), 33 in the central part.

In Table XVII, the W of 6,22-59 are divided according to the actors (cfr. Table V).

Table XVII. words divided acc. to actors John 6,22-59

	Jesus actor	crowd	impersonal
6,22-26	24	75	15
27-34	92/116	57/132	-/15
35-51b	258	42	-
51c-59	143/259/517	15/147/189	-/15

The number of W of the sentences with Jesus as actor in the first and third part is almost equal to their number in the second part: 258 and 259 respectively. For the crowd, these numbers are 147 W, = 7 × 21, and 42 W, = 2 × 21, respectively (42 is also a rectangular number: 6 × 7). When in the first part 6,22-26 is put apart, we obtain, in the case of the crowd, 75 + 57 W for the first part: two numbers made up of the same figures, whose total, 132, is a multiple of 11 (cfr. above, p. 69 with n. 65). In the first part, the sentences with the crowd as actor occupy the largest half of the odd total number of 263 W: 132 W.

In numbers of S, there is a clear relationship between the final sentences spoken by Jesus in each of the three parts (6,33.51ab.58); these sentences turned out to display a remarkable similarity (see above, observation 3.c.). They have a length of 27, 36 and 45 S respectively, i.e., 3 × 9, 4 × 9 and 5 × 9. Moreover, 6,51ab is an isocolon:

ἐγώ εἰμι ὁ ἄρτος ὁ ζῶν ὁ ἐκ τοῦ οὐρανοῦ καταβάς	18 S
ἐάν τις φάγῃ ἐκ τούτου τοῦ ἄρτου ζήσει εἰς τὸν αἰῶνα	18

And 6,58 is made up of three equal parts:

οὗτός ἐστιν ὁ ἄρτος ὁ ἐξ οὐρανοῦ καταβάς	15 S
οὐ καθὼς ἔφαγον οἱ πατέρες καὶ ἀπέθανον	15
ὁ τρώγων τοῦτον τὸν ἄρτον ζήσει εἰς τὸν αἰῶνα	15

So, the numerical analysis confirms our hypothesis concerning the literary structure of John 6,22-59.

c) *Details in John 6,22-59*

Several details concerning numbers of S and W in the discourse on the bread of life attract our attention.

A striking progression is present in Jesus' utterances in 6,29-40:

6,29bc	25 S
32b-33	75 (= 3 × 25)
35b-40	225 (= 3 × 75)

In *6,22-34*, Jesus speaks 100 W, the crowd 50 (including the OT quotation 6,31c; cfr. Table XV above). The first conversation (6,25-27) contains 50 W of discourse, the second one (6,28-29) 20, and the third one, including the final reaction of the crowd (6,30-34), 80. As in 6,1-15, the factors 2 and 5 are present (see above, under 3.a): they are the primary factors of 100, 50, 20 and 80. The first conversation (6,25-27) has a total length (narrative included) of 64 W, = 8^2; the last one (6,30-33) of 81 W, = 9^2. These two conversations are more extensive than the middle one (6,28-29); in both of them, Jesus' answer is introduced by an Amen-formula. In numbers of S, the following pattern emerges (again, the narrative introductions are included):

6,25-27	question + answer	25 +	105 =	130 S
28-29	idem	23 +	36 =	59
30-33	idem	67 +	83 =	150
34	reaction	20	=	20/300/359
		135	224	

59 (total of 6,28-29) is nearly 1/5 of 300 (total of the rest); 135 (total of questions and reaction) is 3 × 45, 224 (total of answers) is nearly 5 × 45. With the articular reading in 6,29 (see p. 139 above) the perfection is realized: 60 S in 6,28-29, 225 for the total of answers. The previous counts, however, do not favour this reading.

The factors 6 and 7 are often found in the discourse in 6,25-34, when measured in numbers of W:

6,25	(4)
26-27	(4 +) 14 + 14 + 7 + 7
28	(2 +) 6
29	6 + 6
30-31	12 + 12 + 7
32-33	42
34	7

The discourse dealing with bread, food and eating is made up mainly of units of 7 W or multiples of 7 W (cfr. the role of the number 7 in 6,1-15, see p. 152 above). The discourse dealing with works, believing and signs is made up mainly of units of 6 W or multiples of 6 W. The rectangular number 42, the number of W of 6,32b-33, is the product of 6 and 7.

6,26c-27a is made up of 30 + 30 S, or 14 + 14 W[90] (both units of 14 W are made up of 6 + 8 W); it is followed in 6,27bc by 12 + 13 = 25 S, or 7 + 7 = 14 W:

		syll.	words
6,26	ζητεῖτέ με οὐχ ὅτι εἴδετε σημεῖα	13	6
	ἀλλ'ὅτι ἐφάγετε ἐκ τῶν ἄρτων καὶ ἐχορτάσθητε	17/30	8/14
27	ἐργάζεσθε μὴ τὴν βρῶσιν τὴν ἀπολλυμένην	14	6
	ἀλλὰ τὴν βρῶσιν τὴν μένουσαν εἰς ζωὴν αἰώνιον	16/30	8/14
	ἣν ὁ υἱὸς τοῦ ἀνθρώπου ὑμῖν δώσει	12	7
	τοῦτον γὰρ ὁ πατὴρ ἐσφράγισεν ὁ θεός	13/25	7/14

The halves of 6,26c-27a are built similarly: a verbal form 2nd plur. pres. is followed by a negative particle and an ἀλλά-clause. The two stichoi of each half are antithetically parallel[91].

Jesus' answer in 6,29 is made up of 10 + 15 = 25 S.

The question of the crowd in 6,30 is made up of two parallel questions, separated by a final clause. In numbers of S:

τί οὖν ποιεῖς σὺ σημεῖον	8 S
ἵνα ἴδωμεν καὶ πιστεύσωμέν σοι	11
τί ἐργάζῃ	4/12

The conversation 6,30-33 has, narrative introductions included, a length of 150 S; Jesus' answer alone (6,32b-33) takes up half of these: 75, made up of 48 + 27 S. To put it otherwise: $3 \times 4^2 + 3 \times 3^2 = 3 \times 5^2$ (see above, p. 29).

6,22-40 may be considered a unit, made up of four times question (or exclamation, 6,34) and answer. In the narrative portions of this passage multiples of 13 appear in the numbers of W. 6,22-24 is made up of 52 + 26 = 78 W, and the narrative in 6,25-40 uses half that number: 39 W. 6,25-27 has a size of 130 S.

In *6,35-51b*, the surplus-technique has been applied: this part contains a self-quotation of Jesus in 6,36 (καὶ ἑωράκατέ με καὶ οὐ πιστεύετε)[92], 13 S on a sum total of 563 S (and on a sum total of 2463 S for John 6 as a whole, or 1363 S for 6,22-59).

According to X. Léon-Dufour[93], 6,36-40 is built chiastically; besides, there is a line of thought from 6,35 via 6,38 to 6,41: 6,41 presupposes 6,35 because of ἄρτος, and 6,38 because of καταβὰς ἐκ τοῦ οὐρανοῦ. Schematically:

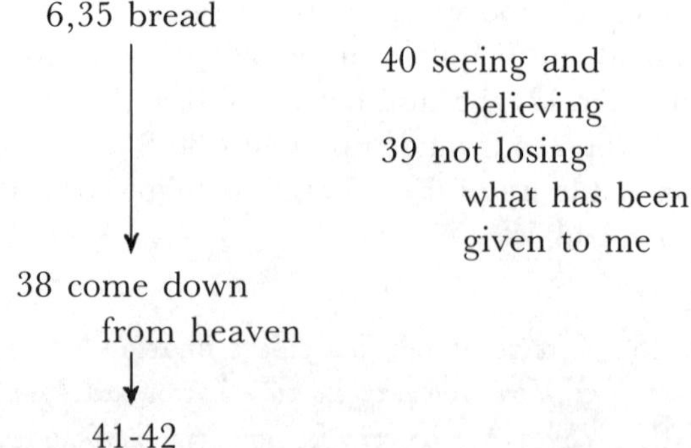

6,35 bread

36 seeing without believing — 40 seeing and believing
37 not driving out what has been given to me — 39 not losing what has been given to me

38 come down from heaven

41-42

Now, it appears that the chiastic pattern corresponds to an exact tripartition of the 225 ($= 3^2 \times 5^2$) S of 6,35b-40. The three groups of corresponding verses amount each to 75 S:

6,35b-d + 38	39 + 36 = 75 S
36 + 40	20 + 55 = 75
37 + 39	29 + 46 = 75

6,37-38 is made up of a main clause and a ὅτι-clause, both having a length of 18 W. The two cola of the main clause are parallel in content: ‘whatever the Father gives to me will come to me/and anyone who comes to me I will never drive out’[94]. They are also of equal length: 9 W.

6,39 is made up of a main clause and a ἵνα-clause, of 8 and 16 W respectively. The ἵνα-clause contains two cola which are parallel in content: ‘that I should lose nothing of what he has given me/but should raise it up on the last day’. These two cola are of equal size: 16 S.

In 6,44-47, a correspondence can be discerned between 6,44-45 and 6,47: ‘to come to me’ and ‘to believe’, ‘to raise up on the last day’ and ‘eternal life’ are the corresponding elements[95]. These elements are not present in 6,46; this verse gives the impression of being an afterthought, intended to correct false consequences from the preceding[96]. In Table XVIII this structure is transposed into numbers of W.

Table XVIII. John 6,44-47

	words	
6,44-45	42	
46		17
47	9/51/68	

6,44-45 and 6,47 have together exactly three times the length of 6,46: 51 and 17 W respectively.

6,44 and 6,45 (6,45c is parallel to 6,44[97]) are of (nearly) equal length: 40 and 41 S, 2 × 21 W. 6,45ab is an isocolon (again the number 11 appears):

ἔστιν γεγραμμένον ἐν τοῖς προφήταις	11 S	5 W
καὶ ἔσονται πάντες διδακτοὶ θεοῦ	11	5

The structure of 6,48-51b may be analysed, at first sight, in two ways:

a) A parallelism is present in 6,48-50.51ab[98]: both halves are made up of an ἐγώ εἰμι-saying, a condition and a promise of salvation, negatively formulated in 6,50, positively in 6,51. The first half is extended by the addition of a reference to the fathers in the wilderness as a negative condition and promise (6,49), and a definition-formula (6,50a), in which 6,48 is taken up. So, 6,48-49.50 are parallel (cfr. ἄρτος, ἔφαγον, ἀπέθανον in 6,48-49, and ἄρτος, φάγῃ, ἀποθάνῃ in 6,50)[99].

b) 6,48-49 and 6,51 are two parallel ἐγώ εἰμι-sayings, followed by condition and promise; these are negatively formulated in 6,49, and positively in 6,51. The enclosed verse 6,50 is a saying introduced by οὗτός ἐστιν; it is, in content, parallel to 6,48-49 and 6,51.

A count of S and W evidently favours the former analysis. 6,48-50 has a length of 63 S, = 7 × 9; 6,51ab of 36 S, = 4 × 9; moreover, both numbers are made up of the same figures, so that their sum is a multiple of 11: 99. Both parts of the parallelism are divided into two (nearly) equal parts (mark the 2 × 11 W in 6,51ab):

6,48-49	32 S	17 W
50	31/63	17
51a	18	11
51b	18/36/99	11

In *6,51c-59*, there is — in numbers of S — a proportion of 1:10 between the parts surrounding the interruption of the Jews 6,52: 6,51c has a length of 23 S, 6,53-59 of 230 S; together 253, triangular number of 22. In numbers of W, the answer 6,53-58 has eight times the length of the question 6,52: 120 and 15 W respectively.

Numerically, 6,55 is the centre of Jesus' words in 6,51c-58: the verse is preceded by 103 S or 58 W of discourse of Jesus, and followed by 102 S or 59 W spoken by him (the sum of 103 and 102 is 205, a number well-known from 6,1-15, see pp. 151-152 above). The verse itself contains 23 S: as long as 6,51c, and 1/10 of 6,53-59 (see Table XIX).

Table XIX. discourse of Jesus in John 6,51c-58

	syllables	words
6,51c	23	16
53b-d	43	23
54	37/103	19/58
55	23	14
56	24	16
57	33	19
58	45/102/228	24/59/131

The central position of 6,55 is brought out also, to some degree, by conventional literary means. The verse, being a definition-formula, is preceded by an antithetic parallelism about having life by eating the flesh of the Son of Man and drinking his blood (6,53-54; see below), and is followed by a synthetic parallelism about remaining in Christ and living by him by eating his flesh and drinking his blood (6,56-57)[100]. Moreover, there is a certain correspondence between 6,51c.58: these are the only verses in this section containing the word ἄρτος. In 6,51c, the bread from the preceding passage is equated to Jesus' flesh; in 6,58, the reverse movement is made: Jesus' flesh is said to be the bread from heaven.

A logical division of 6,53-58 seems to be 6,53-54.55-57.58. 6,53-54 can be considered a thesis: in order to obtain life, it is necessary to eat the flesh and to drink the blood of Jesus. The thesis has the form of an antithetic parallelism[101]:

6,53 ἐὰν μὴ φάγητε τὴν σάρκα τοῦ υἱοῦ τοῦ ἀνθρώπου	54 ὁ τρώγων μου τὴν σάρκα
καὶ πίητε αὐτοῦ τὸ αἷμα	καὶ πίνων μου τὸ αἷμα
οὐκ ἔχετε ζωὴν ἐν ἑαυτοῖς	ἔχει ζωὴν αἰώνιον κἀγὼ ἀναστήσω αὐτὸν τῇ ἐσχάτῃ ἡμέρᾳ

In 6,55-57, a motivation is given for the thesis: 'for my flesh is real food, and my blood is real drink' (6,55); they are such, in so far as they create a connection between Jesus and the believer (6,56), and that connection, 'to live because of me', is ultimately based on Jesus' living because of the Father (6,57). His flesh and blood are real, trustworthy food and drink in so far as God's own life is mediated through them; therefore it is necessary to eat his flesh and to drink his blood in order to obtain life[102]. In 6,58 the identification is made, by way of conclusion, with the bread from heaven. A confirmation of this division can be seen in the fact that the three statements in 6,53-58 speaking of a final eschatology (6,54b. 57b.58c) are found at the end of the three parts.

In Table XX this division is transformed into numbers of S and W.

Table XX. John 6,53b-58	syllables	words
6,53b-d	43	23
54	37/80	19/42
55-56	47	30
57	33/80	19/49
58	45/205	24/115

Thesis and motivation are of equal length in numbers of S: 80. The thesis has a length of 42 W, = 6 × 7 (a rectangular number), the motivation of 49 W, = 7 × 7 (a square number). Both parts end with a sentence of 19 W. In numbers of both S and W, the conclusion 6,58 falls outside the pattern of 6,53b-57. In the sum total of S we meet again the well-known number 205.

6,53cd and 6,54 are antithetically parallel; both sentences have a length of 19 W.

At the end of this analysis of John 6, we can conclude that the author of the Fourth Gospel made use of numbers of S and W in the composition of this section of his work. Evidently, the number 11 has been used as a basic number in John 6. For a general description of the applications of this numerical technique, I refer to the Conclusion.

NOTES TO CHAPTER THREE

1 See W. Michaelis, art. ὁράω etc., *TWNT* V, 315-381; 345. Textual variation between ὁρᾶν and θεωρεῖν is found to occur more often: see the variation at Josh 8,20 LXX; Dan (cfr. LXX and Theod) 2,31.34; 8,15; Acts 8,23; Test Abr (rec. A), ed. James, p. 87 l. 20.

2 So Barrett, 273; Bultmann, 156 n. 2.

3 Turner, *Syntax*, 167; see also Blass-Debrunner-Rehkopf, par. 260_6. The 'set phrase' is, however, no iron rule, cfr. 18,37. Fee, *NTS* 17, 173-175, gives three arguments in favour of the general omission of the article in the idiom ἀπεκρίθη Ἰησοῦς καὶ εἶπεν αὐτ(ῷ) in John, where the manuscript tradition is not unanimous: a) the evidence of P[66.75] (P[66] having the article twice, P[75] never), representing 'two *independent* strains of the Neutral tradition' (174). Besides, P[66], where a corrector *added* the article eight times, shows the recensional tendency to be toward the use of the article; b) 'the other early manuscripts, including those in the Western tradition (Sin in i-viii.38 and D), all tend to support an anarthrous idiom. Where they do have the article before Ἰησοῦς, there is no pattern of agreement' (174); c) 'in similar constructions in the Synoptic Gospels the text is always arthrous. Moreover, variations of anarthrous readings in any of the manuscripts are extremely rare' (175). About 6,29, Fee writes: 'Since the manuscript evidence is indecisive (there is strong Neutral-Western combination for each variant, B D and P[75] Sin), textual choices at such points probably ought to be based on intrinsic probability' (175). Cfr. also the literature mentioned in chapter I, n. 18.

4 Apart from John, the more current usage in the NT seems to be that of πρός με. In *NA*[26], I count outside John 20 instances of πρός με over against 2 instances of πρὸς ἐμέ; in *NA*[25] the figures are 17 and 5. For similar variation in the textual tradition of Melito of Sardis' Περὶ Πασχα, see Smit Sibinga, *VC* 24, 101; for extra-biblical examples of both με and ἐμέ after the preposition πρός (but without textual variation), see Turner, *Syntax*, 39. The statement of R. Kieffer, *Au delà des recensions?* L'évolution de la tradition textuelle dans Jean VI, 52-71 (ConB, NT Series 3; Lund 1968) 186: 'Les mss ... à deux reprises préfèrent nettement εμε (en 6,37 ...)', is simply not true. His opinion: 'Nous estimons donc que εμε est la leçon primitive en 6,37 (deux fois) ...' (*ibid.*), does not take into account the influence exerted by πρὸς ἐμέ in 6,37a on the similar expression in 6,37b.

5 Metzger, *Textual Commentary*, 214. Idem Brown, 282.

6 Cfr. Kieffer, *Au delà des recensions?*, 197: 'L'omission du pronom, si bien attestée dans nos mss grecs, paraît primitive, car elle rend le texte moins clair. On comprend

qu'en Occident, en Syrie et en Égypte, surtout dans les versions, on aît éprouvé le besoin d'ajouter un pronom.'

7 So C. K. Barrett, 'Das Fleisch des Menschensohnes (Joh 6,53)', in: *Jesus und der Menschensohn* (Fs. A. Vögtle; Freiburg etc. 1975) 342-354; 347-349, with 347 n. 1. In his commentary on John, 298, B. adds that 'the short text ... recalls more clearly the complaining of the Israelites (Num. 11.4)'.

8 So also Kieffer, *Au delà des recensions?*, 189; Schnackenburg, II 109 n. 1.

9 At least, this interpretation is a current one, see E. Schweizer, 'Das johanneische Zeugnis vom Herrenmahl', *EvT* 12 (1952-53) 341-363; quoted here from the reprint in id., *Neotestamentica* (Zürich/Stuttgart 1963) 371-396; 388-390; Dodd, *Interpretation*, 341-342; Barrett, 304; X. Léon-Dufour, 'Le mystère du pain de vie (Jean VI)', *RSR* 46 (1958) 481-523; 518-520; H. Schürmann, 'Joh 6,51c — Ein Schlüssel zur grossen johanneischen Brotrede', *BZ* NF 2 (1958) 244-262; 257-259, reprinted in id., *Ursprung und Gestalt*. Erörterungen und Besinnungen zum Neuen Testament (Kommentare und Beiträge zum Alten und Neuen Testament; Düsseldorf 1970) 151-166; Grundmann, *Zeugnis und Gestalt*, 42 n. 81; Hofbeck, *Semeion*, 122; J. Giblet, 'De eucharistie in het evangelie van Johannes. Een lezing van Johannes 6', *Concilium* 4 (1968) nr. 10, 56-65; 63, but cfr. id., 'La chair du Fils de l'homme', *Lumière et Vie* 29 nr. 149 (1980) 89-103; 102; M.-F. Berrouard, 'La multiplication des pains et le discours du pain de vie (Jean, 6)', *Lumière et Vie* 18 nr. 94 (1969) 63-75; 72-73; H. Klos, *Die Sakramente im Johannesevangelium*. Vorkommen und Bedeutung von Taufe, Eucharistie und Busse im vierten Evangelium (SBS 46; Stuttgart 1970) 62-63; J. D. G. Dunn, 'John VI — A Eucharistic Discourse?', *NTS* 17 (1970-71) 328-338; Schnackenburg, II 106; Moloney, *Son of Man*, 106; G. Ferraro, 'Giovanni 6,60-71. Osservazioni sulla struttura letteraria e il valore della pericope nel quarto vangelo', *RivB* 26 (1978) 33-69; 57-60.

10 For Becker, 189-190, 195, the evangelist's faithfulness to his source is the only reason for the presence of 6,16-21 in John 6.

11 Ed. Glatzer, 44-45 (I quote G.'s translation). According to Finkelstein, *HTR* 36, 1sqq, this hymn was composed under Seleucid rule between 198 and 167 B.C.; arguments in favour of this dating are the anti-Egyptian tendency of the hymn and the fact that neither Israel's victories nor Jerusalem are mentioned. The building of the temple as a climax points definitely to the pre-70 C.E.-period.

12 This explanation is given by B. Gärtner, *John 6 and the Jewish Passover* (ConNT 17; Lund 1959) 15-17; Brown, 255-256.

13 So Dodd, *Interpretation*, 344-345; J. Bligh, 'Jesus in Galilee', *HeyJ* 5 (1964) 3-26; 16-17; J. Blank, 'Die johanneische Brotrede', *BibLeb* 7 (1966) 193-207, 255-270; 207; Brown, 255; Giblet, *Concilium* 4 nr. 10, 57; Schnackenburg, II 38; F. Schnider-W. Stenger, *Johannes und die Synoptiker*. Vergleich ihrer Parallelen (Biblische Handbibliothek 6; Munich 1971) 153-154; J. P. Heil, *Jesus Walking on the Sea*. Meaning and Gospel Functions of Matt 14:22-33, Mark 6:45-52 and John 6:15b-21 (AnBib 87; Rome 1981) 149-150.

14 Cfr. esp. F.-M. Braun, 'L'eucharistie selon S. Jean', *RevThom* 70 (1970) 5-29; 17. A similar view is expressed by Bauer, 103; Léon-Dufour, *RSR* 46, 494-496; F.-J. Leenhardt, 'La structure du chapître 6 de l'évangile de Jean', *RHPR* 39 (1959) 1-13; Bligh, *HeyJ* 5, 16-17; P. Zarrella, 'Gesù cammina sulle acque. Significato teologico di Giov. 6,16-21', *BeO* 10 (1968) 181-187. For Bultmann, 161, and H. Schlier, 'Joh. 6 und das johanneische Verständnis der Eucharistie', in: J. Sint, ed., *Bibel und zeitgemässer Glaube* II (Klosterneuburg 1967) 69-95; quoted here from the reprint in H. Schlier, *Das Ende der Zeit* (Freiburg 1971) 102-123; 110, the story expresses Jesus' triumph over the conditions of nature.

15 About the OT background of the epiphany on the sea, see Heil, *Jesus Walking on the Sea*, 37-56, 58-59.

16 See E. Pax, art. 'Epiphanie', *RAC* 5, 832-909, esp. 839, 841, 862, 869-870.

17 Cfr. esp. Zarrella, *BeO* 10, 185.

18 Cfr. H. Zimmermann, 'Das absolute ἐγώ εἰμι als die neutestamentliche Offen-

barungsformel', *BZ* NF 4 (1960) 54-69, 266-276; A. Feuillet, 'Les *Ego eimi* christologiques du quatrième Évangile', *RSR* 54 (1966) 5-22, 213-240; Schnackenburg, II 59-70.

19 So Schnackenburg, II 36-37, cfr. 38; likewise Blank, *BibLeb* 7, 199-200. Differently Heil, *Jesus Walking on the Sea*, 80 (cfr., however, his pp. 154, 160).

20 The connections between 6,16-21 and what follows as discerned by Heil, *Jesus Walking on the Sea*, 144-145, 152-170, are too general: they are applicable to any Johannine miracle story. See, e.g., 145: 'Whereas the discourse of Jesus develops the significance of the sea-walking epiphany as a manifestation of his divine sonship, the power of Jesus to rescue his disciples by walking on the sea authenticates the claim that he has been sent by God, his Father, to serve as *the* medium of eternal life for the world.'

21 Almost all of the text-editions, commentaries and studies consider John 6 to be a literary unit. The only exception known to me is Hoskyns-Davey, 277-288: there, 7,1 is taken as the conclusion of ch. 6.

22 6,60.66 are not included: there, a group of disciples larger than the Twelve only (cfr. 6,66-67) is the subject. I shall suppose here that the disciples mentioned in 6,13.16-17a.20.21a are included in the Twelve: Andrew and Philip, both members of the Twelve according to Mark 3,18, belong to this group of assistants of Jesus (John 6, 12-13; cfr. Mark 3,14); in the parallel story of Mark, Jesus' assistants are clearly singled out as the Twelve (Mark 6,30sqq compared with 6,7). Besides, the fact that the disciples cross the lake in *one* boat (6,22) rules out the possibility that John uses οἱ μαθηταί in 6,1-21 to indicate a large group.

23 Cfr. Schnackenburg, II 56, about 6,35: 'Jetzt spricht Jesus das entscheidende Wort'; see also S. Schulz, *Komposition und Herkunft der johanneischen Reden* (BWANT 5/1; Stuttgart 1960) 72-74; Grundmann, *Zeugnis und Gestalt*, 40-41. F. Hahn, 'Die Worte vom lebendigen Wasser im Johannesevangelium. Eigenart und Vorgeschichte von Joh 4,10.13f; 6,35; 7,37-39', in: *God's Christ and His People* (Fs. N. A. Dahl; Oslo etc. 1977) 51-70; 61sqq, considers 6,35 as the 'Kernlogion' of John 6, serving as a key to the rest of the chapter.

24 Cfr. Heil, *Jesus Walking on the Sea*, 16, 75.

25 Cfr. Bligh, *HeyJ* 5, 3: 'Like every good drama it [scil. John 6] has a beginning, a middle and an end' (n. 1 referring to Aristotle, *Poetica* 7,3 = 1450b); Schnackenburg, II 41: 'Sie [scil. the revelatory discourse in John 6] ist das zentrale Stück und der theologische Höhepunkt von Kap. 6, die Entfaltung der Gedanken, die der Evangelist schon bei der grossen Speisung im Sinne hatte'.

26 See Appendix I.

27 Cfr. Bultmann, 156 n. 4; Strathmann, 114; Barrett, 273; Brown, 235; Schnackenburg, II 18, 27; Schnider-Stenger, *Joh. und die Synoptiker*, 144, 146. The correspondence of 6,1.15 is noticed by Van den Bussche, *Boek der werken*, 100.

28 Noticed by Boismard-Lamouille, *Jean*, 182, 184; D. Marzotto, *L'unità degli uomini nel vangelo di Giovanni* (Supplementi alla RivB 9; Brescia 1977) 158.

29 Cfr. Mark 1,27 par; 2,12 parr; 4,41 parr; 7,37 par; Matt 9,33; 14,33; Luke 18,43, and esp. Luke 7,16: 'A great prophet has arisen among us'; see M. Dibelius, *Die Formgeschichte des Evangeliums* (Tübingen 1933[2]) 54-55, and for John 6,14 Barrett, 277, and Roloff, *Kerygma*, 266.

30 Cfr. Bultmann, 156-157; Strathmann, 111; Dodd, *Interpretation*, 333; Blank, *BibLeb* 7, 206; Schnackenburg, II 16, and the divisions made in the translated text by Hoskyns-Davey and Brown. See Appendix I for divisions in editions of the Greek text. In *NA*[26], 6,5-15 is printed as one paragraph, with spaces before the vv. 14.15. In *UBSGNT*[3] 6,14 begins with a capital letter.

31 Cfr. the division of the translated text by Hoskyns-Davey, and Roloff, *Kerygma*, 265. Marzotto's proposal (*Unità*, 158-159) to divide into 6,1-6.7-9.10-15 neglects the relationship of the question 6,5 and the answer 6,7. Becker, 190, divides into 6,1-4.5-10.10-11.12-13.14-15.

32 Cfr. Bultmann, 157; Hofbeck, *Semeion*, 114-115; Schulz, 99.

33 I mention in passing a most striking observation concerning the number of W of John 6,1-15, which is, however, not of a direct importance for the present investigation: both John 6,1-15 and the parallel story Mark 6,30-44 have a length of 236 W; in John, the narrative takes up 180 W, the discourse 56; for Mark, these numbers are 181 and 55 respectively.

34 Cfr. Quiévreux, *RHPR* 33, 135-136, 147; id., 'Le récit de la multiplication des pains dans le quatrième Évangile', *RevScRel* 41 (1967) 97-108; 98; Boismard-Lamouille, *Jean*, 185.

35 Cfr. Zarrella, *BeO* 10, 184-185; Schnackenburg, II 35.

36 See Bauer, *Wörterbuch*, s.v. ἐκ 3f and 5a; also Lagrange, 189; Bultmann, 343 n. 4; Barrett, 306; Van den Bussche, *Boek der werken*, 151; Schnackenburg, II 109; Ferraro, *RivB* 26, 38.

37 The division at 6,66/67 is defended by Ferraro, *RivB* 26, 37, and also by P. Szczygiel, 'Zum Aufbau der Rede Joh 6,25ff. Ein Beitrag zum sprachlichen Rhythmus bei Johannes', *Pastor Bonus* 24 (1911-12) 257-267; 261, 267. In his analysis 6,60-70 constitutes the final 'Strophengruppe' of John 6,25sqq; it is divided into three strophes of 10, 8 and 10 stichoi: 6,60-63.64-66.67-70. See below, section 4.a., under 1.

38 So Schnackenburg, II 109.

39 See Appendix I for divisions of 6,60-71 in literature and text-editions.

40 So Bligh, *HeyJ* 5, 24.

41 Cfr. G. Stählin, art. σκάνδαλον etc., *TWNT* VII, 338-358; 357, about John 6,61: 'σκανδαλίζω ist wie γογγύζω ... geradezu ein terminus technicus für die Glaubenskrise im Jüngerkreis'; also — about the Synoptic Gospels, but as far as σκανδαλίζειν is concerned, essentially valid for John, too — A. Humbert, 'Essai d'une théologie du scandale dans les Synoptiques', *Bib* 35 (1954) 1-28; 10-11: 'Dans l'Évangile, les concepts σκάνδαλον et πίστις sont inséparablement unis. Σκάνδαλον traduit une idée essentielle du christianisme. À la limite, la formule σκανδαλίζεσθαι ἐν ἐμοί exprime chez le païen le refus absolu de répondre à l'appel du Christ, chez le croyant l'apostasie. À l'actif, σκανδαλίζειν consistera à tuer la foi dans les âmes des croyants.'

42 Also discerned by Ferraro, *RivB* 26, 38; Heil, *Jesus Walking on the Sea*, 167.

43 Ferraro, *RivB* 26, 35-63, proposes this scheme for 6,60-71:

A 6,60	B 61-62	C 63-64a	B' 64b-65	A' 66
	B'' 67-68c	C' 68d-69	B''' 70-71	

Often, the points of similarity between elements as detected by F. are too general to be useful in an analysis of structure. F. mentions, e.g., as a point of similarity between B and B', that both contain an affirmation of Jesus concerning himself and the Father (39). When 6,62 is such an affirmation, why not also 6,63b (cfr. 4,24)?

Heil, *Jesus Walking on the Sea*, 165-166, proposes:

A 59-60	B 61-64a	A' 64b-65	B' 66-69	A'' 70-71

His explanation of this scheme is too vague and inexact to allow of a judgment of it. About criteria to be used in establishing structural correspondences within a passage, see D. J. Clark, 'Criteria for Identifying Chiasm', *Linguistica Biblica* 5 (1975) 63-72; Meynet, 'Comment établir un chiasme?, *NRT* 110, 233-249.

44 Surveys of divisions proposed are given by P. Gächter, 'Die Form der eucharistischen Rede Jesu', *ZKT* 59 (1935) 419-441; 438 (Catholic scholars up to 1935); Brown, 293-294; Schnackenburg, II 41-42; G. Gambino, 'Struttura, composizione e analisi letterario-teologica di Gv. 6,26-51b', *RivB* 24 (1976) 337-358; 337-340; Moloney, *Son of Man*, 89sqq.

45 Szczygiel, *Pastor Bonus* 24, 257-267; Gächter, *ZKT* 59, 419-441.

46 So (with minor variations in the division of 6,22-40): the chapter division of the *Codex Vaticanus*; the text-editions of Tischendorf^{8}, Westcott-Hort, followed by Nestle-Aland (up to and including *NA*^{25}), Von Soden, *UBSGNT*^{3}; to a certain extent also *NA*^{26}. From the literature on John 6: Westcott, I 221; Hoskyns-Davey, 292-299; W. Temple, *Readings in St. John's Gospel* (London 1947) 82; J. Schneider, 'Zur Frage der Komposition von Joh., 6,27-58 (59) (Die Himmelsbrotrede)', in: *In*

Memoriam Ernst Lohmeyer (Stuttgart 1951) 132-142, in abridged form in his commentary on John, 144-146; Strathmann, 118; Barrett, 282-283; Lightfoot, 151-153, 158; Becker, 200-202.

47 Cfr. Léon-Dufour, *RSR* 46, 496-498; Van den Bussche, *Boek der werken*, 110-111; Schnackenburg, II 41-42; L. Schenke, 'Die formale und gedankliche Struktur von Joh 6,26-58', *BZ* NF 24 (1980) 21-41; 25-26.

48 Gärtner, *John 6*, 26-28; E. J. Kilmartin, 'Miscellanea Biblica: Liturgical Influence on John 6', *CBQ* 22 (1960) 183-191; cfr. for the pattern of the four questions and its application to NT texts (but not to John 6) D. Daube, *The New Testament and Rabbinic Judaism* (The Jordan Lectures 1952; London 1956) 158-169.

49 Cfr. Brown, 266-267.

50 E. Galbiati, 'Il pane della vita (Giov. 6,55-58)', *BeO* 5 (1963) 101-110; 101-102.

51 Léon-Dufour, *RSR* 46, 500, 505.

52 Van den Bussche, *Boek der werken*, 53-54, 107-113.

53 J.-N. Aletti, 'Le discours sur le pain de vie (Jean 6). Problèmes de composition et fonction des citations de l'Ancien Testament', *RSR* 62 (1974) 169-197; 170-176.

54 P. Borgen, 'The Unity of the Discourse in John 6', *ZNW* 50 (1959) 277-278; id., 'Observations on the Midrashic Character of John 6', *ZNW* 54 (1963) 232-240; id., *Bread from Heaven*. An Exegetical Study of the Concept of Manna in the Gospel of John and the Writings of Philo (NTS 10; Leiden 1965) 23, 35-38, 59-98. Cfr. Schnackenburg, II 41-42.

55 U. Wilckens, 'Der eucharistische Abschnitt der johanneischen Rede vom Lebensbrot (Joh 6,51c-58)', in: *Neues Testament und Kirche* (Fs. R. Schnackenburg; Freiburg etc. 1974) 220-248; 222-229.

56 Schenke, *BZ* NF 24, 21-41.

57 B. Lindars, *Behind the Fourth Gospel* (Studies in Creative Criticism 3; London 1971) 47-50.

58 Willemse, *Het vierde evangelie*, 190-194.

59 Bligh, *HeyJ* 5, 17-22.

60 G. Segalla, 'La struttura circolare-chiasmatica di Gv. 6,26-58 e il suo significato teologico', *BeO* 13 (1971) 191-198.

61 Segalla, *BeO* 13, 191.

62 So there is a chiasm, according to S., in 6,26-35b, the first one of the five sections (the others are 6,35.41-48; 6,47-51b; 6,51-58, and the inserted passage 6,36-40); he discerns correspondences between 6,26 + 34-35b, 27a + 33, 27c + 32 and 28-29 + 30-31 (*BeO* 13, 192-193). The occurrence, however, of a single identical word (widely used, moreover), such as ἄρτος or πατήρ, and a vague correspondence of content cannot be made the basis for establishing a chiasm. The same criticism is applicable to Heil, *Jesus Walking on the Sea*, 152-165, who discerns four movements, each of which has a concentric structure: 6,26-40.41-47.48-51b.51c-58. The movements end in 'an appeal by Jesus to adhere to him as the medium for gaining eternal life' (152).

63 So, in different ways, S. Temple, 'A Key to the Composition of the Fourth Gospel', *JBL* 80 (1961) 220-232; T. Worden, 'The Holy Eucharist in St. John', *Scr* 15 (1963) 97-103; 16 (1964) 5-16; Schattenmann, *Studien*, 33-39; Gambino, *RivB* 24, 341-358; M. Gourgues, 'Section christologique et section eucharistique en Jean VI. Une proposition', *RB* 88 (1981) 515-531.

64 See Appendix II, for an enumeration of these scholars.

65 Cfr. J. D. Crossan, 'A Structuralist Analysis of John 6', in: *Orientation by Disorientation*. Studies in Literary Criticism and in Biblical Literary Criticism (Fs. W. A. Beardslee; Pittsburgh Theological Monograph Series 35; Pittsburgh 1980) 235-249; 243. This article is identical with 'It Is Written. A Structuralist Analysis of John 6', in: P. J. Achtemeier, ed., *SBL 1979 Seminar Papers* I (SBL Seminar Papers Series 16; Missoula, Mt. 1979) 197-213; 197, 200-208, 212-213.

66 Cfr. Lagrange, 179; Lightfoot, 154; Schnackenburg, II 75; Aletti, *RSR* 62, 173-174; Crossan, in: *Orientation by Disorientation*, 237.

67 Brown, 267; similarly Lagrange, 173, 176; Odeberg, 257; Dodd, *Interpretation*, 337; Léon-Dufour, *RSR* 46, 500-501, 504; Boismard-Lamouille, *Jean*, 203; Gourgues, *RB* 88, 524-526.

68 Brown, 263: 'Verses 25-34 serve as a preface or introduction to the Bread of Life Discourse, and thus the arrangement resembles that of ch. v, where vss. 16-18 set the theme for the long discourse that followed.'

69 The different divisions can be seen in Appendix I (for scholars combining the introduction with the preceding story) and II, or can be derived from the survey under 4.a. In addition, I mention Westcott, I 221 and Lightfoot, 158, who put the caesura after 6,24; Hoskyns-Davey, 291-292, and Schnackenburg, II 43, who put it after 6,25; E. Schweizer, *EGO EIMI*. Die religionsgeschichtliche Herkunft und theologische Bedeutung der johanneischen Bildreden, zugleich ein Beitrag zur Quellenfrage des vierten Evangeliums (FRLANT 56; Göttingen 1939, 1965[2]) 151; Schneider, in: *In Memoriam E. Lohmeyer*, 133, and W. A. Meeks, 'The Man from Heaven in Johannine Sectarianism', *JBL* 91 (1972) 44-72; 58 n. 50, who put it after 6,26. *NA*[26] begins a new paragraph at 6,26.

70 This correspondence is mentioned, with different degrees of clearness, by Bauer, 97; Lagrange, 182; Gächter, *ZKT* 59, 432-433; Schweizer, *EGO EIMI*, 155; Dodd, *Interpretation*, 338; Léon-Dufour, *RSR* 46, 500; Brown, 277; Schlier, in: *Das Ende der Zeit*, 113; Giblet, *Concilium* 4 nr. 10, 60; Schnackenburg, II 81; Segalla, *BeO* 13, 193-194; Schulz, 106; Aletti, *RSR* 62, 173; Wilckens, in: *NT und Kirche*, 225-226; Pancaro, *Law*, 466-467; Gambino, *RivB* 24, 353-354; Boismard-Lamouille, *Jean*, 202-203; Becker, 201, 213-214; Schenke, *BZ* NF 24, 29; Gourgues, *RB* 88, 519, 522.

71 See Norden, *Agnostos Theos*, 186-188, esp. 188 n. 1. Against Norden, however, it has to be said with Bultmann, 170 n. 3 (cfr. 176 n. 8), that in 6,50 οὗτός ἐστιν has a different function: there, οὗτος refers to the ἵνα-clause, within a definition-formula.

72 Noticed by Szczygiel, *Pastor Bonus* 24, 265-266; Bultmann, 176; Strathmann, 125; Van den Bussche, *Boek der werken*, 144; Galbiati, *BeO* 5, 101-102; Borgen, *Bread from Heaven*, 35-38, 87-88; Schlier, in: *Das Ende der Zeit*, 117; Giblet, *Concilium* 4 nr. 10, 59; Schnackenburg, II 96; Aletti, *RSR* 62, 195; Schneider, 155; Schenke, *BZ* NF 24, 36; Gourgues, *RB* 88, 519.

73 This series is noticed by Bultmann, 176; J. McPolin, 'Bultmanni theoria litteraria et Jo 6,51c-58c', *VD* 44 (1966) 243-258; 250; cfr. the series 6,33.50.58 in Westcott, I 255.

74 Cfr. Bengel, *Gnomon*, 368; Schürmann, *BZ* NF 2, 255-256; Schnackenburg, II 56, 83; Riedl, *Heilswerk*, 313 (following Schürmann); Wilckens, in: *NT und Kirche*, 227; Boismard-Lamouille, *Jean*, 203.

75 For the correspondence of 6,36-40 and 6,44-47, cfr. Bengel, *Gnomon*, 370, about 6,44: 'continuat ea ipsa quae v. 40 dixit'; Bauer, 97; Lagrange, 179; E. Ruckstuhl, *Die literarische Einheit des Johannesevangeliums*. Der gegenwärtige Stand der einschlägigen Forschungen (Studia Friburgensia NF 3; Freiburg i.d. Schw. 1951) 254 (6,35-40.44-47); Schneider, in: *In Memoriam E. Lohmeyer*, 135, 141 (6,37-40.44-46); Schlier, in: *Das Ende der Zeit*, 113; W. Wilkens, *Zeichen und Werke*. Ein Beitrag zur Theologie des 4. Evangeliums in Erzählungs- und Redestoff (ATANT 55; Zürich 1969) 92; Schnackenburg, II 75; Wilckens, in: *NT und Kirche*, 223, 225-226; Schenke, *BZ* NF 24, 28-29, with 28 n. 24 (6,37-40.43-47). — It is true that the expressions ἔρχεσθαι πρὸς ἐμέ and πιστεύειν εἰς ἐμέ also occur in 6,35 (cfr. Boismard-Lamouille, *Jean*, 202-203, who make 6,35c-40 correspond to 6,44-47); there, however, they only serve to express the condition for participating in the bread of life within a revelatory formula, whereas in 6,36-40 attention is directed to faith as such. The caesuras (marked by capital letters) at 6,35/36.40/41.43/44.47/48 in *NA*[25] are right; in *NA*[26], the one at 6,43/44 is absent, and the other ones are of a different order (paragraph at 6,35/36 and 6,40/41, capital letter at 6,47/48).

76 Noticed by Schürmann, *BZ* NF 2, 254, followed by Riedl, *Heilswerk*, 312; according

to them, however, 6,32-35 corresponds to 6,48-51; similarly Becker, 201-202. Boismard-Lamouille, *Jean*, 202-203, propose a slightly different scheme which covers 6,31-51 (in which passage a few parts of the text, not very essential to its structure, are omitted, as deriving from the ultimate redactor of the gospel, called by them 'Jean III'):

A 6,31-33 B 34-35b C 35c-40 D 41-43 C' 44-47 B' 48 A' 49-51.

The differences with the scheme I propose arise mainly from the fact that B. and L. do not take into account the caesuras at 6,34/35 and 6,51b/51c. This negligence leads them to anomalies such as making 6,34-35b into one element which corresponds to 6,48, and overlooking the third ἐγώ εἰμι-saying in 6,51 in its relationship to 6,35.48.

77 Noticed (in broad outlines) by Segalla, *BeO* 13, 193-194.

78 Cfr. Crossan, in: *Orientation by Disorientation*, 246.

79 Cfr. Bengel, *Gnomon*, 371, about 'flesh' in 6,51c: 'novus sermonis gradus'.

80 Bauer, 98: 'Die seltene Partikelfolge δέ an vierter Stelle nach καί hebt hier, anders als 8,16.17, das dem schon Gesagten Beigefügte als etwas Neues und Wichtiges hervor; vgl. 1 Jo 1,3; Mt 10,18; PHib. 54,20'; see also Bauer, *Wörterbuch*, s.v. δέ 4b.

81 Similarly Abbott, *Joh. Grammar*, nr. 2076; Gächter, *ZKT* 59, 429-430, referring (430 n. 18) to J. D. Denniston, *The Greek Particles* (Oxford 1934) 201.

82 For the divisions given in text-editions and literature, see under 4.a., and see especially Appendix II.

83 I cannot see any structural significance for the Amen-formulae in 6,26.32.47.53; they only seem to serve to mark important statements of Jesus. The formula might have some structural value in the dialogue 6,22-34: the first and last time Jesus is speaking, his words are introduced by it (6,26.32).

The formula ἀναστήσω κτλ. (6,39.40.44.54) has a clear structural value in 6,39.40.44 (see observation 3.f. above); its occurrence in 6,54 does not seem to have any significance for the structure of the text. As for its content, the formula is only an extension of the theme of (eternal) life present throughout the discourse (see p. 162).

84 Cfr. Dodd, *Interpretation*, 337 ('In verse 35 the ambiguity is cleared up. Jesus expressly claims to be ὁ καταβαίνων ἐκ τοῦ οὐρανοῦ, and, therefore, Himself the Bread of Life'); Hofbeck, *Semeion*, 119 ('Mit V 35 wird das geheimnisvolle Schweigen gelüftet'); Schnackenburg, II 56 (6,35 is 'das entscheidende Wort, das den Schleier um das von ihm gemeinte Brot Gottes zerreisst'); also Pancaro, *Law*, 464.

85 Cfr. Bernard, 197.

86 For αἷμα referring to Jesus' death, cfr. 1 John 1,7; 5,6; for the ὑπέρ-formula of 6,51c in connection with this event, cfr. John 10,11.15; 11,50-52; 15,13; 17,19; 18,14. — It is a widely held opinion, that 6,51c-58 is about the eucharist. It might be preferable to say that this passage is about Jesus' death, and the accepting of it by the believer, in eucharistic terms, see especially Willemse, *Het vierde evangelie*, 191-199; Dunn, *NTS* 17, 328-338. It is clear, anyhow, that the new thought is introduced in 6,51c; so, too, Schürmann, *BZ* NF 2, 244-262, who then, however, considers 6,51c the climax of the preceding, and 6,53-58 a eucharistic discourse.

87 Crossan, in: *Orientation by Disorientation*, 246-247, similarly argues his division of the discourse: 6,25-34.35-48.49-58. In my view, however, 6,49-51b does not go beyond what precedes in 6,31-35.

88 So Bengel, *Gnomon*, 367; D. Buzy, 'Un procédé littéraire de saint Jean', *BLE* 39 (1938) 61-75; 69; Bultmann, 166 n. 10 (cont. 167; B. declares 6,27bc to be a redactional addition, just as 6,51c-58); Léon-Dufour, *RSR* 46, 504 n. 42; Schürmann, *BZ* NF 2, 255; Galbiati, *BeO* 5, 102; Willemse, *Het vierde evangelie*, 190-191; McPolin, *VD* 44, 247-249; Schlier, in: *Das Ende der Zeit*, 111; Schnackenburg, II 50 (cautiously); Wilckens, in: *NT und Kirche*, 226; Becker, 204 (declares 6,27 and 6,51c-58 to be redactional additions); Haenchen, 320 (does so with 6,27bc and 6,51c-58); Gourgues, *RB* 88, 523-524.

89 The inversion of order occurs in the quotation of Jesus' words at the end of 6,42.

For other instances of inversion of order in quotations, see P. C. Beentjes, 'Inverted Quotations in the Bible. A Neglected Stylistic Pattern', *Bib* 63 (1982) 506-523.

90 Cfr. Smit Sibinga's observations concerning Matt 8,14-15: both 8,14 and 8,15 contain 15 W or 30 S (in Gerhardsson, *Mighty Acts*, 41). The difference with the present case is that Matt 8,14-15 is a small literary unit, whereas John 6,26c-27a is not.

91 Cfr. Burney, *The Poetry of Our Lord*, 80 (parallelism); 106, 136, 170 (rhythm and rhyme in a supposed Aramaic original of 6,26-27).

92 Probably the reference is to 6,26, so, e.g., Brown, 269; Schnackenburg, II 71.

93 Léon-Dufour, *NTS* 7, 251-253. See above, p. 114, for criticism of his terminology.

94 Cfr. Burney, *Poetry*, 93 (parallelism), 130 (rhythm in a supposed Aramaic original).

95 So Léon-Dufour, *RSR* 46, 499 n. 40.

96 So Bauer, 97; Schweizer, *EGO EIMI*, 155; Bultmann, 172-173; Barrett, 296; Schnackenburg, II 79; Boismard-Lamouille, *Jean*, 204.

97 So Schneider, 146.

98 Cfr. Westcott, I 237; H. Leroy, *Rätsel und Missverständnis*. Ein Beitrag zur Formgeschichte des Johannesevangeliums (BBB 30; Bonn 1968) 109.

99 Cfr. Schweizer, *EGO EIMI*, 155; Segalla, *BeO* 13, 194-195; Schenke, *BZ* NF 24, 29.

100 The central position of 6,55 within 6,53-57 is confirmed by an observation of Ruckstuhl, *Einheit*, 244-245: in 6,54.56 we have the sequence τρώγων-σάρκα, πίνων-αἷμα, whereas 6,55 has σάρξ-βρῶσις, αἷμα-πόσις; likewise, in 6,54.56 the possessive μου is before the substantive, in 6,55 it is behind it; cfr. also Szczygiel, *Pastor Bonus* 24, 266; Segalla, *BeO* 13, 195. In the strophic divisions of Gächter, *ZKT* 59, 435, and Léon-Dufour, *RSR* 46, 513, 6,55 is also put in the centre, surrounded by 6,53-54.56-57, with 6,58 as a conclusion. The synthetic parallelism of 6,56-57 is mentioned by Schenke, *BZ* NF 24, 31.

101 So Bauer, 98; Lagrange, 184; Ruckstuhl, *Einheit*, 244; Strathmann, 124-125; Moloney, *Son of Man*, 103; Schneider, 153; Boismard-Lamouille, *Jean*, 192; Schenke, *BZ* NF 24, 31; Crossan, in: *Orientation by Disorientation*, 242.

102 Cfr. Schweizer, *EGO EIMI*, 157; Barrett, 299-300; Schnackenburg, II 92-96; Wilckens, in: *NT und Kirche*, 225: 'In diesem Satz V. 57 mündet offensichtlich die mit V. 55 anhebende Begründung der lebenspendenden Kraft der Eucharistie aus: Das Verhältnis von Vater und Sohn findet in dem Verhältnis von Jesus und Mahlteilnehmer seine Entsprechung'.

APPENDIX I

Main divisions of John 6 proposed in literature and text-editions

N.B. In this list divisions of the discourse on the bread of life (6,22-59) are not taken into account.

Westcott	[1 - 15 16-21] [22 - 59] [60-65 66-69 70-71]
Bauer	[1-13] [14 - 21] [22 - 31] [32 - 71]
Windisch, *ΕΥΧΑΡΙΣΤΗΡΙΟΝ*, II 190-191	[1 - 15 16-21 22-24] [25 - 59] [60-65] [66 - 71]
Lagrange	[1-13] [14 - 21] [22 - 59] [60 - 71]
Bernard	[1-13] [14-15] [16-21] [22 - 59] [60-65] [66 - 71]
Bultmann	[1 - 26] [27-59]
	(B. puts 6,60-71 between 8,30-40 and 12,37-43, see pp. 214-215, 321)
Hoskyns-Davey	[1 - 15] [16-21] [22 - 59] [60 - 7,1]
Strathmann	[1 - 21] [22 - 25 26 - 65 66 - 71]
Dodd, *Interpretation*, 333-345 (cfr. *Hist. Tradition*, 213)	[1-13 14-15 16-21] [22 - 59] [60 - 71]
Barrett	[1 - 15] [16-21] [22 - 59] [60 - 71]
Lightfoot	[1 - 15] [16-21] [22 - 59] [60 - 71]
Léon-Dufour, *RSR* 46, 490	[1 - 14 15 16 - 25] [26-58 59 - 65] [66 - 71]
Leenhardt, *RHPR* 39, 1-13	[1-13] [14-15] [16-21] [22 - 70]

Van den Bussche, *Boek der werken*, 98-153	[1 - 15] [16 - 25] [26 - 59] [60 - 71]
Bligh, *HeyJ* 5, 3-26	[1 - 15] [16-21] [22 - 65] [66 - 71]
Blank, *BibLeb* 7, 193-194	[1 - 15 16-21] [22 - 59] [60 - 71]
Brown	[1 - 15] [16-21] [22 - 59] [60 - 71]
Schlier, *Das Ende der Zeit*, 106-107	[1 - 15 16-21 22 - 25] [26 - 59] [60 - 71]
Giblet, *Concilium* 4 nr. 10, 56-65 (also in *Lumière et Vie* 29 nr. 149, 89)	[1 - 21] [22 - 59] [60 - 71]
Berrouard, *Lumière et Vie* 18 nr. 94, 63-75	[1-13] [14-15 16-21] [22 - 58] [60 - 71]
Schnackenburg	[1 - 15] [16-21] [22 - 59] [60-65 66 - 71]
Schulz	[1 - 21] [22 - 59] [60 - 71]
Schneider	[1 - 15] [16-21] [22 - 59] [60 - 71]
Boismard-Lamouille, *Jean*, 178-209	[1 - 15] [16-21] [22 - 59] [60 - 71]
Becker	[1 - 21] [22 - 71]
Haenchen	[1 - 15] [16 - 25] [26 - 59] [60 - 71]

Text-editions:

Tischendorf[8]	[1-13] [14-15] [16-21] [22 - 59] [60-65] [66 - 71]
Westcott-Hort	[1-13 14-15 16-21] [22 - 59 60-65 66 - 71]
Von Soden	[1-13] [14-15 16-21] [22 - 58 59 -65 66 - 71]
NA[25]	[1-13 14-15 16-21] [22 - 59 60-65] [66 - 71]
UBSGNT[3]	[1 - 15] [16-21] [22 - 59] [60-65 66 - 71]
NA[26]	[1-4] [5 - 15] [16-21] [22 - 59] [60-65] [66 - 71]

The chapter division in the *Codex Vaticanus* is 6,1-14.15-21.22-40.41-51.52-71

APPENDIX II

ions of John 6,22-59 into units of thought as found in literature

ange	[22-24] [25 - 40 41-47 48-50] [51 - 59]
ard	[22 - 25] [26 - 40] [41 - 51b] [51c - 59]
, *BLE* 39, ·71	[27] [28 - 40] [41 - 51] [52 - 58]
l, *Interpreta-* ι, 334-340	[22-24] [26 - 34] [35 - 50] [51 - 59]
hardt, *IPR* 39, 1-13	[22 - 35] [36 - 47] [48 - 70]
rmann, *BZ* ' 2, 244-262	[26 - 51] [53-58]
uillet, 'Les mes bibliques majeurs du discours sur le pain de vie', *NRT* 82 (1960) 803-822, 918-939, 40-1062; 803-805	[22 - 25] [26 - 34] [35 - 47] [48 - 58]
uland, 'Sign l Sacrament. John's Bread of Life Discourse', *Int* 18 (1964) 450-462; 450	[26] [27 - 34] [35 - 51b] [51c - 58]
, *BibLeb* 7, -194	[22-24] [25 - 35] [36 - 50] [51 - 59]
n	[22-24] [25 - 34] [35 - 50] [51 - 59]
, *Concilium* 4 10, 57-62	[22 - 34] [35 - 47] [48 - 51] [52 - 59]
uard, *nière et Vie* 18 nr. 94, 63-75	[26 -27] [28 - 51b] [51c-56] [57-58]
f, *Kerygma*, -269	[26 - 51b] [51c - 58]

Schnider-Stenger, *Joh. und die Synoptiker*, 154-166	[26 - 35]	[36 - 51b]	[51c -
Schulz	[22 - 31]	[32 - 51b]	[51c -
Riedl, *Heilswerk*, 312	[26 - 51]	[53	
Pancaro, *Law*, 458-459	[26 - 34]	[35 - 50]	[51 -
Moloney, *Son of Man*, 101-105	[22 - 34]	[35 - 51b]	[51c -

CHAPTER FOUR

JOHN 9,1-10,21: THE HEALING OF THE MAN BORN BLIND AND THE DISCOURSE ON THE SHEPHERD

As for the number of S and W, there is no difference between the text of this passage in *NA25* and that in *NA26*. This common text will be used as a basis for the numerical analysis (including the words that are between square brackets in both editions, οὖν in 9,10 and δέ in 9,16, as well as πρὸ ἐμοῦ in 10,8, a regular part of the text in *NA25* but bracketed in *NA26*), with one exception: instead of ἠνέῳξεν I read in 9,32 the trisyllabic form ἤνοιξεν, with Lachmann, Tischendorf8, Von Soden, Souter (ἤνοιξε), Vogels, *UBSGNT1* and the *Greek-English Diglot*[1]. The reading ἠνέῳξεν is found in B W Δ, ἀνέῳξεν in P75 Θ 565[2]; so, a few representatives of the Alexandrian and the Caesarean type of text have here a quadrisyllabic aorist active indicative of ἀνοίγειν, as well as a representative of the Koinè type of text (Δ). The reading ἤνοιξεν is found in P66 Sin A D (ἤνυξε) and others. In John 9, and elsewhere in the NT, the forms of ἀνοίγειν with augment (single, double or triple) present a very confused picture in the mss.[3]. Nevertheless, this picture can give us a certain indication as to the reading to be adopted in John 9,32. In the words of J. K. Elliott: 'There are no firm examples of ἀνεῳ- or ἠνεῳ-. There are however firm examples (without any *v.ll.*, as far as I can discover) of ἠνοι-. This fact can be used as a touchstone for variants involving this spelling. ἠνοι- seems to be the form natural to the New Testament writers'[4]. When this observation of Elliott is combined with the rather poor attestation to the quadrisyllabic reading in John 9,32 (divided, besides, over two different forms), it seems best in this case to adopt the reading ἤνοιξεν[5].

A second problem of textual criticism, in 9,35, will be dealt with below, under 3.f., in connection with the count of S and W.

1. *The main divisions of John 9,1-10,21 and their coherence*

John 9 starts with the description of the healing of a man born blind performed by Jesus, preceded by a conversation between Jesus and his disciples about the man's illness (9,1-7). The healing is followed by a dialogue between the healed man and his neighbours and those who were accustomed to see him begging (9,8-12), and an examination of the healed man by the Pharisees, which is interrupted by an interrogation of his parents; at the end of the interrogation, the man is cast out (9,13-34). A second meeting of Jesus and the healed man is related, in which the man confesses his faith in Jesus as the Son of Man; this meeting is followed by a short dialogue between Jesus and the Pharisees about the latter's blindness (9,35-41). The dialogue turns into a monologue of Jesus (called a παροιμία, 10,6) about a shepherd and his sheep (10,1-5); the audience does not understand these words (10,6). The monologue is continued, and Jesus explicitly identifies himself with two elements from the *paroimia*: the door (10,7-10), and the shepherd (10,11-18)[6]. Finally, the various reactions of the Jews to Jesus' words are related (10,19-21).

There is no clear unity of place in this passage, neither in itself nor when compared with what precedes and what follows. At the end of ch. 8, Jesus has left the temple (8,59), and the scene of 9,1-12 is laid in the neighbourhood of the temple (cfr. 9,1); the ensuing examination is situated elsewhere, witness 9,13. Another change of place is suggested at 9,34/35. The next episode, 10,22-39, has the temple as its scene again (cfr. 10,23).

Neither does the passage constitute a clear unity of time. There seems to be no lapse of time between 8,59 and 9,1. Within the passage itself, a certain lapse of time could be suggested at 9,12/13[7], and at 9,34/35. When compared with what follows, the passage can be said to constitute a unity of time: 10,22-39 is dated to the Festival of Dedication, whereas 9,1-10,21 is — at least, when we take seriously the evangelist's indications of time in their dramatic function — still part of the events of the last and greatest day of the Festival of Tabernacles (see 7,37).

The unity of John 9,1-10,21 is predominantly a dramatic one. The presence of the man born blind, as subject or as object, is a unifying factor in John 9. He appears on the stage in 9,1, and disappears after 9,38. Jesus' saying in 9,39 is a retrospective conclusion: the sightless who see now are represented by the man born blind, and the seeing ones who become blind by the Pharisees: in the examination of the man born blind they showed their blindness[8]. In 9,40-41, Jesus is conversing with the Pharisees about *their* blindness. The beginning of 9,40: 'Some of the Pharisees, who were with him, heard these things and said to him ...', connects these verses with the preceding context.

A number of words and expressions help to achieve the unity of John 9: τυφλός (13 × in ch. 9; used in John outside ch. 9 only generally in 5,3, and referring to ch. 9 in 10,21; 11,37), ὀφθαλμοὺς ἀνοίγειν (7 × [9]; outside John 9 also only in 10,21; 11,37), βλέπειν, used absolutely (8 × ; not found in John outside ch. 9), and, less strikingly, words of the stem ἁμαρτ-, viz. ἁμαρτάνειν (2 ×), ἁμαρτία (3 ×) and ἁμαρτωλός (4 ×); these words and expressions are found throughout the chapter[10].

The introductory formula καὶ παράγων (9,1) designates a change of scene with respect to what precedes (the same formula with the same function occurs in Matt 9,9.27; Mark 1,16; 2,14). Possibly, it is the introduction of an original 'Einzelgeschichte'[11]; more important, however, is its function of connecting two episodes on a redactional level. Καί at the beginning of a new scene is not uncommon in John[12].

In spite of the traditional division into chapters, 9,40-10,21 constitutes a clear dramatic unity: Jesus and the Pharisees are on the stage[13]. Jesus' words in 9,41 are evidently directed to the Pharisees; so is the ensuing discourse 10,1-18, as the personal pronouns in 10,1.6.7 cannot indicate other persons than the Pharisees mentioned before[14]. The formula ἀμὴν ἀμὴν λέγω ὑμῖν (10,1) is never used in John without a direct connection with what precedes. Its function seems to draw attention to what follows[15]. The formula occurs in John 1-20 in twelve other cases within discourse of Jesus: 3,11; 5,24.25; 6,47; 8,51; 12,24; 13,16.20.38; 14,12; 16,20.23; cfr. 21,18; nowhere, it makes a new beginning. In 10,19, the Pharisees of 9,40 are called οἱ Ἰουδαῖοι; a similar transition from 'the Pharisees' to 'the Jews' occurs elsewhere in John (see 8,13.21.22; 9,13.15.16.18).

9,40-41 is obviously part of the dramatic unit 9,40-10,21, though this is not evident from the vocabulary: the words that are determining 10,1-18 are ποιμήν (6 × in 10,1-18), πρόβατα (13 ×), κλέπτης (3 ×), θύρα (4 ×), to name the more important ones, and none of them is found in 9,40-41.

So far, there seem to be at least two parts in 9,1-10,21: 9,1-41 and 9,40-10,21. 9,40-41 belongs both to 9,1-41 and to 9,40-10,21; it constitutes, in that way, a link between two parts that are different as for vocabulary and theme (and, therefore, probably also as for their origin[16]), viz., ch. 9 and 10,1-21. Another link between the two parts is provided by the back-reference to the healing in 10,21. Then what is the dramatic unity of 9,1-10,21?

To answer this question, the observations of C. H. Dodd referred to earlier (see p. 105) can be helpful. The pattern of narration, dialogue and monologue, all of them related to a single theme, is recognized by Dodd in John 9,1-10,21. According to him, the theme is 'judgment by the light'; he considers 9,1-7 as action, 9,8-41 as dialogues, 10,1-18 as monologue, and 10,19-21 as a brief concluding dialogue (and 10,22-39 as an appendix, but here that passage can be left out of consideration, as it is dated to another occasion)[17].

A slight correction of Dodd's view seems necessary: the narration comprises not only 9,1-7, but 9,1-39. In this story it is told how Jesus heals a man born blind — healing both physical (9,1-7) and spiritual (9,35-38)

— and how the Pharisees condemn this man (and, with him, Jesus) and cast him out (9,13-34). This narration is interpreted in 9,40sqq in the following way[18]:

1. Jesus, condemned by the Pharisees, is in reality 'the door of the sheep' (10,7; cfr. 10,9), 'the good shepherd' (10,11.14). He calls his sheep that hear his voice, he is known to them, and they follow him; he leads his sheep out and goes ahead of them (10,3-4). He gives them life, when they go in through him (10,9-10), he lays down his life for them (10,11.15), and knows them (10,14). What is said here generally about the sheep, has happened paradigmatically to the man born blind.

2. The Pharisees who condemned both the man born blind and Jesus, turn out to condemn themselves by their condemnation: they say that they are seeing, and therefore their sin remains (9,41). When the discourse on the shepherd and his sheep is read in its present context, the reader is simply compelled to think at least *also* of the Pharisees when reading about the characters that are pictured in contrast to the shepherd and the door ('thief and robber', 10,1.8.10; 'stranger', 10,5; 'hireling', 10,12-13). This effect is strengthened as soon as Ezek 34 is acknowledged as (part of the) OT background of John 10,1-18[19]. There, God is passing his verdict on the wicked shepherds of Israel, who are not concerned about the sheep; their function as shepherd will be taken away from them, and God himself will gather the sheep, and appoint his servant David as the one shepherd over them. Then the sheep will know that the Lord is their God and that they are his people. With this background in mind, it is evident that in John 10,1-18 a verdict is passed on the Pharisees as wicked shepherds[20]. Their behaviour as such is evident from their treatment of the man born blind in ch. 9.

The view that 9,1-39 is to be considered as narration, and 9,40-10,18 as dialogue and monologue interpreting this narration, can be corroborated from a comparison of John 5 and John 9[21]:

John 5	*John 9*
1-9 healing (in Jerusalem, 5,2, on a Sabbath, 5,9)	1-7 healing (in Jerusalem, cfr. 8,59, on a Sabbath, 9,14)
10-13 conversation healed man - Jews (no formal interrogation, no change of place), ending with the question who did cure him; the man does not know the answer (οὐκ ᾔδει, 5,13), because Jesus has disappeared	8-12 conversation healed man - neighbours (not yet a formal interrogation, no change of place), in which it becomes evident that Jesus cured him, ending with the question where Jesus is the; the man does not know the answer (οὐκ οἶδα, 9,12)
(no parallel to 9,13-34)	13-34 interrogation
14 Jesus finds him (εὑρίσκει αὐτόν) and tells him to sin no more	35sqq Jesus finds him (εὑρὼν αὐτόν, 9,35) and the man believes in Jesus
15 the man disappears from the stage	39sqq the man does not play an active role any longer

16-18 charge of the Jews, and defence of Jesus
19sqq monologue, beginning with ἀμὴν ἀμὴν λέγω ὑμῖν

40-41 dialogue Jesus-Pharisees (for which 9,39 offers the starting point)
10,1sqq monologue, beginning with ἀμὴν ἀμὴν λέγω ὑμῖν

From this scheme, it will be evident that the sequence of parts of the story is comparable in both episodes. In John 9, the narration is closed with 9,39, as the narration of the healing of the crippled man is closed with 5,15. Then follows, in 9,40-41 and 5,16-18, a brief dialogue or quasi-dialogue that serves as a transition from narration to monologue; in both instances, the latter begins with the same formula[22].

We observed earlier (see p. 106) that in all Johannine examples of the sequence of narration, dialogue and monologue adduced by Dodd, the monologue is a monologue of Jesus, so that the dialogue leading up to it can be expected to be a dialogue of Jesus with others. In ch. 9, this dialogue begins only with 9,40. Of course, 9,8-39 also has the form of a dialogue, but only from 9,40 onward we have a dialogue revealing the meaning of the previous action and passing into monologue.

So, the coherence of John 9,1-10,21 can be summed up in this scheme[23]:

9,1-39	action, ending with Jesus' saying in 9,39, that serves as a starting point for	
9,40-41	dialogue	interpretation of the action[24]
10,1-18	monologue	
10,19-21	concluding reactions	

Now, the composition of the various main parts of John 9,1-10,21 in numbers of S and W has to be dealt with. The story 9,1-39 has a length of 1349 S, made up of 800 S of discourse, and 549 S of narrative[25]. When we suppose a deficit of one S in the narrative portions of the text (other indications for this deficit will be dealt with below), we have 550 S of narrative, and a sum total of 1350 S. Out of the 800 S of discourse, 170 (= 90 W) are put in Jesus' mouth, and 630 in the mouth of other persons, when ὕπαγε ... νίψαι 9,11 is included in Jesus' discourse. In view of what follows, it is important to note here that 1350 and 630 are multiples of 9(0), and 550 of 11(0). A schematic arrangement of the above is given in Table I.

Table I. John 9,1-39	syllables	
narrative in John 9,1-39		549
discourse of Jesus	170	
of others	630/800/1349	

9,40-10,21 has a size of 800 S. This amounts to 404 W (a symmetrical number), made up of 54 W of narrative and 350 W of discourse. When βλέπομεν 9,41 is considered to belong to the discourse of the Pharisees, the discourse of Jesus amounts to 325 W (triangular number of 25), that of the Pharisees/Jews to 25 (see Table II).

Table II. John 9,40-10,21

		words
narrative in John 9,40-10,21		54
discourse of Jesus	325	
of the Pharisees/Jews	25/350/404	

To the 404 W of 9,40-10,21, the surplus-technique has also been applied: Jesus' continuous speech 9,41b-10,5 contains 104 W, from a sum total of 404.

A division of 9,1-39 according to the actors is given in Table III in numbers of W.

Table III. words divided acc. to actors John 9,1-39

	Jesus	dis-ciples	man	neigh-bours	imper-sonal	Phari-sees	parents	
9,1	7							
2		18						
3-7c	75							
7d			7					
8-9d				32				
9e			5					
10				9				
11			29					
12ab				6				
12cd			3					
13				8				
14					16			
15a						9		
15bc			14					
16-17c						48		
17d			6					
18-19						39		
20-23							74	
24						24		
25			15					
26						11		
27			19					
28-29						28		
30-33			63					
34						17		
35	17							
36			12					
37	14							
38			8					
39	22							
total	135 +	18 +	181 +	55 +	16 +	176 +	74	= 655

Here, a symmetrical number appears in the sum of the sentences with the man born blind as actor (181), and also in the total number of W of the passage, when we suppose the hypothetical missing syllable to be a monosyllabic word (656). When this missing word is provisionally located in the narrative portions of the sentences with Jesus and his disciples as actors, these sentences have a length of 154, = 14 × 11, W. Multiples of 11 also occur in the sum of the sentences with the Pharisees/Jews as actor (176, = 16 × 11), and in the sum of those with the neighbours of the man as actor (55, = 5 × 11; 55 is, moreover, triangular number of 10).

It is obvious from the above, that the author of John made 9,1-39 into a literary unit. Now the same is valid for 9,1-41. This is not astonishing, as 9,40-41 is a transition from narration to monologue. The entire chapter has a size of 692 W; reckoning again with the deficit of one W, this number becomes 693, or 7 × 9 × 11. 7, 9 and 11 are three subsequent odd numbers, out of which at least 9 and 11 are essential to the numerical composition of John 9 (see Table I above and its commentary, also Table III, and see below, in the numerical analysis of John 9).

The discourse of Jesus and those who are on his side (the disciples and the man born blind) together in 9,1-41 has a length of 250 W, 100 out of them put in the mouth of Jesus, 11 in the mouth of the disciples and 139 in the mouth of the man born blind (discourse of a speaker includes here quotations by him). The discourse of the other persons in 9,1-41 amounts to 165, = 15 × 11, W; 101 (a symmetrical number) out of them are used for the discourse of the Pharisees (see Table IV).

Table IV. discourse in John 9,1-41	words
discourse of Jesus in John 9,1-41	100
of the disciples	11
of the man born blind	139/250
of his neighbours	23
of the Pharisees/Jews	101
of the parents of the man	38
of anonymous 9,35	3/165/415

Jesus' discourse in 9,1-41 has a length of 200 S, when quotations of his words by others are included (cfr. Table I; to the 170 S mentioned there, 30 S from 9,41 have to be added).

In numbers of S, a division according to the actors has also been applied to 9,1-41 (see Table V).

Table V. syll. divided acc. to actors John 9,1-41

	Jesus	dis-ciples	man	neigh-bours	imper-sonal	Phari-sees	parents
9,1	15						
2		37					
3-7c	154						
7d			14				
8-9d				67			
9e			12				
10				18			
11			64				
12ab				11			
12cd			5				
13				16			
14					31		
15a						19	
15bc			27				
16-17c						94	
17d			11				
18-19						82	
20-23							167
24						47	
25			30				
26						20	
27			42				
28-29						60	
30-33			126				
34						38	
35	34						
36			25				
37	26						
38			18				
39	39						
40						30	
41	40						
total	308 +	37 +	374 +	112 +	31 +	390 +	167 = 1419

The sentences with Jesus *cum suis* as actors in 9,1-41 amount to 308 + 37 + 374 = 719 S, those with other actors amount to exactly 700 S (112 + 31 + 390 + 167 = 700). When we suppose a missing syllable in the narrative portions of the sentences in which Jesus and his disciples are the actors (see the comment following Table III), the 719 S become 720 S — which is a multiple of 9(0).

Story (9,1-39) and interpretation (9,40-10,21) are connected by a numerical *concatenatio*: Jesus' final saying in the story (9,39bc) and his first saying in the interpretation (9,41b-e) are of equal length, 33 S (= 3 × 11).

Monologue and concluding reactions together (10,1-21) have a length of 730 S. The ἐγώ εἰμι-saying of 10,11 constitutes the centre of this passage. It contains the two elements that will be worked out in the following verses: 'I am the good shepherd' — 'the good shepherd lays down his life for the sheep'. It is connected, on the other hand, with what precedes, because now the most important element from the *paroimia* (10,1-5), the shepherd, is identified, after the (shorter) identification of a less important element, the door (10,7-10). Besides, an inclusion can be discerned between 10,1-2 and 10,10, because of the antithesis shepherd = Jesus versus thief (and robber)[26]. 10,11 has a length of 30 S; within 10,1-21, it is preceded and followed by 350 S (see below, Table XX, and cfr. p. 146 above, about John 6,35b).

Finally, a few numerical observations concerning the entire episode John 9,1-10,21. The discourse of Jesus *cum suis* (the disciples and the man born blind) amounts to 560 W, so that the rest (discourse of other characters and narrative) comprises 499 W (see Table VI; discourse of a speaker includes here quotations of his words by others). Reckoning with the deficit of one W in the narrative, this number has to be 500. The 120 W (triangular number of 15) of discourse of the Pharisees/Jews are equivalent to 250 S.

Table VI. John 9,1-10,21		words
discourse	of Jesus in John 9,1-10,21	410
	of the disciples	11
	of the man born blind	139/560
	of his neighbours	23
	of the Pharisees/Jews	120
	of the parents of the man	38
	of anonymous 9,35	3
narrative		315/499/1059

2. *John 9: the healing of the man born blind*

John 9 is easily divided into dramatic scenes, when notice is taken of the changes of *dramatis personae*[27]:

1. In 9,1-7, the healing of the man born blind is narrated. Protagonists are Jesus and the man born blind; the disciples do no more than ask a question (9,2).

2. In 9,8-12, the neighbours of the man and those who were accustomed to see him begging are, together with him, on the stage; their conversation is about the identity of the healed man, his healing and the whereabouts of his healer.

3. In 9,13, the man born blind is brought to the Pharisees, to be officially questioned by them about his healing (9,13-17). Strictly speaking, this interrogation begins in 9,15[28], after an indication of the situation in 9,13-14[29].

4. In 9,18, the parents of the man are called in, to be questioned about the healing of their son (9,18-23). 9,18 is a transitional passage connecting this scene with the preceding one: it describes the reaction of 'the Jews' to what has been told before, and motivates, in that way, the summoning of the parents[30].

5. In 9,24-34, the man is summoned and examined 'for the second time' (9,24); this examination ends with his being cast out (9,34).

6. Finally, in 9,35-39, Jesus is on the stage again, and the healed man confesses his faith in him as the Son of Man. From the direct connection of 9,39 with what precedes, it is obvious that this verse belongs together with 9,35-38. 9,40-41 is, as a transitional dialogue, on the one hand connected with 9,35-39, on the other hand the beginning of the interpretation of the action (see under 1. above).

This division is rather obvious; it is given (with the restriction made in n. 23 above) by many authors and text-editions[31]. It is confirmed by the observation, that the healed man's belief in Jesus is progressing through the scenes, judging from the titles and other predicates by which he is designating Jesus. In the first scene, he does not say anything at all; in the second one he is talking about 'the man called Jesus' (9,11). In the third scene he calls Jesus 'a (or: the?[32]) prophet' (9,17). In the fourth scene the man is not on the stage; nevertheless, we meet a title there: 'the Christ' (9,22). In the fifth scene Jesus is described by the man as 'from God' (9,33), and in the final scene the man confesses his faith in Jesus as the Son of Man (cfr. 9,35), and addresses him as 'Lord' (9,38)[33]. While the man's faith in Jesus is growing, the Pharisees' rejection of the man and of Jesus shows more clearly (cfr. 9,13-17 with 9,24-34).

What are the relationships between these scenes? It is evident, first of all, that 9,13-34 constitutes a whole: the interrogation of the man born blind and of his parents by the Pharisees. These three scenes are situated at the same place, and are distinguished in that way from what precedes and follows. The first scene of the three, 9,13-17 (with 9,18, as a transition to the next scene) corresponds to the third one, 9,24-34, for three reasons:

1. 'Εκ δευτέρου (9,24) is a back-reference in the third scene to the first one.

2. The *dramatis personae* are identical in both scenes: the healed man and the Pharisees.

3. The themes of the conversation are identical: the way the cure happened, and the interpretation of the person of Jesus to be derived from it. Their sequence is, however, different: in the first scene, the Pharisees start by asking how the man has gained his sight (9,15), and afterwards, after dissension among them, they ask for the blind man's opinion about

Jesus (9,16-17). At the beginning of the third scene, this sequence is reversed: firstly, the interpretation of Jesus is discussed (9,24-25), and then the way the healing happened is asked for (9,26); in his answer (9,27) the man refers to what he previously said (in 9,15)[34].

Besides, both scenes show a series of more superficial agreements:

13 the man appears before the Pharisees	34 he is cast out by them
13 'the man who formerly had been blind'	34 'you were altogether born in sins'
(in 9,2-3, the relationship of blindness and sin is asked for; cfr. also 9,40-41)	
14 violation of the Sabbath: transgression of the Law	28-29 appeal to the Lawgiver: Moses
15 ὁ δὲ εἶπεν αὐτοῖς	27 εἶπον ὑμῖν ἤδη
15 βλέπω	25 ἄρτι βλέπω
16 παρὰ θεοῦ	33 παρὰ θεοῦ (cfr. 9,29.30: πόθεν)
16 ἄνθρωπος ἁμαρτωλός	24 οὗτος ὁ ἄνθρωπος ἁμαρτωλός ἐστιν (cfr. 9,25.31)
18 ὅτι ἦν τυφλός	24 ὃς ἦν τυφλός
18 ἐφώνησαν	24 ἐφώνησαν

The sequence of these agreements — at least of the majority of them — is reversed in 9,24-34 when compared with the sequence in 9,13-17(18). Taken together with the inversion of the sequence: the way the healing happened — interpretation of Jesus, this points to a 'mirrored symmetry'.

A similar correspondence exists between 9,1-7 and 9,35-39(41). The main agreements are:

1. The *dramatis personae* are identical: Jesus and the man born blind (the disciples are present in 9,2 only to ask a question; for the rest, nothing points to their presence[35]). Both times, the initiative to their meeting is taken by Jesus. In the other scenes, Jesus is not on the stage.

2. With the physical cure of the man in 9,1-7 corresponds his coming to faith in 9,35-39[36]; so, Jesus' saying of 8,12 is illustrated in two ways.

In the relationship of these two scenes, too, something of a 'mirrored symmetry' is present[37]:

1. 9,1-7 begins with a question of the disciples about the relationship of sin and blindness (9,2). 9,35-41 ends with the same theme, explicitly in 9,40-41, where the Pharisees ask about their blindness, implicitly already in 9,39: the real sin is lying in the spiritual blindness that thinks itself seeing.

2. Jesus' sayings in 9,3-5 and 9,39 are corresponding on certain points. The *works* of God should be made manifest in the man; Jesus has come into this world for *judgment*[38] (according to 5,20sqq, 'judging' is one of the works of the Son; possibly, the agreement of sound between -ργ-

in ἔργον and χρ- in χρίμα plays its role as well). The *light* of 9,5 is also connected with the judgment of 9,39 (cfr. 3,19: 'and this is the judgment, that the light has come into the world'; also 12,46-48). Only in these two passages of John 9 the κόσμος is mentioned (9,5.39).

3. 9,1-7 ends with the physical healing of the man (9,6-7); 9,35-39(41) begins with his spiritual healing: he comes to belief in Jesus as the Son of Man.

Moreover, there are a few more superficial agreements between the two scenes:

1. From 9,6 it can be derived that Jesus stoops; in 9,38 the man is kneeling before him.

2. In both scenes, Jesus reveals his identity, in 9,5 as 'light of the world', in 9,35-37 as 'Son of Man'.

3. The part. βλέπων occurs in John only in these two scenes (9,7.39*bis*).

4. There is similarity between the question of the disciples in 9,2 and that of the man in 9,36: Jesus is addressed as ῥαββί or κύριε; this address is followed by a τίς-clause and a ἵνα-clause.

Now, two scenes remain: 9,8-12 and 9,18-23. The latter evidently constitutes a unity together with the preceding and following scene: the juridical interrogations. The former constitutes a unity together with the other two corresponding scenes, 9,1-7.35-39(41). No change of place or time is suggested between 9,7 and 9,8. In 9,8-12 the neighbours are wondering whether the healed man is really the same one as the former blind beggar, and how he has been cured; in that way, the fact of the healing is clearly established[39]. The conversation of 9,8-12 seems to be an application and expansion of the motif, common in miracle stories, of the reaction of the public (cfr., e.g., Mark 1,27; 2,12)[40]. The beginning of the final scene (9,35) is directly linked up with the end of this scene (9,12): the man does not know where Jesus is; Jesus finds him[41].

A comparison of John 9 with John 5 can clarify even more the belonging together of 9,1-7.8-12.35-39(41): from the survey on pp. 192-193, it can be observed that in John 9 the three scenes of interrogation (9,13-34) are the surplus in the composition of the story, in comparison with John 5.

The scenes 9,8-12 and 9,18-23 have a similar function:

1. In both scenes, 'outsiders' are speaking, the neighbours and former acquaintances of the man in 9,8-12, his parents in 9,18-23.

2. In both scenes, questions are asked about his identity, and about the way he was cured.

3. Both scenes end in embarrassment: in 9,12 'I do not know' in answer to the question where Jesus is; in 9,23 'ask him', viz., for the way he was cured.

Our conclusion is, that John 9 is made up of two groups of three scenes: a) 9,1-7.8-12.35-39(41) (A-B-A'), and b) 9,13-17.18-23.24-34 (C-D-C'); in both groups, there is a correspondence of the first and third scenes (A and A', C and C'). Group a) is marked by the constant presence of the man born blind; group b) by the constant presence of the Pharisees. Schematically, these results can be arranged as follows:

scene				*main characters*
1	9,1-7	A		Jesus + man
2	8-12	B		man + neighbours
3	13-17		C	man + Pharisees
4	18-23		D	Pharisees + parents
5	24-34		C'	man + Pharisees
6	35-39(41)	A'		Jesus + man

Group b) is placed within group a), in such a way that a perfect concentric symmetry is not reached (there is no scene B'). We can only guess at the exact reasons for which the author arranged his materials in this way; a probable reason seems that in a perfect concentric symmetry, the dramatic effect would have disappeared which is achieved by the direct sequence of the blind man's being cast out by the Pharisees, and his being found by Jesus. The climax of the linear dramatic development of the story is lying in scenes C' and A': the man, formerly blind but now seeing, is cast out — and with him, Jesus — as a sinner by the Pharisees, but he is accepted by Jesus; the Pharisees, thinking that they are seeing, are really blind and sinful[42].

In Table VII, the numbers of S are given for the (groups of) scenes of John 9,1-39 as described above.

Table VII. John 9,1-39

			syllables	
9,1-7	A		220	
8-12	B		177	
13-17		C		198
18-23		D		249
24-34		C'		363/810
35-39	A'		142/	539/1349

When the missing syllable is provisionally located somewhere in the scenes A-B-A', then the total number of S of these scenes is 540. There is, in that case, a proportion of 540:810 = 2:3 between the scenes A-B-A' and C-D-C', 540 and 810 being multiples of 9(0). When the missing syllable is in 9,35-39, then the numbers of S of the exterior scenes of both groups of three (A, C, C' and A') are, all of them, divisible by 11 (20, 18, 33 and 13×11). A and A' together are, then, as long as C' ($363, = 3 \times 11^2$, S).

In Table VIII the results are given of a combination of the above division with a division into narrative and discourse.

Table VIII. John 9,1-39 syllables

			narrative			discourse		
9,1-7	A		104			116		
8-12	B		66			111		
13-17		C		112			86	
18-23		D		134			115	
24-34		C'		84/330			279/480	
35-39	A'		49/		219/549	93/		320/800

The proportion of 2:3 for (A + B + A'):(C + D + C') exactly returns in the numbers of S of the narrative in both groups of scenes (219 and 330; the former number presumably has to be 220), and in those of the discourse in both groups of scenes (320 and 480). Apparently, framing-technique has been applied by the author in various ways.

A similarity between scenes A and A' is that the discourse of the disciples in A is as long as that of the man born blind in A': 21 S (cfr. p. 200 above, for the similarity between the questions in 9,2 and 9,36).

In the central part of the episode, scenes C-D-C', the discourse of the protagonists, the healed man and the Pharisees, is of equal length: both the man and the Pharisees speak in 197 S (see Table IX).

Table IX. discourse of man and Pharisees John 9,13-34 syllables

	man	Pharisees
9,15c	21	
16bc		22
16e		19
17bc		19
17d*b*	5	
19b-d		29
24bc		25
25bc	22	
26bc		15
27b-d	36	
28b-29		49
30b-33	113	
34b		19
total	197	197

A division of the sentences of 9,13-34 according to the actors results in numbers of S (see Table V above) in 360 S for the sentences in which the Pharisees are actor, and 450 S for the other sentences. Again, two multiples of 9(0) appear.

The results of the same kind of division in numbers of W (cfr. Table III above) are given in Table X.

Table X. words divided acc. to actors John 9,13-34

neighbours actor		8		
impersonal				16
Pharisees	176			
man born blind		117/125		
parents	74/		250/375/391	

Without the impersonal sentence 9,14, the total number of W is 375, 250 for the sentences with the Pharisees and the parents as actors, half this number, 125, for the sentences with the man and his neighbours as actors. The number of W of the sentences with the Pharisees as actor is 176, = 16 × 11.

It has been observed above, that 9,13-17 is closely connected with 9,18-23 because of the transition 9,18, and that 9,13-14 is an introductory indication of situation, the proper interrogation beginning at 9,15 (cfr. the inclusion, chiastically constructed, of 9,15.23: ἠρώτων αὐτόν-αὐτὸν ἐπερωτήσατε). 9,13-14 has a size of 47 S, 9,15-23 of 400 S (= 190 W, triangular number of 19), to be divided into 151 S (= 77 W) for 9,15-17, and 249 for 9,18-23. A similar combination of numbers (a round number plus one and a round number less one) appears when 9,15-23 is divided into narrative and discourse: 199 S of narrative, 201 S of discourse (see Table XI). Omission of δέ in 9,16d (between square brackets in *NA*[25] and *NA*[26]) would result in 150 S for 9,15-17.

Table XI. John 9,13-23 syllables

	total	narrative	discourse
9,13-14	47	47	
15-17	151	65	86
18-23	249/400/447	134/199/246	115/201

The two scenes 9,13-17 and 9,18-23 contain both 60 W of narrative, together 120 (triangular number of 15); the introduction 9,13-14 has a length of 8 + 16 = 24 W, i.e., 2/5 of 60; so, 9,15-17 contains 36 (= 4 × 9, and triangular number of 8) W of narrative. The discourse of the two scenes has a size of 41 + 53 = 94 W (see Table XII).

Table XII. John 9,13-23 words

	narrative	discourse
9,13-14	24	
15-17	36/60	41
18-23	60/120	53/94

So, the division in scenes of John 9,1-39, and the relationships between these scenes, are recognizable in numbers of S, and to a certain extent also in numbers of W.

3. *The sections of John 9 separately and their details*

a) *John 9,1-7: the healing of the man born blind*

The passage 9,1-7 has a length of 220 S, to be divided into 95 S for the discourse of Jesus (80 in 9,3b-5, and 15 in 9,7b), and 125, = 5^3, for the discourse of the disciples and the narrative.

The passage has a length of 107 W, to be divided into 47 W of narrative and 60 W of discourse. Out of these 60 W, 11 are spoken by the disciples, and 49, = 7^2, by Jesus (42, = 6×7, a rectangular number, in 9,3b-5, and 7 in 9,7b; see Table XIII).

Table XIII. John 9,1-7	syllables		words
narrative in 9,1-7	104		47
discourse of the disciples	21/125		11
of Jesus		95/220	49/60/107

Surplus-technique has been applied in 9,1-7 in various ways:

1. In 9,1, the situation of the scene is drawn: passing by, Jesus sees a man born blind. This verse contains 7 W, so 9,2-7 has a size of 100 W.

2. Jesus' command in 9,7 also has a length of 7 W, so the rest of the scene amounts to 100 W; these are divided into 53 W of discourse (question and answer in 9,2-5) and 47 W of narrative (see the discussion of 9,8-12 below for another occurrence of the 47 + 53-combination).

3. A division of the W of the text according to the actors results in 7 W for the one sentence with the man born blind as actor (9,7d), and 100 for the other sentences (those with Jesus as actor: 7 W in 9,1, and 75 in 9,3-7c; cfr. Table III).

Both the first and the last sentence of this scene (9,1.7d) have a length of 7 W.

The composition of the question of the disciples and Jesus' answer to it in 9,2-5 asks for attention:

		syllables		words	
9,2	ῥαββί, τίς ἥμαρτεν	6		3	
	οὗτος ἢ οἱ γονεῖς αὐτοῦ	8/14		5/ 8	
	ἵνα τυφλὸς γεννηθῇ	7/ 7/	21	3/ 3/	11
3	οὔτε οὗτος ἥμαρτεν	7		3	
	οὔτε οἱ γονεῖς αὐτοῦ	7/14		4/ 7	
	ἀλλ'ἵνα φανερωθῇ	7		3	
	τὰ ἔργα τοῦ θεοῦ ἐν αὐτῷ	9/16/30		6/ 9/16	
4	ἡμᾶς δεῖ ἐργάζεσθαι	7		3	
	τὰ ἔργα τοῦ πέμψαντός με	8		5	
	ἕως ἡμέρα ἐστίν	7/22		3/11	

ἔρχεται νύξ	4	2
ὅτε οὐδεὶς δύναται ἐργάζεσθαι	11/15	4/ 6
ὅταν ἐν τῷ κόσμῳ ὦ	7	5
φῶς εἰμι τοῦ κόσμου	6/13/50/80	4/ 9/26/42

The question in 9,2 is made up of 14 + 7 = 21 S (triangular number of 6). The first part of Jesus' monologue (9,3bc) is a direct answer to it; it contains 14 + 16 = 30 S (5 × 6: a rectangular number). The second part of his monologue (9,4-5), connected with the first one by means of the *Stichwort* ἔργα, amounts to 50 S. Between the numbers of W of these parts, there is a proportion according to the golden section: 16:26 = 26:42 = 0,62 (see above, p. 29). In numbers of S, the proportion is somewhat less perfect.

The factors 11 and 9 are used a few times in the dialogue 9,2-5: the question in 9,2 has a size of 11 W, and the sentence 9,4a amounts to 22 S or 11 W. Both 9,3c and 9,5 have a size of 9 W.

The factor 7 is also found in 9,2-5: we meet several cola of 7 S, among which an isocolon in 9,3b, while 9,2b-d has a size of 14, = 2 × 7, S. The narrative introduction 9,2a amounts to 7 W; so does 9,3b.

There is a very close relationship (already mentioned) between the question 9,2 and the first part of Jesus' answer 9,3. Question and introductory formula together (9,2), and answer and introductory formula together (9,3) have both a size of 18 W, and of 37 and 36 S respectively.

In 9,7, there is a close correspondence between Jesus' command 9,7b, and its execution 9,7d. Both elements have a length of 7 W; they contain 15 and 14 S respectively (cfr. above, p. 111 with n. 42).

b) *John 9,8-12: the man and his neighbours*

The second scene is made up of three times question and answer: 9, 8-9 (with 9,9a-d as an 'intermezzo', showing the dissension among the public).10-11.12.

9,8-12 has a size of 177 S, made up of 66 S of narrative, and 111 S of discourse (both 66 and 111 are numbers made up of identical figures; 66 is 6 × 11, and triangular number of 11). Out of these 111 S, 11 are a quotation by the healed man of words of Jesus (in 9,11b: ὕπαγε εἰς τὸν Σιλωὰμ καὶ νίψαι). Of the remaining 100 S of discourse, 53 are spoken by the healed man, and 47 by his neighbours[43].

The intermezzo 9,9a-d has a size of 27 S, = 3^3; it is preceded by 40 S and followed by 110 S (10 × 11: a rectangular number).

9,8-12 contains 54 W of discourse; the words of the healed man in 9,11bc occupy half of these, 27 W. The passage contains 30 W of narrative (a rectangular number: 5 × 6).

The conversation in 9,8-9 and that in 9,10-11, about the man's identity and cure respectively (these two topics will return in 9,18-23), are in number of W of almost equal length: 37 and 38 W, together 75. The third conversation (9,12) has a length of 9 W, and contains 9 S of discourse. The second conversation (9,10-11) contains 33 W of discourse, the first one (9,8-9) half that number, 16 (= 33 S). A schematic arrangement of the above is given in Table XIV.

Table XIV. John 9,8-12

	syllables				
	narr.	discourse			total
		neighbours	man		
9,8	26	14			40
9a-d	12	15			27
9e	8		4	12	
10-11b (... ὅτι)	13	12	33	58	
11b (ὕπαγε ...)			11	11	
11c			13	13	
12	7	6	3	16/110	
	66	47	64		177
		111			

	words			
	narr.	discourse		total
		neighbours	man	
9,8	13	7		20
9a-d	5	7		12
9e	3		2	5/37
10-11b (... ὅτι)	5	6	16	27
11b (ὕπαγε ...)			6	6
11c			5/27	5/38
12	4	3	2	9
	30	23	31	84
		54		

The total length of the questions is half that of the answers given by the man (both without introductory formulae), in numbers of W as well as S, as will be evident from Table XV.

Table XV. discourse in John 9,8-12

	words		syllables	
	questions	answers	questions	answers
9,8b	7		14	
9e: ἐγώ εἰμι		2		4
10b	6		12	
11bc		27		57
12b	3/	16	6/	32
12d		2/31		3/64

In 9,11b the healed man describes what Jesus did to him in 44 S; 11 out of these are — as already mentioned — a quotation of Jesus' words. The 44 S are arranged according to this pattern:

ὁ ἄνθρωπος ὁ λεγόμενος Ἰησοῦς πηλὸν ἐποίησεν	17 S
καὶ ἐπέχρισέν μου τοὺς ὀφθαλμούς	10
καὶ εἶπέν μοι ὅτι ὕπαγε εἰς τὸν Σιλωὰμ καὶ νίψαι	17/44

c) *John 9,13-17: the first interrogation of the man*

The scene 9,13-17, of 101 W (a symmetrical number), is made up of an introduction of 24 W (9,13-14), and a corpus of 77 W (9,15-17), being 36 ($= 6^2$, triangular number of 8) W of narrative and 41 of discourse (see above, Table XII).

9,15-17 contains two conversations, about the way the cure was performed, and concerning the person of Jesus respectively (9,15.17); they enclose a description of the dissension among the Pharisees (9,16). This description has a size of 33 W (= 66 S); so, the two conversations together amount to 44 W: 22 W of discourse and 22 W of narrative. Again and again, the factor 11 appears (see Table XVI).

Table XVI. John 9,15-17 words

	narr.	discourse	total
9,15	13	10	23
16	14	19	33
17	9/22	12/22	21/44/77

9,15 contains a question (in indirect discourse) of 2 W and an answer of 10 W; 9,17 contains a question of 10 W and an answer of 2 W.

Without δέ in 9,16d (in *NA*[25] and *NA*[26] between square brackets), the scene 9,13-17 has a size of exactly 100 W; however, the omission would spoil not only the 33 W of 9,16, but also the overall balance of 9,1-39 as set forth above, under 2.

d) John 9,18-23: the interrogation of the man's parents

The scene 9,18-23 begins with a description of what 'the Jews' do (9,18-19): they do not believe that the man before them is the one who was born blind; therefore, they summon his parents and question them. In 9,20-21 the parents give their answer, and in 9,22-23 their answer is motivated.

The scene contains 53 W of discourse, and 60 W of narrative, made up of 24 W (= 53 S) in the part where the Jews are actor (9,18-19), and 36 W (= 81 S) in the part where the parents are actor (9,20-23). The 60 W of narrative of the preceding scene were divided in exactly the same way: 24 in 9,13-14, 36 in 9,15-17.

In numbers of S, a sandwich-pattern is present in 9,18-23: 9,18-19 and 9,22-23 contain 82 and 81 ($= 9^2$) S respectively, 9,20-21 contains 86 S. 86 S is also the length of the discourse of the parents in this scene (and of the discourse in the previous scene). The 81 syllables of 9,22-23 are made up of 54 S in 9,22, and half that number, 27, in 9,23. In numbers of W, the total for 9,22-23 is 33, divided into 22 W in 9,22 and 11 W in 9,23.

54 out of 81 S of narrative for 9,20-23 are in 9,22; the narrative in 9,20.23 amounts to 14 + 13 = 27 S, half of 54. A schematic arrangement of the above is given in Table XVII.

Table XVII. John 9,18-23

	words			syllables			
					discourse		
	narr.	discourse	total	narr.	Jews	parents	total
9,18-19	24	15	39	53	29		82
20-21	7	34	41	14		72	86
22	22		22	54			54
23	7/36/60	4/38/53	11/33/113	13/81		14/86	27/81/249

In 9,20b-21, the parents give their answer in 72 S (8×9: a rectangular number), arranged as follows:

οἴδαμεν ὅτι οὗτός ἐστιν ὁ υἱὸς ἡμῶν καὶ ὅτι τυφλὸς ἐγεννήθη	23 S
πῶς δὲ νῦν βλέπει οὐκ οἴδαμεν, ἢ τίς ἤνοιξεν αὐτοῦ τοὺς ὀφθαλμοὺς ἡμεῖς οὐκ οἴδαμεν	26
αὐτὸν ἐρωτήσατε, ἡλικίαν ἔχει, αὐτὸς περὶ ἑαυτοῦ λαλήσει	23/72

Several multiples of 9 are present among the numbers of S and W of this passage: we meet 27, 36, 54, 72 and 81.

e) *John 9,24-34: the second interrogation of the man*

No doubt, the climax of the second interrogation of the healed man by the Pharisees (9,24-34) is the monologue (the longest one of John 9) of the man in 9,30b-33, in which he draws the only possible conclusion from what happened to him: his healer is 'from God'. This monologue contains 113 S from a total of 363 S for 9,24-34; so there remain 250 S for the rest of the scene (in numbers of W, the application of the surplus-technique is less clear: 57 words on a total of 177).

A division of the sentences of this scene according to the actors results in 198 S, $= 18 \times 11$ or 6×33, for the sentences with the healed man as actor, and 165 S, $= 15 \times 11$ or 5×33, for the sentences with the Pharisees as actor (see Table V).

The discourse of the healed man in this scene has a length of 171 S, $= 19 \times 9$; that of the Pharisees of 108 S, $= 12 \times 9$ (see Table IX).

In 9,24-25, the man is summoned by the Pharisees to acknowledge that Jesus is a sinner; he answers, that he does not know whether Jesus is a sinner or not, but that the only thing he knows is that he was formerly blind and is now seeing. Table XVIII gives a schematic arrangement of these two verses.

Table XVIII. John 9,24-25

	syllables		words	
9,24a narrative introduction	22		12	
24bc command of the Pharisees		25		12
25a narrative introduction	8		3	
25bc reaction of the man		22		12
	30 + 47 = 77		15 + 24 = 39	

Command and reaction have together, narrative introductions included, a size of 77 S; the man's answer amounts to 22 S, as does the introductory clause 9,24a. We meet again multiples of 11. In numbers of W, the Pharisees' command in 9,24bc is as long as the man's answer in 9,25bc: 12 W; this is also the size of the narrative introduction 9,24a. In numbers of both S and W, the proportion between 9,24 and 9,25 is equal to the proportion between discourse and narrative (47:30, and 24:15). In numbers of W, this proportion is a proportion according to the golden section: 15:24 = 24:39 = 0,62.

The saying in 9,28-29, about Jesus versus Moses, their disciples and their authority, shows a chiastic construction[44]:

9,28	A	σὺ μαθητὴς εἶ ἐκείνου	8 S
	B	ἡμεῖς δὲ τοῦ Μωϋσέως ἐσμὲν μαθηταί	13/21
29	B′	ἡμεῖς οἴδαμεν ὅτι Μωϋσεῖ λελάληκεν ὁ θεός	17
	A′	τοῦτον δὲ οὐκ οἴδαμεν πόθεν ἐστίν	11/28/49

A and B deal with discipleship and oppose 'you' and 'that fellow'[45] to 'we' and 'Moses'. B′ and A′ deal with the origin of authority, and oppose Moses, to whom God spoke, to Jesus, whose origin is unknown. Within both halves of the chiasm, there is a secondary chiasm: in A + B, we meet the sequence μαθητής - ἐκείνου - τοῦ Μωϋσέως - μαθηταί, and in B′ + A′, the sequence οἴδαμεν - Μωϋσεῖ - τοῦτον - (οὐκ) οἴδαμεν.

The chiasmus 9,28b-29 has a total length of 49 S, = 7^2. With these 49 S, the Pharisees answer to the 12 + 9 + 15 = 36 S, = 6^2, of the man in 9,27b-d. Elements A and B of the chiasmus amount together to 8 + 13 = 21 S (3 × 7), triangular number of 6; B′ and A′ amount together to 28 S (4 × 7), triangular number of 7 and a perfect number. We meet here two successive triangular numbers, whose sum is a square number (see above, p. 28).

The monologue of the healed man in 9,30b-33 also shows a structure that asks for attention:

9,30	A	ἐν τούτῳ γὰρ τὸ θαυμαστόν ἐστιν	6 W	10 S
		ὅτι ὑμεῖς οὐκ οἴδατε πόθεν ἐστίν	6	12
		καὶ ἤνοιξέν μου τοὺς ὀφθαλμούς	5/17	9
31	B	οἴδαμεν ὅτι ἁμαρτωλῶν ὁ θεὸς οὐκ ἀκούει	7	16
		ἀλλ' ἐάν τις θεοσεβὴς ᾖ	5	9
		καὶ τὸ θέλημα αὐτοῦ ποιῇ	5	9
		τούτου ἀκούει	2/19	5
32	A′	ἐκ τοῦ αἰῶνος οὐκ ἠκούσθη	5	9
		ὅτι ἤνοιξέν τις ὀφθαλμοὺς τυφλοῦ γεγεννημένου	6	16
33		εἰ μὴ ἦν οὗτος παρὰ θεοῦ	6	9
		οὐκ ἠδύνατο ποιεῖν οὐδέν	4/21/57	9/113

Elements A and A′ are corresponding: in A, the man expresses his amazement that the Pharisees do not know where Jesus is from, whereas he opened his eyes[46]; in A′, he says that it is unheard of that anyone opened the eyes of a man born blind, and that there is only one explanation for his healing: Jesus is 'from God'. Note also the chiastic order: πόθεν ἐστίν - ἤνοιξεν ... ὀφθαλμούς - ἤνοιξεν ... ὀφθαλμούς - παρὰ θεοῦ. Element B, on the other hand, is a general thesis, a 'dogmatic' sentence, that should be endorsed, witness οἴδαμεν, by the speaker as well as by his opponents[47]. There are numerous parallels to this sentence; indeed the OT parallels make it obvious that a common starting point is given here[48].

Now, the three elements have a size of 17, 19 and 21 W respectively: B is longer than A by 2 W, and A′ is longer than B by 2 W. Consequently, the size of B is exactly 1/3 of the sum total of 57 W: 19 W.

In numbers of S, we meet 6 cola with a size of 9 S. The monologue ends with an isocolon of 2 × 9 S.

f) *John 9,35-39(41): the faith of the man and the blindness of the Pharisees*

The scene 9,35-39(41) is made up of a conversation of Jesus and the healed man (9,35-38), followed by a retrospective conclusion in 9,39; a short dialogue of Jesus and the Pharisees directly ensues (9,40-41).

The conversation of Jesus and the healed man is made up of two questions (9,35.36) and two answers (9,37.38); the first answer is a reaction to the second question, and the second answer is a reaction to the first question:

35 question of Jesus: 'Do you believe in the Son of Man?'
36 question of the man: 'Who is he ...?'
37 answer of Jesus: 'You have seen him, and it is he who is speaking to you.'
38 answer of the man: 'I believe ....'

In the preceding sections of this chapter, a strong suspicion has arisen that the text of John 9 used as a basis for the present investigation has a deficit of one monosyllabic word. This word has to be looked for, so was suspected, in the narrative portions with Jesus or his disciples as actors; more precisely, it has to be in those portions in 9,35-39.

This hypothesis is confirmed by an analysis of the numbers of S and W of 9,35-39(41):

1. When one monosyllabic word is added to the narrative portions of 9,35-39, we obtain 50 S of narrative and 93 S of discourse in this passage: an example of the technique of rounding off one part (see Table VIII).

2. When one monosyllabic word is added to the sentences with Jesus as actor, another example of rounding-off-technique appears in 9,35-39: the sentences with Jesus as actor have a length of 100 S, those with the man as actor of 43 S (see Table V). It is possible, of course, to locate the missing monosyllabic word in the sentences with the man as actor, to obtain a 99 + 44-division; that would spoil, however, at least some of the results rendered in Table III and its commentary, apart from the difficulty of finding the missing monosyllabic word in 9,36a.38a.d.

3. With the addition of one monosyllabic word to the narrative portions, an application of the surplus-technique appears in 9,35-39: Jesus' final saying 9,39bc has a size of 33, = 3 × 11, S; so, there remain 110, = 10 × 11, S for the rest of the scene, 50 for the discourse, 60 for the narrative.

4. With the addition of one word in 9,35-39, this passage has a length of 74 W. The ensuing dialogue, 9,40-41, has exactly half that length: 37 W. 9,35-41 as a whole contains, then, 111 W. Without the addition of one word this number would be 110, made up of 73 and 37; that result, interesting in itself, would spoil, however, much of what was previously found (see esp. Tables VII and VIII, with the commentary accompanying them).

The missing monosyllabic word can be located more exactly by means of the following observation concerning the meeting between Jesus and the man, 9,35a*b*-38. This passage contains the two questions and two answers described above, including their introductory clauses and the *proskynèsis* of 9,38d. The first half — the two questions 9,35a*b*-36 — and the second half — answer and reaction 9,37-38 — are of (almost) equal length: 44 S, 23 and 22 W respectively. Moreover, corresponding questions and answers are, in numbers of S, of almost equal length (see Table XIX).

Table XIX. John 9,35*ab*-38	syllables	words
9,35 (from καί onward)	19	11
36	25/44	12/23
37	26	14
38	18/44/88	8/22/45

These numbers do not suggest that the missing monosyllabic word is to be looked for anywhere in this part. Nor is it in 9,39a, it seems: 9,39 contains 22 W, = 2 × 11, and is as long, in that way, as the preceding verses 9,37-38. There remains the opening sentence of 9,35: ἤκουσεν Ἰησοῦς ὅτι ἐξέβαλον αὐτὸν ἔξω. There, indeed, a suitable variant reading exists: ὁ Ἰησοῦς is read by P[66] Sin[2] A D L W Θ Ψ 0124 0250 *f*[1.13] *Mehrheitstext*; anarthrous Ἰησοῦς by P[75] Sin* B *pc*. The articular reading (also present in the *Textus Receptus* and in the editions of Lachmann, Von Soden, Souter and Vogels) very well suits the findings concerning numbers of S and W.

It has to be asked, of course, whether other arguments support the choice of the articular reading in 9,35. I refer here to the investigations of G. D. Fee concerning the use of the article with the name Ἰησοῦς, when this name directly follows the verb; his results have been rendered above, pp. 44-45, where the presence of the article ὁ in 1,47a was discussed. In 9,35 (and in 1,47), the name follows a verb of the mental processes (ἤκουσεν in 9,35); in such cases, Fee inclines to suppose that the personal names tend to be anarthrous, but he is very cautious in this conclusion. In the present case, the numerical evidence suggests the articular reading. In the similar instance in 1,47a, the numerical evidence suggested the anarthrous reading. Maybe, then, we may replace Fee's caution concerning these instances by the suspicion that the author of John was not consistent in his use of the article with Ἰησοῦς when this name immediately follows verbs of the mental processes.

The adoption of the articular reading in 9,35, based on the convergence of several numerical observations, shows the use that can be made of the analysis of a text's numerical composition in textual criticism.

Jesus' saying in 9,39, of 33 S, concluding the narrative, contains an isocolon in the subordinate clause:

εἰς κρίμα ἐγὼ εἰς τὸν κόσμον τοῦτον ἦλθον	13 S	8 W
ἵνα οἱ μὴ βλέποντες βλέπωσιν	10	5
καὶ οἱ βλέποντες τυφλοὶ γένωνται	10/33	5/18

Finally, the composition of Jesus' saying in 9,41 deserves our attention. It is made up of two parts that are parallel, certainly as to their meaning, though they are not strictly parallel grammatically speaking. In the first part, an unreal condition and consequence are stated; in the second one, a real state of affairs and its consequence. In both parts, the first clause concerns blindness and seeing, the consequence concerns the sin, whether or not connected with it:

εἰ τυφλοὶ ἦτε	5 S	3 W
οὐκ ἂν εἴχετε ἁμαρτίαν	9	4
νῦν δὲ λέγετε ὅτι βλέπομεν	10 (5 + 5)	5/ 8
ἡ ἁμαρτία ὑμῶν μένει	9/33	4/8/16

The consequence-clauses are of equal length, in numbers of S and W. The two other clauses together are, in W, as long as the two consequence-clauses together. In S, the first clause has exactly half the length of the third one, that can be divided into two equal parts.

4. *John 10,1-21: the discourse on the shepherd*

John 10,1-18 is made up of two parts[49]:

1. 10,1-5, called a *paroimia* in 10,6, is a separate unit, marked off from what follows by the comment of the evangelist in 10,6 and the new opening in 10,7.
2. In 10,7-18, Jesus explicitly identifies himself with two elements from the *paroimia*. This part is subdivided into two smaller parts[50]:

a. 10,7-10, about Jesus as 'the door', and
b. 10,11-18, about Jesus as 'the good shepherd'.

Both smaller parts contain two ἐγώ εἰμι-sayings (10,7.9; 10,11.14). A recurrent theme in the second smaller part is 'laying down his life (for the sheep)', 10,11.15.17-18.

The division 10,1-5.7-18 is also discernible in numbers of W: in 10,1-5 Jesus speaks 88 W (again a multiple of 11); in 10,7-18, he speaks 222 W. Both numbers are made up of identical figures.

The arrangement of the parts of 10,1-21 in numbers of S is shown in Table XX.

Table XX. John 10,1-21 syllables

10,1-5	186	
6a	14/200	
6b	17	
7a	8	
7b-10	125/150/350	
11		30
12-18	268	
19-21	82/	350/730

The *paroimia* 10,1-5, of 186 S, is completed up to 200 S by the clause 10,6a: 'Jesus told them this *paroimia*'. It is followed by a clause about the incomprehension of the audience (10,6b), of 17 S, an introduction to direct discourse (10,7a) of 8 S, and the first part of the explanation (10,7b-10), of 125 S, = 5^3; together 150 S. The second part of the explanation (10,11-18) and the ensuing reactions (10,19-21) have together a size of 380 S. We already saw that Jesus' saying 10,11 constitutes the centre of 10,1-21, as it is preceded and followed by 350 S (see above, under 1., *in fine*).

5. *The sections of John 10,1-21 separately and their details*

a) *John 10,1-6: the* paroimia *on the shepherd and his sheep*

The *paroimia* 10,1-5 begins and ends with an antithetic parallelism (10,1-2.4b*b*-5):

10,1	ὁ μὴ εἰσερχόμενος διὰ τῆς θύρας (εἰς τὴν αὐλὴν τῶν προβάτων) (ἀλλὰ ... ἀλλαχόθεν) ἐκεῖνος κλέπτης ἐστὶν καὶ ληστής	2	ὁ δὲ εἰσερχόμενος διὰ τῆς θύρας ποιμήν ἐστιν τῶν προβάτων
4	καὶ τὰ πρόβατα αὐτῷ ἀκολουθεῖ ὅτι οἴδασιν τὴν φωνὴν αὐτοῦ	5	ἀλλοτρίῳ δὲ οὐ μὴ ἀκολουθήσουσιν (ἀλλὰ ... ἀπ' αὐτοῦ) ὅτι οὐκ οἴδασιν τῶν ἀλλοτρίων τὴν φωνήν

In 10,1b-2, Jesus speaks first about the 'thief and robber', who enters the sheepfold in an illegal way, and secondly about the 'shepherd of the sheep', who enters in a legal way; in 10,4b*b*-5 he speaks first about the shepherd whom the sheep follow, and secondly about the 'stranger' whom they will not follow. So, the two parallelisms together constitute in 10,1-5 an inclusion in chiastic order: thief and robber - shepherd (10,1b.2) - shepherd - stranger (10,4b*b*-c.5)[51]. 10,1b and 10,5 also correspond because both elements are enlarged, over against their counterparts, with an ἀλλά-clause positively stating what the first clause of the sentence negatively stated[52].

Paying attention to the spatial aspects of the *paroimia* can be helpful in determining its composition. This point of view is suggested by the imagery of the *paroimia* itself (to enter the sheepfold by the door, to open, to lead out, to go ahead, to follow, to flee), and also by the spatial categories used in its explanation (10,9.12.16)[53]. 10,1-3*a* deals with entering the sheepfold: the true shepherd enters by the door[54] and not 'in some other way', as does the 'thief and robber', and for him the door-keeper opens[55]. In 10,3 one reads what happens within the sheepfold: the door-keeper opens the door for the shepherd, the sheep hear his voice, he calls his own[56] sheep by name (it seems supposed that they recognize their shepherd) and leads them out of the sheepfold. 10,4-5, finally, is about what happens outside the sheepfold[57]: the sheep follow their shepherd going ahead of them, because they know his voice, whereas they will not follow a stranger whose voice they do not know.

So we have three parts, the first and third part containing the antithetic parallelisms described above. The first clause of 10,3 ('for him the door-keeper opens') seems to have a double function (as will be clear from the above): it closes the first part, by telling that the door-keeper opens for the shepherd who comes in a legal way, and it begins the second part because the opening of the door-keeper makes possible the action of the shepherd (and the reaction of the sheep) inside the sheepfold (the threefold καί-connection within 10,3 suggesting the latter interpretation)[58]. So, the first part is 10,1-2 or 10,1-3*a*, and the second part 10,3 or 10,3*b*-*d*[59].

The halves of the antithetic parallelism 10,1b.2 have a length of 20 + 10 + 10 = 40 S and half that number, 20 S, respectively. The halves of the antithetic parallelism 10,4b*b*-c.5 have a length of 21 S, = 3 × 7, and 35 S, = 5 × 7, respectively (the 35 S are divided into 21 S for 10,5ab, and 14 S for 10,5c; 21 is triangular number of 6). In numbers of W, we meet a multiple of 11 in the total number of W of the chiastic construction 10,1b.2.4*b*b-c.5: 55 W (triangular number of 10). The two elements dealing with the shepherd (10,2.4b*b*-c) have both a size of 10 W.

The literary division of 10,1-5 as a whole clearly corresponds to a division into numbers of S and W, in such a way, that in the division of S 10,3*a* forms part of the preceding section, and in the division of W it forms part of the following section. The division into numbers of S is given in Table XXI.

Table XXI. John 10,1-5

			syllables			
10,1a	Amen-formula		8			
1b	how the thief and robber enters	77		40		
2-3*a*	how the shepherd enters				29	
3*b*-*d*	inside the sheepfold	33				33
4	the sheep follow the shepherd	76			41	
5	they will not follow the stranger			35		
			8 +	75 +	70 +	33 = 186

First and third part (10,1-3*a*.4-5) are of almost equal length: 77 (a multiple of 11, as the 33 S of the second part) and 76 S. The sum total for 10,2-3*a*.4 (about the shepherd) is 70 S, for 10,1b.5 (about his counterpart) it is 75 S. Besides multiples of 11, we meet in 10,1-5 multiples of 7. The same factors occur in the passage directly preceding 10,1-5, viz., 9,40-41. It has a size of 70 S, 30 in 9,40, 40 in 9,41; the introduction 9,41a has a length of 7 S. The narrative in 9,40 amounts to 22 S, the discourse in 9,41 to 33 S. The factor 7 is also found in 10,6a, which has a length of 14 S; this clause, referring to the preceding *paroimia*, completes it up to 200 S. One could compare the (multiples of) 10 S in 10,1-2, and the 30 + 40 = 70 S of 9,40-41, as well as the 70 S of 10,2-3*a*.4; clauses of 10 S are also 9,41d; 10,4d. 9,40-10,6 is framed by corresponding clauses of 17 S: 9,40a*a* (up to ὄντες inclusive), and 10,6b, about the Pharisees' hearing and not understanding of Jesus' words respectively. The numbers of S of the first and last sentence spoken by Jesus in 9,41-10,5 are multiples of 7 (14 in 9,41bc; 21 + 14 = 35 in 10,5).

The division of 10,1-5 into numbers of W is given in Table XXII.

Table XXII. John 10,1-5

			words			
10,1a	Amen-formula		4			
1b	how the thief and robber enters	33		19		
2	how the shepherd enters				10	
3	inside the sheepfold	21				21
4	the sheep follow the shepherd	34			18	
5	they will not follow the stranger			16		
			4 +	35 +	28 +	21 = 88

First and third part are again of almost equal length: 33 (a multiple of 11) and 34 W. In the sum totals on the bottom line, a series appears of 5 × 7, 4 × 7 and 3 × 7 W; 28 is, moreover, triangular number of 7 and a perfect number; 21 is triangular number of 6.

The factor 8 seems prominent in the numbers of W of the *paroimia* and the passages directly surrounding it (9,40-41; 10,6). 10,1-5 has a size of 88 W, preceded by 16 W spoken by Jesus in 9,41b-e, and followed by 16 W in 10,6; moreover, 9,40-41 contains 16 W of narrative. 10,5 has a length of 16 W, 10,4ab*a* of 8 W.

b) *John 10,7-10: 'I am the door'*

One theme dominates, and so unites, 10,7-10: Jesus is 'the door'. In contrast to others — 'thieves and robbers', 10,8 cfr. 10 — he came to give his followers life (10,9.10)[60].

The passage answers to an alternating pattern a-b-a′-b′-a″. It contains three sentences about Jesus starting with ἐγώ: at the beginning

(10,7b, preceded by the Amen-formula), in the middle (10,9; ἐγώ is continued in δι' ἐμοῦ), and at the end (10,10b). Between these, sentences have been put about the 'thieves and robbers' and the 'thief' (10,8.10a). 10,9 is the centre of the passage; it contains an ἐγώ εἰμι-saying and a conditioned promise of life, and so it sums up the other sentences about Jesus in the passage, viz., 10,7b ('I am the door') and 10,10b ('I came that they may have life')[61].

Moreover, the passage displays a bipartition: 10,7-8.9-10. Both parts begin with an ἐγώ εἰμι-saying, and contain a sentence about the 'thieves and robbers' or the 'thief'. In the first part, the sentences end in προβάτων and πρόβατα respectively; the second part begins and ends with a sentence starting with ἐγώ[62]. 10,10 contains a clear antithetic parallelism[63].

The structure of 10,7b-10 in numbers of S is schematically rendered in Table XXIII.

Table XXIII. John 10,7b-10

			syllables a			syllables b
10,7b*a*	a	Amen-formula	10			10
7b*b*		'I am the door ...'	11/21			11
8	b	on thieves and robbers		27		27/38/48
9	a'	'I am the door'			38	38
10a	b'	on the thief		21/	48	21
10b	a″	'I came ...'	18		39/77/125	18/39/77/125

As mentioned before, 10,7b-10 has a length of 125 S, = 5^3. Elements a and a″ (10,7b.10b) are together almost as long as a' (10,9; this verse sums up the contents of 10,7b.10b): 39 and 38 S respectively, together 77, a multiple of 11. Elements b and b' (10,8.10a) have together a size of 48 S; 10,1, another saying about the 'thief and robber', has the same length (see Table XXIIIa). Because of the equal length of elements a and b' (21 S), the division into 48 + 77 S returns in the bipartition of the passage: 10,7b-8 has a size of 48 S, 10,9-10 of 77. Of course, the two halves of 77 also return: 38 S in 10,9; 39 S in the antithetic parallelism 10,10. 10,7b*b*-8 also has a size of 38 S; 11 S are used in the ἐγώ εἰμι-saying 10,7b*b*. There is a division, then, into three parts of 38, 38 and 39 S (a + b, without the Amen-formula; a'; b' + a″; see Table XXIIIb). The proportion between 48 and 77, present in two ways in the passage under consideration, is a proportion according to the golden section: 48:77 = 77:125 = 0,62.

The factor 7 occurs several times in numbers of S in 10,7b-10: 21 S in 10,7b and 10,10a; 7 S in 10,9a; 77 for 10,7b + 9 + 10b, and for 10,9-10.

Elements a, a′ and a″ have together a length of 36 W (4 × 9, 6^2, triangular number of 8); b and b′ amount together to 27 W (3 × 9, and 3^3; see Table XXIV).

Table XXIV. John 10,7b-10

			words	
10,7b	a	'I am the door ...'	11	
8	b	on thieves and robbers		15
9	a′	'I am the door'	17	
10a	b′	on the thief		12/27
10b	a″	'I came ...'	8/	36/63

Again, the factor 9 appears, and in the sum total of 63 W the factor 7 is present as well.

c) *John 10,11-21: 'I am the good shepherd', and reactions to the discourse*

As has been said above, there are two recurrent themes in this passage: 'I am the good shepherd', and 'laying down his life (for the sheep)'. 10,11 contains both themes, and nothing more, and is, in that way, a programmatic sentence at the beginning of the passage. In 10,12-13, a contrast to 10,11 is drawn: the hireling, not being the shepherd, does not care for the sheep. We meet the word μισθωτός at the beginning and at the end of this passage (10,12a.13). 10,14-15 is the next unit: here the two elements of 10,11 return, but now the sentence 10,14*b*-15a has been inserted between them. The inserted sentence is built according to a chiastic pattern[64]: Jesus is subject in the first and the last clause, and object in the two middle clauses (the word order is the same in the corresponding clauses). Jesus is the 'good shepherd', because he and his sheep 'know' each other (10,14), which mutual knowledge has as its model (and cause[65]) the mutual knowledge of the Father and Jesus (10,15a). The mutual knowledge of Jesus and his sheep (and of the Father and Jesus) ends in Jesus' laying down his life for the sheep (10,15b; cfr. 15,13: the climax of love is to lay down his life for his friends; also 1 John 3,16). So, there is an internal coherence in 10,14-15. All three units of 10,11-15 end in the refrain ὑπὲρ τῶν προβάτων, varied as περὶ τῶν προβάτων in the contrasting middle part (10,11b.13.15b). In 10,16, a new theme appears: the other sheep, not from this fold. Πρόβατα in 10,16a takes up, by way of *concatenatio*, προβάτων at the end of 10,15b; εἷς ποιμήν 10,16d makes up an inclusion with 10,11a.14a: ἐγώ εἰμι ὁ ποιμὴν ὁ καλός. In 10,17-18, we read that Jesus lays down his life of his own free will, and takes it up again. Πατήρ at the beginning of 10,17 makes up an inclusion with πατρός at the end of 10,18. In contrast to what precedes, no figurative language is used in this unit, nor is it connected with what precedes it by means of *concatenatio* or a refrain. So it seems to be a relatively independent unit in 10,11-18[66].

John 10,11-18 is made up, then, of five units: 10,11.12-13.14-15. 16.17-18. The first, third and fifth unit are connected by the occurrence of 'laying down his life (for the sheep)'. The first and third unit are also connected by 'I am the good shepherd', and the third and fifth unit are also connected, because in both the relationship of Jesus and the Father is dealt with (mutual knowledge, and the love of the Father for Jesus and Jesus' obedience)[67].

The remaining units (10,12-13.16) are connected as well, albeit less clearly. In 10,12-13, we are told that because of the carelessness of the hireling, the wolf gets a chance of scattering (σκορπίζειν) the sheep. In 10,16, the contrasting behaviour of the shepherd is dealt with: he leads (ἄγειν) the sheep from 'this fold' together with 'other sheep', and they become one flock (μία ποίμνη). Scattering and gathering are contrasted. Both ideas are also combined in 11,52, where the goal of Jesus' death is said to be ἵνα καὶ τὰ τέκνα τοῦ θεοῦ τὰ διεσκορπισμένα συναγάγῃ εἰς ἕν[68].

10,11 and 10,14-15 together have a length of 88 S (a multiple of 11); 10,17-18 is of almost equal length: 89 S. 10,12-13 has a length of 74 S, 10,16 of 47 S: two numbers made up of the same figures, whose sum is 121, = 11^2. So, the number of S of 10,11-16 is also a multiple of 11: 209, divided as well as possible into two equal halves of 104 and 105 S (105 is triangular number of 14) for 10,11-13 and 10,14-16, two parallel parts (10,11 corresponding to 10,14-15, and 10,12-13 to 10,16, see above). A schematic arrangement of the above is given in Table XXV.

Table XXV. John 10,11-18 syllables

10,11	30		
12-13		74	104
14-15	58/88		
16		47/121	105/209
17-18	89/	177/298	

A few details in 10,11-18 deserve our attention. First of all, the programmatic verse 10,11: it is made up of an ἐγώ εἰμι-saying of 10 S, and a clause qualifying the good shepherd of 20 S; together, then, 30 S.

10,12-13, about the hireling, is constructed as follows[69]:

12	ὁ μισθωτὸς καὶ οὐκ ὢν ποιμήν, οὗ οὐκ ἔστιν τὰ πρόβατα ἴδια			20 S
	θεωρεῖ τὸν λύκον ἐρχόμενον		10	
	καὶ ἀφίησιν τὰ πρόβατα	9		
	καὶ φεύγει	3/12		
	καὶ ὁ λύκος ἁρπάζει αὐτά	9		
	καὶ σκορπίζει	4/13/25/35		
13	ὅτι μισθωτός ἐστιν καὶ οὐ μέλει αὐτῷ περὶ τῶν προβάτων			19/74

10,12ab begins with a characteristic of the hireling, and 10,13 ends with it. Both elements have the word μισθωτός at the beginning, and πρόβατα/ -ων at the end. They are of almost equal length: 20 and 19 S. Between them, the doings of hireling and wolf are described. Firstly, the confrontation of hireling and wolf, in 10 S; then their acting towards the sheep, in two times two clauses (all of them beginning with καί); both times a longer clause with an object is followed by a shorter one without. The two clauses about the hireling have a length of 9 + 3 = 12 S; those about the wolf, of 9 + 4 = 13 S; together 25 S.

The clauses about the mutual knowledge of Jesus and his own, and of the Father and Jesus in 10,14-15, constitute a chiasm (see above); the corresponding sentences are of equal length in numbers of W, and consequently, the two halves of the chiasm are of equal length, 9 W:

14	a	καὶ γινώσκω τὰ ἐμά	4 W
	b	καὶ γινώσκουσί με τὰ ἐμά	5/9
15	b′	καθὼς γινώσκει με ὁ πατήρ	5
	a′	κἀγὼ γινώσκω τὸν πατέρα	4/9

10,17-18 displays a concentric structure[70]:

17	A	διὰ τοῦτό με ὁ πατὴρ ἀγαπᾷ			11 S		6 W
	B1	ὅτι ἐγὼ τίθημι τὴν ψυχήν μου		11		6	
		ἵνα πάλιν λάβω αὐτήν		8/19		4/10	
18	B′	οὐδεὶς αἴρει αὐτὴν ἀπ’ ἐμοῦ	9			5	
		ἀλλ’ ἐγὼ τίθημι αὐτὴν ἀπ’ ἐμαυτοῦ	12/		21	6/11	
	B2	ἐξουσίαν ἔχω θεῖναι αὐτήν		10		4	
		καὶ ἐξουσίαν ἔχω πάλιν λαβεῖν αὐτήν		13/23/42		6/10	
	A′	ταύτην τὴν ἐντολὴν ἔλαβον παρὰ τοῦ πατρός μου			15/89		8/45

Elements A and A′ deal with the relationship of Jesus and the Father[71]. In A, διὰ τοῦτο refers to what follows; in A′, ταύτην refers to what precedes. Both times, these words are at the beginning of the clause. In the B-elements, Jesus speaks about laying down and taking up again his life. Elements B1 and B2 have in their first colon the expression τιθέναι τὴν ψυχήν/αὐτήν, and in their second colon λαμβάνειν αὐτήν; in all four cola of B1 and B2, the object is at the end of it. This is not the case, however, in B′; there, too, both cola end in a similar way, and they are, in contrast to B1 and B2, formulated as an antithetic parallelism. In numbers of S, B1 and B2 together are twice the length of B′: 42 and 21 S respectively, together 63, = 7 × 9. As 21 is a triangular number (of 6), 42 is a rectangular number (6 × 7; see above, p. 28). Note the sequence of units of 19, 21 and 23 S.

B1 and B2 have both a length of 10 W (made up of 6 + 4 and 4 + 6 W respectively), whereas B′ has a length of 11 W.

The statement of the ‘others’ in 10,21, giving a positive reaction to Jesus’ words, is made up of two clauses of (almost) equal length:

ταῦτα τὰ ῥήματα οὐκ ἔστιν δαιμονιζομένου	15 S	6 W
μὴ δαιμόνιον δύναται τυφλῶν ὀφθαλμοὺς ἀνοῖξαι	16	6

At the end of this chapter, we can conclude that the author of the Fourth Gospel made use of numbers of S and W in the composition of John 9,1-10,21. For a description of the different ways he does so, I refer to the Conclusion. Basic numbers used in 9,1-10,21 are 9 and 11, and — to a less extent — 7.

NOTES TO CHAPTER FOUR

1 G. D. Kilpatrick, *A Greek-English Diglot for the Use of Translators*: John (issued for private circulation by the British and Foreign Bible Society, London 1960).

2 I derive this information mainly from J. K. Elliott, 'Temporal Augment in Verbs with Initial Diphthong in the Greek New Testament', *NT* 22 (1980) 1-11; 10; he does not mention P[75].

3 See the survey in Elliott, *NT* 22, 9-11.

4 Elliott, *NT* 22, 11.

5 Elliott seems to go too far in making an iron rule out of his observation. I should be reluctant to adopt the reading ἤνοιξεν in John 9,14 (with D 0141 *al*), or in John 9,17 (with L Θ Ψ 565 *al*). The results of the numerical analysis suggest — as will appear later — that the evangelist chose now the quadrisyllabic, now the trisyllabic form.

6 The exact determination of the literary genre of 10,1-5 (parable, allegory, 'Bildrede'?), as well as the relationship between 10,7-18 and 10,1-5, are disputed questions, of major consequence for the exegesis of 10,1-18, but of minor importance in an analysis of the structure of the text; they will be treated here only in so far as they are connected with this analysis. See about these problems, besides the commentaries on John: J. Quasten, 'The Parable of the Good Shepherd (Jn 10,1-21)', *CBQ* 10 (1948) 1-12, 151-169; 153sqq; O. Kiefer, *Die Hirtenrede*. Analyse und Deutung von Joh 10,1-18 (SBS 23; Stuttgart 1967) 37sqq; Simonis, *Hirtenrede*, 68-96, 110-118, 183-188, 195-200; I. de la Potterie, 'Le bon pasteur', in: *Populus Dei* II (Fs. A. Ottaviani; Rome 1970) 927-968; 930-934. To indicate John 10,1-5, I will use the term *paroimia*, in conformity with 10,6.

7 Bernard, 331, derives such a lapse of time from ποτε in 9,13.

8 Cfr. Barrett, 365: 'The narrative being now completed Jesus sums up its meaning'; likewise Hofbeck, *Semeion*, 126; Roloff, *Kerygma*, 137; Haenchen, 382, who considers 9,40-41 as a 'verdeutlichendes Nachspiel'; cfr., however, Haenchen's division of John 9 rendered in the Appendix.

9 This sevenfold occurrence is given a symbolic meaning by Boismard-Lamouille, *Jean*, 252, 260.

10 Cfr. S. Sabugal, *La curación del ciego de nacimiento (Jn 9,1-41)*. Análisis exegético y teológico (Biblioteca Escuela Bíblica 2; Madrid 1977) 31.

11 So Bultmann, 250; Schnackenburg, II 304; Schulz, 141; Haenchen, 377; cfr. K. L. Schmidt, *Der Rahmen der Geschichte Jesu*. Literarkritische Untersuchungen zur ältesten Jesusüberlieferung (Berlin 1919²; repr. Darmstadt 1964) 18-20, 44.

12 See above, p. 61 with n. 52.

13 Cfr. Simonis, *Hirtenrede*, 29.

14 Bengel, *Gnomon*, 394, about 10,1: 'arcte haec cohaerent cum praecedentibus', arguing from the reference in 10,6 to the Pharisees of 9,40.

15 See Simonis, *Hirtenrede*, 30-31, esp. 30: 'Den Beginn im strengen Sinn einer *Rede* bildet die Formel nie'; also Bernard, 67; Strathmann, 164; A. Feuillet, 'La com-

position littéraire de Jn 9-12', in: *Mélanges Bibliques*, rédigés en l'honneur de A. Robert (Paris 1957) 478-493; 486.

16 So, e.g., Dodd, *Interpretation*, 355; Brown, 388, and esp. P.-R. Tragan, *La parabole du 'pasteur' et ses explications: Jean 10,1-18*. La genèse, les milieux littéraires (Studia Anselmiana 67; Rome 1980) *passim*, who sees also in 10,1-18 itself a collection of different materials.

17 Dodd, *Interpretation*, 354-356, 400; cfr. Feuillet, in: *Mélanges Robert*, 484-486.

18 Cfr. for this view of the relationship of John 9 and 10,1-18, and for making the 'contrast-characters' of 10,1-18 refer to the Pharisees: Hoskyns-Davey, 366, 368; Quasten, *CBQ* 10, 3-5, 12, 153, 159-160; Strathmann, 154; Barrett, 367; Lightfoot, 205-206; Van den Bussche, *Boek der werken*, 217-218; Grundmann, *Zeugnis und Gestalt*, 54-55; Brown, 388; Kiefer, *Hirtenrede*, 38; J. L. de Villiers, 'The Shepherd and His Flock', in: A. B. du Toit, ed., *The Christ of John*. Essays on the Christology of the Fourth Gospel = *Neot* 2 (1968) 89-103; 90-91; Sabugal, *ΧΡΙΣΤΟΣ*, 325 n. 327; J. D. M. Derrett, 'The Good Shepherd: St. John's Use of Jewish Halakah and Haggadah', *ST* 27 (1973) 25-50; 40, reprinted in id., *Studies in the New Testament* II (London 1978) 121-147; Schneider, 198; Haenchen, 394. Willemse, *Het vierde evangelie*, 311, is also of the opinion, that in John 10,1-18 the Pharisees are meant by the thieves and robbers, and the hireling. J. J. O'Rourke, 'Jo 10,1-18: Series Parabolarum?', *VD* 42 (1964) 22-25, divides John 10,1-18 into a series of separate parables, all of which, according to him, find their most appropriate context in the dispute between Jesus and the Pharisees.

19 See esp. Dodd, *Interpretation*, 358-360; besides, Quasten, *CBQ* 10, 168; Barrett, 373-374; Lightfoot, 205-206; Van den Bussche, *Boek der werken*, 223; D. Mollat, 'Le bon pasteur — Jean 10:1-18, 26-30', *BVC* 52 (1963) 25-35; 28-29; Brown, 397; Simonis, *Hirtenrede*, 167. For other possible aspects of the OT background, see, e.g., Barrett, 373-374; Van den Bussche, *Boek der werken*, 220-223; Mollat, *BVC* 52, 25-29; Derrett, *ST* 27, 25-50.

20 Simonis, *Hirtenrede*, 129-130, is of the opinion, that the Pharisees cannot be meant by 'thieves and robbers', because in Ezek 34, usually considered as background of John 10,1-18, the wicked shepherds do not themselves steal the sheep, but because of their lack of care others get a chance of doing so. Likewise, it is not said in John that the wicked shepherds are stealing the sheep; and nowhere does Jesus explicitly call the Pharisees 'thieves and robbers'. It seems to me, that, as far as Ezek 34 is concerned, the view of Simonis is contradicted by, e.g., 34,10: 'I will rescue my sheep from their jaws, and they shall feed on them no more' (*NEB*) (cfr. also 34,3). As far as the application of 'thieves and robbers' to the Pharisees is concerned, the context (i.e., John 9) seems decisive. When one is considering, moreover, how the Pharisees and 'the Jews' are qualified in John 8 ('from beneath', 'of this world', 8,23; 'you will die in your sins', 8,24; 'your father is the devil and you choose to carry out your father's desires', 8,44; 'not of God', 8,47; 'a liar', 8,55), then it is not astonishing that they are passing here for 'thieves and robbers', nor that they are pictured as intruders in 10,1 (which would be impossible as well, according to Simonis).

21 The relationship of John 5 and John 9 is pointed out by, e.g., R. Mackintosh, 'Two Johannine Miracles', *ExpTim* 37 (1925-26) 43-44; Bultmann, 249-250; Hoskyns-Davey, 360-362; Strathmann, 103; Van den Bussche, *Boek der werken*, 209; Bligh, *HeyJ* 4, 123 n. 3; Brown, 377; Martyn, *History and Theology*, 71-72; Duprez, *Jésus et les dieux guérisseurs*, 151-153; Schneider, 187; Boismard-Lamouille, *Jean*, 154, 157, 262; Becker, 315; Haenchen, 382; M. Gourgues, 'L'aveugle-né (*Jn* 9). Du miracle au signe: typologie des réactions à l'égard du Fils de l'homme', *NRT* 104 (1982) 381-395; 381-382.

22 Cfr. Dodd, *Interpretation*, 356.

23 The main caesura commonly made in John 9,1-10,21 is at 9,41/10,1, in conformity with the traditional chapter-division. A major break at 9,39/40 is made in Nestle's *NT Graece*, 10th-25th ed. (the 10th ed. was the first one to be edited by Erw. Nestle),

and by Strathmann, 156-157, and Hofbeck, *Semeion*, 126. In the Nestle-editions just mentioned, 9,40-10,21 is printed in one paragraph, as is 9,1-39. No major break at all, neither at 9,39/40 nor at 9,41/10,1, is made in the text-editions of Griesbach, Lachmann, Von Soden and Vogels. Cfr. F. Hahn, 'Die Hirtenrede in Joh. 10', in: *Theologia crucis — signum crucis* (Fs. E. Dinkler; Tübingen 1979) 185-200; 186: '... unverkennbar, dass 9,1-10,21 zusammengehören'; cfr. also 195 (the present order of the text is ascribed by him, however, to a 'deutero-Johannine' redaction, see also n. 60 of this chapter). See further the Appendix.

24 Two remarks concerning the background of this coherence:
1. L. Cerfaux, 'Le thème littéraire parabolique dans l'évangile de saint Jean', *ConNT* 11 (Fs. A. Fridrichsen; 1947) 15-25; 16-18; also in: *Receuil L. Cerfaux* II (Gembloux 1954) 17-26 (followed by Feuillet, in: *Mélanges Robert*, 487-488), and Simonis, *Hirtenrede*, 82-85, recognize in John 9,39sqq a pattern similar to that of Mark 4,2sqq: Jesus tells a parable (Mark 4,3-8; cfr. John 10,1-5, called a *paroimia* in 10,6), Isa 6,9-10 is quoted (Mark 4,12; recognizable in John 9,39-41), the parable is not understood (Mark 4,13; cfr. John 10,6) and is explained (Mark 4,14-20; cfr. John 10,7sqq); cfr. also Hoskyns-Davey, 366; Lightfoot, 210; Brown, 391.
2. Simonis, *Hirtenrede*, 161-168, considers 1 Enoch 88-90 as the background that plausibly explains the connection of the various themes that are interwoven in John 9,1-10,21; in the passage from 1 Enoch are found together: blindness and seeing, the opening of eyes, shepherd and sheep, the new house of the sheep.
The coherence of John 9,1-10,21 is clarified once more from this twofold background.

25 The words ἐξέβαλον αὐτὸν ἔξω in 9,35 are discourse of an anonymous speaker.

26 So Kiefer, *Hirtenrede*, 19; Simonis, *Hirtenrede*, 230. Hahn, in: *Theologia crucis*, 191, considers the parallel ἐγώ εἰμι-saying with its explanation in 10,14-15 to be the 'Kernlogion' of 10,1-18, 'von dem aus die anderen Teile der Bildrede verständlich werden'.

27 Large parts of the Fourth Gospel can be read as a kind of stage-play, with dialogue and something as staging indications (e.g., 9,18); see already chapter I, n. 25, and p. 50. See about the dramatic composition of John 9: J. M. Thompson, 'An Experiment in Translation', *The Expositor*, 8th Series, 16 (1918) 117-125; Windisch, in: *ΕΥΧΑΡΙΣΤΗΡΙΟΝ*, II 181-183; Noack, *Zur joh. Tradition*, 115; Martyn, *History and Theology*, 24-36. Among the elements characteristic of the structure of the Fourth Gospel are, according to Windisch, in: *ΕΥΧΑΡΙΣΤΗΡΙΟΝ*, II, 'die breit ausgeführten, dramatisch ausgestalteten Erzählungen' (175-176), distinguishing themselves from the synoptic pericopes in the extent of the dialogue and the changes of scenes. He reckons John 9 among these (181-183).

28 Πάλιν 9,15: in comparison with the unofficial questions of the neighbours, cfr. Lagrange, 263; Boismard-Lamouille, *Jean*, 251.

29 So Sabugal, *Curación*, 34, 41. Cfr. Barrett, 360, ad 9,15: 'The examination of the blind man, and through him of Jesus, now begins'.

30 Cfr. the text-editions of Tischendorf[8], Von Soden, Nestle (ed. 1a-25a), Vogels, Merk and Bover, where 9,13-23 is printed in one paragraph.

31 See the survey in the Appendix. Simonis, *Hirtenrede*, 18-19, distinguishes as literary units 9,24-33 and 9,34-41, because of the triple occurrence of a number of words and expressions within each of these parts (this argument is derived, according to Simonis, from E. A. Abbott, *Johannine Vocabulary* [London 1905] nr. 2587; presumably Abbott's *Johannine Grammar* [London 1906] is meant; see *Hirtenrede*, 17 n. 35). His only argument, however, to locate the caesura at 9,33/34 precisely, is the triple occurrence of ἁμαρτία in 9,34-41, an inclusion being constituted by the occurrences of ἁμαρτία in 9,34b.41e. The other words and expressions taken into account by Simonis allow of a caesura at 9,34/35 as well. Moreover, one should question the value of the triple occurrence of one word over against the evident dramatic indications of the text (and: Simonis' inclusion can be a *responsio* as well).

32 Cfr. Zerwick, *Biblical Greek*, par. 175 (referring to E. C. Colwell, 'The Definite

Article', *JBL* 52 [1933] 12-21). See also M. de Jonge, 'Jesus as Prophet and King in the Fourth Gospel', *ETL* 49 (1973) 160-177; 170, reprinted in id., *Jesus: Stranger from Heaven and Son of God*, 49-76.

33 Cfr. Bengel, *Gnomon*, 392, 393; Bultmann, 257; Lightfoot, 199-200; D. Mollat, 'La guérison de l'aveugle-né', *BVC* 23 (1958) 22-31; 29-30; Grundmann, *Zeugnis und Gestalt*, 52-53; J. Bligh, 'Four Studies in St. John, I: The Man Born Blind', *HeyJ* 7 (1966) 129-144; 141-143; Brown, 377; Martyn, *History and Theology*, 32 n. 32; Schnackenburg, II 303; Schulz, 146; Moloney, *Son of Man*, 147-148; Schneider, 187; Boismard-Lamouille, *Jean*, 257, 260; Becker, 319-321; Gourgues, *NRT* 104, 383, 391.

34 Cfr. Sabugal, *Curación*, 34.

35 Cfr. Lagrange, 258; Willemse, *Het vierde evangelie*, 161.

36 Cfr., e.g., Strathmann, 160, ad 9,35-39: 'Aber die leibliche Heilung des Blindgeborenen bedarf noch der geistlichen Krönung'; Schneider, 187; Boismard-Lamouille, *Jean*, 256-257.

37 Also observed by Gourgues, *NRT* 104, 382.

38 Cfr. M. de Jonge, *ETL* 49, 171.

39 So also Gourgues, *NRT* 104, 387.

40 Cfr. Bultmann, 253, ad 9,8-12: 'Es ist darin das für die Wundergeschichte typische Motiv der "Zeugen" verwendet, jedoch nicht als Abschluss der Geschichte zu ihrer Beglaubigung, sondern als Vorspiel der Haupterzählung: in der Ratlosigkeit der Leute spiegelt sich schon die Verlegenheit der Autoritäten'; similarly Martyn, *History and Theology*, 25-26; Nicol, *Sēmeia*, 36 (see for materials for comparison concerning the motif of the reaction of the public R. Bultmann, *Die Geschichte der synoptischen Tradition* [FRLANT 29; Göttingen 1970[8]] 241). The prelude-function does not, however, exclude the closing function, and a new start is evidently made in 9,13: now the *juridical* interrogation, that is situated elsewhere, begins, so Barrett, 355, 360; Blank, *Krisis*, 255 (referring to W. Beilner, *Christus und die Pharisäer.* Exegetische Untersuchung über Grund und Verlauf der Auseinandersetzung [Vienna 1959] 161); Pancaro, *Law*, 19; Sabugal, *Curación*, 41, 76. For that reason, it is wrong to combine 9,8-34 (or 38) into one episode: the discussion about the miracle (so Bultmann, Strathmann, Brown, Hofbeck, Bornkamm, Schnackenburg, Sabugal, Schulz, M. de Jonge; see the Appendix).

41 Cfr. Blank, *Krisis*, 255.

42 See the Appendix, for the main caesuras of John 9 in literature and text-editions. Boismard-Lamouille, *Jean*, 254-255, detect a structure comparable to the one I found in their hypothetically reconstructed text of an earlier stage of development of the Fourth Gospel ('Jean II-A'): to the dialogue 9,2-3 corresponds that of 9,35-37; to the dialogue of 9,15.17 corresponds that of 9,24a.26b.27-30.33-34; 9,18-21 is the central dialogue.

43 The numbers 53 and 47 are important in the structure in numbers of S of Matt 24-25, according to Smit Sibinga, *ST* 29, 77. He cautiously suggests, that in Matt 24-25 the number 53 is associated with the election of the righteous, and 47 with the disastrous end of the wicked. In John 9,8-12, the discourse of the healed man amounts to 53 S, and that of his sceptic public to 47 S. Other occurrences of these numbers in John do not, however, fit this association very well, e.g., Peter's confession in 6,68b-69 amounts to 47 S, whereas the discourse in 9,18-23 (speakers: the Pharisees and the blind man's parents) contains 53 W.

44 Cfr. Barrett, 362: 'Jesus and Moses, with their disciples, are intentionally thrown into sharp contrast'; likewise Sabugal, *Curación*, 48; the chiasm within 9,28 is noticed by Abbott, *Joh. Grammar*, nr. 2554.

45 'Ἐκεῖνος can be used contemptuously, see Blass-Debrunner-Rehkopf, par. 291_2.

46 In 9,30d, καί is used adversatively, see Blass-Debrunner-Rehkopf, par. 442.1; Zerwick, *Biblical Greek*, par. 455. The amazing thing is the opposition between the fact of the healing and the negative point of view of the Jews with regard to what happened, cfr. Westcott, II 42; Noack, *Zur joh. Tradition*, 49: '... wo das θαυμαστόν

nicht das οὐκ οἴδατε, auch nicht das ἤνοιξεν, sondern der Widerspruch zwischen den beiden Tatsachen ist'.

47 Cfr. Lagrange, 268; Grundmann, *Zeugnis und Gestalt*, 53; Blank, *Krisis*, 260; Schneider, 194; Becker, 321; Haenchen, 381; differently Hoskyns-Davey, 357-358.

48 The best parallel is, as far as I know, Prov 15,29; there, too, a negative statement is followed by a positive one. More OT parallels in, e.g., Barrett, 363; Greek parallels in Bauer, 136; rabbinic parallels in Str-B, II 534-535.

49 The division given here is rather obvious and it is supported, as far as I can see, by the great majority of text-editions, commentaries, and other literature (a notable exception is Schnackenburg, II 375-381, where 10,16-21 is made into a unit). According to Tragan, *Parabole*, 91 n. 22, 'une certaine convergence' can be discerned among authors as to this division; cfr. esp. Gächter, *ZKT* 60, 412; J. Schneider, 'Zur Komposition von Joh. 10', *ConNT* 11 (Fs. A. Fridrichsen; 1947) 220-225; 221-222; in abridged form in his commentary on John, 196-198 (followed by Feuillet, in: *Mélanges Robert*, 487); Kiefer, *Hirtenrede*, 10-26; Simonis, *Hirtenrede*, 22-39; Sabugal, *ΧΡΙΣΤΟΣ*, 320-322. In the *Còdex Vaticanus* the chapter-division is: 9,24-10,6; 10,7-13; 10,14-21.

50 Cfr. Simonis, *Hirtenrede*, 35. Kiefer, *Hirtenrede*, 48 n. 41, notices that ἐγώ occurs 7 × in 10,7-18: 4 × in an ἐγώ εἰμι-saying (10,7.9.11.14), further in 10,10.17.18, i.e. at the end of the parts 10,7-10.11-18 (apparently, Kiefer does not count κἀγώ in 10,15). Another connecting factor in 10,7-18 is, according to Kiefer, *Hirtenrede*, 48-49, the absence of the second person (with the exception of ὑμῖν in the Amen-formula 10,7b) over against the 'I' of Jesus.

51 In view of this structure, one could suspect that 'thief and robber' and 'stranger' mean the same person or group, cfr. Barrett, 370, ad 10,5: 'Presumably a thief or robber is in mind'; Sabugal, *ΧΡΙΣΤΟΣ*, 325 n. 327. De la Potterie, in: *Populus Dei* II, 937, is sure about this identification.

52 Cfr. for the inclusion in chiastic form Kiefer, *Hirtenrede*, 12; Simonis, *Hirtenrede*, 31-32; Becker, 325.

53 Cfr. Simonis, *Hirtenrede*, 201.

54 Evidently, the 'door' is not only a peripheral element in 10,1-5: it decides about the attribution of the title 'shepherd', see P. W. Meyer, 'A Note on John 10,1-18', *JBL* 75 (1956) 232-235. This is important in view of 10,7-10, see n. 60 below.

55 Simonis, *Hirtenrede*, 24, discerns an inclusion between θύρα (10,1) and θυρωρός (10,3), confirming the unity of 10,1-3*a*.

56 The introduction of ἴδια in the third clause of 10,3 leads to the suspicion that from the larger group meant in the second clause the particular flock of the shepherd in question is separated. Another indication supporting this interpretation is the presence of a door-keeper, suggesting that the sheepfold of 10,1 has to be conceived of as a courtyard where the flocks of various shepherds were gathered at night and where the shepherds came to in the morning to take along their own flock. See Simonis, *Hirtenrede*, 104-106; the same interpretation of ἴδια in Westcott, II 51; Bernard, 350; Barrett, 369; Lightfoot, 206-207; Schnackenburg, II 352; De la Potterie, in: *Populus Dei* II, 940-941; Becker, 325; differently Bauer, 134; Lagrange, 276; Bultmann, 284 n. 1; Brown, 385; Kiefer, *Hirtenrede*, 40; Boismard-Lamouille, *Jean*, 269; Haenchen, 387.

57 Cfr. Simonis, *Hirtenrede*, 108, ad 10,4b ('he goes ahead of them'): 'Es ist, als ob damit ein Ortswechsel des Hirten angegeben wird'.

58 Cfr. for the double function of 10,3*a* De Villiers, *Neot* 2, 95, and esp. Tragan, *Parabole*, 198-199, with 198 n. 39. 10,3 and 10,4 are not connected by means of such a transition-clause, but there ἐξάγει 10,3 is picked up in ἐκβάλῃ 10,4.

59 The division given here is partially and indirectly confirmed by the genesis of the *paroimia* as it is supposed to have been by J. A. T. Robinson, 'The Parable of John 10,1-5', *ZNW* 46 (1955) 233-240, reprinted as 'The Parable of the Shepherd (John 10.1-5)' in id., *Twelve New Testament Studies* (SBT 34; London 1962) 67-75 (R. is followed in the main lines by Dodd, *Historical Tradition*, 382-385): two parables

should have been united, one about the legitimation of the shepherd (10,1-3*a*, with its point in 10,3*a*: the watchmen of Israel should recognize the true shepherd), and one about his relationship with the sheep (10,3*b*-5). A similar view is found in L. Soubigou, 'Le pasteur, la porte et les brebis (Étude de Jean, X,1-21)', *L'Année Théologique* 7 (1946) 244-253; 246-248; A. George, 'Je suis la porte des brebis. Jean 10,1-10', *BVC* 51 (1963) 18-25; 18; Brown, 391-393; as a possibility in Lindars, *Behind the Fourth Gospel*, 51-52. O'Rourke, *VD* 42, 22-25, even makes a separate parable out of 10,3*a*, starting from a very strict application of the principle that a parable has only two terms of comparison.

Divisions of the present text of John 10,1-5 are given by Schweizer, *EGO EIMI*, 146-147 (10,1-2.3-5); Quasten, *CBQ* 10, 5 (10,1-2: 'the door to the fold'; 10,3-5: 'the shepherd and his flock'); Kiefer, *Hirtenrede*, 11-14 (10,1-3*a*.3*b*-5); De Villiers, *Neot* 2, 94-96 (as Kiefer); De la Potterie, in: *Populus Dei* II, 937 (10,1.2-3*b*.3*c*-4.5, displaying an a-b-b′-a′-pattern, a and b dealing with the entrance of the 'thief and robber' and the shepherd, b′ and a′ with their leaving); Sabugal, *ΧΡΙΣΤΟΣ*, 321 (10,1b-2: 'the door'; 10,2-5: 'the shepherd of the sheep'); Hahn, in: *Theologia crucis*, 187-188 (10,1-3*b*.3*c*-5, about legitimate entrance and leading out of the sheep respectively); Becker, 325 (as Kiefer); Tragan, *Parabole*, 197-198 (10,1.2.3-4.5, displaying an a-b-b′-a′-pattern).

Gächter, *ZKT* 60, 412, and Simonis, *Hirtenrede*, 12-39, divide 10,1-5 into strophes. Gächter's division is 10,1-2.3.4.5, that of Simonis 10,1-3*a*.3*b*-4.5. Arguments of Simonis to consider 10,3*b*-4.5 as units are: the triple occurrence of τὰ πρόβατα and the inclusion τῆς φωνῆς αὐτοῦ - τὴν φωνὴν αὐτοῦ in 10,3*b*-4, the inclusion ἀλλοτρίῳ - ἀλλοτρίων and the disconnecting δέ in 10,5. By means of this division, however, he breaks the antithetic parallelism in 10,4-5 (observed by him, too, pp. 31-32), whereas δέ in 10,2 does not lead him to a similar operation in the antithetic parallelism 10,1-2. Without questioning the correctness of the observations of Simonis, one should ask what their value is in comparison with other indications for the composition of the text.

60 At first sight, there seems to be an inconsistency between 10,7-8 on the one hand and 10,9-10 on the other: 10,7-8 (read in connection with the preceding *paroimia*) is about the door *to* the sheep, 10,9-10 about the door *for* the sheep. Inconsistency also seems to exist between 10,1-5 and 10,7-10 (the identification of Jesus with 'the door' is unexpected after 10,1-5), and between 10,7-10 and 10,11-18 (how can Jesus be 'door' and 'shepherd' at the same time?). In the exegesis of 10,1-10 as given by Simonis, *Hirtenrede*, the inconsistency is decreasing a great deal in favour of the unity of the text. According to Simonis, αὐλή in 10,1 refers to the temple and Temple-Judaism (120-127); against this background, he considers θύρα in 10,7.9 as a *pars pro toto* for the temple. Jesus is identified here, then, with the 'new Temple', the place where salvation can be found, with the new Ark of the Covenant going ahead of his own — whereby the distance between the predicates 'door' and 'shepherd' is smaller than it is usually supposed to be (194-254). Anyhow, the way Simonis is looking for the consistency of the text should be preferred to the proposal of Hahn, in: *Theologia crucis*, 194-197, to ascribe the present order of the text and the passage 10,7-10 to a 'deutero-Johannine' redaction. Too quickly, Hahn supposes real and not only seeming inconsistency of the text.

61 Cfr. Schneider, *ConNT* 11, 222; Simonis, *Hirtenrede*, 34, 194 (noticing the triple occurrence of ἔρχεσθαι in 10,7-10). Boismard-Lamouille, *Jean*, 265 (who read in 10,7b ὁ ποιμήν instead of ἡ θύρα), discern in 10,7b-10 a 'structure en chiasme', on the level anterior to the final redaction of the gospel ('Jean II-B'; 10,9 should have been absent on this level): 10,7b corresponds to 10,10b; 10,8a to 10,10a; 10,8b is the centre. In a case as this, one should speak of 'concentric structure' instead of 'chiastic structure'.

62 Cfr. Schneider, *ConNT* 11, 222; Grundmann, *Zeugnis und Gestalt*, 54-55; Brown, 393-395; Kiefer, *Hirtenrede*, 15-19; Simonis, *Hirtenrede*, 25; Sabugal, *ΧΡΙΣΤΟΣ*, 321; Hahn, in: *Theologia crucis*, 186; Becker, 324. Gächter, *ZKT* 60, 412, divides the passage into four strophes: 10,7.8.9.10.

63 Cfr. Kiefer, *Hirtenrede*, 18-19; Simonis, *Hirtenrede*, 31.
64 Cfr. Kiefer, *Hirtenrede*, 22; Simonis, *Hirtenrede*, 289; Tragan, *Parabole*, 218-219.
65 See Blass-Debrunner-Rehkopf, par. 453.2; also Bultmann, 291 n. 3, and Simonis, *Hirtenrede*, 294 (with n. 129).
66 Cfr. for this division and its argumentation esp. Simonis, *Hirtenrede*, 25-26, 35-37, 39 (followed by Marzotto, *Unità*, 112), and also De la Potterie, in: *Populus Dei* II, 951-966; further Gächter, *ZKT* 60, 413, who gives the same division, with one exception: he makes two strophes out of 10,17-18, viz., 10,17-18b.18c-e. A rather general division, into 10,11-13.14-18, is given by Schneider, *ConNT* 11, 223; Kiefer, *Hirtenrede*, 20-26; Sabugal, *ΧΡΙΣΤΟΣ*, 321; Hahn, in: *Theologia crucis*, 186; Becker, 324; also *UBSGNT*[3]. A tripartition into 10,11-13.14-16.17-18, is given by Quasten, *CBQ* 10, 6, and in *NA*[26]. A bipartition into 10,11-16.17-18 is given by Westcott, II 56-62; Lagrange, 273-274, and Brown, 395-399, Westcott and Brown subdividing the first part into 10,11-13.14-16.
67 Cfr. for these connections Hoskyns-Davey, 377, and Kiefer, *Hirtenrede*, 70-71.
68 Cfr. Bernard, 364; Mollat, *BVC* 52, 34; Schnackenburg, II 371. The association of 11,52 with 10,16 could explain the *l.v.* συναγαγεῖν for ἀγαγεῖν in 10,16 (P[66] Clement of Alexandria[pt]), so Simonis, *Hirtenrede*, 23 n. 27.
69 Cfr. Kiefer, *Hirtenrede*, 20-21.
70 Cfr. Kiefer, *Hirtenrede*, 25-26; De la Potterie, in: *Populus Dei* II, 964; Riedl, *Heilswerk*, 107-108; Boismard-Lamouille, *Jean*, 271; Tragan, *Parabole*, 219-220.
71 Cfr. Schnackenburg, II 378.

APPENDIX

ions of John 9 proposed in literature and text-editions

cott	[1 - 12] [13 - 17 18-23 24-34] [35 - 41]
npson, *The Expo-r*, 8th Series, 119-123	[1 - 7] [8-12] [13 - 17] [18-23] [24-34] [35-38] [39 - 41]
lisch, ΧΑΡΙΣΤΗΡΙΟΝ, II 181-183	[1 - 7] [8-12] [13 - 17] [18-23] [24-34] [35-38] [39 - 41]
ange	[1 - 12] [13 - 34] [35 - 41]
ard	[1 - 12] [13 - 34] [35-38] [39 - 41]
nann	[1 - 7] [8-12 13 - 17 18-23 24-34 35-38] [39 - 41]
yns-Davey	[1 - 12] [13 - 34] [35 - 41]
nmann	[1 - 7] [8-12 13 - 17 18-23 24-34] [35 - 39]
k, *Zur joh. dition*, 115	[1 - 5] [6-7] [8-12] [13 - 17] [18-23] [24-34] [35-38] [39 - 41]
foot	[1 - 12] [13 - 17 18-23 24-34] [35 - 41]
den Bussche, *k der werken*, 206-208	[1 - 7] [8-12] [13 - 17] [18-23] [24-34] [35 - 41]
, *Krisis*, 254	[1 - 5] [6-7] [8-12] [13 - 34] [35-38] [39 - 41]
, *HeyJ* 7, -144	[1 - 7] [8 - 13] [14 - 17] [18-23] [24-34] [35-38] [39 - 41]
n	[1 - 5] [6-7] [8-12 13 - 17 18-23 24-34] [35 - 41]
eck, *Semeion*,	[1 2 - 5 6-7] [8-12 13 - 17 18-23 24-34 35-38] [39]
yn, *History and ology*, 26-27	[1 - 7] [8-12] [13 - 17] [18-23] [24-34] [35-38] [39 - 41]
rnkamm, 'Die lung des Blindgeborenen. Johannes 9', in: id., *Geschichte und ube* II. Gesammelte Aufsätze IV (BEvT 53; Munich 1971) 65-72	[1 - 7] [8-12 13 - 17 18-23 24-34] [35-38] [39 - 41]
ckenburg	[1 - 7] [8-12 13 - 17 18-23 24-34] [35 - 41]

<table>
<tr><td>Sabugal, ΧΡΙΣΤΟΣ,
304-308 (idem in his Curación, 31-34)</td><td>[1-2</td><td>3 - 5</td><td>6-7]</td><td>[8-12</td><td>| 13</td><td>- 14</td><td>15-17</td><td>18-23</td><td>24-34</td><td>| 35</td><td></td><td>-</td><td></td><td></td></tr>
<tr><td>Schulz</td><td>[1</td><td>-</td><td>7]</td><td>[8-12</td><td>| 13</td><td>-</td><td>17</td><td>18-23</td><td>24-34</td><td>| 35</td><td>-</td><td>39</td><td></td><td>| 40</td></tr>
<tr><td>M. de Jonge, ETL
49, 170-171</td><td>[1</td><td>-</td><td>7]</td><td>[8-12</td><td>13</td><td>-</td><td>17</td><td>18-23</td><td>24-34]</td><td>[35-38</td><td></td><td>39</td><td></td><td>40</td></tr>
<tr><td>Riedl, Heilswerk,
291 n. 3</td><td>[1</td><td>- 5</td><td>6-7]</td><td>[8-12]</td><td>[13</td><td></td><td>-</td><td></td><td>34]</td><td>[35-38]</td><td></td><td>[39</td><td>-</td><td></td></tr>
<tr><td>Moloney, Son of
Man, 142-149</td><td>[1</td><td>- 5]</td><td>[6-7]</td><td>[8-12]</td><td>[13</td><td>-</td><td>17]</td><td>[18-23]</td><td>[24-34]</td><td>[35-38]</td><td></td><td>[39</td><td>-</td><td></td></tr>
<tr><td>Schneider</td><td>[1</td><td>-</td><td>7]</td><td>[8-12]</td><td>[13</td><td>-</td><td>17]</td><td>[18-23]</td><td>[24-34]</td><td>[35-38]</td><td></td><td>[39</td><td>-</td><td></td></tr>
<tr><td>Becker</td><td>[1</td><td>-</td><td>7]</td><td>[8-12]</td><td>[13</td><td>-</td><td>17]</td><td>[18-23]</td><td>[24-34]</td><td>[35-38]</td><td></td><td>[39</td><td>-</td><td></td></tr>
<tr><td>Haenchen
(cfr., however, my n. 8 above)</td><td>[1</td><td>-</td><td>7]</td><td>[8-12]</td><td>[13</td><td>-</td><td>17]</td><td>[18-23]</td><td>[24-34]</td><td>[35-38]</td><td></td><td>[39</td><td>-</td><td></td></tr>
<tr><td>Gourgues, NRT
104, 382</td><td>[1</td><td>-</td><td>7]</td><td>[8-12]</td><td>[13</td><td>-</td><td>17]</td><td>[18-23]</td><td>[24-34]</td><td>[35</td><td></td><td>-</td><td></td><td></td></tr>
<tr><td>Text-editions:</td><td></td><td></td><td></td><td></td><td></td><td></td><td></td><td></td><td></td><td></td><td></td><td></td><td></td><td></td></tr>
<tr><td>Tischendorf[8]</td><td>[1</td><td>-</td><td>7</td><td>8-12]</td><td>[13</td><td>-</td><td></td><td>23</td><td>24-34]</td><td>[35</td><td></td><td>-</td><td></td><td></td></tr>
<tr><td>Westcott-Hort</td><td>[1</td><td>-</td><td>7]</td><td>[8-12]</td><td>[13</td><td>-</td><td>17</td><td>18-23</td><td>24-34]</td><td>[35</td><td>-</td><td>39</td><td></td><td>40</td></tr>
<tr><td>Von Soden</td><td>[1</td><td>-</td><td>7</td><td>8-12</td><td>13</td><td>-</td><td></td><td>23</td><td>24-34]</td><td>[35</td><td></td><td>-</td><td></td><td></td></tr>
<tr><td>NA 25</td><td>[1</td><td>-</td><td>7]</td><td>[8-12]</td><td>[13</td><td>-</td><td></td><td>23]</td><td>[24-34]</td><td>[35</td><td>-</td><td>39]</td><td></td><td></td></tr>
<tr><td>UBSGNT 3*</td><td>[1</td><td>-</td><td>7</td><td>8-12]</td><td>[13</td><td>-</td><td>17</td><td>18-23</td><td>24-34]</td><td>[35</td><td>-</td><td>39</td><td></td><td>40</td></tr>
<tr><td>NA 26</td><td>[1</td><td>-</td><td>7]</td><td>[8-12]</td><td>[13</td><td>-</td><td>17]</td><td>[18-23]</td><td>[24-34]</td><td>[35-38]</td><td></td><td>[39</td><td>-</td><td></td></tr>
</table>

* The secondary caesura at 9,7/8 is of a lower order than the other secondary caesuras.
The chapter division of the *Codex Vaticanus* is: 9,1-23; 9,24-10,6.

CHAPTER FIVE

JOHN 17: JESUS' PRAYER TO HIS FATHER

1. *John 17 as a literary unit*

John 17 contains a prayer of Jesus to his Father. He begins by asking for his glorification (17,1-5). Then he looks back upon his work of revelation and its results and prays for those whom this work concerned, that they may be kept safe and be sanctified (17,6-19). He prays not only for them, but also for those who will believe in him through their word, that they may all be one (17,20-23). Finally, he expresses his will that they may be with him where he is to behold his glory (17,24). They have reached the insight that Jesus was sent by God; to them he has revealed God's name, and he will continue to do so in the future (17,25-26).

The unity of John 17, already suggested by this description of contents, is made even more evident by the difference in literary genre between John 17 and what precedes and follows. The preceding section (13,31-16,33) is commonly named the 'farewell discourses': Jesus is addressing his disciples before leaving them. The following section (18-19) is the Johannine passion account. Intervening these is John 17, whose literary genre is a prayer of Jesus to his Father, delivered in the presence of his disciples. This is obvious from several indications: Jesus looks up to heaven (17,1) which is an attitude of prayer (cfr. 11,41; Ps 123,1; Mark 6,41 parr; Luke 18,13); in the entire chapter, the Father is referred to in the 2nd pers. sg., and he is addressed with the vocative πάτερ (17,1.5.11.21.24.25), with imperatives (17,1.5.11.17) and by means of the verb ἐρωτᾶν (17,9.15.20)[1].

These considerations suffice as a legitimation to look upon John 17 as a unit; 17,1a*a* concludes, then, the preceding discourses, and 17,1a*b* introduces the prayer.

Does the unity of John 17 also appear in numbers of S and W? The chapter has a length of 941 S, made up of 25 S of narrative (17,1a) and 916 S of discourse (17,1b-26). The number of W is 498[2] for the entire chapter, made up of 12 for 17,1a, and 486 for 17,1b-26. The technique of making the whole unit or one of its components (narrative or discourse) count a round number of S and/or W does not seem to have been applied to John 17. One of the above numbers is, however, significant in another way. 486, the number of W of 17,1b-26, is also the numerical value of the vocative πάτερ (80 + 1 + 300 + 5 + 100 = 486), present six times in the text (the first time as its first word) and characterizing it as a prayer to the Father. The size of 486 W suits a prayer to the Father[3].

2. *The sections of John 17 and their connections*

Because of its scanty vocabulary, simple syntax and frequently recurring themes, John 17 makes the impression of being a very coherent whole. For the same reasons, it is difficult to determine the sections of this whole and their connections. Several words (e.g., διδόναι, κόσμος, ἵνα) occur so frequently all over the chapter, that they seem to offer hardly any starting point to describe the structure of John 17[4].

Several efforts have been made to bring to light the literary structure of John 17. In what follows, the methods used and the results achieved in these efforts will be briefly discussed; then, in the light of these efforts, I will propose my own analysis of the structure of John 17, and confront its results with a count of S and W.

a) *Extant analyses of the literary structure of John 17*[5]

1. Divisions of the text of John 17 given in text-editions, commentaries and other literature are usually based mainly on the contents of the text. So there is a division according to the object of Jesus' prayer: in 17,1-5 he prays for himself, in 17,6-19 for his disciples, and in 17,20-26 for all future believers[6]. Slightly different is the division 17,1-8.9-19.20-26, in which the retrospective passage 17,6-8 is considered as motivating Jesus' prayer for glorification (cfr. 17,4)[7]. Elsewhere, we meet a combination of these two divisions: 17,1-5.6-8.9-19.20-26[8]. The two divisions are also found with a bipartition of the final section (17,20-26) into 17,20-23.24-26; the part 17,24-26 is mostly considered as the climax and conclusion of the entire prayer, in which the eschatological achievement is prayed for[9]. They are also found with a bipartition of the final section into 17,20-24.25-26[10]. Combinations of various divisions result in divisions such as 17,1-5.6-8.9-19.20-23.24-26[11], or 17,1-8.9-23.24-26[12], or (with the peculiarity of a caesura at 17,3/4) 17,1-3.4-8.9-19.20-23.24-26[13]. For others, 17,6-26 is in its entirety a prayer for the believers[14]. In some instances, main parts are subdivided into smaller units which may coincide with what are considered to be main parts in other divisions[15].

The differences between these proposals to divide John 17 make it evident that, in order to trace the literary structure of this chapter, considerations based only on the contents of the text — important though they may be — are insufficient. Formal indications for the composition of the text, which have the advantage of being more easily checked, have to play the first role in structural analysis, if one wants to reduce at least the risk that one's own interpretation determines the composition of the text[16].

2. In handling formal indications, however, one runs the risk of using too few of them or only the less important, and of overlooking the others. O. Merlier[17], for instance, corrects the current division based on the contents of the text only from the formal point of view that the vocative πάτερ (17,1.5.11.21.24.25) has its role in the structure of the text. The resulting division is: 17,1-5.6-11c.11d-19.20-23.24.25-26.

Another instance is the analysis of A. Laurentin[18]. His starting point is the occurrence of the particles καὶ νῦν, νῦν, νῦν δέ (17,5.7.13), which mark, in his opinion, the stages of the text. He combines this with the correspondences between 17,5 ('before the world existed') and 17,24 ('before the creation of the world'), and between 17,6 ('I revealed your name') and 17,26 ('I made known your name'). In this way he arrives at the following division: 17,1-4 (introduction).5-6 (transition).7-12 (first part).13-23 (second part).24 (transition).25-26 (conclusion). The particles mentioned above introduce a new perspective, thanks to a forceful résumé of the preceding. Both parts contain in the same order the themes of word, prayer and unity, and contain moreover the themes of world, mission, faith, and the unity of Father and Son. The main theme of the prayer is the revelation of God's name, announced in 17,6, developed at the end of the first part (17,11-12) and taken up in 17,26. It evokes in the second part the theme of sanctification (17,19), suggested by 'Holy Father' (17,11) in the first part. The progression of the two parts consists in that the glorification begins with the revelation of God's name, and is accomplished in the sanctification of the believers.

The formal observations, on which Laurentin bases his structural analysis, are no doubt correct. His analysis is, nevertheless, subject to criticism on three points:

a) He uses only a few formal indications out of a larger series.

b) He supposes without sufficient reason, that one indication, rather weak in itself (the particle νῦν), has the same function and the same importance wherever it is used in John 17.

c) This one weak indication is made the decisive factor in his analysis[19].

3. Another way to trace the structure of John 17, close to form-criticism, is to determine the various literary forms or 'Gattungselemente' present in the text ('form' is understood here not as the in-

dividual shape of a text, but as a set of characteristics it shares with other texts). Its most prominent representative is J. Becker[20]. He distinguishes four 'Gattungselemente' in John 17:

a) The statement of accounts: 17,4.6-8.14.22-23. Its characteristics are: it starts with a main clause normally made up of ἐγώ, a verb of revelation in the 1st pers. sg. aor.[21], the object of revelation in the acc., and its recipients in the dat. Subsequent clauses unfold the work of revelation in various directions.

b) The introduction to the petition: 17,9-11c.15-16, characterized by ἐρωτῶ. It has to remove possible misunderstandings before the petition.

c) The petition, 17,1b-e.5.11d-f.17.24, characterized by the πάτερ-address (absent in 17,17), the imperative (θέλω in 17,24), and a ἵνα-clause and/or further specification of what is prayed for.

d) The motivation which is appended to the petition: 17,2.12-13.18-19.25-26; this is the least uniform element. It ends with a final ἵνα-clause, dealing with the salvation of the believers.

The 'Gattungselemente' occur only in the order indicated above. John 17 contains five series of successive 'Gattungselemente' (not all series are complete; only element c) is present in all of them), and these five series determine the composition of the prayer. The first series, 17,1b-2, contains the main petition (it stands apart from the rest because of Jesus' use of the 3rd pers. sg. concerning himself); its key-words are glorification and eternal life. The contents of this main petition are unfolded in the following parts:

1) 17,4-5: the Son prays for his glorification (key-word: glory).

2) 17,6-13: the revelation of God's name and the preservation of the church on earth in unity (key-word: name).

3) 17,14-19: the revelation of God's word and the preservation of the church on earth over against the world's hatred (key-words: word and truth).

4) 17,22-26: the beholding of Jesus' heavenly glory by his church in the future of salvation, determined by agapè (key-words: glory and agapè).

17,3.20-21 do not fit into this scheme and are considered to be secondary additions to the text, from another hand.

It seems to me that Becker is basically right in looking for literary forms within the prayer John 17. The reader cannot fail to notice the difference of form between, e.g., the petitions to the Father in 17,1.5, and the recalling of Jesus' past work in 17,6-8. In so far, Becker has drawn attention to a principle of structure that is present beyond doubt in John 17. The way he elaborates this principle is, however, subject to criticism on several points:

a) The distinction of literary forms and the determination of their sequence should not be so rigid as to consider as secondary additions those elements which do not fit into the scheme. When elements do not fit, the scheme has to be adapted[22].

b) Becker handles only one category of indications for the composition of the text; he neglects literary data such as repetition, inclusion and chiasmus.

c) The four 'Gattungselemente' distinguished by Becker are not so self-evident as he supposes them to be. The category 'appended motivation' includes materials which are too disparate to constitute a separate form. Besides, their motivating character is not very clear, and the occurrence of final ἵνα-clauses is by no means restricted to these parts (see 17,1.11.21-24). The category 'petition' is formally recognizable. Becker includes in it, however, 17,24, where instead of an imper. aor. θέλω ἵνα is used, which formula has the same force as an imper. aor. But in that case the sentences with ἐρωτῶ ... ἵνα (17,15.20-21) should also be qualified as petitions, even though they are worded as a statement and 17,15 may be a repetition or specification of 17,11d-f. After all, there is little difference as to the contents of the petition between 'keep them safe' (17,11), or 'I pray you to keep them safe' (17,15), or 'I wish you to keep them safe' (cfr. 17,24)[23]. So it seems that in John 17 two ways are found to formulate a petition: an imper. aor., or ἐρωτῶ/θέλω ἵνα, resulting in what I would call 'imperative petitions' and 'petitionary statements' respectively. An introductory function might be ascribed to 17,9, seen in its relationship with 17,11d-f. The distance between introduction and petition is, however, rather large, and 17,9 can also be understood as a general petitionary statement, unfolded in what follows. It seems preferable, then, to follow H. Ritt and to consider all verses in question as expressing a petition, which can be put into words either as an imperative (17,1.5.11d-f.17) or as an indicative (17,9.15.20-21.24)[24]. Both categories of petition can be documented from biblical and Jewish usage[25].

Becker's 'statement of accounts' can also be considered as a separate category, with formal characteristics. There are, however, next to the passages mentioned by Becker, other parts of John 17 as well which might also be qualified as 'statement of accounts', viz., 17,12.18.25-26, when the contents of such a statement are broadened from Jesus' work of revelation in a strict sense to his earthly work in general (this is already the case in 17,4, considered by Becker as a statement of accounts). The passages in question cannot be said not to meet Becker's requirements, when it is noticed that the passages listed by Becker himself do not meet all his requirements[26]. The retrospect on the petitioner's past actions is an element of prayer frequently found in biblical and Jewish prayers[27].

When these corrections are right, the basis of Becker's division of John 17 partly falls (apart from the circumstance that his key-words are hardly a valid criterion for distinguishing sections, because in most instances they are not restricted to only one section). His starting point, the search for literary forms, should nevertheless be taken seriously.

Other scholars agree with Becker in considering the presence of different literary forms the basic principle of composition of John 17, and in neglecting other indications for the structure of the text. M. L. Appold[28] distinguishes two literary forms: petition (17,1-2 [expanded by 3].5.9-11.15-17.20-21.24) and retrospect (17,4.6-8.12-14.18-19.22-23.25-26); about the composition of John 17, he remarks: 'If any literary principle at all is apparent in the construction of ch. 17, then it is the constant exchange between retrospect or review on the one hand and petition on the other'[29]. J.-A. Bühner[30] distinguishes between statement of accounts in 17,1-8, and petition in 17,9sqq; he concedes, however, that both forms are interwoven as far as their motifs are concerned: in the statement of accounts we meet Jesus' charge concerning his community (17,2.3.6-8), and the petition links up with Jesus' charge and his deeds (17,9-14.17.18.24.25.26).

According to H. Ritt[31], there are three different kinds of formulae ('Formeln' or 'geprägte Elemente') in the prayer John 17: the πάτερ-invocation (17,1b.5b.11d.21c.24a.25a); the intention of prayer, worded either as an imperative (17,1de.5a + c.11ef.17a) or as a statement (17,9.15.20-21.24); the anamnesis (17,2.4.6-8.10b-11c.12ab.13-14.18-19.22-23.25-26). Ritt combines another approach with this search for forms, differing thereby from Becker, Appold and Bühner. In an earlier part of his study, about the textsyntactical analysis of John 17[32], he has been looking for signals of articulation ('Gliederungssignale'); he lists: the πάτερ-invocation (see above), the 'syntagmem' οὐκ ... ἐρωτῶ ... ἀλλά (17,9ab.15ab.20ab), the theme of the mutual glorification of Father and Son (17,1de; cfr. 17,4.5a + c.10b.22a.24de), the conjunction καθώς (17,2a.11f.14b.16.18a.21b.22b.23c), the intentions of prayer, worded either as an imperative or as a statement (see above), the indicative clauses in the 1st pers. sg. about Jesus himself and in the 3rd pers. pl. about those for whom he is praying (passim). Neither of the two (partly overlapping) ways of distinguishing elements leads Ritt to the detection of a more or less elaborate literary structure in John 17[33]. Ritt rightly combines the form-critical approach with a search for signals of articulation, but his list of the latter is incomplete. As Becker, he unjustly considers parts of the text as secondary additions[34].

4. A different analysis of the literary structure of John 17 has been presented by E. Malatesta[35]. According to him, the Greek text of John 17 (and of other parts of John and 1 John) possesses a free rhythm, mainly determined by the thought content; the various members of a sentence can be of similar length in numbers of words and syllables. Successive grammatical units are often in parallel structure. Several such units together can form a larger unit, having its own grammatical and rhythmical consistency: a strophe. Within a given passage, strophes can be compared in regard to themes or formal disposition[36]. In his actual analysis, he also pays attention to literary techniques such as inclusion, chiasmus, concentric symmetry, and to literary forms such as petition. In the end, he arrives at a division of John 17 into five sections: 17,1b-5.6-8.9-19.20-24.25-26. Each of them displays a concentric structure; so does the chapter as a whole according to the scheme A (17,1b-8) — B (9-19) — A′ (20-26). This division is confirmed by a short analysis of the contents of the prayer[37].

A full rendering and discussion of Malatesta's very detailed analysis is not necessary here, because much of it will return in my own analysis (under b.). A few general remarks may now suffice.

An important advantage of Malatesta's method is that he wants to base his structural analysis on as many indications as possible, primarily concerning the literary form of the text, and not on one single word or one single formal criterion[38]. Nevertheless, Malatesta also seems to fall a victim to a tendency of systematizing that goes too far, where he discovers almost everywhere concentric symmetry as a principle of composition[39]. It should be noted, moreover, that his division of the text into lines and strophes is hardly motivated, but is given at the same time a considerable weight in his argumentation[40].

5. In his analysis of the structure of John 17, R. Schnackenburg[41] also wants to start from formal elements, using the 'structuralist method' and, if necessary, other methods[42]. The words δόξα and δοξάζειν occurring at the beginning and at the end of John 17, determine the prayer. Witness 17,10.22.24, the disciples, who are meant in the formula 'whom you have given him/me' (17,2.6.9.24), are involved in the glorification. Apparently, they are in view from the beginning of the prayer (cfr. 17,1b-2). Therefore, the traditional division of John 17 according to the objects of prayer is incorrect[43].

Schnackenburg's own division of John 17 (much of it will return below, under b.) is as follows: 17,1b-5 is the first unit (cfr. the inclusion constituted by 17,1b-e and 5, via 17,4 as a connecting link). In 17,6-11c the gift of eternal life to those whom the Father gave to Jesus from 17,2 is worked out; here the prayer of the departing Christ for his own is motivated. 17,11d-23 is the proper petition, determined by the imperatives τήρησον and ἁγίασον (17,11.17). Key-word of 17,11d-15 is τηρεῖν; of 17,17-19 ἁγιάζειν and ἀλήθεια. 17,22-23, in which the prayer for unity of 17,11 is worked out, is the third unit within the petition. The chapter is concluded with 17,24-26, with its double vocative (17,24.25); this section is referring back to the beginning of the chapter[44].

Schnackenburg's analysis contains a number of useful observations concerning the structure of John 17. Apart from a few dubious literary-critical observations[45], the main points of criticism are these:

a) Schnackenburg wrongly neglects a series of formal indications, such as the occurrence of ἐρωτῶ in 17,9.15.20, the relationship between 17,6a and 26a, and the fivefold occurrence of the radix γνω- in 17,25-26. Attention to these might have changed his scheme.

b) In a structural analysis the contents of the text cannot be totally left aside. It is important, then, to render these contents in a correct way. When Schnackenburg considers the entire prayer as a prayer for the disciples, he wrongly makes what is mentioned only marginally in 17,2 into the main point of 17,1b-5.

6. M.-É. Boismard and A. Lamouille[46] have proposed a scheme of structure for John 17, in which the prayer, after removal of secondary additions[47], is divided into two parts: 17,1-5, where Jesus prays for himself, and 17,6-26, in which he prays for his disciples. Both parts are built in what they call 'the form of a chiasmus'[48]. The pattern of the first part is: A (17,1b-d) — B (1e) — C (2) — B′ (4) — A′ (5). The second part is built in the following way: A (17,6-10) — B (11-13) — C (14-17) — B′ (18-23) — A′ (24-26). Each one of the five sections of the second part displays on a smaller scale also 'the form of a chiasmus'.

Whereas the concentric structure of the first part does not seem to be too much beside the mark, the detection of numerous concentric structures in the second part can hardly be said to be successful. A few critical remarks have to be made here:

1) In the scheme of Boismard and Lamouille, only very few formal indications from the text are used. Their scheme is actually based on a few more or less identical clauses, while a series of obvious correspondences is left aside. So the correspondence of elements B and B′ in the second part is established only on the basis of the ἵνα-clauses about unity 17,11f.22b.23b; on the other hand, an obvious correspondence such as that of the imperative petitions 17,11e.17a is not observed by them.

2) In the scheme of Boismard and Lamouille, the text of John 17 is forced into a mould of concentric symmetry. They seem to suppose that the author of John makes use of only this one pattern in composing his text, and not of others.

7. Recently, Y. Simoens[49] has presented an analysis of the structure of John 17. In his view, the prayer is made up of five elements, and it displays a concentric structure[50]:

17,1-5 Glorification Knowledge — Mission Glorification	A	A′	17,24-26 Agapè Knowledge — Mission Agapè
17,6-11 Keeping the word Gift of the words Keeping in the name — Unity	B	B′	17,20-23 Faith by the word Gift of the glory Agapè — Unity

C
17,12-19
Keeping in the name
Gift of the word
Keeping from the evil one —
Word — Truth

Elements A, C and A′ in themselves show a concentric structure; elements B and B′ show 'concentric parallelism', i.e., a structure in which two parallel parts surround a centre. The scheme proposed for John 17 is part of a larger scheme, for John 13-17 as a whole.

Simoens correctly observes the concentric structure of 17,1b-5. For the rest, his scheme is based on vague correspondences, mostly consisting in one or a few identical words. In the relationship of 17,6 and 11 for instance, 'keeping the word' in 17,6 and 'keeping in the name' in 17,11 are important[51]. However, Simoens does not mention that in the former case the disciples are the subject, and in the latter case the Father. He also neglects, for the most part, the differences in literary form which occur within the prayer[52], and of which petition and retrospect are the most important ones. Many evident correspondences are simply neglected (e.g., that between 17,6 and 17,26).

Despite his sound methodological principles ('the delicate methodological point is to establish a hierarchy in the finding of the formal indices'[53], 'to follow step by step the maximum of its signals and indices [i.e., of the stylistic structure]'[54]), Simoens does not arrive at a correct scheme of structure for John 17.

At the end of this survey, a few methodological principles for the analysis of the structure of John 17 may be stated, as a basis for what follows:

a) One should start from the present text of John 17, without literary-critical operations.

b) Formal indications, which as such can be objectively established, should primarily be used in the analysis.

c) As many indications as possible should be used.

d) The value of the various indications should be weighed: they do not all have the same importance.

e) An author may use various models to compose his text: various kinds of parallelism, concentric symmetry, inclusion, etc. One should not suppose too rapidly that he uses only one type of structure.

b) *An analysis of the structure of John 17*

1. It cannot escape the attentive reader of John 17, that the imperative petition at the beginning of the prayer (17,1) is repeated a few verses later (17,5), and that both petitions together make up a chiasm because of the inversion of the sequence of vocative and imperative, while a minor chiasm is constituted by the indications of Father and Son directly following the imperative:

17,1	πάτερ	×	δόξασόν σου τὸν υἱόν
5	δόξασόν με σύ		πάτερ

Both imperative petitions are evidently corresponding. Their correspondence is reinforced by their being preceded by an indication of time (ἐλήλυθεν ἡ ὥρα 17,1; καὶ νῦν 17,5), and by another chiasm: in 17,1 the imperative 'glorify', whose subject is the Father and whose object the Son, is followed by a final clause about the glorification of the Father by the Son; in 17,5 the same imperative, with the same subject and object, is preceded by a clause about the glorification of the Father by the Son (see for details below, under 3.)[55].

As, moreover, 17,2 depends upon 17,1de, and 17,3 is an explanation of the final words of 17,2, 17,1b-5 can rightly be said to be a literary unit.

2. Just as in 17,1b-5, so in 17,20-24 a chiasm is constituted, now by two petitionary statements (introduced by ἐρωτῶ/θέλω) and two vocatives:

17,20-21	ἐρωτῶ ... ἵνα	×	πάτερ
24	πάτερ		θέλω ἵνα[56]

Between these two petitionary statements (and the subordinate clauses dependent upon them), we find the long sentence 17,22-23, which is connected by a number of correspondences both with 17,20-21 and with 17,24. The correspondence to 17,20-21 is evident from the remarkable parallelism between the subordinate clauses in 17,21 and 17,22b-23: ἵνα ... καθώς ... ἵνα ... ἵνα ... ὅτι ... (see below, under 3., for details; for our purposes, the obvious similarities between the two sentences 17,20-21 and 17,22-23 are most important, but it should be noted that there is actually a very intricate network of relations between 17,20-21 and 17,22-23). The correspondence to 17,24 is evident as this sentence repeats from 17,22-23 in similar order τὴν δόξαν (...) ἣν δέδωκάς μοι and ἐμὲ ἠγάπησας (with inversion of verb and pronoun; cfr. 17,26, see below, p. 247)[57]. So it seems that there are reasons to consider 17,20-24 as a literary unit, whose unity of contents might be described as follows: Jesus prays for the unity of the believers (17,20-21), which unity is the goal of the glory he gave them and which he received from the Father (17,22-23), and which he wants them to behold in his and their heavenly state (17,24).

3. The two literary units established up to now correspond at several points. They display a similar structure: they begin and end with a combination of vocative and petition (imperative petition in the first unit, petitionary statement in the other one); these combinations make up a chiasm in both units. Moreover, the two units reflect each other: 17,1b-5 begins with a vocative followed by an imperative petition, and ends with an imperative petition followed by a vocative; 17,20-24 begins with a petitionary statement followed by a vocative, and ends with a vocative followed by a petitionary statement (the vocative πάτερ without a nearer qualification does not occur in John 17 outside these units). In both cases, the imperative petitions or petitionary statements enclose passages about Jesus' past work (17,2.4.22). In addition to this correspondence of structure, the two units share the important theme of glorification, expressed in the substantive δόξα (17,5.22.24) and the cognate verb δοξάζειν (17,1.4.5). In 17,1.4-5, the Son asks the Father to glorify him; he, in turn, will glorify and has glorified the Father. In 17,22.24, the glory given by the Father to the Son is mentioned; there, the glorification of the Son by the Father is presented as a past event. Witness 17,22, Jesus in his turn gave this glory to the believers. (Another kind of glorification, viz., of the Son in the disciples, is mentioned in 17,10; see

below, p. 246.) So there is a correspondence of key-words and consequently of theme between the units 17,1b-5 and 17,20-24[58].

The correspondence of the two units is supported by a few similarities on minor points:

a) In 17,2.24 (and only there within John 17), the disciples or believers are indicated with a remarkable relative clause in the 3rd pers. sg. neutr., used as a pendent nominative: (πᾶν) ὃ δέδωκας αὐτῷ/μοι (cfr. 17,6.9)[59].

b) In 17,5.24 (and only there within John 17) we meet a reference to the primeval character of Jesus' glory, in the words πρὸ τοῦ τὸν κόσμον εἶναι; πρὸ καταβολῆς κόσμου[60].

4. The clause following 17,1b-5: ἐφανέρωσά σου τὸ ὄνομα τοῖς ἀνθρώποις ... (17,6), has its counterpart at the end of the prayer: καὶ ἐγνώρισα αὐτοῖς τὸ ὄνομά σου (17,26). These statements are equivalent as for their contents, as the verbs φανεροῦν and γνωρίζειν have almost the same meaning, and the indirect object refers in both instances to the disciples[61].

Both times, the revelation by Jesus is — logically — connected with its acceptance by the disciples. In the case of 17,6, the reaction of the disciples follows, in 17,6b*b*-8 (interrupted by a second reference, in different words, to Jesus' revelation in 17,8a); in the case of 17,26 it precedes, in 17,25d, which clause looks like an abbreviation of 17,8bc:

17,8	καὶ αὐτοὶ ἔλαβον	17,25	καὶ οὗτοι
	καὶ ἔγνωσαν ἀληθῶς		ἔγνωσαν
	ὅτι παρὰ σοῦ ἐξῆλθον		
	καὶ ἐπίστευσαν		
	ὅτι σύ με ἀπέστειλας		ὅτι σύ με ἀπέστειλας

In 17,6-8 as well as in 17,25-26, the verb γινώσκειν more often occurs: in 17,7 it also indicates the disciples' belief that Jesus is God's envoy; in 17,25 it is used twice more, to indicate that the world did not know God, but that Jesus did, and in this way the disciples are aligned with Jesus over against the world[62].

Both in 17,6-8 and in 17,25-26, indicative and preterite dominate in the description of Jesus' revelation and the disciples' answer[63]. In this way, these passages distinguish themselves from the petitions which precede or follow them.

It seems, then, that 17,6-8 and 17,25-26 are corresponding literary units. The unity of 17,6-8 is mainly a unity of contents. The unity of 17,25-26 is also a unity of contents; it is formally marked, moreover, by the fivefold use of the radix γνω-[64]. This passage displays, however, two peculiarities not found in the corresponding unit: the vocative πάτερ δίκαιε at its beginning, and the future γνωρίσω at its end. These peculiarities may be explained by the position of 17,25-26 at the end of the entire prayer. The passage begins with the vocative πάτερ to make it correspond to the opening of the prayer (17,1); it is qualified here by δίκαιε because of the judgment implicitly present in the following words: the world did not know God, whereas the disciples recognized that God sent Jesus (cfr. 3,18-19)[65]. The passage ends with the future γνωρίσω to give the prayer a concluding perspective on the future in which Jesus will continue to reveal God's name[66].

5. So far, two combinations of corresponding units have been traced: 17,1b-5 corresponds to 17,20-24, and 17,6-8 to 17,25-26. The pattern according to which these four units are corresponding is: A (17,1b-5) — B (6-8) — A′ (20-24) — B′ (25-26).

A confirmation of these findings, which is at the same time an indication of the coherence of the four units, is the way in which the definition 17,3 is echoed in other parts of the prayer. This definition is in the middle of the unit 17,1b-5. Eternal life is said to be ἵνα γινώσκωσιν σὲ τὸν μόνον ἀληθινὸν θεὸν καὶ ὃν ἀπέστειλας Ἰησοῦν Χριστόν. After a very faint echo in 17,7, a clear echo is heard at the end of 17,6-8: ἔγνωσαν ἀληθῶς ... ὅτι σύ με ἀπέστειλας (17,8); the two clauses beginning with καὶ ἔγνωσαν and καὶ ἐπίστευσαν are evidently parallel. The motif of Jesus' being sent by the Father returns in 17,18, but there without the motif of the believers' 'knowing'. It appears also in 17,21, there as the object of the verb πιστεύειν (cfr. 17,8). A clear echo of 17,3 is found in the middle part of 17,20-24, viz., in 17,23: ἵνα γινώσκῃ ὁ κόσμος ὅτι σύ με ἀπέστειλας. A final echo is heard in 17,25: καὶ οὗτοι ἔγνωσαν ὅτι σύ με ἀπέστειλας, i.e., in the first half of the unit 17,25-26. So 'knowing that the Father sent Jesus' is found:

— in the middle of part A (17,3);
— at the end of part B (17,8);
— in the middle of part A′ (17,23);
— at the beginning of part B′ (17,25).

At the end of part B and at the beginning of part A′, Jesus' being sent by the Father is connected with the verb 'to believe'. A clear pattern emerges in all this, and it confirms the previous analysis.

6. The next step will be an analysis of the remaining part 17,9-19. What is the structure of this section, and is this structure consistent with what has been found up to now?

The first remark to be made has to do with the contents of the text, and it has to be confirmed by considerations of a formal nature; nevertheless, it suggests that 17,9-19 is a separate unit. It is easy to observe that the object of Jesus' praying changes in the course of his prayer. In 17,1b-5 he asks for his own glorification. In 17,9-19 he prays for his disciples, for those given to him by the Father, to whom he revealed the name of the Father and who accepted his revelation by believing that the Father sent him (cfr. 17,6-8). He asks the Father to keep them safe (17,11.15) and to sanctify them (17,17). In 17,20, there is a second change, or better an extension, of the object of his praying: he also prays for those who will believe in him through the word of those for whom he prayed in the preceding part. His prayer 17,20-24 concerns *all* believers: his disciples and the future believers. It is possible that οὗτοι in 17,25 refers again only to the disciples present at Jesus' prayer, just as they were referred to by τούτων in 17,20[67]. 17,9-19 has so its own object of prayer, differing in this respect from what precedes and what follows.

7. The section 17,9-19 is made up of two parts, 17,9-13 and 17,15-19, surrounding a central sentence 17,14. The two parts are parallel to each other, according to a pattern A - B - C - D - E - (17,14) - A′ - B′ - C′ - D′ - E′. To point out the parallelism in detail, I will start from the most striking correspondences.

a. There are obvious similarities between the petitions 17,11d-f and 17,17:

— The imperative petitions in the strict sense display parallelism:

17,11e τήρησον αὐτοὺς ἐν τῷ ὀνόματί σου
17a ἁγίασον αὐτοὺς ἐν τῇ ἀληθείᾳ[68]

Moreover, the verbs τηρεῖν and ἁγιάζειν are related as for their meaning: both verbs indicate here that people are taken from the sphere of power of the world and put into the sphere of power of God (indicated here by his 'name' and 'truth')[69].

— The predicate ἅγιε in 17,11 corresponds to ἁγίασον in 17,17[70]. In addition to the imperative petitions, both elements contain one or more clauses dependent upon the petition: in 17,11 a relative clause (dependent upon ὀνόματι) and a final clause; in 17,17 a second main clause explaining ἀληθείᾳ.

b. The petition 17,11d-f is followed in 17,12 by a retrospective sentence, in which Jesus says that, as long as he was with his disciples, he did what he asks the Father to do from now on. The parallelism is obvious indeed:

17,11e τήρησον αὐτοὺς ἐν τῷ ὀνόματί σου ᾧ δέδωκάς μοι
12*ab* ἐγὼ ἐτήρουν αὐτοὺς ἐν τῷ ὀνόματί σου ᾧ δέδωκάς μοι[71]

In a comparable way, 17,17 is followed in 17,18 by a retrospective sentence, in which Jesus' sending of the disciples is paralleled to the Father's sending of Jesus (with inversion of direct object and verb):

17,18a καθὼς ἐμὲ ἀπέστειλας εἰς τὸν κόσμον
18b κἀγὼ ἀπέστειλα αὐτοὺς εἰς τὸν κόσμον[72]

Here, too, Jesus says that he did what he asks the Father to do now, in so far as ἁγιάζειν and ἀποστέλλειν are closely related: 'to sanctify' is to separate from the sphere of power of the world in view of a mission into the world. The close association of both verbs is obvious in John 10,36, the only other text in John outside 17,17-19, where the verb ἁγιάζειν is used[73]. The Father is asked to sanctify the disciples in the truth; Jesus sent them into the world.

So 17,12 and 17,18 are corresponding as for their contents: in both verses Jesus says that he did the same as, or something closely related to, what he asked the Father to do in the previous verse.

c. A similar correspondence of contents is present in 17,13.19. After the retrospective sentences 17,12.18 the speaker returns to the present (emphatically in 17,13: νῦν δὲ πρὸς σὲ ἔρχομαι, to be contrasted with ὅτε ἤμην μετ' αὐτῶν in 17,12[74]), more precisely to his imminent departure from this world (evidently in 17,13; somewhat more covertly in 17,19, in so far as ἁγιάζω ἐμαυτόν means: 'I dedicate myself as a sacrifice'[75]). Both times, the reference to what Jesus is doing in the present is connected with a final ἵνα-clause, dealing with the positive effect of his present acting in the disciples: 'that they may have my joy within them in full measure' (17,13); 'that they too may be sanctified in truth' (17,19).

So the three elements: imperative petition, retrospect and statement about present action in 17,11d-13, correspond to the same elements in the same order in 17,17-19.

d. Both in 17,9 and in 17,15, Jesus is presented as praying, by means of the verb ἐρωτᾶν, and as specifying the object of his prayer, by means of an οὐκ ... ἀλλά-construction:

17,9 οὐ περὶ τοῦ κόσμου ἐρωτῶ ἀλλὰ περὶ ὧν δέδωκάς μοι
15 οὐκ ἐρωτῶ ἵνα ἄρῃς αὐτοὺς ἐκ τοῦ κόσμου ἀλλ' ἵνα τηρήσῃς αὐτοὺς ἐκ τοῦ πονηροῦ[76]

Both times, the specification has to do with the relationship between the disciples and the world.

e. In both instances, the petitionary statement is followed by an explanation. This is evident in 17,15-16: Jesus does not ask the Father to take the disciples out of the world, but to keep them safe from the evil one, because they do not belong to the world as he does not belong to the world, which is dominated by the evil one (cfr. John 12,31; 14,30; 16,11; 1 John 5,18-19)[77]. An explanation is also given for the petitionary statement of 17,9: Jesus does not pray for the world, but only for his disciples; the Father, to whom they belong, gave them to him (he and the Father share all possessions), and he is glorified in them. He prays for them, because they remain in the world and he goes to the Father[78]. The main reason for Jesus' prayer is his departure from the world and his disciples' remaining in it (as is also evident from 17,12-13), expressed in 17,11a-c. The ὅτι-clause 17,9c: 'because they belong to you', 'is explicative both of why Jesus is praying for them and of why Jesus can say that it was the Father who gave them to him'[79]. This clause gives rise to the parenthesis 17,10a: 'and all that is mine is thine, and what is thine is mine'[80]. The next clause: 'and I am glorified in them/these' (17,10b) is either a continuation of the parenthesis, when a neuter αὐτοῖς refers to τὰ ἐμά/τὰ σά[81], or — more probably — an explanation of why Jesus is praying for the disciples, who are indicated by a masculine αὐτοῖς. So the explanation for the petitionary statement 17,9ab begins with 17,9c, but the main reason is given in 17,11a-c[82].

The explanations given in 17,11a-c and 17,16 are at the same time preparing the imperative petitions which follow, in 17,11d-f and 17,17. That 17,11a-c has such a function is evident in the light of 17,12; for 17,16 it is obvious as far as 'to sanctify' means 'to separate from the world', which does not exclude but includes a mission to the world (see n. 73 above).

So we find both in 17,9-13 and in 17,15-19 a sequence of five elements:
A + A′) A petitionary statement in which ἐρωτῶ is used, and in which a specification is given by means of an οὐκ ... ἀλλά-construction (17,9ab.15).
B + B′) An explanation for this petitionary statement (17,9c-11c, or at least 17,11a-c, and 17,16).
C + C′) A petition, using an aorist imperative (17,11d-f.17).
D + D′) A sentence reviewing Jesus' past work: he himself did what he asked the Father to do in the preceding petition (17,12), or he did something closely related to what he asked the Father to do in the preceding petition (17,18).
E + E′) A sentence about the present in the 1st person, concerning Jesus' imminent departure from this world, and ending with a final clause about the positive effect of his present acting in the disciples (17,13.19).

The cohesion of 17,9-13 is strengthened by the almost literal repetition of 17,11c: κἀγὼ πρὸς σὲ ἔρχομαι, in 17,13 (cfr. also ἐν τῷ κόσμῳ in 17,11.13)[83]. The parallelism of 17,9-13 and 17,15-19 is mitigated because the petitionary statement in 17,15 is a repetition of the imperative petition in 17,11d-f:

17,11e τήρησον αὐτούς
15 ... ἐρωτῶ ... ἵνα τηρήσῃς αὐτούς[84]

So an abba-pattern emerges:

17,11 πάτερ ἅγιε, τήρησον αὐτούς
15.17 ... ἵνα τηρήσῃς αὐτούς .... ἁγίασον αὐτούς

The element standing in the middle of 17,9-19 is then 17,14: 'I have given them your word, and the world hated them, because they do not belong to the world any more than I belong to the world'. Its first part makes one think of the references to Jesus' work of revelation in 17,6-8.25-26 (cfr. esp. 17,6b*b*.8a)[85], but here Jesus' completed work of revelation is not connected with the belief of the disciples, but with the world's hatred of them. The basic condition of the disciple in the world is described here: he has God's word, given to him by Jesus, and he is hated by the world, because he does not belong to the world, just as Jesus does not. In its quality of a reference to Jesus' past acting towards the disciples, 17,14 is — within 17,9-19 — similar to 17,12.18, but it differs from these verses as these are connected with the imperative petitions preceding them, whereas 17,14 is not connected with a petition. This middle verse of 17,9-19 reflects elements both from what precedes and from what follows. Its first half (17,14a) reflects 'and these things I speak in the world' from 17,13; a contrast between Jesus' joy and the hatred of the world may also be intended (cfr. 16,20; Luke 6,22-23). God's word is mentioned again in 17,17[86]. The second half of 17,14 is repeated almost *ad litteram* in 17,16[87].

So John 17,9-19 appears to be a coherent and well-structured unit, and its structure is consistent with what was previously found concerning the rest of the chapter[88].

It is possible now to describe the structure of John 17. The chapter is made up of five units: 17,1b-5.6-8.9-19.20-24.25-26 (and, of course, the narrative introduction 17,1a). Their relations can be rendered schematically as follows:

A 17,1b-5 A' 20-24
C 9-19
B 6-8 B' 25-26

First part (A) and fourth part (A') are corresponding; so are second part (B) and fifth part (B'). The third part (C) is the central one; it is enclosed by two combinations of two parts, which combinations display parallelism as for their structure (A + B // A' + B'). Concentric and parallel symmetry are combined.

Parts A, C and A' show formal similarity in so far as they are built concentrically (in part C two parallel parts surround a middle verse). B and B' constitute together a chiasm according to the pattern: revelation-reaction-reaction-revelation[89].

The results of the structural analysis are confirmed by two features of John 17 not considered in their totality up to now:

1) It has been observed above, in discussing Becker's analysis (p. 233), that in John 17 two ways are used to express a petition: either with an aorist imperative, or with ἐρωτῶ/θέλω ἵνα. Now it appears that the distribution of the two kinds of petition over the various parts of John 17 is very regular:

— in part A: imperative petitions at beginning and end (17,1.5);
— in part C: two petitionary statements and two imperative petitions, alternately (17,9.11.15.17);
— in part A': petitionary statements at beginning and end (17,20.24)[90].

2) Six times, the vocative πάτερ is used to address the Father (17,1.5.21.24; + ἅγιε 17,11; + δίκαιε 17,25)[91]. The vocatives without qualification accompany the imperative petitions in part A, and the petitionary statements in part A'. In part C, only the first imperative petition is combined with a (qualified) vocative. The final vocative does not occur in the framework of a petition (see p. 241 above, about its function).

On the level of form as well as of contents, numerous connections can be observed between the parts of John 17, in addition to what has already been mentioned:

a) Parts A and B are connected because 17,6-8 is an elaboration of the 'accomplishment' of the 'work' mentioned in 17,4, and of the glorification of the Father implied in it[92]. Moreover, ὃ δέδωκας αὐτῷ 17,2 is taken up in οὓς ἔδωκάς μοι 17,6[93].

b) A very similar expression returns in 17,9b: περὶ ὧν δέδωκάς μοι; it is followed there by ὅτι σοί εἰσιν, taking up σοὶ ἦσαν from 17,6b. In this way parts B and C are connected[94].

c) Δεδόξασμαι (17,10) is an obvious link between part C on the one side, and parts A and A' on the other (17,1.4.5.22.24)[95].

d) 'Εν τῷ ὀνόματί σου (17,11.12) connects part C with parts B and B', where σου τὸ ὄνομα/τὸ ὄνομά σου is found (17,6.26)[96].

e) The clause ἵνα ὦσιν ἓν καθὼς ἡμεῖς (17,11f) is an announcement within part C of the theme of unity so prominent in part A' (17,20-23)[97].

f) On the level of contents, the end of part C and the beginning of part A' are connected because of the relationship between the mission of the disciples (17,18) and 'their word' (17,20)[98].

g) There is a formal agreement between the first petitionary statements of C (17,9) and of A' (17,20):

17,9 οὐ περὶ τοῦ κόσμου ἐρωτῶ ἀλλὰ περὶ ὧν δέδωκάς μοι
20 οὐ περὶ τούτων δὲ ἐρωτῶ μόνον ἀλλὰ καὶ περὶ τῶν πιστευόντων ...

An οὐκ ἐρωτῶ ... ἀλλά-construction is also found in the second petitionary statement of part C (17,15)[99].

h) Parts A' and B' are connected by means of the words ἀγάπη/ἀγαπᾶν (17,23.24.26), and the theme of 'being in' (17,21.23.26)[100].

Nrs. a), b), e), f), g) and h) of the above series have to do with the connection of successive parts, whereas nrs. c) and d) have to do with the symmetric construction of John 17.

The next step will be to see whether the structure described above also appears in numbers of W and S. In Table I, these numbers are given for the various parts of the prayer spoken by Jesus (17,1b-26).

Table I. John 17,1b-26

		words			syllables		
17,1b-5	A	79			155		
6-8	B		56			111	
9-19	C			201			370
20-24	A'	111/		190	210/		365
25-26	B'		39/	95/486		70/	181/916

The length of parts A and A' together is twice the length of parts B and B' together, exactly in numbers of W (2 × 95 = 190), approximately in numbers of S. The conspicuous number 111 appears twice: it is the number of W of A', and the number of S of B. The size of part B is — in numbers of S — exactly 3/10 of the size of part C (111 = 3/10 × 370). The number of S of A' is three times that of B' (3 × 70 = 210). 190 (number of W of parts A + A') and 210 (number of S of A') are triangular numbers, of 19 and 20 respectively. 210 is, moreover, a rectangular number (14 × 15); the same is valid for 56, the number of W of part B (7 × 8).

A different organization of the data of Table I is given in Table II: parts A and B on the one side, and A' and B' on the other, are now considered as entities, as two blocks built in parallel and surrounding the central part C.

Table II. John 17,1b-26

		words	syllables
17,1b-8	A + B	135	266
9-19	C	201	370
20-26	A' + B'	150/486	280/916

A + B amount to 135 W, = 9 × 15; A' + B' amount to 150 W, = 10 × 15. A + B have a length of 266 S, = 19 × 14, and A' + B' of 280 S, = 20 × 14. There is a numerical relationship between the blocks A + B and A' + B'[101].

The 135 W of parts A + B are also interesting for another reason: 135 is the numerical value of δόξα (4 + 70 + 60 + 1), an important word in John 17 (*vv.* 5.22.23), together with the cognate verb δοξάζειν (*vv.* 1*bis*.4.5). The rest of the prayer (C + A' + B') has a size of 351 W. 135 and 351 are — to say it in modern terms — numbers written with the same digits: 1, 3 and 5, being the three lowest odd numbers. Both are multiples of 3^3: $135 = 5 \times 3^3$, $351 = 13 \times 3^3$[102].

One more aspect of the numerical composition of John 17 has to be dealt with here. As we saw earlier (p. 246), 17,11f announces the theme of unity in part A'. The words ἵνα ὦσιν ἓν καθὼς ἡμεῖς are repeated, with the addition of a final ἕν, in 17,22b; compare 17,21a.23b. The unity among the believers is said to be the goal of Jesus' gift of glory in 17,22, and in 17,24 Jesus prays that the believers may behold his glory. So the beholding of his glory there where he is may be the final completion of the believers' unity. In this way 17,24 is related to the preceding on the level of contents; the formal relations have been dealt with earlier (p. 239). The passage 17,11d-24, enclosed between the first prayer for unity and the prayer for the final completion of unity, has a size of exactly 500 S.

3. *The sections of John 17 separately and their details*

a) *John 17,1-5: Jesus prays for his glorification*[103]

The correspondence of 17,1b-e and 17,5 has already been described (see p. 238). 17,2 is connected with 17,1b-e by the conjunction καθώς. 17,4 is connected with 17,5 by means of καὶ νῦν, and also because of the evident correspondence of the first halves of both verses, displaying a combination of parallelism and chiasm:

17,4 ἐγώ σε ἐδόξασα ἐπὶ τῆς γῆς
5 καὶ νῦν δόξασόν με σύ, πάτερ, παρὰ σεαυτῷ

In the second halves of both verses, there is a parallelism between ὃ δέδωκάς μοι and ᾗ εἶχον[104]. On the level of contents, a correspondence can be detected between 17,2 and 17,4: in 17,4, Jesus looks back upon his completed work, and the purport of this work is to give eternal life to his own (cfr. John 4,34sqq; 5,20-22), as mentioned — also in retrospect — in 17,2. A formal correspondence between 17,2 and 17,4 is the occurrence of the verb διδόναι; in the passage 17,1b-5 this verb, frequently occurring in John 17, is used only in 17,2.4 (cfr. especially ὃ δέδωκας αὐτῷ 17,2 with ὃ δέδωκάς μοι 17,4).

So 17,3, elucidating the meaning of 'eternal life' and in that way linked up with 17,2, is in the middle of the passage 17,1b-5. This verse stands out by its form (a definition), and by its use of the indications 'Jesus Christ' for the speaker and 'the one true God' for the addressee of the prayer[105]. The verbs δοξάζειν and διδόναι, characteristic of the rest of 17,1b-5 (both four times in 17,1b-2.4-5) do not occur in 17,3, where we find the verb γινώσκειν, and where Jesus is qualified as sent by God: two traits characteristic of 17,6-8.23 (cfr. 21).25-26 (see p. 241 above).

In Table III, the numbers of S and part of the numbers of W are given for the structure of 17,1b-5 as set out above, with addition of 17,1a.

Table III. John 17,1-5	syllables			words
17,1a			25	
1b-e	25			
2	34/59			6 + 9
3		38		6 + 12
4	28			6 + 8
5	30/58/155/180			

Narrative introduction (17,1a) and first petition (17,1b-e) are of equal length: 25 S, = 5^2. It is obvious that 17,3 is in the middle of 17,1b-5: it is preceded by 59 S and followed by 58 S. 17,2-4, enclosed by the two corresponding verses 17,2 and 17,4, has a size of exactly 100 S. Each of its three parts begins with a clause of 6 W. The number of S of 17,4 (28) is both a perfect number and triangular number of 7. The number of S of 17,5 (30) is a rectangular number (5 × 6).

Numerical techniques have been applied to details of 17,1b-5 as well:

1. The correspondence according to a chiastic pattern between 17,1b.d and 17,5ab (see p. 238 above) is also realized in numbers of S:

17,1b	πάτερ	2 S
1d	δόξασόν σου τὸν υἱόν	7
5a	καὶ νῦν δόξασόν με σύ	7
5b	πάτερ	2

The indication of time 17,1d: ἐλήλυθεν ἡ ὥρα, corresponding as such to καὶ νῦν in 17,5a, has a size of 7 S as well.

2. 17,1de displays concentric symmetry (combined with parallelism) round the conjunction ἵνα[106], a symmetry which is also discernible in numbers of W and S:

17,1d	δόξασόν σου τὸν υἱόν	4 W	7 S
1e ἵνα		1	2
	ὁ υἱὸς δοξάσῃ σέ	4	7

The sentence 17,1b-e as a whole shows a pattern of 9 + 7 + 9 S.

3. 17,1d-2 displays parallel symmetry round the conjunction καθώς, which symmetry is discernible in numbers of S:

17,1de	δόξασον ... ἵνα ... δοξάσῃ	16 S
2 καθὼς		2
	ἔδωκας ... ἵνα ... δώσῃ	32/50

There is a proportion of 1:2 between the corresponding parts. The total number of S of this sentence amounts to 50.

4. The two objects of 'that they know' in 17,3*b* are formulated in an isocolon:

17,3*b*	σὲ τὸν μόνον ἀληθινὸν θεόν	10 S	5 W[107]
	καὶ ὃν ἀπέστειλας Ἰησοῦν Χριστόν	10	5

The ἵνα-clause in 17,3 has twice the length of the main clause: 12 and 6 W respectively. 17,3 has a size of 38 S, = 2 × 19; the factor 19 appeared several times in Tables I and II above.

b) *John 17,6-8: Jesus looks back to his past work*[108]

The passage 17,6-8 is made up of three parts, of four cola each.

1. 17,6 contains several instances of concentric symmetry; the verse as a whole is built chiastically, and there is concentric symmetry within corresponding cola, combined with parallelism in the case of the middle cola:

		words
17,6a*a*	ἐφανέρωσά σου τὸ ὄνομα τοῖς ἀνθρώποις	6
6a*b*	οὓς ἔδωκάς μοι ἐκ τοῦ κόσμου	6
6b*a*	σοὶ ἦσαν κἀμοὶ αὐτοὺς ἔδωκας	5/11
6b*b*	καὶ τὸν λόγον σου τετήρηκαν	5 /11/22

17,6a*a* and 17,6b*b* deal with Jesus' revelation and the disciples' answer to it respectively; 17,6a*b* and 17,6b*a* with God's giving of the disciples to

Jesus. Because the verse is made up of two times two cola of equal length in numbers of W, the combinations of corresponding cola are of equal length: 11 W. The verse has a size of 42 S, which is a rectangular number (6 × 7).

2. A comparable literary structure is found in 17,7-8b*a*:

		words	syll.
17,7*a*	νῦν ἔγνωκαν	2	4
7*b*	ὅτι πάντα ὅσα δέδωκάς μοι παρὰ σοῦ εἰσιν	8	15
8a	ὅτι τὰ ῥήματα ἃ ἔδωκάς μοι δέδωκα αὐτοῖς	8/16	16/31
8b*a*	καὶ αὐτοὶ ἔλαβον	3/ 5/21	6/ 10/41

17,7*a*.8b*a* indicate the disciples' reaction. The clauses 17,7*b*.8a begin both with ὅτι, and are at least in their first halves parallel. 17,7*b* is about the divine origin of God's gift to Jesus; 17,8a is about the destination of this gift: Jesus gave it to the disciples. These two clauses are of equal length: 8 W (or 15 and 16 S). This part as a whole is almost as long as the preceding one (21 and 22 W, 41 and 42 S respectively).

3. Both in form and in contents, 17,8b*b*-c displays (synonymous) parallelism[109]:

		words	syll.
17,8b*b*	καὶ ἔγνωσαν ἀληθῶς	3	7
8b*c*	ὅτι παρὰ σοῦ ἐξῆλθον	4	8
8c*a*	καὶ ἐπίστευσαν	2/ 5	5/ 12
8c*b*	ὅτι σύ με ἀπέστειλας	4/8/13	8/16/28

First and third colon are about respectively the knowledge and the belief of the disciples; second and fourth colon are about the contents of their knowledge and belief. The latter two cola are of equal length (4 W, 8 S). The former two cola have a size of 3 and 2 W respectively, and are corresponding in length according to a chiastic pattern to the two cola indicating the disciples' reaction in the preceding part: νῦν ἔγνωκαν and καὶ αὐτοὶ ἔλαβον, of 2 and 3 W. The number of S of this third part is 28, a perfect number, a multiple of 7 and triangular number of 7; the number of S of the first part of the present section (17,6) is also a multiple of 7: 42. The total number of W of 17,6-8 is the rectangular number 56, = 8 × 7.

Next to this tripartition, it should be observed that 17,7*b* is the numerical middle of the passage. The clause ὅτι πάντα ὅσα δέδωκάς μοι παρὰ σοῦ εἰσιν, of 8 W, is preceded and followed by 24 W (cfr. the correspondence between 'your word' in 17,6 and 'the words which you have given me' in 17,8).

c) *John 17,9-19: Jesus prays for his disciples*

The structure of 17,9-19 has already been discussed under 2. (pp. 242-245), because it proved to be necessary within the framework of the analysis of the entire chapter's structure to analyse the composition of this passage. On the basis of what has been found there, it is possible to make up a scheme of structure of 17,9-19 as given in Table IV, where the numbers of S are given for the various elements, in two arrangements.

Table IVa. John 17,9-19

			syllables			
17,9ab	petitionary statement	A	27			
9c-11c	explanation	B	53/80			
11d-f	imperative petition	C		31		
12	retrospect	D			59	
13	present action	E			36/95	
14	central reviewing sentence	X				41
15	petitionary statement	A'	27			
16	explanation	B'	18/45/			125
17	imperative petition	C'		23/		54
18	retrospect	D'			24	
19	present action	E'			31/55/150/370	

Table IVb. John 17,9-19

			syllables		
17,9ab	petitionary statement	A	27		
9c-11c	explanation	B	53/80		
11d-f	imperative petition	C		31	
12	retrospect	D	59		
13	present action	E	36/95/175/206		
14	central reviewing sentence	X			41
15	petitionary statement	A'	27		
16	explanation	B'	18/45		
17	imperative petition	C'		23	
18	retrospect	D'	24		
19	present action	E'	31/55/100/123/370		

The above numbers need a few words of comment. Concerning Table IVa, the following remarks should be made:
— Elements A and A' are of equal length: 27 S, = 3^3.
— The proportion of numbers of S for elements B and B' is approximately 3:1.
— The 80 S of elements A and B together (they belong together as statement and explanation) are divided as well as possible into two parts having a proportion between them of 1:2.
— The proportion of numbers of S for elements A' and B' (also belonging together as statement and explanation) is 3:2.
— The sum of numbers of S is 80 for elements A + B, and 45 for A' + B'. These two sum totals amount together to 125.

— The sum of numbers of S is 95 for elements D + E (belonging together because of the contrast of review and present action), and 55 for elements D' + E' (belonging together in the same way). These two sum totals amount together to 150.

— The sum of numbers of S for D + E is 95, which is a multiple of 19. Other multiples of 19 appeared in Tables I and II above. 95 is also the number of S of elements C, X and C' together, i.e., of those elements not comprised in the sum numbers of 125 and 150 just mentioned.

Concerning Table IVb:

— Both in 17,9-13 and in 17,15-19, the surplus-technique has been applied. In 17,9-13 the middle element C stands out by its size of 31 S over against 175 S for the other four elements. In 17,15-19, the middle element C' has a size of 23 S, whereas the four other elements together amount to 100 S.

— These 100 S are made up of 45 S for elements A' + B', and 55 S for elements D' + E'. Both 45 and 55 are triangular numbers, of 9 and 10 respectively. The sum of two successive triangular numbers makes up a square number: $100 = 10^2$ (see above, p. 28).

— The middle element of the whole passage, X (17,14), has a size of 41 S. The first half (A, B, C, D and E) has a size of 206 S, being approximately 5×41, whereas 123, the number of S of the second half (A', B', C', D' and E'), is exactly 3×41.

It should also be noted that elements A, B and C together have a length of 111 S, being exactly 3/10 of the sum total of 370 S for 17,9-19. 111 S is also the length of the preceding section (17,6-8).

The words νῦν δέ at the beginning of 17,13 may be considered as marking a division of the text; in that case a bipartition appears into 170 + 200 S, for 17,9-12.13-19[110].

An application of the surplus-technique to John 17 as a whole becomes visible as soon as it is realized that the verse 17,14 is in the middle of 17,9-19, and also in the middle of the entire chapter, 17,9-19 being the middle one of the five sections of John 17. The entire chapter has a length of 941 S; 17,14 contains 41 S, so the rest uses 900 S. When the narrative introduction 17,1a is left aside, the rest uses 875 S, $= 7 \times 5^3$ (= 17,1b-13.15-26).

In Table V (see page 254), an arrangement is given of the numbers of W for 17,9-19, according to the same scheme as used in Table IV.

The numerical arrangement which appears here is very similar to that of Table IVa. Elements A, B, A' and B' together amount to 74 W, and elements D, E, D' and E' together amount to 76 W. So the total number of W of these eight elements is 150.

Table V. John 17,9-19

			words				
17,9ab	petitionary statement	A	14				
9c-11c	explanation	B	33/47				
11d-f	imperative petition	C		16			
12	retrospect	D			31		
13	present action	E			20/51		
14	central reviewing sentence	X					24
15	petitionary statement	A'	15				
16	explanation	B'	12/27/			74	
17	imperative petition	C'		11/			27
18	retrospect	D'			12		
19	present action	E'			13/25/76/150/201		

A few more remarks concerning the numbers of W of 17,9-19:
— 17,9-12, the part of the passage up to νῦν δέ, is made up of 2 × 47 W: both elements A and B together and elements C and D together have a size of 47 W. When element A extends up to the end of 17,10 (see p. 244 above), there is a sequence of units of 31, 16, 16 and 31 W.
— 17,12-16 is made up of 2 × 51 W: both elements D and E together and elements X, A' and B' together amount to 51 W. Elements C, C', D' and E' may be taken together because of the correspondence of ἅγιε (17,11) to ἁγίασον (17,17), ἁγιάζω, ἡγιασμένοι (17,19); together they amount to 52 W, or 51 W with omission of ἐγώ in 17,19 (see n. 101).
— 17,15-19 is made up of 27 W (= 3 × 9) for 17,15-16, and 36 W (= 4 × 9) for 17,17-19, together 63 W, which is also the size of 17,9-11.
— Another striking sequence of numbers of W is this: 47 W for 17,9-11c, 67 W for 17,11d-13, and 87 W for 17,14-19. Or, to put it otherwise: 17,11d-13 is, in numbers of W, half as long as 17,9-11c.14-19 (67 = ½ × 134).

Several details from 17,9-19 ask for attention:
1. 17,9-11c contains a petitionary statement and an explanation:

			syll.			words
17,9a	ἐγὼ περὶ αὐτῶν ἐρωτῶ				9	4
9b*a*	οὐ περὶ τοῦ κόσμου ἐρωτῶ	a			9	5
9b*b*	ἀλλὰ περὶ ὧν δέδωκάς μοι				9/27	5/14
9c	ὅτι σοί εἰσιν			5		3
10a*a*	καὶ τὰ ἐμὰ πάντα σά ἐστιν	b	9			6
10a*b*	καὶ τὰ σὰ ἐμά		5/		14	4
10b	καὶ δεδόξασμαι ἐν αὐτοῖς				8/13/27	4/17
11a	καὶ οὐκέτι εἰμὶ ἐν τῷ κόσμῳ				10	6
11b	καὶ αὐτοὶ ἐν τῷ κόσμῳ εἰσίν	c			9	6
11c	κἀγὼ πρὸς σὲ ἔρχομαι[111]				7/26/80	4/16/47

As for their formal structure, parts a and c reflect each other. Part a consists of 1 + 2 cola: 17,9a is elucidated in a *correctio* in 17,9b. Part c is made up of 2 + 1 cola, because 17,11a and 11b are in antithetic parallelism (and contain a chiasm εἰμί-ἐν τῷ κόσμῳ-ἐν τῷ κόσμῳ-εἰσίν). Cola which belong together contain the same number of W: 5 + 5 W in 17,9b, and 6 + 6 W in 17,11ab, whereas first and last colon (17,9a.11c) are of equal length: 4 W.

Each part contains three verbs, the first two of which are identical in each of the three parts. Moreover, each part contains a plural form of αὐτός, in the first, last and middle colon respectively. In first and third part, these αὐτοί (the disciples) are put in relation to the world: according to part a, Jesus prays for the disciples and not for the world, and according to part c, the disciples are in the world, whereas Jesus is not any longer in the world. In part b, the disciples are put in relation to God and Jesus: they belong to the Father, and Jesus is glorified in them. In numbers of S, the three parts are of (nearly) equal length: 27, 27 and 26 S.

Each colon of part a has the preposition περί (+ gen.) as its second word, and has a size of 9 S (as do 17,10a*a*.11b).

In the second part, the first three cola contain a pronoun 2nd pers. sg. This part is built according to a chiastic pattern: first and fourth colon are about the disciples, in their relationship to the Father and Jesus respectively; second and third colon are about the relationship of Father and Son (and contain a chiasm in the sequence of possessive pronouns: ἐμά-σά-σά-ἐμά). The 27 S of part b are divided into two halves, according to the chiastic pattern: first and fourth colon together amount to 13 S, second and third colon together to 14 S.

Within parts a and b taken together (see p. 244 above) and measured in numbers of W, the clause ὅτι σοί εἰσιν stands exactly in the middle: it is preceded and followed by 14 W.

2. The petition 17,11d-f is linked up with the preceding unit 17,11a-c: the petition has a size of 5 (= πάτερ ἅγιε) + 26 S, and 17,11a-c has a size of 26 S.

3. The first clauses of 17,12 and 17,13 are opposed to each other (see p. 243 above), and are of equal length in numbers of S:

17,12a*a*	ὅτε ἤμην μετ'αὐτῶν	7 S
13*a*	νῦν δὲ πρὸς σὲ ἔρχομαι	7

In 17,12a, Jesus says that he did in his earthly ministry what he asked the Father to do in the preceding petition (17,11d-f): to keep the disciples safe. 17,12a has a size of 26 S or 14 W, and is in that way linked up with

17,11d-f, made up of 5 + 26 S or 2 + 14 W (cfr. the preceding remark, about 17,11d-f).

17,12 is made up of five clauses: a subordinate clause, three main clauses, two long ones and a short one in between[112], and a subordinate clause. In numbers of W, the verse displays a balanced structure:

17,12a*a*	subordinate clause	4 W
12a*b*	long main clause	10
12b	short main clause	2
12c	long main clause	11
12d	subordinate clause	4

4. 17,14 is made up of four cola. First and second colon together constitute a main clause; third and fourth colon together make up a causal subordinate clause. The main clause has a size of 21 S, the subordinate clause of 20 S. First and fourth colon, both with Jesus as subject (indicated by ἐγώ), are of equal length:

		syll.
17,14a*a*	ἐγὼ δέδωκα αὐτοῖς τὸν λόγον σου	11
14a*b*	καὶ ὁ κόσμος ἐμίσησεν αὐτούς	10/21
14b*a*	ὅτι οὐκ εἰσὶν ἐκ τοῦ κόσμου	9
14b*b*	καθὼς ἐγὼ οὐκ εἰμὶ ἐκ τοῦ κόσμου	11/20

5. 17,15[113] is made up of two parallel cola, of almost equal length:

17,15a	οὐκ ἐρωτῶ ἵνα ἄρῃς	αὐτοὺς ἐκ τοῦ κόσμου	8 W	14 S
	ἀλλ' ἵνα τηρήσῃς	αὐτοὺς ἐκ τοῦ πονηροῦ	7	13

6. 17,17-19 is a literary unit, because of the inclusion constituted by 17,17.19. In 17,17, ἁγιάζειν occurs once and ἀλήθεια twice; in 17,19, ἁγιάζειν is found twice and ἀλήθεια once (within John 17, both words occur only here). Combining with the personal pronoun αὐτοί, present three times as well in 17,17.19, we obtain this scheme:

	a	b	c	c	
17,17	ἁγίασον —	αὐτούς —	ἀληθείᾳ —	ἀλήθεια	
	b	a	b	a	c
19	αὐτῶν —	ἁγιάζω —	αὐτοί —	ἡγιασμένοι —	ἀληθείᾳ

The enclosed verse 17,18 displays symmetrical parallelism (see p. 243 above)[114].

In Table VI, the numbers of W are given for 17,17-19 in accordance with the structure described above.

Table VI. John 17,17-19 words

	words		
17,17a	5		
17b	6/	11	
18a		6	
18b		6/	12
19a	6		
19b	7/	13/24/36	

There is a climbing sequence of 11, 12 and 13 W, for 17,17.18.19. In that way, the corresponding verses 17,17 and 17,19 are together twice as long as the middle verse 17,18. A climbing sequence is also visible in the successive separate cola: 5, four times 6, and 7 W. First and last clause are evidently corresponding:

17,17a ἁγίασον αὐτοὺς ἐν τῇ ἀληθείᾳ

19b ἵνα ὦσιν καὶ αὐτοὶ ἡγιασμένοι ἐν ἀληθείᾳ

Together, they have a length of 5 + 7 = 12 W, and in that way they are together as long as the middle verse 17,18, which constitutes, moreover, an isocolon:

17,18a	καθὼς ἐμὲ ἀπέστειλας εἰς τὸν κόσμον	6 W	12 S
18b	κἀγὼ ἀπέστειλα αὐτοὺς εἰς τὸν κόσμον	6	12

Apparently, the (perfect) number 6 is prominent in the numbers of W of 17,17-19: four clauses of 6 W, and a sum total of 36 W, = 6^2 (and triangular number of 8).

d) *John 17,20-24: Jesus prays for all believers*[115]

The passage 17,20-24 is made up of three long sentences: 17,20-21. 22-23.24. The first two of these have together a size of 154 S, = 22 × 7; the third one has a size of 56 S, = 8 × 7. 17,25-26, the final section of John 17, has a size of 70 S, = 10 × 7. So the factor 7 seems to be prominent in John 17,20-26.

From the above numbers, it may be derived that 17,24 is relatively independent from 17,20-23. This independence is confirmed by the conventional literary analysis, in which 17,20-21 and 17,22-23 will appear to be parallel (see below). Now, 17,20-23 has a size of 83 W, and 17,24-26 of 67 W (which is also the size of 17,11d-13, see p. 254 above). In this way the 150 W of 17,20-26 are divided as well as possible into parts having a proportion between them of 5:4.

The parallelism of 17,20-21 and 17,22-23[116] will be evident from a schematic rendering of the Greek text, to which the numbers of S and W are added:

		syll.	wrd.			syll.	wrd.
17,20ab	οὐ περί ... εἰς ἐμέ	31	17	22a	κἀγώ ... δέδωκα αὐτοῖς	15	8
21a	ἵνα πάντες ἓν ὦσιν	7	4	22b*a*	ἵνα ὦσιν ἕν	5	3
21b-d	καθὼς σύ, πάτερ, ἐν ἐμοὶ κἀγὼ ἐν σοί	12	8	22b*b* -23a	καθὼς ἡμεῖς ἕν, ἐγὼ ἐν αὐτοῖς καὶ σὺ ἐν ἐμοί	15	10
21e	ἵνα καὶ αὐτοὶ ἐν ἡμῖν ὦσιν	10	6	23b	ἵνα ὦσιν τετελειωμένοι εἰς ἕν	12	5
21f*a*	ἵνα ὁ κόσμος πιστεύῃ	8	4	23c*a*	ἵνα γινώσκῃ ὁ κόσμος	8	4
21f*b*	ὅτι σύ με ἀπέστειλας	8	4	23c*b*	ὅτι σύ με ἀπέστειλας	8	4
				23c*c*	καὶ ἠγάπησας αὐτούς	7	3
				23c*d*	καθὼς ἐμὲ ἠγάπησας	8	3
		76	43			78	40

17,20-21 begins with a main clause (17,20) of 31 S, and ends with a final clause (17,21f) of 16 S (or 8 W); 17,22-23 begins with a main clause (17,22a) of 15 S (or 8 W), and ends with a final clause (17,23c) of 31 S. So there is, in 17,20-21 and 17,22-23, a proportion of 2:1 and 1:2 respectively between main clause and last ἵνα-clause (an approximate proportion, of course, 31 being an odd number).

In both parts of 17,20-23, the length of the series of ἵνα-clauses amounts to a multiple of 9 S: 45 S, = 5 × 9, in 17,21, and 63 S, = 7 × 9, in 17,22b-23, half of which (31) are used in the final clause 17,23c.

In both parts, the first two ἵνα-clauses together (17,21a-e.22b-23b) have a size of 18 W. In both instances these two clauses are similar not only as for their contents, but also formally: in 17,21a-e because both end in ὦσιν, and in 17,22b-23b because both end in ἕν. The parallel clauses 17,21a and 17,22b*a* display a chiasm: ἓν ὦσιν-ὦσιν ἕν. In both instances the first ἵνα-clause is enlarged with a καθώς-clause.

The final clause 17,21f is made up of 8 + 8 S, or 4 + 4 W. The longer final clause 17,23c, in its first part parallel to 17,21f (with inversion of the sequence of subject and verb in 17,23c*a* in comparison with 17,21f*a*[117]), is made up of 8 + 8 + 7 + 8 S, or 4 + 4 + 3 + 3 W. In this way, the structure of this clause in numbers of W reflects to a certain extent in reversed order the structure in numbers of W of the first final clause in this part, which clause is made up, moreover, of 5 + 5 + 5 + 5 S (preceded by 15 S, = 3 × 5, in 17,22a)[118]:

17,22b*a*	ἵνα ὦσιν ἕν	3 W	5 S
22b*b*	καθὼς ἡμεῖς ἕν	3	5
23a*a*	ἐγὼ ἐν αὐτοῖς	3	5
23a*b*	καὶ σὺ ἐν ἐμοί	4	5

17,24 has a size of 56 S, = 8 × 7 (a rectangular number), or 28 W, = 4 × 7 (also triangular number of 7, and a perfect number), to be arranged as follows:

17,24a	πάτερ	2 S	1 W
24b	ὃ δέδωκάς μοι	5	3
24c*a*	θέλω ἵνα ὅπου εἰμὶ ἐγώ	10	5
24c*b*	κἀκεῖνοι ὦσιν μετ'ἐμοῦ	8	4
24d	ἵνα θεωρῶσιν τὴν δόξαν τὴν ἐμήν	12	6
24e*a*	ἣν δέδωκάς μοι	5	3
24e*b*	ὅτι ἠγάπησάς με	7	3
24e*c*	πρὸ καταβολῆς κόσμου	7/56	3/28

The number 7 is found again at the end of this verse, in the causal clause 17,24e*bc*, made up of 7 + 7 S (= 3 + 3 W). Leaving aside the vocative at the beginning, the verse appears to be made up of units of (multiples of) 3 W: 3 + 9 (= 5 + 4) + 6 + 3 + 3 + 3 W.

The final clause 17,24de has a size of 31 S, i.e., as long as the first main clause and last final clause of 17,20-23 (see above).

e) *John 17,25-26: Jesus looks back to his past work, and looks forward to the future*[119]

		syll.	words
17,25a	πάτερ δίκαιε	5	2
25b	καὶ ὁ κόσμος σε οὐκ ἔγνω	8	6
25c	ἐγὼ δέ σε ἔγνων	6/14	4
25d*a*	καὶ οὗτοι ἔγνωσαν	6	3
25d*b*	ὅτι σύ με ἀπέστειλας	8/14	4/19
26a*a*	καὶ ἐγνώρισα αὐτοῖς τὸ ὄνομά σου	12	6
26a*b*	καὶ γνωρίσω	4/16	2
26b*a*	ἵνα ἡ ἀγάπη ἣν ἠγάπησάς με	12	6
26b*b*	ἐν αὐτοῖς ᾖ	4	3
26b*c*	κἀγὼ ἐν αὐτοῖς	5/21/70	3/20/39

The factor 7 is prominent in the numbers of S of this passage. It has a size of 70 S (cfr. the 42 + 28 = 70 S of first and last part of the corresponding section 17,6-8, see p. 251 above). The final clause 17,26b has a length of 21 S, = 3 × 7, and is made up, moreover, of 6 (to be divided into 3 + 3) + 3 + 3 W, to be compared with the units of (multiples of) 3 in the preceding verse 17,24. In 17,25b-d, the knowledge of the disciples (and of Jesus) is contrasted with the world's ignorance about God in two times

14 S, = 2 × 7, arranged according to a pattern of 8 + 6 + 6 + 8 S; both groups of 14 S begin with καί[120].

The first and last colon (17,25a.26b*c*) have a length of 5 S. What is enclosed between these two cola, is made up of 8 + 6 + 6 + 8 + 12 + 4 + 12 + 4 S, or 14 + 14 + 16 + 16 S.

In numbers of W, 17,25-26 is made up of two almost equal halves: 19 W for 17,25, and 20 W for 17,26.

We may conclude, that the author of the Fourth Gospel used numbers of S and W in the composition of John 17. A résumé of the various applications of this technique will be given in the Conclusion.

NOTES TO CHAPTER FIVE

1 Cfr. Hoskyns-Davey, 497; Barrett, 501; E. Käsemann, *Jesu letzter Wille nach Johannes 17* (Tübingen 1966, 1971[3]) 17; Brown, 744; M. Lattke, *Einheit im Wort.* Die spezifische Bedeutung von ἀγάπη, ἀγαπᾶν und φιλεῖν im Johannesevangelium (SANT 41; Munich 1975) 198-199; Schnackenburg, III 189, 192; M. L. Appold, *The Oneness Motif in the Fourth Gospel.* Motif Analysis and Exegetical Probe into the Theology of John (WUNT, 2. Reihe, 1; Tübingen 1976) 194-211; H. Ritt, *Das Gebet zum Vater.* Zur Interpretation von Joh 17 (FzB 36; Würzburg/Stuttgart 1979) 182-183, 424-426; Haenchen, 512.

2 E. Malatesta, 'The Literary Structure of John 17', *Bib* 52 (1971) 190-214; 192 n. 1, reaches a sum total of 500 W, but can do so only at the cost of two rash and unmotivated corrections of the text: the addition of σου in 17,1e, and of ἕν in 17,21e (cfr. Ritt, *Gebet*, 137 n. 256). M.'s count of numbers of S and W in John 17 (given on a folding chart which accompanies his article) contains a few anomalies: a) M. counts 'Ἰησοῦς (17,1.3) at 3 S. b) In 17,6a*a*, M. counts by mistake 13 S; the correct number is 14. c) In 17,21e, M. counts 10 S and 7 W; I presume that ἕν has been included in the number of W, but not in the number of S.

3 I owe this observation to J. Smit Sibinga, who pointed out to me that Luke 11,1-13, a teaching of Jesus about prayer, also has a length of 486 S, = 6 × 81 (both in *NA*[25] and in *NA*[26], when 'Ἰωάννης in 11,1 is counted at 4 S), within which units of 81 S occur: 11,1-2b and 2c-4 (the Lord's prayer) both have a size of 81 S. He also notes that in John 17, with its size of 6 × 81 W, the vocative πάτερ occurs 6 times, and that the number 81 is written in Greek characters as πα', being the first two letters of πάτερ. — A comparison of Luke 11,2-4 and John 17 is made by W. Thüsing, 'Die Bitten des johanneischen Jesus in dem Gebet Joh 17 und die Intentionen Jesu von Nazareth', in: *Die Kirche des Anfangs* (Fs. H. Schürmann; Leipzig 1977) 307-337; 313-321. He compares: the πάτερ-address and the theocentric tenor in both prayers; the prayer for the glorification of the Father (John 17,1) with that for the hallowing of God's name and the coming of his kingdom (Luke 11,2); the prayer for the preservation of the disciples (John 17,11d-16) with the prayer 'and lead us not into temptation' (Luke 11,4c). On these points, John 17 is, according to Th., a 'nachösterlich transformierende Konzentration' (318) or 'johanneische Transformation' (319) of the Lord's prayer, a judgment which can be confirmed by the above considerations of a numerical character. W. O. Walker, Jr., 'The Lord's Prayer in Matthew and in John', *NTS* 28 (1982) 237-256, considers John 17 as 'a type of "midrash" on the Matthean version of the Lord's Prayer' (238).

4 See J. Becker, 'Aufbau, Schichtung und theologiegeschichtliche Stellung des Gebetes in Johannes 17', *ZNW* 60 (1969) 56-83; 56-57 (with quotations from other authors); Malatesta, *Bib* 52, 190-191, with 191 n. 1.

5 Surveys of opinions about the structure of John 17 are given by Becker, *ZNW* 60, 57-60; Malatesta, *Bib* 52, 191 n. 2; Ritt, *Gebet*, 92-140.

6 Cfr. already Thomas Aquinas, *Super Evangelio S. Johannis lectura*, ed. Marietti (Rome/Turin 1952) 411: Jesus prays 'primo pro seipso, secundo pro discipulorum collegio, tertio pro universo fideli populo'; in later times the text-editions of Tischendorf[8], Westcott-Hort and *UBSGNT*[3]; Westcott, II 240; W. Thüsing, *Herrlichkeit und Einheit*. Eine Auslegung des hohepriesterlichen Gebetes Jesu (Joh. 17) (Die Welt der Bibel; Düsseldorf 1962) 7-8; see further the surveys mentioned in the preceding note. A. Feuillet, *Le sacerdoce du Christ et de ses ministres d'après la prière sacerdotale du quatrième Évangile et plusieurs donneés parallèles du Nouveau Testament* (Paris 1972) 47, who supposes the liturgy of the Day of Atonement to constitute the background of John 17, sees a confirmation for a tripartition of John 17 on this basis in Lev 16,17: Aaron has to make 'expiation for himself, his household, and the whole assembly of Israel'.

7 So Bernard, 559; Hoskyns-Davey, 496-507 (with 17,19 as a separate part); O. Michel, 'Das Gebet des scheidenden Erlösers', *ZST* 18 (1941) 521-534; 522; Lightfoot, 296; Grundmann, *Zeugnis und Gestalt*, 77-80; J. Perret, 'Notes Bibliques. La Prière sacerdotale (Jean 17)', *VCaro* 18, nr. 69 (1964) 119-126; Brown, 547; Riedl, *Heilswerk*, 71, 132; Haenchen, 498-513. See further Becker, *ZNW* 60, 58.

8 Von Soden's edition; also Dodd, *Interpretation*, 417.

9 With 17,1-5 as first section: the Nestle(-Aland)-editions 1914[10]-1963[25]; Bengel, *Gnomon*, 431; Bauer, 202-208; Lagrange, 436; Strathmann, 231; G.-M. Behler, *Les paroles d'adieux du Seigneur (S. Jean 13-17)* (LD 27; Paris 1960) 219, 258; Schulz, 213-220; Schneider, 283 (see further Becker, *ZNW* 60, 58-59). With 17,1-8 as first section: Van den Bussche, *Jezus' woorden*, 148.

10 With 17,1-5 as first section: Barrett, 499; with 17,1-8 as first section: A. Loisy, *Le quatrième évangile* (Paris 1903) 798.

11 So *NA*[26].

12 So B. Rigaux, 'Les destinataires du IVe Évangile à la lumière de Jn 17', *RTL* 1 (1970) 289-319; 293-295.

13 So J. L. Boyle, 'The Last Discourse (Jn 13,31-16,33) and Prayer (Jn 17): Some Observations on Their Unity and Development', *Bib* 56 (1975) 210-222; 219.

14 So Bultmann, 373, 380, and Lattke, *Einheit im Wort*, 197.

15 As an example I adduce Thüsing, *Herrlichkeit*, 65, 82, 99, who divides 17,6-19 into 17,6-8.9-11c.11d-16.17-19, and 17,20-26 into 17,20-23.24.25-26. Cfr. also Becker, *ZNW* 60, 59-60.

16 Cfr. R. Schnackenburg, 'Strukturanalyse von Joh 17', *BZ* NF 17 (1973) 67-78, 196-202; 68.

17 O. Merlier, *Le Quatrième Évangile*. La Question Johannique (Paris 1962) 421.

18 A. Laurentin, '*Weʿattah-Kai nun*. Formule caractéristique des textes juridiques et liturgiques (à propos de Jean 17,5)', *Bib* 45 (1964) 168-197, 413-432; 426-432.

19 A similar criticism of Laurentin's position in Ritt, *Gebet*, 116-117, 276-279.

20 Becker, *ZNW* 60, 60-70; in abridged form in his commentary on John, 508-516.

21 Becker does not notice that in 17,14.22 the perfect is used.

22 It should be noted, to do justice to Becker, that there are other parts of the text as well which are, in his view, secondary additions, viz., 17,12b-d.16, about which he is fairly sure, and 17,8.10a.11a-c, about which he is less sure; and that he has other arguments for his opinion, besides that of not fitting into the scheme of some supposed additions. These other arguments are: a) The additions contain words and thoughts which are unique within John 17 (*vv.* 3.12b-d.20-21) or within John in its entirety (*v.* 12b-d). b) They are doublets to other parts of John 17 (*vv.* 8.11a-c.16.20-21). c) They are addressed to the reader and move, in that way, outside the framework of the prayer (17,3.10a.12b-d). d) They disrupt connections between sentences (17,12b-d.16). These arguments are, however, hardly valid; ad a): it is not astonishing, that in a piece of text of 26 verses words are used only once, or thoughts are expressed only once. Real Johannine hapaxlegomena are only the ex-

pression ὁ υἱὸς τῆς ἀπολείας in 17,12 (but cfr. υἱοὶ φωτός in 12,36), and ἡ αἰώνιος ζωή in 17,3, over against the normal ζωὴ αἰώνιος (but here the definition-formula, taking up the end of 17,2, leads to the use of the article — so also F. Mussner, *ΖΩΗ*. Die Anschauung vom 'Leben' im vierten Evangelium unter Berücksichtigung der Johannesbriefe [Münchener Theologische Studien I/5; Munich 1952] 48 —, cfr. 3,19; 6,39; 15,12; this, in turn, leads to the inversion of substantive and adjective). Ad b): the doublets are in fact repetitions, such as occur in John 17 also outside the so-called additions (e.g., 17,1d + 5a; 6a + 26a; 11f + 21a.22b). Ad c): the whole prayer is, as a literary composition of the evangelist, indirectly addressed to the reader; 17,12b-d is so no more than, e.g., 17,6. Ad d): the elimination of 17,12b-d.16 hardly improves connections. Cfr. for similar criticisms of Becker's position: Appold, *Oneness Motif*, 224 n. 4, 225 n. 1 and 2, 226 n. 1 and 2; Ritt, *Gebet*, 254-256.

23 Cfr. for θέλειν in the sense of 'to wish': LXX 3 Reg 10,13 (parallel to αἰτεῖν); Sir 23,14; in the NT Matt 12,38; Mark 6,22.25 (also in combination with αἰτεῖν); John 12,21. See Bauer, *Wörterbuch*, s.v. θέλω 1: '*wollen* v. Wunsch, Begehren (...), *haben wollen*, *wünschen*, *begehren*'; G. Schrenk, art. θέλω etc., *TWNT* III, 43-63; 48, about John 17,24: 'betende Willenserklärung'; cfr. moreover Bengel, *Gnomon*, 434; Lagrange, 451-452; Bernard, 579; Bultmann, 397; Barrett, 514; Lightfoot, 299; Thüsing, *Herrlichkeit*, 113; Perrett, *VCaro* 18, nr. 69, 125; C. Evans, 'Le Christ en prière dans l'évangile selon S. Jean', *Lumen Vitae* 24 (1969) 411-428; 422; Brown, 772; Malatesta, *Bib* 52, 208; Schulz, 218; Schnackenburg, III 222; Schneider, 291; Boismard-Lamouille, *Jean*, 400.

24 Ritt, *Gebet*, 248, 393-399; R. speaks of a 'Gebetsintention', which is in my opinion too weak a qualification. Cfr. also Bultmann, 384; Michel, *ZST* 18, 529; Evans, *Lumen Vitae* 24, 422; Brown, 750.

25 Imperative petitions are numerous, both with and without a vocative; a few instances: Deut 9,26-27; Dan 9,16-19; LXX Esth 4,17f-h.l.q-t.z; Jdt 9,8-14; 2 Macc 1,26-29; 3 Macc 2,2.17.19-20; Sir 36,1-17; 1QH XVI, 18; XVIII, 9; John 12,27; Acts 4,29. Petitionary statements, introduced by ἐρωτῶ and the like, are rather scarce, but they are not absent; instances can be found in LXX Num 12,13 (δέομαι + imper. aor.); 1 Esdr 4,46 (to king Darius; δέομαι + ἵνα); Or Man 13 (αἰτοῦμαι δεόμενος + imper. aor. and conj. aor. 2 sg. with negation); Ps.-Philo, *Lib. Ant. Bibl.* 19,8 (peto + conj.); Luke 8,28 (δέομαι + conj. aor. 2 sg. with negation); 9,38 (δέομαι + inf. aor.; + imper. aor. in *l.v.*; cfr. Matt 17,15); 16,27 (to Abraham in heaven; ἐρωτῶ + ἵνα; cfr. 16,24).

26 The characteristics summed up on p. 232 above are not found in all instances of statement of accounts listed by Becker. A similar criticism of B. in Appold, *Oneness Motif*, 219-221.

27 See, e.g., Dan 9,5-15; LXX Esth 4,17d-e.n.u-y; Tob 3,5.14-15; Or Man 9-12; Ps.-Philo, *Lib. Ant. Bibl.* 19,8-9 (Moses before his death); 21,3.

28 Appold, *Oneness Motif*, 202-204, 223-227.

29 Appold, *Oneness Motif*, 223-224.

30 J.-A. Bühner, *Der Gesandte und sein Weg im 4. Evangelium*. Die kultur- und religionsgeschichtlichen Grundlagen der johanneischen Sendungschristologie sowie ihre traditionsgeschichtliche Entwicklung (WUNT, 2. Reihe, 2; Tübingen 1977) 225.

31 Ritt, *Gebet*, 389-405.

32 Ritt, *Gebet*, 236-261.

33 Cfr. Ritt, *Gebet*, 432: '... dass sich in Joh 17 *keine wohlgegliederte und einheitlich beschreibbare Themenfolge* ablesen lässt, ja dass überhaupt all das, was man unter "Gliederung des Textes" versteht, kaum rezeptartig vorgelegt werden kann'.

34 These are: 17,3.10a.12c*b*d.16. Ritt's arguments (see esp. *Gebet*, 183-188) do not essentially differ from Becker's.

35 Malatesta, *Bib* 52, 190-214. See for a criticism mainly arising from incomprehension with regard to the literary techniques of the fourth evangelist: Ritt, *Gebet*, 135-138.

36 Malatesta, *Bib* 52, 192-194.

37 Malatesta, *Bib* 52, 194-214. M. is followed by Ferraro, *L'"ora" di Cristo*, 263-264, and by Marzotto, *Unità*, 170-171.

38 Cfr. Malatesta's criticism of his predecessors Laurentin and Becker, *Bib* 52, 191-192.
39 Two texts where Malatesta discovers concentric symmetry while there really is none, are 17,6-8 (in which 17,6 should correspond to 17,8b*b*-c, because these two parts 'correspond respectively to the knowledge of the Father and the Son highlighted in 3, while the center sub-division speaks of the mediation of the Son', p. 199), and 17,25-26 (where M. only posits concentric symmetry but does not prove it, pp. 209-210).
40 Cfr. his words on p. 194: 'Other divisions into lines and strophes might be proposed and defended'. Numbers of lines are used in the argumentation on, e.g., pp. 202 (17,12-14), 209-210 (17,25-26), and esp. 210-211 (where numbers of lines and strophes are used to argue the structure of John 17 as a whole). A few examples of conflicting divisions into lines: 17,11 πάτερ ἅγιε τήρησον αὐτούς 1 line, 17,25 πάτερ δίκαιε 1 line; 17,11 ἵνα ὦσιν ἓν καθὼς ἡμεῖς 1 line, 17,22 ἵνα ὦσιν ἕν/καθὼς ἡμεῖς ἕν 2 lines; 17,8 ὅτι τὰ ῥήματα ἃ ἔδωκάς μοι δέδωκα αὐτοῖς 1 line, 17,22 κἀγὼ τὴν δόξαν/ἣν δέδωκάς μοι/δέδωκα αὐτοῖς 3 lines.
41 Schnackenburg, *BZ* NF 17, 67-78, 196-202. In his commentary on John (III 191), S. refers to this article as far as the structure of John 17 is concerned. Where article and commentary are overlapping, I give only the references to the article.
42 Schnackenburg, *BZ* NF 17, 68-70.
43 Schnackenburg, *BZ* NF 17, 72-74.
44 Schnackenburg, *BZ* NF 17, 74-78, 196-202. The division proposed by S. returns, with one modification (17,24 is a fourth petition, and 17,25-26 is the conclusion to the prayer), in Thüsing, in: *Die Kirche des Anfangs*, 314. Th. apparently changed his former position (see p. 230, with n. 6).
45 Secondary additions are, according to Schnackenburg, *BZ* NF 17, 75, 197-199, 202: 17,3.12b-d.16.20-21. His arguments do not essentially differ from Becker's.
46 Boismard-Lamouille, *Jean*, 392-401, esp. 395-396.
47 Boismard and Lamouille consider as secondary additions: 17,3.8b*c*-c*a* (ὅτι[2] ... ἐπίστευσαν).12b-d.19-21 (*Jean*, 392-394). Their arguments do not essentially differ from those of Becker. The main difference is that B. and L. make an extensive use of characteristics of style. As an example illustrating B.'s and L.'s working with stylistic arguments in John 17, I adduce their argument for the secondary character of 17,8b*c*-c*a*: the verb ἐξέρχεσθαι is Johannine, but 'Jean II' uses it with ἀπό, and 'Jean III' with παρά (*Jean*, 393). In fact, the verb is used in John six times to indicate Jesus' coming from God. In 13,3; 16,30 it is found with ἀπό, in 16,27; 17,8 with παρά, and in 8,42 with ἐκ, while in 16,28 mss. vary between παρά (so *NA*[26]) and ἐκ (so *NA*[25]). According to B. and L., 8,42 is from 'Jean II-A', 13,3 and 16,30 are from 'Jean II-B', and 16,27 and 17,8 are from 'Jean III'; 16,28 comes from a collection of Johannine logia; it was inserted here by 'Jean III', but it was redacted at an earlier date, possibly by 'Jean II-A' (see *Jean*, 390 and 494). It will be evident from this example, that at least in the case of John 17,8b*c*-c*a*, the evidence for assigning a phrase to one of the stages in the development of the Fourth Gospel is rather scanty.
48 It would be preferable to speak here of 'concentric symmetry'.
49 Y. Simoens, *La gloire d'aimer*. Structures stylistiques et interprétatives dans le Discours de la Cène (Jn 13-17) (AnBib 90; Rome 1981), esp. 174-199.
50 I reproduce the scheme from Simoens, *La gloire d'aimer*, 187.
51 Simoens, *La gloire d'aimer*, 184.
52 Simoens, *La gloire d'aimer*, 176-180, offers something of the kind, but is inexact.
53 Simoens, *La gloire d'aimer*, 182.
54 Simoens, *La gloire d'aimer*, 193.
55 The relationship of 17,1 and 5 also in Bengel, *Gnomon*, 431; Westcott, II 244; Lagrange, 439; Bultmann, 378; J. Giblet, 'Sanctifie-les dans la vérité (Jn 17,1-26)', *BVC* 19 (1957) 58-73; 61; Behler, *Paroles d'adieux*, 228; Laurentin, *Bib* 45, 425; Brown, 742, 751; Malatesta, *Bib* 52, 195-198; Riedl, *Heilswerk*, 79; Schnackenburg,

BZ NF 17, 74-75; Schneider, 284; Boismard-Lamouille, *Jean*, 396; Ritt, *Gebet*, 238; Haenchen, 502; Simoens, *La gloire d'aimer*, 178, 188.

56 Cfr. Malatesta, *Bib* 52, 205, 208, who only notices the correspondence of the two petitions.

57 Cfr. Malatesta, *Bib* 52, 208; Ritt, *Gebet*, 370-371.

58 Cfr. Giblet, *BVC* 19, 71, 72; Behler, *Paroles d'adieux*, 262; Laurentin, *Bib* 45, 425 n. 3; Becker, *ZNW* 60, 68-69; Brown, 750, 771, 772; Rigaux, *RTL* 1, 314; Malatesta, *Bib* 52, 196; Schnackenburg, *BZ* NF 17, 72-73; Boyle, *Bib* 56, 220-221; Ritt, *Gebet*, 238; Simoens, *La gloire d'aimer*, 64 *et alibi*.

59 See for this construction Blass-Debrunner-Rehkopf, parr. 138.1; 466.3; Zerwick, *Biblical Greek*, parr. 25; 31; Turner, *Syntax*, 21. Cfr. for the relationship of 17,2 and 24: Westcott, II 242; Bernard, 561; Barrett, 502, 514; Brown, 750; Malatesta, *Bib* 52, 208; Feuillet, *Sacerdoce*, 46; Schnackenburg, *BZ* NF 17, 73-74; Haenchen, 508.

60 This correspondence has been noticed by many scholars: Bengel, *Gnomon*, 432; Westcott, II 245; Bauer, 207; Lagrange, 437; Bernard, 563; Bultmann, 399 n. 1; Michel, *ZST* 18, 522-523; Barrett, 514; Lightfoot, 300-301; Behler, *Paroles d'adieux*, 262; Van den Bussche, *Jezus' woorden*, 147; Thüsing, *Herrlichkeit*, 42, 116; Laurentin, *Bib* 45, 426-427; Brown, 750, 772; Malatesta, *Bib* 52, 196; Riedl, *Heilswerk*, 79; Schnackenburg, *BZ* NF 17, 73; Ferraro, *L' "ora" di Cristo*, 269; Lattke, *Einheit im Wort*, 205-206; Haenchen, 500, 502; Simoens, *La gloire d'aimer*, 64. That the verb τελειοῦν occurs within John 17 only in *vv*. 4.23 (cfr. Thüsing, *Herrlichkeit*, 108 n. 2; Brown, 771; Rigaux, *RTL* 1, 294 n. 19, 315; Schnackenburg, *BZ* NF 17, 70-72; Boyle, *Bib* 56, 220-221) is true; the rather divergent way it is used in these verses makes it however hardly support the correspondence of 17,1b-5 and 20-24.

61 This correspondence is noticed by Bauer, 207; Lagrange, 452; Bernard, 564, 581; Bultmann, 380 n. 2, 400 n. 3; Barrett, 505, 515; Behler, *Paroles d'adieux*, 264; Thüsing, *Herrlichkeit*, 24, 118-119; Laurentin, *Bib* 45, 427-428, 430; Perret, *VCaro* 18, nr. 69, 125; Brown, 750, 773; Rigaux, *RTL* 1, 305; Malatesta, *Bib* 52, 199, 212; Riedl, *Heilswerk*, 96; Schnackenburg, *BZ* NF 17, 201; Ferraro, *L' "ora" di Cristo*, 269; Lattke, *Einheit im Wort*, 200; Boismard-Lamouille, *Jean*, 396; Ritt, *Gebet*, 310.

62 Cfr. Thüsing, *Herrlichkeit*, 118; Schnackenburg, *BZ* NF 17, 200-201; Boismard-Lamouille, *Jean*, 396; Simoens, *La gloire d'aimer*, 181.

63 It is not necessary here to go into the curiosities in the use of tenses in John 17 (preterite used to indicate events which had, strictly speaking, not yet occurred, cfr. 17,18 in connection with 20,21), originating with the unclear situation of the prayer (before, during or after Jesus' exaltation?); see about this problem: A. George, '"L'Heure" de Jean XVII', *RB* 61 (1954) 392-397; W. J. P. Boyd, 'The Ascension according to St. John', *SE* VI (TU 112; Berlin 1973) 20-27; Schnackenburg, III 208; Haenchen, 511. In a structural analysis such as the present one, differences in tense have to be taken as a datum.

64 Cfr. Malatesta, *Bib* 52, 209-210. Another argument for the unity of 17,25-26 is, according to M. (p. 210), that the Father, Jesus and the disciples are each referred to four times by personal pronouns in these two verses.

65 Cfr. esp. Malatesta, *Bib* 52, 209; for the signification of δίκαιε in the present context also Bauer, 207; Lagrange, 452; Bernard, 580; Hoskyns-Davey, 506-507; Strathmann, 235; Barrett, 514; Ferraro, *L' "ora" di Cristo*, 274; Ritt, *Gebet*, 349.

66 Cfr. Ritt, *Gebet*, 257, about 17,25-26: '... eine *retrospektive und prospektive Sprecherperspektive* (bildet) den krönenden Abschluss der gesamten Texteinheit'.

67 So Bernard, 581. See for οὗτος as referring to someone actually present: Blass-Debrunner-Rehkopf, par. 290.1; Turner, *Syntax*, 44.

68 Cfr. Bultmann, 384; Malatesta, *Bib* 52, 204; Schnackenburg, *BZ* NF 17, 197; J. Delorme, 'Sacrifice, sacerdoce, consécration. Typologie et analyse sémantique du discours', *RSR* 63 (1975) 343-366; 359; I. de la Potterie, *La vérité dans Saint Jean*, II: Le croyant et la vérité (AnBib 74; Rome 1977) 721; Thüsing, in: *Die Kirche des Anfangs*, 325; Ritt, *Gebet*, 335-336; Simoens, *La gloire d'aimer*, 178-180.

69 Cfr. 2 Macc 14,36; 1 Thess 5,23; 1 Tim 5,22; Jude 1.3. Sanctification is 'die

positive Seite der Bewahrung', so A. Wikenhauser, *Das Evangelium nach Johannes* (RNT 4; Regensburg 1957[2]) 307; see also Bultmann, 384, and esp. De la Potterie, *Vérité*, 721-758.

70 This correspondence has been noticed by Bengel, *Gnomon*, 433; Lagrange, 445; Bultmann, 384; Barrett, 507; Giblet, *BVC* 19, 63; Thüsing, *Herrlichkeit*, 91; R. Poelman, 'La prière sacerdotale, Jn 17', *Lumen Vitae* 19 (1964) 653-678; 665-666; Brown, 761; Malatesta, *Bib* 52, 202; Feuillet, *Sacerdoce*, 55, 123-124; Schnackenburg, *BZ* NF 17, 197; De la Potterie, *Vérité*, 721; Ritt, *Gebet*, 335; Simoens, *La gloire d'aimer*, 178-179.

71 Cfr. Bengel, *Gnomon*, 433; Westcott, II 250; Becker, *ZNW* 60, 67; Malatesta, *Bib* 52, 202, 203; Boismard-Lamouille, *Jean*, 396.

72 Cfr. Brown, 762; Malatesta, *Bib* 52, 204; Schnackenburg, III 212; Ritt, *Gebet*, 241.

73 Expositions about sanctification as separation and mission can be found in almost all commentaries on John 17,17-19. OT texts to be compared are Exod 28,41; Jer 1,5 (cfr. Sir 49,7). Somewhat differently De la Potterie, *Vérité*, 740-744, 775-781, who wants to dissociate both verbs and for whom sanctification is only the condition for mission. Strikingly, there is no reference to John 10,36 in his discussion of the link between the two verbs.

74 Cfr. esp. Malatesta, *Bib* 52, 202; also Bengel, *Gnomon*, 433; Barrett, 509; Schnackenburg, III 208.

75 Cfr. for this meaning LXX Exod 13,2.12; Lev 22,2.3; Num 18,8.9; Deut 15,19 (cfr. 21); 2 Chr 29,33; 31,6. Ἁγιάζω in John 17,19 is interpreted in this way by, e.g., Bultmann, 391 (with n. 3); Hoskyns-Davey, 502-505; Barrett, 511; Van den Bussche, *Jezus' woorden*, 161; Brown, 766-767; Schnackenburg, III 212-213; Haenchen, 507; also Bauer, *Wörterbuch*, s.v. 2. This interpretation is strongly suggested by the combination of ἁγιάζω ἐμαυτόν with ὑπὲρ αὐτῶν, as ὑπέρ + gen. is used elsewhere in John (10,11.15; 11,50.51.52; 15,13; 18,14) and in other parts of the NT (e.g., Mark 14,24; Luke 22,19.20; Rom 5,6.7.8; 8,32; 14,15; 1 Tim 2,6; Heb 2,9; 1 Pet 2,21; 3,18; 1 John 3,16) in connection with Jesus' death to indicate its vicarious or salvific character. To compare also 4 Macc 17,20, where the martyrs are called ἁγιασθέντες; in the previous verse LXX Deut 33,3 is quoted and applied to them: καὶ πάντες οἱ ἡγιασμένοι ὑπὸ τὰς χεῖράς σου. This interpretation is compatible with John 10,36, where ἁγιάζειν and ἀποστέλλειν are parallel, since in John and 1 John the idea of Jesus' being sent by the Father implies his death (cfr. 3,14-17; 1 John 4,9-10). De la Potterie, *Vérité*, 758-771, wants to understand 17,19a as referring to Jesus' whole earthly existence in obedience to the Father; yet De la P. cannot escape looking upon Jesus' death as the climax of this existence (see esp. pp. 761, 771; cfr. also Delorme, *RSR* 63, 361-362).

76 Cfr. Laurentin, *Bib* 45, 427; Simoens, *La gloire d'aimer*, 176-177, 180.

77 Cfr. Evans, *Lumen Vitae* 24, 422.

78 17,9-11c is considered to be a unit by Behler, *Paroles d'adieux*, 233; Thüsing, *Herrlichkeit*, 65; Becker, *ZNW* 60, 63 (with elimination of 17,10a); Malatesta, *Bib* 52, 200-201.

79 Brown, 758.

80 The parenthetical function of 17,10a is probably the reason to put a full stop or a semicolon at the end of 17,9, and again a full stop or a semicolon after 17,10a, as is done in, e.g., the *Textus Receptus*, Souter's edition, and in several translations (*Authorized Version*, *New English Bible*, the Dutch *Statenvertaling* of 1637, *Petrus Canisiusvertaling* of 1929 and *Willibrordvertaling* of 1975). Full stop or semicolon seem, however, too strong an interruption of the sequence of thought.

81 A possibility noted by Barrett, 507.

82 Thüsing, *Herrlichkeit*, 71, 73, may be right in making the whole of 17,10-11 depend upon ὅτι 17,9c, but as the result is an unusually long causal clause, it seems preferable to put a full stop after 17,10 (as all modern editions consulted by me do). 17,10b may be dependent upon ὅτι, but it may be a main clause as well. It is evident anyhow that the whole of 17,9c-11c has a causal function with respect to the petition 17,9ab, and that the main reason is given in 17,11a-c (cfr. 17,11d-13).

83 Cfr. Bernard, 567, 572; Laurentin, *Bib* 45, 429; Brown, 758, 761; Schneider, 288; Boismard-Lamouille, *Jean*, 396.
84 Cfr. Malatesta, *Bib* 52, 200, 201-202; Schnackenburg, *BZ* NF 17, 197.
85 Cfr. Bernard, 572; Barrett, 509; Laurentin, *Bib* 45, 427-429; Lattke, *Einheit im Wort*, 200.
86 Cfr. Barrett, 509.
87 Cfr. Bengel, *Gnomon*, 433; Westcott, II 253; Lagrange, 447; Behler, *Paroles d'adieux*, 244-245; Thüsing, *Herrlichkeit*, 88; Malatesta, *Bib* 52, 202, 203; Boismard-Lamouille, *Jean*, 396; Ritt, *Gebet*, 243-244.
88 Some elements of the structure I found for 17,9-19 are also present in the parallelism proposed by Simoens, *La gloire d'aimer*, 180 *et alibi*, for 17,6-11.12-19:

17,6	remembrance of the past	17,12
7	actualization	13
9	formulation on the prayer	15
11d-f	formulation of the prayer	17-19

The vagueness of the correspondences in this scheme is, in my view, problematical. Simoens' scheme for John 17 in its entirety (see above, p. 237) is comparable with mine in so far as in his scheme 17,14*a* is the centre of the entire prayer (see his p. 190), while it my scheme it is 17,14.
89 This division of John 17 agrees with Malatesta's (*Bib* 52, 210-211), and, as far as the division into three parts is concerned, with the one of the scholars mentioned in n. 7. The chiasm constituted by B and B' is also observed by Boismard-Lamouille, *Jean*, 396.
90 This series of petitions has been observed in part by Bultmann, 384; Michel, *ZST* 18, 529; Evans, *Lumen Vitae* 24, 422; Becker, *ZNW* 60, 63; Brown, 750; De la Potterie, *Vérité*, 776; Simoens, *La gloire d'aimer*, 177. The entire series has been detected by Appold, *Oneness Motif*, 204, 224-227, and Ritt, *Gebet*, 248, 393-399.
91 Observed also by Bengel, *Gnomon*, 431; Lagrange, 451; Michel, *ZST* 18, 522; Merlier, *Quatrième Évangile*, 421; Thüsing, *Herrlichkeit*, 99 n. 1; Poelman, *Lumen Vitae* 19, 656; Becker, *ZNW* 60, 63; Brown, 750; Malatesta, *Bib* 52, 196, 202, 207-208, 209; Schnackenburg, *BZ* NF 17, 70-72; Ritt, *Gebet*, 237, 389-392; Simoens, *La gloire d'aimer*, 177.
92 Cfr. Bernard, 564; Bultmann, 380; Barrett, 505; Giblet, *BVC* 19, 61; Thüsing, *Herrlichkeit*, 24, 65; Brown, 743; Malatesta, *Bib* 52, 199; Schulz, 215; Riedl, *Heilswerk*, 96; Schnackenburg, *BZ* NF 17, 73; Boyle, *Bib* 56, 219-220; Boismard-Lamouille, *Jean*, 398; Haenchen, 512-513.
93 Stressed by Schnackenburg, *BZ* NF 17, 73, 75, 76-77.
94 Cfr. Brown, 758; Schnackenburg, *BZ* NF 17, 75, 77; Boismard-Lamouille, *Jean*, 396.
95 Cfr. Thüsing, *Herrlichkeit*, 71; Brown, 750, 771; Malatesta, *Bib* 52, 213; Riedl, *Heilswerk*, 80; Schnackenburg, *BZ* NF 17, 73, 75.
96 Cfr. Laurentin, *Bib* 45, 430; Becker, *ZNW* 60, 67; Malatesta, *Bib* 52, 198; Schnackenburg, *BZ* NF 17, 196-197; Simoens, *La gloire d'aimer*, 180.
97 Cfr. Bengel, *Gnomon*, 433; Bultmann, 385; Strathmann, 233; Barrett, 508, 512; Giblet, *BVC* 19, 61; Laurentin, *Bib* 45, 427-429; J. F. Randall, 'The Theme of Unity in Jn 17,20-23', *ETL* 41 (1965) 373-394; 390-391; Brown, 750; Malatesta, *Bib* 52, 202, 206; Schulz, 216, 217; Schnackenburg, *BZ* NF 17, 196; Schneider, 287, 289; Boismard-Lamouille, *Jean*, 396; De la Potterie, *Vérité*, 731; Ritt, *Gebet*, 242-243; Simoens, *La gloire d'aimer*, 180, 187.
98 Cfr. Strathmann, 234; Barrett, 511.
99 Cfr. Malatesta, *Bib* 52, 205; Ritt, *Gebet*, 237; Simoens, *La gloire d'aimer*, 176-177.
100 Cfr. Bernard, 581; Barrett, 515; Brown, 773; Schnackenburg, *BZ* NF 17, 200; Boismard-Lamouille, *Jean*, 396; Ritt, *Gebet*, 370-371; Simoens, *La gloire d'aimer*, 186-187.
101 In addition it should be mentioned that part C has a length of exactly 200 W, when ἐγώ in 17,19 is omitted, with Sin A W 700 *pc* it sa ac^2 pbo bo^{ms}. The word is put

between square brackets in Westcott and Hort's edition, indicating their doubt, and consequently in *NA*[25], given the difference of opinion between Tischendorf[8] (who omits it) and B. Weiss (who accepts it in the text). It was also put between square brackets by Lachmann, and was accepted by Souter, Von Soden and Merk, and in *NA*[26]. It is very difficult to reach a satisfactory textual decision in this case. The pronoun may have been added by a scribe in order to have an explicit subject, as many other clauses in the vicinity of 17,19 do (17,14.16.18.22.24.25). On the other hand, stylistic considerations favour the originality of ἐγώ: the emphatic καὶ αὐτοί in 17,19b implies a comparison and requires the presence of an equally emphatic subject in 17,19a (cfr. John 7,10: ὡς δὲ ἀνέβησαν οἱ ἀδελφοὶ αὐτοῦ ... τότε καὶ αὐτὸς ἀνέβη, and esp. 1 John 2,6: ὁ λέγων ἐν αὐτῷ μένειν ὀφείλει καθὼς ἐκεῖνος περιεπάτησεν καὶ αὐτὸς [οὕτως] περιπατεῖν; also Rom 11,31; 1 Thess 2,14; Heb 4,10; Rev 6,11; I suppose that the intended contrast is not only between 'myself' and 'they too'); but cfr. 17,18, where κἀγώ in the second half has no counterpart in the first half. If we accept nevertheless because of the stylistic consideration adduced that the reading with ἐγώ has the best chances of being the original one, the omission of ἐγώ can be explained in two ways: a) by its omission, a hiatus is avoided (see Blass-Debrunner-Rehkopf, par. 486; Radermacher, *Grammatik*, 35-36; Moulton-Howard, *Accidence*, 62-63); b) ἐγώ may have disappeared because of parablepsis, caused by its similarity to the word following it: ΕΓΩΑΓΙΑΖΩ. All in all, a slight preference for the reading with ἐγώ seems justified.

102 I owe these observations to J. Smit Sibinga (see for a similar phenomenon in Matt 24,1-31: Smit Sibinga, *ST* 29, 78-79), who pointed out to me that the numerical value of δίκαιος used in John 17,25, is 4 + 10 + 20 + 1 + 10 + 70 + 200 = 315, also made up of only 1,3 and 5. According to C. E. Donker, the number 351 is also of importance in the Epistle of James, where 1,1-11; 1,19-27 and 5,12-20 have a size of 351 S.

103 Cfr. for what follows Malatesta, *Bib* 52, 195-199; besides, Laurentin, *Bib* 45, 424-425; Schnackenburg, *BZ* NF 17, 74-76; Boismard-Lamouille, *Jean*, 396; Ritt, *Gebet*, 405; Simoens, *La gloire d'aimer*, 188.

104 Cfr. for the correspondence of 17,4 and 5, in addition to the literature mentioned in n. 103: Bengel, *Gnomon*, 432; Bultmann, 378 n. 9; Ferraro, *L'"ora" di Cristo*, 267-268.

105 The peculiar form of 17,3 — possibly a confession of faith — has been noticed by many scholars: see above p. 232, and nn. 22, 34, 45 and 47; further Bauer, 203; Lagrange, 440; Bernard, 561; Bultmann, 378 n. 1 and 2; Hoskyns-Davey, 498; Barrett, 503; Lightfoot, 300; Giblet, *BVC* 19, 60; Thüsing, *Herrlichkeit*, 50 n. 1; Van den Bussche, *Jezus' woorden*, 151; Poelman, *Lumen Vitae* 19, 658; Evans, *Lumen Vitae* 24, 421; Brown, 741; Schulz, 214. The striking character of 17,3 is in itself no argument to consider the verse as secondary.

106 Cfr. Ferraro, *L'"ora" di Cristo*, 265-266; Ritt, *Gebet*, 271.

107 Numbers of W also observed in this case by Malatesta, *Bib* 52, 197. Cfr. further Barrett, 504.

108 Cfr. for this section Malatesta, *Bib* 52, 198-200; for 17,6 also De la Potterie, *Vérité*, 749 n. 306.

109 Cfr. also Lagrange, 433; Bultmann, 381-382; Barrett, 506; Brown, 744; Rigaux, *RTL* 1, 304; Schnackenburg, *BZ* NF 17, 78; Schneider, 286; Simoens, *La gloire d'aimer*, 189.

110 For Laurentin, *Bib* 45, 427, νῦν δέ in 17,13 marks the main division of John 17 as a whole (see p. 231 above). Malatesta, *Bib* 52, 200-202, 210-211, considers 17,11d-16 as middle section of 17,9-19. Within this section, 17,11d-f corresponds to 17,15-16; both parts have a length of one strophe. The section 17,12-14, enclosed by these two strophes, is made up, according to M., of two parts of two strophes each: 17,12.13-14. In this rather artificial scheme, no account is taken of the obvious literary correspondences of, e.g., 17,9 and 15, and 17,11d-f and 17.

111 A division differing somewhat from the one proposed here, is given by Malatesta,

Bib 52, 200-201 (see also the folding chart at the end of his article): he considers 17,9c as part of the first strophe. I have argued my division into three parts above, see pp. 243-244.

112 Schnackenburg, III 206-207, speaks of a 'Neuansatz' with καὶ ἐφύλαξα.

113 Cfr. Malatesta, *Bib* 52, 203.

114 Cfr. Malatesta, *Bib* 52, 204-205; Schnackenburg, *BZ* NF 17, 197 (the unit 17,17-19 'ist geradezu klassisch gerundet'); De la Potterie, *Vérité*, 743; Ritt, *Gebet*, 335-336. See also n. 15 above.

115 Cfr. Malatesta, *Bib* 52, 205-209. In his division, the petitions 17,20 and 24 are corresponding, and so are 17,21 and 22b-23; 17,22a is then the centre of 17,20-24. M. seems to fall a victim here to a constraint of detecting concentric structures everywhere; both sentence structure and numbers of S and W oppose this division.

116 Noticed by many authors: Bengel, *Gnomon*, 434; Bauer, 206-207; Lagrange, 450; Bernard, 578; Bultmann, 394 n. 8; Barrett, 513; Giblet, *BVC* 19, 70; Van den Bussche, *Jezus' woorden*, 162; Thüsing, *Herrlichkeit*, 99-100; Randall, *ETL* 41, 388-389; Brown, 769; Rigaux, *RTL* 1, 300, 304; Malatesta, *Bib* 52, 206-207; Feuillet, *Sacerdoce*, 41; Boyle, *Bib* 56, 222; Appold, *Oneness Motif*, 157-158; Schneider, 290; De la Potterie, *Vérité*, 777; Marzotto, *Unità*, 184; Ritt, *Gebet*, 242-243, 253-254, 295, 330, 357-364 (where also the differences between 17,20-21 and 17,22-23 are worked out); Simoens, *La gloire d'aimer*, 191.

117 Noticed by Abbott, *Joh. Grammar*, nr. 2554.

118 Also noticed by Schattenmann, *Studien*, 15.

119 Malatesta, *Bib* 52, 209-210, divides 17,25-26 into three strophes of 3, 4 and 5 lines respectively: 17,25a-c (because of the antithetic parallelism 17,25b.c).25d-26a*a* (because of parallelism, with a chiasm caused by inversion of the sequence of pronoun and verb in the main clauses; 17,26a*a* is divided by M. into καὶ ἐγνώρισα αὐτοῖς/τὸ ὄνομά σου).26a*b*-b (about the future, in contrast to what precedes; symmetric parallelism in the final clause; 17,26b*a* is divided by M. into ἵνα ἡ ἀγάπη/ἣν ἠγάπησάς με). It seems to me that 17,25d rather belongs to what precedes than to what follows, because of the verb γινώσκειν and the opposition between the disciples and the world. For M.'s division into three strophes, the numbers of S are 19, 25 and 26, and the numbers of W are 12, 13 and 14.

120 This numerical arrangement seems a confirmation of the view of several scholars, that 17,25c is a parenthetic clause, and that 17,25b and 25d are opposed: Westcott, II 260; Lagrange, 452; Bernard, 580; Barrett, 515; Brown, 773; Schnackenburg, III 224.

CONCLUSION AND SUMMARY

In the composition of the passages analysed in this thesis (John 1,19-2,11; 5; 6; 9,1-10,21; 17) the author of the Fourth Gospel made use of numbers of syllables and words. The results of an analysis of this numerical composition are convergent with the results of a conventional analysis of literary structure; the numerical analysis offers, moreover, possibilities to refine the conventional literary analysis, and to make it more concrete.

In applying his quantitative technique, the author of John has employed two basic methods. The syllables and words can be divided according to a 'transverse section' and according to a 'longitudinal section'. In the former case, the text is divided into its successive parts: scenes, parts of a discourse, sentences, and the like. In the latter case, the text is divided into portions which are present all over the literary unit and throughout its successive parts; such a division is a division of the syllables and words of a given passage into narrative and discourse, in which case the discourse can be divided according to the various speakers. Such a division is also a division of the syllables and words of a given passage according to the actors, i.e., the acting and speaking subjects.

There are two basic patterns of relationship between the parts of the text arising from a transverse section, i.e., the successive parts of the text, measured in numbers of syllables and words:

1. The A-A'-pattern: two successive parts have a numerical relationship. Examples:

— John 1,35-42 is made up of two parts, of 164, = 4 × 41, and 123, = 3 × 41, syllables respectively (see Chapter I, under 3.a.).

— John 9,35*ab*-38 is made up of two parts of (almost) equal length: 44 and 44 syllables, 23 and 22 words (see Chapter IV, under 3.f., with Table XIX).

2. The A-B-A'-pattern: the first and last part have a numerical relationship. Application of it may be termed 'framing-technique'. Examples:

— In John 6, the central part (6,22-59) is surrounded by parts whose number of syllables is a multiple of 44 (704, = 16 × 44, for 6,1-21, and 396, = 9 × 44, for 6,60-71); the sum total of syllables for the two surrounding parts together is the round number of 1100 (see Chapter III, under 2., with Table III).

— The words of the steward in John 2,10bc display this pattern on a small scale. They are made up of 7 + 5 + 7 words, or 14 + 11 + 14 syllables. The same pattern is present in the entire sentence 2,9-10, made up of 22 + 5 + 22 words (see Chapter I, under 5., *in fine*).

Of course, the number of members in each of the patterns can be enlarged, and patterns can be combined. An example is afforded by John 5,19b-30, which passage displays a pattern a-b-c-d-d'-c'-b'-a'. Elements a and a' amount together to 110 syllables, and all the other combinations of corresponding elements result in sum totals of syllables which are divisible by 7, and in which the factor 7 is also present in another way. In numbers of words, elements a and a' are of equal length, and all the other combinations of corresponding elements result in sum totals which are divisible by 11 (see Chapter II, under 3.b., with Tables VII and VIII). Here, the A-B-A'-pattern is enlarged, and it is combined with the A-A'-pattern, as there is no single central element, but the middle of the passage is constituted by two elements (d and d').

Longitudinal and transverse sections can be combined, too. An example is to be found in John 9,1-39, where there is a proportion of 2:3 between the numbers of syllables of 9,1-12.35-39 and 9,13-34 (supposing the articular reading in John 9,35a, see Chapter IV, under 3.f.). The same proportion is present in the numbers of syllables for the narrative portions of 9,1-12.35-39 and 9,13-34, and in those for the discourse in these passages (see Chapter IV, under 2., with Table VIII).

The numbers of syllables and words of the various parts arising from a transverse or longitudinal section of the text display the following arrangements:

a. A part stands out by containing a round or otherwise significant (triangular, rectangular, square, symmetric) number of syllables or words. Examples:

— In John 6,22-59, the central passage 6,41-43 has a size of exactly 100 syllables (see Chapter III, under 4.b., with Table XIII).

— In John 1,29-34, the discourse amounts to exactly 100 words (see Chapter I, under 2.b., with Table II).

b. Parts supplement each other, and together they amount to a round or otherwise significant number of syllables or words. Examples:

— John 1,35-2,11 is made up of three scenes; together, these amount to 1000 syllables (see Chapter I, under 6.).

— In John 9, the discourse of Jesus and those who are on his side (the disciples and the man born blind) together amounts to 250 words (see Chapter IV, under 1., with Table IV).

c. Parts are of equal length, in numbers of syllables or words. Examples:

— In John 5,31-47, both 5,31-36 and 5,41-47 contain 210 syllables, so that 5,31-40 and 5,37-47 are also of equal length: 345 syllables (see Chapter II, under 3.c., with Table IX).
— In John 6,1-15, the sentences with Jesus as actor are, in numbers of words, as long as the sentences with other actors: 118 words (see Chapter III, under 3.a., with Table VII).

d. Parts have a relationship of proportion, in numbers of syllables or words. Examples:
— Between the numbers of syllables of John 10,7b-8 and 10,9-10, there is a proportion according to the golden section: 48:77 = 77:125 = 0,62. The same proportion exists between 10,8.10a and 10,7b.9.10b (see Chapter IV, under 5.b., with Table XXIII).
— The 789 words of John 5 are divided as well as possible according to a proportion of 1:3 into 197 words of narrative and 592 words of discourse, and also into 197 words for the sentences with actors other than Jesus, and 592 words for the sentences with Jesus as actor (see Chapter II, under 1., with Tables I and II).

Within a given pattern, similar relationships are possible between all A-parts taken together over against all B-parts taken together, etc. An example is to be found in John 17,1b-26, built according to the pattern A-B-C-A'-B'. A and A' together are (almost) twice as long as B and B' together: 190 and 95 words, 365 and 181 syllables (see Chapter V, under 2.b., *in fine*, with Table I).

A few special varieties of numerical technique have to be mentioned:

1. One small but important part of a literary unit, e.g., an OT quotation or an important saying of Jesus, contains exactly the number of syllables or words which this unit has above a round or otherwise significant figure (the 'surplus-technique'). Examples:
— In John 1,19-28, the OT quotation 1,23bc contains 22 syllables from a sum total of 322 syllables for the entire pericope (see Chapter I, under 2.a.).
— In the miracle story John 9,1-7, Jesus' command to the man born blind to go and to wash in the pool of Siloam 9,7b contains 7 words from a sum total of 107 words for the entire pericope (see Chapter IV, under 3.a.).

2. Cola of equal length succeed one another; the result is an isocolon, a phenomenon which has frequently been described in antiquity (see Introduction, under 2.c., ad *2.*). Examples:
— John 5,45 is made up of two clauses, which have both a size of 20 syllables or 9 words (see Chapter II, under 3.c., *in fine*).
— John 6,58 is made up of three clauses; each one contains 15 syllables. This isocolon marks the end of the discourse on the bread of life (see Chapter III, under 4.b., *in fine*).

3. Certain basic numbers are used in a literary unit: many figures which occur in its numbers of syllables and words are multiples of the same factor. Examples:
— In John 1,19-34, the factor 11 is used as basic number (see Chapter I, under 2.c.).
— In John 9,1-39, the factors 9 and 11 are used as basic numbers (see Chapter IV, under 2. and 3., *passim*).

4. There is a relationship between numbers of syllables and words of a passage and the figures mentioned in that passage. Examples:
— In John 5,1-18, the text mentions the figures 5 (5,2) and 38 (5,5). In the numbers of syllables and words, the factors 5, 19 (= ½ × 38) and 43 (= 5 + 38) are prominent (see Chapter II, under 3.a.).
— In John 6, the factor 11 is prominent. An explanation for this phenomenon is to be found at the end of John 6: out of the Twelve, one is a devil (6,70); so, there remain eleven (see Chapter III, under 3.c., *in fine*).

5. The sum total of syllables or words for a passage is equal to the numerical value of an important name or title occurring in that passage. Examples:
— John 1,19-2,11 has a size of 1550 syllables, which number is the numerical value of ὁ χριστός (see Chapter I, under 7.).
— John 17,1b-26 contains 486 words, which number is the numerical value of the vocative πάτερ, which is found six times in the text (see Chapter V, under 1.).

The results of this investigation of five selected passages from the Fourth Gospel are, strictly speaking, only valid for these five passages. Nevertheless, they strongly suggest that it might be worth while to study other passages in John from the same point of view.

It is not my intention to claim that the present numerical analysis is a complete numerical analysis. It is possible that other counts than a count of syllables and words are significant as well in the composition of a text. In a recent contribution concerning Matt 14,22-33, J. Smit Sibinga counts not only syllables and words, but also the different forms of the verb; he points out that these are distributed over the story in a balanced way[1]. There is no *a priori* reason to assume this and similar counts have not been applied by other authors as well.

Much remains to be done in the investigation of the significance of the numbers found in the analysis. We found a few ψῆφοι: numbers which are equal to the numerical value of names or titles; it is not unlikely that other ψῆφοι have remained hidden. Sometimes, it proved to be possible to connect the use of certain basic numbers with numbers used in the text itself; in other instances, however, the question remains why the author uses specific basic numbers in specific passages. Of course, one should always take into account the possibility that basic numbers are used for purely aesthetic reasons; on the other hand, there is probably much we do not or not yet know about the significance numbers could have in antiquity.

The numerical analysis carried out in this thesis evokes at least three questions: (a) What is the relevance of this analysis for biblical exegesis? (b) How does it relate to those methods of investigation of biblical texts, which try to elucidate the pre-history of the written text as we know it? (c) Have these numerical techniques been applied consciously or unconsciously by the author of the Fourth Gospel?

Ad (a): When numerical techniques have been used by an author, they are *ipso facto* relevant for the exegesis of his work. They are simply an aspect of it which has to be taken into account in explaining it — just as other aspects have to. Numerical analysis such as the one presented here is, moreover, especially important for two reasons:

1. It can be used in textual criticism, as a part of what is commonly called 'internal evidence'. When numerical techniques can be proved to have been used in a text, it may be possible to determine whether or not a passage in the textual state in which we know it is identical to what an author originally wrote, as far as its size is concerned. The use of numerical analysis in textual criticism should proceed very cautiously, as there is always the danger that unwarranted presumptions concerning what the size of a text should be, determine textual decisions. In my opinion, at least two conditions should be fulfilled, to guarantee a correct use of numerical analysis in textual criticism: there should be more evidence in support of a reading than only that which is supplied by the numerical analysis, and a series of numerical observations should converge in supporting one and the same reading. See for examples Chapter I, under the preliminary problems, and under 3.b., 3.c. and 4.; Chapter IV, under 3.f.

2. Numerical analysis can also be used as a means of verifying a conventional analysis of a text's literary structure. Frequently, divergent schemes are proposed for the literary structure of the same passage (see, e.g., Chapter III, under 4.a., and Chapter V, under 2.a.). Numerical analysis affords an additional criterion to judge about the correctness of a proposed scheme of structure, and it gives, in that way, a more objective basis to structural analysis.

Quantitative analysis also makes it possible to determine where the mathematical centre of a passage is. This centre often appears to be the main point of the text. In that way, numerical analysis may confirm or correct our exegetical presumptions about what is the most important element in a passage. So we observed that the words 'And he said to him: We have found the Messiah' in John 1,41 constitute the centre of John 1,19-2,11 (see Chapter I, under 7.), and that John 6,35b: 'I am the bread of life', is the centre of John 6 when measured in numbers of S (see Chapter III, under 1., *in fine*).

Ad (b): The use of numerical techniques on the part of an author does not exclude his having used traditional materials and having incorporated these in his text. It may be possible to arrive at reasonable presumptions concerning the size and character of these materials. His use of numerical techniques shows, however, that he incorporated the traditional materials in a thorough fashion. His final redaction created a new literary work, and not only a simple compilation of older materials. Numerical analysis helps to show the radical character of the final redaction.

Ad (c): About the question whether numerical techniques are used consciously or unconsciously by an author, two things can be said:

1. *We* can imagine large-scale application of numerical techniques only as a conscious process. The existence of ancient theories about size and proportion in works of literature (see Introduction, under 2.a.) may suggest the same. Only small-scale applications, such as an isocolon, can, in *our* estimation, be done unconsciously.

2. In the case of the Fourth Gospel (and of many other ancient works of literature), we know nothing about the author outside his literary work, let alone that we know something about the mental processes operative in the making of his literary work. The only thing we know is the final product of these processes. Inductive analysis of it reveals the presence of numerical patterns. How these came into being, escapes our perception[2].

NOTES

1 Smit Sibinga, 'Matthew 14:22-33 — Text and Composition', in: *NT Textual Criticism*, 19-21.

2 Syllable- and word-count were not only used in antiquity in the making of works of literature (see Introduction, n. 130). A quotation of the well-known American journalist C. L. Sulzberger shows that he applies word-count to his columns. When interviewed in 1974 (the interview, by the Dutch journalist M. Ruyter, was published under the title 'De beroemde journalist had geen commentaar' in the Dutch newspaper *De Volkskrant* of Saturday, February 16th, 1974), he told about his way of working: 'Three times a week, I write a column, always on a fixed day. I write on Tuesday, Friday and Saturday. The next day, they are in the newspaper. Every column contains exactly 725 words. When I started, they said at the newspaper's: Write *approximately* so many words. I said: *Approximately*, that is nothing for me. Please tell *exactly* how many. When I have more than 725 words, I delete the surplus. When I have less, I write a few words in addition.'

A MATHEMATICAL EXTRA: PROBABILITY ANALYSIS

Questions which present themselves in the course of an investigation such as the one described in this thesis, are: what is the probability that certain numerical patterns occur in a passage? Is there a risk that we declare fortuitous occurrences of a pattern to be intentional occurrences?

Dr. A. Ollongren, of the *Rijksuniversiteit* at Leiden, has set up a formulation of the probability that sentences of a given length occur in a given text, and of the probability that sentences which have a given length in numbers of words, contain a certain number of syllables. In theory, it is possible to set up such formulations for more complicated numerical patterns as well, but it is a very difficult task.

I give Dr. Ollongren's formulations (I quote from his letter to me of January 20th, 1983):

'We are given a collection of sentences. Every sentence has a certain length, a positive integer, measured according to the number of syllables or of words. Let x be a variable which ranges over the positive integers, and let p(x) be the frequency distribution of the sentences from the given collection. p(x) is normalized so that the sum of p(x), in which x runs through the positive integers, is equal to 1. When a sentence is arbitrarily selected from the collection, the probability that this sentence has the length n is equal to p(n). When two sentences are arbitrarily selected, the probability that one sentence has the length n and the other has the length m, is equal to $p(n) \times p(m)$. In this way, the question concerning the probability of the occurrence of sentences with given lengths has been formally answered. Of course, one has to look at the material, in order to determine the function p(x).

Another problem is the question concerning the probability that a sentence of a given length, measured according to the number of words, is made up of a certain number of syllables. Let q(x) be the probability that a word from the text is made up of x syllables. For q, there is again a normalization: x runs through the positive integers and the sum of q(x) is equal to 1. This problem is treated as follows: let n be the number of words of which the sentence should be made up and m be the number of syllables, and let x_1, x_2, ..., x_n be variables which range over the positive integers. The probability that the first word is made up of x_1 syllables, the second word of x_2 syllables, etc., is (see the above formulation)

$$q(x_1) \times q(x_2) \times \ldots \times q(x_n).$$

The sentence which is made up of these words put behind each other, has a length of $x_1 + x_2 + \ldots + x_n$ syllables. This sentence takes part in the probability computation when this sum is equal to m. We obtain the requested probability by making up the sum of all terms of the above form under the condition

$$x_1 + x_2 + \ldots + x_n = m.$$

With this, the question concerning the probability of the occurrence of sentences containing a given number of words that are made up of a certain number of syllables, has been answered.

Of course, one has to look at the material in order to determine the function q(x). The actual computation of the requested probability cannot be carried out without a computer program: I showed you that for $n = 9$ $m = 20$ we need 75582 summations, and per summation 8 multiplications.'

By way of illustration, the above formulation has been applied to John 5,45, a verse made up of two sentences of 20 syllables or 9 words (see above, p. 129). The frequency distributions p(x) measuring sentences in numbers of words and syllables, have been determined by counting the numbers of words and syllables of each sentence in the Fourth Gospel. The frequency distribution q(x) measuring words in numbers of syllables, has been determined by counting the numbers of syllables of each word in a representative part of John. Using these functions, the results for the Fourth Gospel are as follows:

— The probability that a sentence has a length of 20 syllables is 0.026, and so the probability that two successive sentences have both a length of 20 syllables is much less than 1% and is insignificant.

— The probability that a sentence has a length of 9 words is 0.052, and so the probability that two successive sentences have both a length of 9 words is much less than 1% and is insignificant.

The above results derive directly from the frequency distributions. For the next result a computer program was written and run at the *Centraal Reken Instituut* of Leiden University.

— The probability that a sentence of 20 syllables has a length of 9 words is 0.096, which is significant. In other words: it is not *a priori* unlikely that such a sentence occurs in material with the probability distributions of John. The probability, however, that two successive sentences of 20 syllables from the Fourth Gospel have both a length of 9 words, is approximately 1% and can be considered to be insignificant.

The above may at least give an impression of the possibilities (and difficulties) of applying probability analysis in a relatively simple form to numerical features of a text; in our case the numerical features are derived from measuring the lengths of sentences or parts thereof in appropriate units[1].

NOTES

1 Cfr. for a comparable use of probability analysis in a study of ancient texts: D. M. L. Philippides, 'Euripides: Meter and Dramatic Effect', *Perspectives in Computing* 2, nr. 1 (March 1982) 16-25. Ph. studies the distribution of resolutions, i.e., 'the substitution of two short syllables for a single long syllable in the regular iambic metrical pattern' (17), in Euripides' plays, and finds, using probability analysis, that 'Euripides apparently manipulates the distribution of a particular metrical variation to reinforce, in an innovative fashion, the dramatic effect of certain kinds of scenes' (24). I thank Dr. Ollongren for having drawn my attention to Philippides' article.

INDEX OF AUTHORS

N.B. The number of the page where full bibliographic information about a work is given, appears in italics.

INDEX OF REFERENCES

N.B. 1. As a rule, no single verses are indicated from discussions of smaller units or from those parts where opinions of other scholars are discussed.

N.B. 2. The numbers of the pages where passages are discussed in detail, appear in italics.

1. *Old Testament*

2. *New Testament*

3. *Jewish Literature*

4. *Early Christian Literature*

5. *Pagan Literature*

The passages discussed rendered in numbers of syllables and words

N.B. 1. For the text-edition used, see the Introduction, p. 25; the results of the textual discussions at the beginning of the various chapters are supposed in the below lists.

N.B. 2. The division of verses by means of punctuation marks agrees with that in *NA*[26].

N.B. 3. Subtotals correspond to the division of the passages into pericopes in *UBSGNT*[3].

I. *John 1,19-2,11*

verse	syllables		words	
1,19	14,36·3;	53	7,14·3;	24
20	12,16.	28	5,8.	13
21	7·2;5;3·3.6;5·1.	32	3·2;3;2·2.4;2·1.	19
22	5·2;14·8;	29	3·2;6·4;	15
23	2·12·10,12.	36	1·6·4,5.	16
24	14.	14	6.	6
25	12·23;	35	6·14;	20
26	12·9·13,	34	5·4·7,	16
27	9,25.	34	4,12.	16
28	17,10.	27/322	7,5.	12/157
29	20·19.	39	10·11.	21
30	11·17,6.	34	6·8,4.	18
31	7,26.	33	4,12.	16
32	40.	40	17.	17
33	7,18·18,15.	58	4,10·11,7.	32
34	24.	24/228	11.	11/115
35	24	24	12	12
36	14·8.	22	6·5.	11
37	24.	24	11.	11
38	23·4;6·2,15,3;	53	10·2;4·1,4,2;	23
39	4·7.23·7.	41	2·3.13·4.	22
40	37·	37	17·	17
41	23·8,12.	43	11·3,4.	18
42	9.10·10,6,8.	43/287	5.5·6,3,3.	22/136
43	25.8·5.	38	10.5·2.	17
44	12,11.	23	6,6.	12
45	16·20,13.	49	7·10,7.	24
46	9·13;8·5.	35	4·6;4·3.	17
47	23·17.	40	11·8.	19
48	8·6;11·19.	44	3·3;5·11.	22
49	10·2,8,9.	29	3·1,6,5.	15
50	11·17,3;6.	37	5·9,1;3.	18
51	5·8,40.	53/348	3·4,17.	24/168
2,1	22,10·	32	11,7·	18
2	19.	19	12.	12
3	19·6.	25	10·3.	13
4	8·5,2;8.	23	5·4,1;5.	15
5	12·11.	23	6·5.	11
6	26,12.	38	12,6.	18
7	7·11.11.	29	4·4.5.	13

8	5˙15˙5.	25	3˙6˙3.	12
9	30,17,12	59	14,8,5	27
10	5˙25˙14.	44	3˙12˙7.	22
11	34,14.	48/365/1550	16,7.	23/184/760

II. *John 5*

verse	syllables		words	
5,1	25.	25	11.	11
2	43.	43	16.	16
3	14,2,2,2.	20	6,1,1,1.	9
5	27˙	27	14˙	14
6	24,4˙8;	36	12,2˙3;	17
7	10˙3,25˙8,9.	55	4˙1,13˙5,4.	27
8	7˙15.	22	4˙7.	11
9	30.13.	43	13.7.	20
10	15˙5,12.	32	6˙2,7.	15
11	8˙14˙12.	34	4˙7˙6.	17
12	6˙11˙7;	24	2˙7˙3;	12
13	11,16.	27	7,9.	16
14	22˙8,7,10.	47	12˙3,2,6.	23
15	29.	29	14.	14
16	16,11.	27	8,5.	13
17	9˙18˙	27	4˙8˙	12
18	20,12,25.	57/575	9,6,12.	27/274
19	15˙8,27˙8,11.	69	7˙4,15˙5,6.	37
20	22,12,8.	42	13,6,3.	22
21	17,13.	30	9,7.	16
22	11,13,	24	6,7,	13
23	19.20.	39	9.12.	21
24	43,16.	59	23,8.	31
25	46.	46	24.	24
26	14,17.	31	8,9.	17
27	14,9.	23	6,4.	10
28	7,26	33	3,14	17
29	22,15.	37	9,7.	16
30	14˙7,12,23.	56/489	7˙3,7,13.	30/254
31	12,12˙	24	5,6˙	11
32	12,23.	35	6,11.	17
33	11,11˙	22	4,4˙	8
34	17,13.	30	8,6.	14
35	15,23.	38	8,10.	18
36	16˙20,25.	61	8˙11,13.	32
37	19.25,	44	9.9,	18
38	16,10,9.	35	9,4,4.	17
39	7,18˙15˙	40	3,8˙7˙	18
40	16.	16	9.	9
41	11,	11	5,	5
42	24.	24	12.	12
43	16,7˙16,6.	45	8,4˙8,2.	22
44	20,16;	36	8,10;	18
45	20˙12,8.	40	9˙5,4.	18
46	10,8˙11.	29	4,3˙5.	12
47	14,11;	25/555/1619	7,5;	12/261/789

III. *John 6*

verse	syllables		words	
6,1	27.	27	12.	12
2	11,20.	31	5,9.	14
3	25.	25	13.	13
4	7,8.	15	5,4.	9
5	35·16;	51	17·6;	23
6	11·11.	22	5·6.	11
7	10·27.	37	4·11.	15
8	12,12·	24	7,5·	12
9	25·11;	36	11·6;	17
10	5·12.10.19.	46	3·4.7.8.	22
11	41.	41	18.	18
12	7,8·14,8.	37	3,4·4,4.	15
13	40.	40	17.	17
14	41.	41	19.	19
15	28,15.	43/ 516	12,7.	19/236
16	25	25	11	11
17	21.23,	44	10.11,	21
18	19.	19	7.	7
19	48,6.	54	20,2.	22
20	6·4·4.	14	4·2·2.	8
21	12,20.	32/ 188	7,11.	18/ 87
22	69·	69	37·	37
23	37.	37	15.	15
24	25,26.	51	14,12.	26
25	16·2,7;	25	8·1,3;	12
26	12·8,13,17.	50	6·4,6,8.	24
27	30,12·13.	55	14,7·7.	28
28	6·17;	23	4·8;	12
29	11·10,15.	36	5·6,6.	17
30	5·8,11;4;	28	3·5,5;2;	15
31	17,8·14.	39	9,3·7.	19
32	8·8,17,23·	56	5·4,9,13·	31
33	27.	27	16.	16
34	6·3,11.	20	4·1,6.	11
35	7·10·13,16.	46	4·6·7,9.	26
36	20.	20	10.	10
37	14,15,	29	9,9,	18
38	36.	36	18.	18
39	14,16,16.	46	8,9,7.	24
40	13,25,17.	55	8,13,8.	29
41	17·16,	33	8·9,	17
42	4·12,15;16;	47	2·7,8;8;	25
43	11·9.	20	5·4.	9
44	24,16.	40	14,7.	21
45	11·11·19.	41	5·5·11.	21
46	21,10.	31	13,4.	17
47	8,12.	20	4,5.	9
48	10.	10	6.	6
49	22·	22	11·	11
50	17,14.	31	9,8.	17
51	18·18,23.	59	11·11,16.	38
52	16·15;	31	7·8;	15
53	8·8,25,10.	51	5·4,14,5.	28

54	22,15.	37	13,6.	19
55	11,12.	23	7,7.	14
56	24.	24	16.	16
57	20,13.	33	11,8.	19
58	15,15·15.	45	8,7·9.	24
59	17.	17/1363	7.	7/721
60	16·9·9;	34	8·5·4;	17
61	30·8;	38	15·3;	18
62	26;	26	12;	12
63	10,8·22.	40	5,5·11.	21
64	14.30.	44	8.17.	25
65	4·34.	38	2·18.	20
66	31.	31	15.	15
67	10·10;	20	6·5;	11
68	10·3,9;11,	33	4·1,3;4,	12
69	24.	24	12.	12
70	9·14;11.	34	4·6;6.	16
71	15·13,6.	34/ 396/2463	6·5,4.	15/194/1238

IV. *John 9,1-10,21*

verse	syllables		words	
9,1	15.	15	7.	7
2	16·2,4,8,7;	37	7·1,2,5,3;	18
3	6·14,16.	36	2·7,9.	18
4	22·15.	37	11·6.	17
5	7,6.	13	5,4.	9
6	37	37	18	18
7	5·15(11).14.	45	3·7(3).7.	20
8	26·14;	40	13·7;	20
9	11,5·2,9.12.	39	5,2·1,4.5.	17
10	6·12;	18	3·6;	9
11	7·44·13.	64	2·22·5.	29
12	5·6;2·3.	16/397	3·3;1·2.	9/191
13	16.	16	8.	8
14	31.	31	16.	16
15	19.6·21.	46	9.4·10.	23
16	12·13,9.6·19;7.	66	6·7,5.3·7;5.	33
17	9·8,11;11.	39	5·5,5;6.	21
18	43	43	20	20
19	10·9,14;6;	39	4·5,6;4;	19
20	14·23·	37	7·11·	18
21	9,17·7,6,10.	49	6,9·2,2,4.	23
22	19·26,9.	54	9·11,2.	22
23	19,8.	27	9,2.	11
24	22·6·19.	47	12·4·8.	24
25	8·10·12.	30	3·5·7.	15
26	5·6;9;	20	3·3;5;	11
27	6·12·9;15;	42	2·6·4;7;	19
28	11·8,13·	32	5·4,6·	15
29	17,11.	28	7,6.	13
30	13·10,12,9.	44	6·6,6,5.	23
31	16,23.	39	7,12.	19
32	25·	25	11·	11
33	9,9.	18	6,4.	10
34	10·19;9.	38/810	4·9;4.	17/391
35	22·12;	34	10·7;	17

36	10·4,3,8;	25	4·3,1,4;	12
37	7·19.	26	4·10.	14
38	4·3,3·8.	18	3·1,1·3.	8
39	6·13,20.	39	4·8,10.	22
40	22·8;	30	12·5;	17
41	7·5,9·10,9.	40/212	4·3,4·5,4.	20/110
10,1	8,40·	48	4,19·	23
2	20.	20	10.	10
3	42.	42	21.	21
4	11,20,10·	41	5,8,5·	18
5	13,8,14.	35	5,4,7.	16
6	14,17.	31/217	7,9.	16/104
7	8·21.	29	5·11.	16
8	16,11.	27	9,6.	15
9	7·31.	38	4·13.	17
10	21·18.	39	12·8.	20
11	10.20·	30	6.11·	17
12	9,11,22-13-	55	6,6,10-7-	29
13	19.	19	10.	10
14	26,	26	15,	15
15	18,14.	32	9,8.	17
16	18·17,9,3.	47	11·9,4,2.	26
17	22,8.	30	12,4.	16
18	9,12.10,13·15.	59	5,6.4,6·8.	29
19	20.	20	10.	10
20	9·10·7;	26	5·4·3;	12
21	5·15·16;	36/513/2149	2·6·6;	14/263/1059

V. *John 17*

verse	syllables		words	
17,1	25·2,7·7,9,	50	12·1,3·4,5,	25
2	15,19.	34	6,9.	15
3	38.	38	18.	18
4	28·	28	14·	14
5	7,2,21.	30	5,1,13.	19
6	23.19.	42	12.10.	22
7	19·	19	10·	10
8	16,21,13.	50	8,10,6.	24
9	9,18,5,	32	4,10,3,	17
10	14,8.	22	10,4.	14
11	10,9,7.5,17,9.	57	6,6,4.2,9,5.	32
12	26,5,20,8.	59	14,2,11,4.	31
13	36.	36	20.	20
14	21,20.	41	11,13.	24
15	14,13.	27	8,7.	15
16	18.	18	12.	12
17	12·11.	23	5·6.	11
18	12,12·	24	6,6·	12
19	14,17.	31	6,7.	13
20	11,20,	31	6,11,	17
21	7,3,2,7,10,16.	45	4,2,1,5,6,8.	26
22	15,10·	25	8,6·	14
23	10,12,31.	53	7,5,14.	26
24	2,5,18,12,19.	56	1,3,9,6,9.	28
25	5,8,6,14·	33	2,6,4,7·	19
26	16,21.	37/941	8,12.	20/498